TUCKER · FREE · LIBRARY
HENNIKER, N.H.

AMERICAN
REGIONAL COOKING

AMERICAN
REGIONAL COOKING

More than 400 delicious recipes shown step by step in over 1750
stunning photographs that guide you clearly through each recipe

Carole Clements, Laura Washburn & Patricia Lousada

LORENZ BOOKS

This edition is published by Lorenz Books

Lorenz Books is an imprint of Anness Publishing Ltd
Hermes House, 88–89 Blackfriars Road, London SE1 8HA; tel. 020 7401 2077; fax 020 7633 9499
www.lorenzbooks.com; www.annesspublishing.com

If you like the images in this book and would like to investigate using them for publishing, promotions
or advertising, please visit our website www.practicalpictures.com for more information.

© Anness Publishing Ltd 1998, 2006

UK agent: The Manning Partnership Ltd, 6 The Old Dairy, Melcombe Road, Bath BA2 3LR
tel. 01225 478444; fax 01225 478440; sales@manning-partnership.co.uk

UK distributor: Grantham Book Services Ltd, Isaac Newton Way, Alma Park Industrial Estate, Grantham
Lincs NG31 9SD; tel. 01476 541080; fax 01476 541061; orders@gbs.tbs-ltd.co.uk

North American agent/distributor: National Book Network, 4501 Forbes Boulevard, Suite 200, Lanham
MD 20706; tel. 301 459 3366; fax 301 429 5746; www.nbnbooks.com

Australian agent/distributor: Pan Macmillan Australia, Level 18, St Martins Tower, 31 Market St, Sydney
NSW 2000; tel. 1300 135 113; fax 1300 135 103; customer.service@macmillan.com.au

New Zealand agent/distributor: David Bateman Ltd, 30 Tarndale Grove, Off Bush Road, Albany, Auckland
tel. (09) 415 7664; fax (09) 415 8892

A CIP catalogue record for this book is available from the British Library

Publisher: Joanna Lorenz
Editor: Sophy Friend
Indexer: Pat Coward
Designer: Sheila Volpe
Photography: Amanda Heywood
Food for Photography: Elizabeth Wolf-Cohen, Carla Capalbo
Steps by Marilyn Forbes, Cara Hobday, Teresa Goldfinch, Nicola Fowler

Previously published as *The Ultimate American Cookbook*

1 3 5 7 9 10 8 6 4 2

NOTES
Standard spoon and cup measures are level.
Large eggs are used unless otherwise stated.
Electric oven temperatures in this book are for conventional ovens. When using a fan oven, the
temperature will probably need to be reduced by about 20–40°F. Since ovens vary, you should
check with your manufacturer's instruction book for guidance.

CONTENTS

THE BEST OF AMERICA

American families – with their diverse culinary traditions – have always been on the move. Hardy immigrants crossed oceans, and pioneers followed a trail or a river to the West. Today we chase down jobs far from where we grew up and retire to where the sun shines. As people criss-cross the country, they adapt their favorite recipes to the local produce and, in mixed communities, adopt entirely new foods and flavors. What has evolved is the richest and most varied cuisine imaginable. Even now, new dishes are continually entering the changing repertoire.

This unique volume explores this gastronomic heritage. We take you through America's regional cooking, passing on historical tastes with vintage recipes as well as offering new dishes made with local ingredients. All the recipes are presented in a simple step-by-step format with pictures to guide you every inch of the way.

We have taken the compass points as general divisions and look at each region in terms of its most important and characteristic ingredients and its unique traditions, offering a varied and representative selection of the food from each area.

Cooking from New England and the Mid-Atlantic seaboard evokes some of our oldest food traditions, from the first Thanksgiving to Thomas Jefferson's waffle iron. With such a long coastline, seafood has always played a key role, and cold winters promoted the hearty fare we associate with this region. For many people, the South conjures up Spanish moss, French quarter architecture, and plantations. In fact, the Spanish, French, and African-American influences are the most important ones in terms of local food, and Cajun, Creole, and soul food mingle with customs of gracious dining carried over from earlier times.

Moving westward, the Midwest has always been the breadbasket of the country and, although much fertile farmland has been urbanized today, raising crops and animals for the table is still important. The Southwest draws on heirloom traditions, gleaned from Native Americans and Spanish settlers of the areas. Since the state of California occupies much of the West coast and has had such an influence on culinary trends, we have treated it on its own. With well stocked coastal waters and orchards laden with apples, the Pacific Northwest and the Mountain States conclude the culinary tour.

Today cooking at home has changed from an everyday event starting from scratch to more of a hobby. But whether you're preparing for a festive meal to share with friends or simply putting together a quick dinner, this wonderful cookbook has recipes to suit.

NEW ENGLAND & THE MID-ATLANTIC STATES

THE FIRST SETTLERS FOUND
REFUGE IN THIS PART OF THE
COUNTRY AND WORKED THE
FERTILE LAND, CREATING A RICH
CULINARY HERITAGE. SINCE
COLONIAL DAYS, THE TRADITION OF
GOOD EATING THAT DEVELOPED
HERE SPREAD TO OTHER AREAS.
WITH SO MUCH COASTLINE,
SEAFOOD HAS ALWAYS BEEN A KEY
INGREDIENT IN THE COOKING OF
THIS REGION.

New England Clam Chowder

SERVES 8

4 dozen cherrystone or littleneck clams, scrubbed

6 cups water

¼ cup finely diced salt pork or bacon

1½ cups minced onions

1 bay leaf

2½ cups diced peeled potatoes

salt and pepper

2 cups milk, warmed

1 cup light cream

chopped fresh parsley, for garnishing

1 Rinse the clams well in cold water. Drain. Place them in a deep kettle with the 6 cups of water and bring to a boil. Cover and steam until the shells open, about 10 minutes. Remove from the heat.

2 When the clams have cooled slightly, remove them from their shells. Discard any clams that have not opened. Chop the clams coarsely. Strain the cooking liquid through a strainer lined with cheesecloth, and reserve it.

3 In a large heavy saucepan, fry the salt pork or bacon until it renders its fat and begins to brown. Add the onions and cook over low heat until softened, 8–10 minutes.

4 ▲ Add the bay leaf, potatoes, and clam cooking liquid. Stir. Bring to a boil and cook 5–10 minutes.

5 ▲ Stir in the chopped clams. Continue to cook until the potatoes are tender, stirring occasionally. Season with salt and pepper.

6 Reduce the heat to low and stir in the warmed milk and cream. Simmer very gently 5 minutes more. Discard the bay leaf, and taste and adjust the seasoning before serving, sprinkled with parsley.

~ COOK'S TIP ~

If clams have been dug, purging helps to rid them of sand and stomach contents. Put them in a bowl of cold water, sprinkle with ½ cup cornmeal and some salt. Stir lightly and let stand in a cool place for 3–4 hours.

Chilled Asparagus Soup

Serves 6

2 pounds fresh asparagus
4 tablespoons butter or olive oil
1½ cups sliced leeks or scallions
3 tablespoons flour
6 cups chicken stock or water
salt and pepper
½ cup light cream or plain yogurt
1 tablespoon minced fresh tarragon or chervil

1 ▲ Cut the top 2½ inches off the asparagus spears. Blanch these tips in boiling water until just tender, 5–6 minutes. Drain. Cut each tip into 2 or 3 pieces, and set aside.

2 Trim the ends of the stalks, removing any brown or woody parts. Chop the stalks into ½-inch pieces.

3 ▲ Heat the butter or oil in a heavy saucepan. Add the leeks or scallions and cook over low heat until softened, 5–8 minutes. Stir in the chopped asparagus stalks, cover, and cook 6–8 minutes more.

4 Add the flour and stir well to blend. Cook 3–4 minutes, uncovered, stirring occasionally.

5 ▼ Add the stock or water. Bring to a boil, stirring frequently, then reduce the heat and simmer 30 minutes. Season with salt and pepper.

6 ▲ Purée the soup in a food processor or food mill. If necessary, strain it to remove any coarse fibers. Stir in the asparagus tips, most of the cream or yogurt, and the herbs. Chill well. Stir thoroughly before serving, and check the seasoning. Garnish with swirled cream or yogurt.

Chesapeake Melon and Crab Meat Salad

Serves 6

1 pound fresh lump crab meat

½ cup mayonnaise

¼ cup sour cream or plain yogurt

2 tablespoons olive oil

2 tablespoons fresh lemon or lime juice

¼ cup minced scallions

2 tablespoons minced fresh coriander (cilantro)

¼ teaspoon cayenne

salt and pepper

1½ canteloupe or small honeydew melons

3 medium-size heads of Belgian endive

fresh coriander (cilantro) sprigs, for garnishing

1 ▲ Pick over the crab meat very carefully, removing any bits of shell or cartilage. Leave the pieces of crab meat as large as possible.

2 ▲ In a medium-size bowl, combine all the other ingredients except the melon and endive. Mix well. Fold the crab meat into this dressing.

3 ▲ Halve the melons and remove the seeds. Cut into thin slices, and remove the rind.

4 ▲ Arrange the salad on individual serving plates, making a decorative design with the melon slices and whole endive leaves. Place a mound of dressed crab meat on each plate. Garnish each salad with fresh coriander sprigs.

Long Island Scallop and Mussel Kabobs

SERVES 4

5 tablespoons butter, at room temperature

2 tablespoons minced fresh fennel fronds or parsley

1 tablespoon fresh lemon juice

salt and pepper

32 bay or small sea scallops

24 large mussels in shell

8 bacon slices

1 cup fresh bread crumbs

¼ cup olive oil

hot toast, for serving

1 ▲ Make the flavored butter by combining the butter with the minced herbs, lemon juice, and salt and pepper to taste. Mix well. Set aside.

2 ▲ In a small saucepan, cook the scallops in their own liquor until they begin to shrink. (If there is no scallop liquor – retained from the shells after shucking – use a little fish stock or white wine.) Drain and pat dry with paper towels.

3 Scrub the mussels well, and rinse under cold running water. Place in a large saucepan with about 1 inch of water in the bottom. Cover and steam the mussels over medium heat until they open. Remove them from their shells, and pat dry on paper towels. Discard any mussels that have not opened.

4 ▼ Take 8 6-inch wooden or metal skewers. Thread on each one, alternately, 4 scallops, 3 mussels, and a slice of bacon, weaving the bacon between the scallops and mussels.

5 Preheat the broiler.

6 ▲ Spread the bread crumbs on a plate. Brush the seafood with olive oil and roll in the crumbs to coat all over.

7 Place the skewers on the broiler rack. Broil until crisp and lightly browned, 4–5 minutes on each side. Serve immediately with hot toast and the flavored butter.

Oyster Stew

SERVES 6

2 cups milk

2 cups light cream

1 quart shucked oysters, drained, with
  their liquor reserved

⅛ teaspoon paprika

salt and pepper

2 tablespoons butter

1 tablespoon minced fresh parsley

1 Combine the milk, cream, and
oyster liquor in a heavy saucepan.

2 ▼ Heat the mixture over medium
heat until small bubbles appear around
the edge of the pan. Do not allow it to
boil. Reduce the heat to low and add
the oysters.

3 Cook, stirring occasionally, until
the oysters plump up and their edges
begin to curl. Add the paprika, and
salt and pepper to taste.

4 Meanwhile, warm 6 soup plates or
bowls. Cut the butter into 6 pieces
and put one piece in each bowl.

5 Ladle in the oyster stew and
sprinkle with parsley. Serve
immediately, with soda crackers if
desired.

Oysters Rockefeller

SERVES 6

1 pound fresh spinach leaves

½ cup chopped scallions

½ cup chopped celery

½ cup chopped fresh parsley

1 garlic clove

2 anchovy fillets

4 tablespoons butter or margarine

½ cup dry bread crumbs

1 teaspoon Worcestershire sauce

2 tablespoons anise-flavored liqueur
  (Pernod or Ricard)

½ teaspoon salt

hot pepper sauce

36 oysters in shell

fine strips of lemon rind, for garnishing

~ COOK'S TIP ~

To open an oyster push the point
of an oyster knife about ½ inch
into the "hinge". Push down
firmly. The lid should pop open.

1 ▲ Wash the spinach well. Drain,
and place in a heavy saucepan. Cover
and cook over low heat until just
wilted. Remove from the heat. When
the spinach is cool enough to handle,
squeeze it to remove excess water.

2 ▲ Put the spinach, scallions,
celery, parsley, garlic, and anchovy
fillets in a food processor and process
until finely chopped.

3 Heat the butter or margarine in a
skillet. Add the spinach mixture,
bread crumbs, Worcestershire sauce,
liqueur, salt, and hot pepper sauce to
taste. Cook 1–2 minutes. Let cool,
and refrigerate until ready to use.

4 Preheat the oven to 450°F. Line a
baking sheet with crumpled foil.

5 ▲ Open the oysters and remove
the top shells. Arrange them, side by
side, on the foil (it will keep them
upright). Spoon the spinach mixture
over the oysters, smoothing the tops
with the back of the spoon.

6 Bake until piping hot, about 20
minutes. Serve immediately,
garnished with lemon rind.

Oyster Stew (top), Oysters Rockefeller

Cape Cod Fried Clams

SERVES 4

36 cherrystone clams, scrubbed

1 cup buttermilk

¼ teaspoon celery salt

¼ teaspoon cayenne

oil for deep-frying

1 cup dry bread crumbs

2 eggs, beaten with 2 tablespoons water

lemon wedges and tartar sauce or
    catsup, for serving

1 Rinse the clams well. Put them in a large kettle with 2 cups of water and bring to a boil. Cover and steam until the shells open.

2 ▼ Remove the clams from their shells, and cut away the black skins from the necks. Discard any clams that have not opened. Strain the cooking liquid and reserve.

3 ▲ Place the buttermilk in a large bowl and stir in the celery salt and cayenne. Add the clams and ½ cup of their cooking liquid. Mix well. Let stand 1 hour.

4 Heat oil in a deep-fryer or large saucepan to 375°F. (To test the temperature without a thermometer, drop in a cube of bread; it should be golden brown in 40 seconds.)

5 ▲ Drain the clams and roll them in the bread crumbs to coat all over. Dip them in the beaten egg and then in the bread crumbs again.

6 Fry the clams in the hot oil, a few at a time, stirring, until they are crisp and brown, about 2 minutes per batch. Remove with a slotted spoon and drain on paper towels.

7 Serve the fried clams hot, accompanied by lemon wedges and tartar sauce or catsup.

Eggs Benedict

SERVES 4

1 teaspoon vinegar

4 eggs

2 English muffins or 4 rounds of bread

butter, for spreading

2 slices of cooked ham, ¼-inch thick,
   each cut in half crosswise

fresh chives, for garnishing

FOR THE SAUCE

3 egg yolks

2 tablespoons fresh lemon juice

¼ teaspoon salt

½ cup (1 stick) butter

2 tablespoons light cream

pepper

4 ▼ Bring a shallow pan of water to a boil. Stir in the vinegar. Break each egg into a cup, then slide it carefully into the water. Delicately turn the white around the yolk with a slotted spoon. Cook until the egg is set to your taste, 3–4 minutes. Remove to paper towels to drain. Very gently cut any ragged edges off the eggs with a small knife or scissors.

5 ▲ While the eggs are poaching, split and toast the muffins or toast the bread slices. Butter while still warm.

6 Place a piece of ham, which you may brown in butter if you wish, on each muffin half or slice of toast. Trim the ham to fit neatly. Place an egg on each ham-topped muffin. Spoon the warm sauce over the eggs, garnish with chives, and serve.

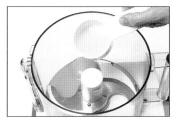

1 ▲ For the sauce, put the egg yolks, lemon juice, and salt in the container of a food processor or blender. Blend 15 seconds.

2 Melt the butter in a small saucepan until it bubbles (do not let it brown). With the motor running, pour the hot butter into the food processor or blender through the feed tube in a slow, steady stream. Turn off the machine as soon as all the butter has been added.

3 Scrape the sauce into the top of a double boiler, over just simmering water. Stir until thickened, 2–3 minutes. (If the sauce curdles, whisk in 1 tablespoon of boiling water.) Stir in the cream and season with pepper. Keep warm over the hot water.

Maryland Crab Cakes with Tartar Sauce

SERVES 4

1½ pounds fresh lump crab meat

1 egg, beaten

2 tablespoons mayonnaise

1 tablespoon Worcestershire sauce

1 tablespoon sherry wine

2 tablespoons minced fresh parsley

1 tablespoon minced fresh chives or dill

salt and pepper

3 tablespoons olive oil

FOR THE SAUCE

1 egg yolk

1 tablespoon white wine vinegar

2 tablespoons Dijon-style mustard

1 cup vegetable or peanut oil

2 tablespoons fresh lemon juice

¼ cup minced scallions

2 tablespoons chopped drained capers

¼ cup minced sour dill pickles

¼ cup minced fresh parsley

1 ▲ Pick over the crab meat, removing any shell or cartilage. Keep the pieces of crab as large as possible.

~ COOK'S TIP ~

For easier handling and to make the crab meat go further, add 1 cup fresh bread crumbs and 1 more egg to the crab mixture. Divide the mixture into 12 cakes to serve 6.

2 ▲ In a mixing bowl, combine the beaten egg with the mayonnaise, Worcestershire sauce, sherry, and herbs. Season with salt and pepper. Gently fold in the crab meat.

3 ▲ Divide the mixture into 8 portions and gently form each one into an oval cake. Place on a baking sheet between layers of wax paper and refrigerate at least 1 hour.

4 ▲ Meanwhile, make the sauce. In a medium-size bowl, beat the egg yolk with a wire whisk until smooth. Add the vinegar, mustard, and salt and pepper to taste, and whisk about 10 seconds to blend. Whisk in the oil in a slow, steady stream.

5 ▲ Add the lemon juice, scallions, capers, pickles, and parsley and mix well. Check the seasoning. Cover and chill.

6 Preheat the broiler.

7 ▲ Brush the crab cakes with the olive oil. Place on an oiled baking sheet, in one layer.

8 ▲ Broil 6 inches from the heat until golden brown, about 5 minutes on each side. Serve the crab cakes hot with the tartar sauce.

Baked Scrod

Serves 6

2½ pounds scrod or bluefish fillets, skinned

3 tablespoons olive oil

1 teaspoon drained capers

2 garlic cloves

2 medium-size ripe tomatoes, peeled, seeded, and finely diced

2 tablespoons minced fresh basil, or 2 teaspoons dried basil

salt and pepper

1 cup dry white wine

1 Preheat the oven to 400°F.

2 ▲ Arrange the fillets in one layer in a shallow oiled baking dish. Brush the fish with olive oil.

3 Chop the capers with the garlic. Mix with the tomatoes and basil. Season with salt and pepper.

4 ▼ Spoon the tomato mixture over the fish. Pour in the wine. Bake until the fish is cooked, 15–20 minutes. Test for doneness with the point of a knife; the fish should be just opaque in the center. Serve hot.

Old Westbury Flounder with Crab

Serves 6

4 tablespoons butter or margarine

¼ cup flour

1 cup fish stock, or ¾ cup fish stock mixed with ¼ cup dry white wine

1 cup milk

1 bay leaf

salt and pepper

12 flounder fillets, about 2½ pounds

1½ cups fresh crab meat, flaked

½ cup freshly grated Parmesan cheese

1 Preheat the oven to 425°F.

~ **VARIATIONS** ~

Other flat white fish, such as sole, can be substituted for the flounder. Raw peeled and deveined shrimp, chopped if large, can be used instead of crab meat.

2 ▲ In a medium-size heavy saucepan, melt the butter or margarine over medium heat. Stir in the flour and cook 2–3 minutes.

3 ▲ Pour in the fish stock (or mixed fish stock and wine) and the milk. Whisk until smooth.

4 Add the bay leaf. Raise the heat to medium-high and bring to a boil. Cook 3–4 minutes more. Remove the sauce from the heat, and add salt to taste. Keep hot.

5 ▲ Butter a large baking dish. Twist each fillet to form a "cone" shape and arrange in the dish. Sprinkle the crab meat over the fish. Pour the hot sauce evenly over the top and sprinkle with the cheese.

6 Bake until the top is golden brown and the fish is cooked, 10–12 minutes. Test for doneness with the point of a knife: the fish should be just opaque in the center. Serve hot.

Baked Scrod (top), Old Westbury Flounder with Crab

Scallops Thermidor

SERVES 6

2 pounds sea scallops

½ cup flour

½ cup (1 stick) butter or margarine

1 cup quartered small mushrooms

½ cup fresh bread crumbs

2 tablespoons minced fresh parsley

2 tablespoons minced fresh chives

½ cup sherry wine

¼ cup cognac

1 teaspoon Worcestershire sauce

½ teaspoon salt

¼ teaspoon black pepper

1½ cups whipping cream

2 egg yolks

chives, for garnishing

1 Preheat the oven to 400°F.

2 ▲ Roll the scallops in the flour, shaking off the excess. Heat half of the butter or margarine in a medium-size skillet. Add the scallops and sauté until they are barely golden all over, about 3 minutes. Remove from the skillet and set aside.

3 ▲ Melt 2 more tablespoons of butter or margarine in the pan. Add the mushrooms and bread crumbs and sauté 3–4 minutes, stirring. Add the parsley, chives, sherry, cognac, Worcestershire sauce, salt, and pepper. Cook 3–4 minutes more, stirring well.

4 ▲ Add the cream, and cook another 3–4 minutes, stirring occasionally. Remove from the heat and mix in the egg yolks. Fold in the sautéed scallops.

5 Divide the mixture among 6 greased individual gratin or other baking dishes. Or, if you prefer, put it all in one large shallow baking dish. Dot with the remaining 2 tablespoons of butter or margarine.

6 Bake until bubbling and lightly browned, about 10 minutes. Serve immediately, in the dishes. Garnish with chives, if desired.

Spaghetti with Clams

SERVES 4

2 dozen hard-shell clams, such as littlenecks, scrubbed
1 cup water
½ cup dry white wine
salt and pepper
1 pound spaghetti, preferably Italian
5 tablespoons olive oil
2 garlic cloves, minced
3 tablespoons minced fresh parsley

1 ▲ Rinse the clams well in cold water and drain. Place in a large kettle with the water and wine and bring to a boil. Cover and steam until the shells open, about 6–8 minutes.

2 Discard any clams that have not opened. Remove the clams from their shells. If large, chop them roughly.

3 ▲ Strain the cooking liquid through a strainer lined with cheesecloth. Place in a small saucepan and boil rapidly until it has reduced by about half. Set aside.

4 Bring a large pot of water to a boil. Add 2 teaspoons of salt. When the water is boiling rapidly, add the spaghetti and stir well as it softens. Cook until the spaghetti is almost done, and still firm to the bite (check package directions for timing).

5 ▼ Meanwhile, heat the olive oil in a large skillet. Add the garlic and cook 2–3 minutes, but do not let it brown. Add the reduced clam liquid and the parsley. Let cook over low heat until the spaghetti is ready.

6 ▲ Drain the spaghetti. Add it to the skillet, raise the heat to medium, and add the clams. Cook 3–4 minutes, stirring constantly to cover the spaghetti with the sauce and to heat the clams.

7 Season with salt and pepper and serve. No cheese is needed with this sauce.

Maine Broiled Lobster Dinner

SERVES 4

4 live lobsters, 1½ pounds each

3 tablespoons minced mixed fresh herbs, such as parsley, chives, and tarragon

1 cup (2 sticks) butter, melted and kept warm

8 ears of tender fresh corn, shucked

salt and pepper

lemon halves, for serving

1 Preheat the broiler.

2 Kill each lobster quickly by inserting the tip of a large chef's knife between the eyes.

3 ▲ Turn the lobster over onto its back and cut it in half, from the head straight down to the tail. Remove and discard the hard sac near the head, and the intestinal vein that runs through the middle of the underside of the tail. All the rest of the lobster meat is edible.

4 ▲ Combine the minced herbs with the melted butter.

5 ▲ Place the lobster halves, shell side up, in a foil-lined broiler pan or a large roasting pan. (You may have to do this in two batches.) Broil about 8 minutes. Turn the lobster halves over, brush generously with the herb butter, and broil 7–8 minutes more.

6 ▲ While the lobsters are cooking, drop the corn into a large pot of rapidly boiling water and cook until just tender, 4–7 minutes. Drain.

7 Serve the lobsters and corn hot, with salt, freshly ground black pepper, lemon halves, and individual bowls of herb butter. Provide crackers for the claws, extra plates for cobs and shells, finger bowls and lots of napkins.

Shrimp Soufflé

SERVES 4–6

| 1 tablespoon dry bread crumbs |
| 2 tablespoons butter or margarine |
| ⅔ cup coarsely chopped cooked shrimp |
| 1 tablespoon minced fresh tarragon or parsley |
| ¼ teaspoon pepper |
| 3 tablespoons sherry or dry white wine |
| FOR THE SOUFFLE MIXTURE |
| 3 tablespoons butter or margarine |
| 2½ tablespoons flour |
| 1 cup milk, heated |
| ¾ teaspoon salt |
| 4 egg yolks |
| 5 egg whites |

1 ▲ Butter a 6- or 8-cup soufflé mold. Sprinkle with the bread crumbs, tilting the mold to coat the bottom and sides evenly.

2 Preheat the oven to 400°F.

~ **VARIATIONS** ~

For Lobster Soufflé, substitute 1 large lobster tail for the cooked shrimp. Chop it finely and add to the saucepan with the herbs and wine in place of the shrimp. For Crab Soufflé, use 1 cup fresh lump crab meat, picked over carefully to remove any bits of shell, in place of the shrimp.

3 ▲ Melt the butter or margarine in a small saucepan. Add the chopped shrimp and cook 2–3 minutes over low heat. Stir in the herbs, pepper, and wine and cook 1–2 minutes more. Raise the heat and boil rapidly to evaporate the liquid. Remove from the heat and set aside.

4 For the soufflé mixture, melt the butter or margarine in a medium-size heavy saucepan. Add the flour, blending well with a wire whisk. Cook over low heat 2–3 minutes. Pour in the hot milk and whisk vigorously until smooth. Simmer 2 minutes, still whisking. Stir in the salt.

5 ▼ Remove from the heat and immediately beat in the egg yolks, one at a time. Stir in the shrimp mixture.

6 In a large bowl, beat the egg whites until they form stiff peaks. Stir about one-quarter of the egg whites into the shrimp mixture. Gently fold in the rest of the egg whites.

7 Turn the mixture into the prepared mold. Place in the oven and turn the heat down to 375°F. Bake until the soufflé is puffed up and lightly browned on top, 30–40 minutes. Serve immediately.

Chicken Brunswick Stew

Serves 6

4-pound broiler chicken, cut in
   serving pieces

salt and pepper

paprika

2 tablespoons olive oil

2 tablespoons butter

2 cups chopped onions

1 cup chopped green or yellow bell
   pepper

2 cups chopped peeled fresh or canned
   plum tomatoes

1 cup white wine

2 cups chicken stock or water

¼ cup chopped fresh parsley

½ teaspoon hot pepper sauce

1 tablespoon Worcestershire sauce

2 cups corn kernels (fresh, frozen, or
   canned)

1 cup lima beans (fresh or frozen)

3 tablespoons flour

biscuits, rice, or potatoes, for serving
   (optional)

1 ▲ Rinse the chicken pieces under
cool water and pat dry with paper
towels. Sprinkle each piece lightly
with salt and paprika.

2 In a large heavy saucepan or Dutch
oven, heat the olive oil with the
butter over medium-high heat. Heat
until the mixture is sizzling and just
starting to change color.

3 ▲ Add the chicken pieces and fry
until golden brown on all sides.
Remove the chicken pieces with tongs
and set aside.

4 ▲ Reduce the heat to low and add
the onions and bell pepper to the pan.
Cook until softened, 8–10 minutes.

5 Raise the heat. Add the tomatoes
and their juice, the wine, stock or
water, parsley, and hot pepper and
Worcestershire sauces. Stir and bring
to a boil.

6 ▲ Return the chicken to the pan,
pushing it down in the sauce. Cover,
reduce the heat, and simmer 30
minutes, stirring occasionally.

7 ▲ Add the corn and lima beans
and mix well. Partly cover and cook
30 minutes more.

8 ▲ Tilt the pan, and skim off as
much of the surface fat as possible. In
a small bowl, mix the flour with a
little water to make a paste.

9 ▲ Gradually stir in about ¼ cup of
the hot sauce from the pan. Stir the
flour mixture into the stew, and mix
well to distribute it evenly. Cook 5–8
minutes more, stirring occasionally.

10 Check the seasoning. Serve the
stew in shallow soup plates or large
bowls, with biscuits, rice, or potatoes,
if desired.

Yankee Pot Roast

SERVES 8

4-pound chuck roast, or bottom round roast or brisket

3 garlic cloves, cut in half or in thirds

½-pound piece of salt pork or slab bacon

2 cups chopped onions

1 cup chopped celery

1½ cups chopped carrots

1 cup diced turnips

2 cups beef or chicken stock

2 cups dry red or white wine

1 bay leaf

1 teaspoon fresh thyme leaves, or
   ½ teaspoon dried thyme

8 small whole potatoes, or 3 large
   potatoes quartered

½ teaspoon salt

½ teaspoon pepper

4 tablespoons butter or margarine, at
   room temperature

¼ cup flour

watercress, for garnishing

1 Preheat the oven to 325°F.

2 ▲ With the tip of a sharp knife, make deep incisions in the chuck roast, on all sides, and insert the garlic pieces.

3 In a large flameproof casserole or Dutch oven, cook the salt pork or bacon over low heat until it renders its fat and begins to brown.

4 ▲ Remove the salt pork with a slotted spoon and discard. Raise the heat to medium-high and add the chuck roast. Brown it on all sides. Remove and set aside.

5 ▲ Add the onions, celery, and carrots to the casserole and cook over low heat until softened, 8–10 minutes. Stir in the turnips. Add the stock, wine, and herbs and mix well. Return the roast. Cover and place in the oven. Cook 2 hours.

6 ▲ Add the potatoes, pushing them down under the other vegetables. Season with salt and pepper. Cover again and cook until the potatoes are tender, about 45 minutes.

7 ▲ In a small bowl, combine the butter or margarine with the flour and mash together to make a paste.

8 Transfer the meat to a warmed serving platter. Remove the potatoes and other vegetables from the casserole with a slotted spoon and arrange around the roast. Keep hot.

9 ▲ Discard the bay leaf. Tilt the casserole and skim off the excess fat from the surface of the cooking liquid. Bring to a boil on top of the stove. Add half of the butter and flour paste and whisk to blend. Cook until the gravy is thickened, 3–4 minutes. Add more of the paste if the gravy is not sufficiently thick. Strain into a gravy boat. Serve with the sliced meat and vegetables, garnished with watercress.

~ VARIATION ~

Add 1½ cups frozen peas to the casserole about 5 minutes before the potatoes are done.

Philadelphia Scrapple

Serves 10

3 pounds pork neck bones or pigs' knuckles

3 quarts water

2 teaspoons salt

1 bay leaf

2 fresh sage leaves

1 teaspoon pepper

2¾ cups yellow cornmeal

maple syrup, fried eggs, and broiled tomatoes, for serving (optional)

1 Put the pork bones or knuckles, water, salt, and herbs in a large pot. Bring to a boil and simmer 2 hours.

2 ▲ Remove the meat from the bones and chop it finely or grind it. Set aside. Strain the broth and skim off any fat from the surface. Discard the bones.

3 Put 2 quarts of the broth in a large heavy saucepan. Add the chopped or ground meat and the pepper. Bring to a boil.

4 ▲ There should be about 1 quart of broth left. Stir the cornmeal into this. Add to the boiling mixture in the pan and cook until thickened, about 10 minutes, stirring constantly.

5 Reduce the heat to very low, cover the pan, and continue cooking about 25 minutes, stirring often. Check the seasoning.

6 ▲ Turn the mixture into 2 loaf pans and smooth the surface. Let cool, then refrigerate overnight.

7 To serve, cut the loaves into ½-inch slices. Sprinkle with flour and brown on both sides in butter or other fat over medium heat. Serve with warmed maple syrup, fried eggs, and broiled tomato halves, if desired.

Red Flannel Hash with Corned Beef

SERVES 4

6 bacon slices

¾ cup minced onion

2½ cups peeled, boiled, and diced potatoes

1½ cups chopped corned beef

1½ cups diced cooked beets (not in vinegar)

¼ cup light cream or half and half

¼ cup minced fresh parsley

salt and pepper

3 ▼ Heat 4 tablespoons of the reserved bacon fat, or other fat, in the skillet. Add the hash mixture, spreading it evenly with a spatula. Cook over low heat until the base is brown, about 15 minutes. Flip the hash out onto a plate.

4 ▲ Gently slide the hash back into the skillet and cook on the other side until lightly browned. Serve immediately.

1 ▲ Cook the bacon in a large heavy or nonstick skillet until golden and beginning to crisp. Remove with a slotted spatula and drain on paper towels. Pour off all but 2 tablespoons of the bacon fat in the pan, reserving the rest for later.

2 ▲ Cut the bacon into ½-inch pieces and place in a mixing bowl. Cook the onion in the bacon fat over low heat until softened, 8–10 minutes. Remove it from the pan and add to the bacon. Mix in the potatoes, corned beef, beets, cream, and the minced parsley. Season with salt and pepper and mix well.

Boston Baked Beans

SERVES 8

3 cups dried navy or Great Northern beans

1 bay leaf

4 cloves

2 medium-size onions, peeled

½ cup molasses

¾ cup dark brown sugar, firmly packed

1 tablespoon Dijon-style mustard

1 teaspoon salt

1 teaspoon pepper

1 cup boiling water

½-pound piece of salt pork

1 Rinse the beans under cold running water. Drain and place in a large bowl. Cover with cold water and let soak overnight.

2 Drain and rinse the beans. Put them in a large kettle with the bay leaf and cover with fresh cold water. Bring to a boil and simmer until tender, 1½–2 hours. Drain.

3 Preheat the oven to 275°F.

4 ▲ Put the beans in a large casserole. Stick 2 cloves in each of the onions and add them to the pot.

5 In a mixing bowl, combine the molasses, sugar, mustard, salt, and pepper. Add the boiling water and stir to blend.

6 Pour this mixture over the beans. Add more water if necessary so the beans are almost covered with liquid.

7 ▲ Blanch the piece of salt pork in boiling water for 3 minutes. Drain. Score the rind in deep ½-inch cuts. Add the salt pork to the casserole and push down just below the surface of the beans, skin-side up.

8 Cover the casserole and bake in the center of the oven for 4½–5 hours. Uncover for the last half hour, so the pork rind becomes brown and crisp. Slice or shred the pork and serve hot.

Harvard Beets

SERVES 6

5 medium-size cooked beets (about 1½ pounds)

⅓ cup sugar

1 tablespoon cornstarch

½ teaspoon salt

¼ cup cider or white wine vinegar

½ cup beet cooking liquid or water

2 tablespoons butter or margarine

1 Peel the beets and cut into medium-thick slices. Set aside.

2 ▲ In the top of a double boiler, combine all the other ingredients except the butter or margarine. Stir until smooth. Cook over hot water, stirring constantly, until the mixture is smooth and clear.

3 ▼ Add the beets and butter or margarine. Continue to cook over the hot water, stirring occasionally, until the beets are heated through, about 10 minutes. Serve hot.

Boston Baked Beans (top), Harvard Beets

Coleslaw

Serves 8

1 cup mayonnaise

½ cup white wine vinegar

1 tablespoon Dijon-style mustard

2 teaspoons sugar

1 tablespoon caraway seeds

salt and pepper

8 cups finely sliced green cabbage, or a
 mixture of green and red cabbage

1 cup grated carrots

1 cup finely sliced yellow or red onions

1 Combine the mayonnaise, vinegar,
mustard, sugar, and caraway seeds.
Season with salt and pepper.

2 ▼ Put the cabbage, carrots, and
onions in a large bowl.

3 ▲ Add the dressing to the
vegetables and mix well. Taste for
seasoning. Cover and refrigerate 1–2
hours. The cabbage will become more
tender the longer it marinates.

Pennsylvania Dutch Fried Tomatoes

Serves 4

2–3 large green or very firm red
 tomatoes (about ½ pound)

⅓ cup flour

4 tablespoons butter or bacon fat

salt and pepper

sugar, if needed

4 slices of hot buttered toast

¾ cup half and half

1 ▼ Slice the tomatoes into ½-inch
rounds. Coat lightly with flour.

2 ▲ Heat the butter or bacon fat in a
skillet. When it is hot, add the tomato
slices and cook until browned. Turn
them once, and season generously
with salt and pepper.

3 If the tomatoes are green, sprinkle
each slice with a little sugar. Cook
until the other side is brown, 3–4
minutes more.

4 Divide the tomatoes among the
slices of toast and keep hot.

5 ▲ Pour the half and half into the
hot skillet and bring to a simmer.
Cook 1–2 minutes, stirring to mix in
the brown bits and cooking juices.
Spoon the gravy over the tomatoes,
and serve immediately.

~ VARIATION ~

For Fried Tomatoes with Ham,
top the toast with ham slices
before covering with the tomatoes.

Coleslaw (top), Pennsylvania Dutch Fried Tomatoes

Boston Brown Bread

MAKES 2 SMALL LOAVES

1 tablespoon butter or margarine, at
    room temperature

1 cup yellow cornmeal

1 cup graham or whole-wheat flour

1 cup rye flour

2 teaspoons baking soda

1 teaspoon salt

2 cups buttermilk, at room temperature

¼ cup molasses

1 cup chopped raisins

butter or cream cheese, for serving

1 ▲ Grease two 1-pound food cans,
or two 1-quart pudding molds, with
the soft butter or margarine.

2 ▲ Sift all the dry ingredients
together into a large bowl. Tip in any
bran from the whole-wheat flour. Stir
well to blend.

3 In a separate bowl, combine the
buttermilk, molasses, and raisins. Add
to the dry ingredients and mix well.

4 ▲ Pour the batter into the
prepared molds, filling them about
two-thirds full. Cover the tops with
buttered foil, and tie or tape it down
so that the rising bread cannot push
the foil lid off.

5 Set the molds on a rack in a large
kettle with a tight-fitting lid. Pour in
enough warm water to come halfway
up the sides of the molds. Cover the
pan, bring to a boil, and steam 2½
hours. Check occasionally that the
water has not boiled away, and add
more if necessary.

6 Unmold the bread on a warmed
serving dish. Slice and serve with
butter or cream cheese for spreading.

Sweet Potato Biscuits

MAKES ABOUT 24

1¼ cups flour

4 teaspoons baking powder

1 teaspoon salt

1 tablespoon brown sugar

¾ cup mashed cooked sweet potatoes

⅔ cup milk

4 tablespoons butter or margarine, melted

1 Preheat the oven to 450°F.

2 ▲ Sift the flour, baking powder, and salt into a bowl. Add the sugar and stir to mix.

3 ▲ In a separate bowl, combine the sweet potatoes with the milk and melted butter or margarine. Mix well until evenly blended.

4 ▼ Stir the dry ingredients into the sweet potato mixture to make a dough. Turn onto a lightly floured surface and knead lightly just to mix, 1–2 minutes.

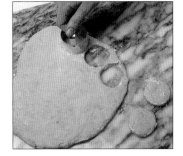

5 ▲ Roll or pat out the dough to ½-inch thickness. Cut out rounds with a 1½-inch cookie cutter.

6 Arrange the rounds on a greased cookie sheet. Bake until puffed and lightly golden, about 15 minutes. Serve the biscuits warm.

Boston Cream Pie

Serves 8

2 cups cake flour

1 tablespoon baking powder

½ teaspoon salt

½ cup (1 stick) butter, at room temperature

1 cup granulated sugar

2 eggs

1 teaspoon vanilla extract

¾ cup milk

For the filling

1 cup milk

3 egg yolks

½ cup granulated sugar

¼ cup flour

1 tablespoon butter

1 tablespoon brandy or 1 teaspoon vanilla extract

For the chocolate glaze

1-ounce square unsweetened chocolate

2 tablespoons butter or margarine

½ cup confectioners' sugar, plus extra for dusting

½ teaspoon vanilla extract

about 1 tablespoon hot water

1 Preheat the oven to 375°F.

2 Grease 2 8- × 2-inch round cake pans, and line the bottoms with rounds of greased wax paper.

3 Sift the flour with the baking powder and salt.

4 Beat the butter and granulated sugar together until light and fluffy. Add the eggs one at a time, beating well after each addition. Stir in the vanilla. Add the milk and dry ingredients alternately, mixing only enough to blend thoroughly. Do not over-beat the batter.

5 Divide the cake batter between the prepared pans and spread it out evenly. Bake until a cake tester inserted in the center comes out clean, about 25 minutes.

6 Meanwhile, make the filling. Heat the milk in a small saucepan to boiling point. Remove from the heat.

7 ▲ In a heatproof mixing bowl, beat the egg yolks until smooth. Gradually add the granulated sugar and continue beating until pale yellow. Beat in the flour.

8 ▲ Pour the hot milk into the egg yolk mixture in a steady stream, beating constantly. When all the milk has been added, place the bowl over, not in, a pan of boiling water, or pour the mixture into the top of a double boiler. Heat, stirring constantly, until thickened. Cook 2 minutes more, then remove from the heat. Stir in the butter and brandy or vanilla. Let cool.

9 ▲ When the cake layers have cooled, use a large sharp knife to slice off the domed top to make a flat surface. Place one layer on a serving plate and spread on the filling in a thick layer. Set the other layer on top, cut side down. Smooth the edge of the filling layer so it is flush with the sides of the cake layers.

10 ▲ For the glaze, melt the chocolate with the butter or margarine in the top of a double boiler. When smooth, remove from the heat and beat in the sugar to make a thick paste. Add the vanilla. Beat in a little of the hot water. If the glaze does not have a spreadable consistency, add more water, 1 teaspoon at a time.

11 Spread the glaze evenly over the top of the cake, using a metal spatula. Dust the top with confectioners' sugar. Because of the custard filling, refrigerate any leftover cake.

Shaker Summer Pudding

SERVES 6–8

1 loaf of white farmhouse-type bread,
  1–2 days old, sliced

1½ pounds fresh red currants

¼ cup plus 2 tablespoons sugar

¼ cup water

1½ pounds berries: raspberries,
  blueberries, and blackberries

juice of ½ lemon

whipped cream, for serving (optional)

1 ▲ Trim the crusts from the bread slices. Cut a round of bread to fit in the bottom of a 6-cup domed pudding mold or mixing bowl. Line the sides of the mold with bread slices, cutting them to fit and overlapping them slightly. Reserve enough bread slices to cover the top of the mold.

2 Combine the red currants with ¼ cup of the sugar and the water in a non-reactive saucepan. Heat gently, crushing the berries lightly to help the juices to flow. When the sugar has dissolved, remove from the heat.

3 Tip the currant mixture into a food processor and process until quite smooth. Press through a fine-mesh nylon strainer set in a bowl. Discard the fruit pulp left in the strainer.

4 Put the berries in a bowl with the remaining sugar and the lemon juice. Stir well.

5 One at a time, remove the cut bread pieces from the mold and dip in the red-currant purée. Replace to line the mold evenly.

6 ▲ Spoon the berries into the lined mold, pressing them down evenly. Top with the reserved cut bread slices, which have been dipped in the currant purée.

7 Cover the mold with plastic wrap. Set a small plate, just big enough to fit inside the rim of the mold, on top of the pudding. Weigh it down with cans of food. Refrigerate 8–24 hours.

8 To unmold, remove the weights, plate, and plastic wrap. Run a knife between the mold and the pudding to loosen it. Turn out onto a serving plate. Serve in wedges, with whipped cream if desired.

Apple Brown Betty

SERVES 6

1 cup fresh bread crumbs

¾ cup light brown sugar, firmly packed

½ teaspoon ground cinnamon

¼ teaspoon ground cloves

¼ teaspoon grated nutmeg

4 tablespoons butter

2 pounds tart-sweet apples

juice of 1 lemon

⅓ cup finely chopped walnuts

1 Preheat the broiler.

5 ▲ Peel, core, and slice the apples. Toss immediately with the lemon juice to prevent the apple slices from turning brown.

6 Sprinkle about 2½ tablespoons of bread crumbs over the bottom of the prepared dish. Cover with one-third of the apples and sprinkle with one-third of the sugar-spice mixture. Add another layer of bread crumbs and dot with one-third of the butter. Repeat the layers two more times, ending with a layer of bread crumbs. Sprinkle with the nuts, and dot with the remaining butter.

7 Bake until the apples are tender and the top is golden brown, 35–40 minutes. Serve warm. Good with cream or ice cream.

2 ▲ Spread the bread crumbs on a cookie sheet and toast under the broiler until golden, stirring so they color evenly. Set aside.

3 Preheat the oven to 375°F. Butter a 2-quart baking dish.

4 ▲ Mix the sugar with the spices. Cut the butter into pea-size pieces; set aside.

Maryland Peach and Blueberry Pie

SERVES 8

2 cups flour

½ teaspoon salt

2 teaspoons sugar

10 tablespoons (1¼ sticks) cold butter or margarine

1 egg yolk

2–3 tablespoons ice water

2 tablespoons milk, for glazing

FOR THE FILLING

3 cups peeled, pitted, and sliced fresh peaches

2 cups fresh blueberries

¾ cup sugar

2 tablespoons fresh lemon juice

⅓ cup flour

⅛ teaspoon grated nutmeg

2 tablespoons butter or margarine, cut in pea-size pieces

1 For the pastry, sift the flour, salt, and sugar into a bowl. Using a pastry blender or 2 knives, cut the butter or margarine into the dry ingredients as quickly as possible until the mixture resembles coarse meal.

2 Mix the egg yolk with 2 tablespoons of the ice water and sprinkle over the flour mixture. Combine with a fork until the dough holds together. If the dough is too crumbly, add a little more water, 1 teaspoon at a time. Gather the dough into a ball and flatten into a disk. Wrap in wax paper and refrigerate at least 20 minutes.

3 Roll out two-thirds of the dough between 2 sheets of wax paper to a thickness of about ⅛ inch. Use to line a 9-inch pie pan. Trim all around, leaving a ½-inch overhang. Fold the overhang under to form the edge. Using a fork, press the edge to the rim of the pie pan.

4 ▲ Gather the trimmings and remaining dough into a ball, and roll out to a thickness of about ¼ inch. Using a pastry wheel or sharp knife, cut strips ½ inch wide. Refrigerate both the pie shell and the strips of dough for 20 minutes.

5 Preheat the oven to 400°F.

6 ▲ Line the pie shell with wax paper and fill with dried beans. Bake until the pie shell is just set, 7–10 minutes. Remove from the oven and carefully lift out the paper with the beans. Prick the bottom of the pie shell all over with a fork, then return to the oven and bake 5 minutes more. Let the pie shell cool slightly before filling. Leave the oven on.

7 ▲ In a mixing bowl, combine the peach slices with the blueberries, sugar, lemon juice, flour, and nutmeg. Spoon the fruit mixture evenly into the pie shell. Dot with the pieces of butter or margarine.

8 ▲ Weave a lattice top with the chilled pastry strips, pressing the ends to the baked pie-shell edge. Brush the strips with the milk.

9 Bake the pie 15 minutes. Reduce the heat to 350°F, and continue baking until the filling is tender and bubbling and the pastry lattice is golden, about 30 minutes more. If the pastry gets too brown, cover loosely with a piece of foil. Serve the pie warm or at room temperature.

Brethren's Cider Pie

SERVES 6

1½ cups flour

¼ teaspoon salt

2 teaspoons sugar

½ cup (1 stick) cold butter or margarine

3–4 tablespoons ice water

FOR THE FILLING

2½ cups apple cider

1 tablespoon butter

1 cup maple syrup

¼ cup water

¼ teaspoon salt

2 eggs, at room temperature, separated

1 teaspoon grated nutmeg

1 ▲ For the pastry, sift the flour, salt, and sugar into a bowl. Using a pastry blender or 2 knives, cut the butter or margarine into the dry ingredients as quickly as possible until the mixture resembles coarse meal.

2 Sprinkle 3 tablespoons of the ice water over the flour mixture. Combine with a fork until the dough holds together. If the dough is too crumbly, add a little more water, 1 teaspoon at a time. Gather the dough into a ball and flatten into a disk. Wrap in wax paper and refrigerate at least 20 minutes.

3 ▲ Meanwhile, place the cider in a medium-size heavy saucepan. Boil until only ¾ cup remains. Let cool.

4 ▲ Roll out the dough between 2 sheets of wax paper to a thickness of about ⅛ inch. Use to line a 9-inch pie pan.

5 ▲ Trim all around, leaving a ½-inch overhang. Fold the overhang under to form the edge. Using a fork, press the edge to the rim of the pan and press up from under with your fingers at intervals for a ruffle effect. Refrigerate 20 minutes.

6 Preheat the oven to 350°F.

7 ▲ For the filling, add the butter, maple syrup, water, and salt to the cider and simmer gently 5–6 minutes. Remove the pan from the heat and let the mixture cool slightly, then whisk in the beaten egg yolks.

8 ▲ In a large bowl, beat the egg whites until they form stiff peaks. Add the cider mixture and fold gently together until evenly blended.

9 ▲ Pour into the prepared pie shell. Dust with the grated nutmeg.

10 Bake until the pastry is golden brown and the filling is well set, 30–35 minutes. Serve warm.

Vermont Baked Maple Custard

SERVES 6

3 eggs

½ cup maple syrup

2½ cups milk

⅛ teaspoon salt

⅛ teaspoon grated nutmeg

~ COOK'S TIP ~

Baking delicate mixtures such as
custards in a water bath helps
protect them from uneven heating
which could make them rubbery.

1 Preheat the oven to 350°F.

2 ▼ Combine all the ingredients in a
bowl and mix well.

3 ▲ Set individual custard cups or
ramekins in a roasting pan half filled
with hot water. Pour the custard
mixture into the cups. Bake until the
custards are set, ¾–1 hour. Test by
inserting the blade of a knife in the
center: it should come out clean.
Serve warm or chilled.

Cranberry Ice

MAKES ABOUT 1½ QUARTS

2 quarts fresh or frozen cranberries

2 cups water

1¾ cups sugar

¼ teaspoon grated orange rind

2 tablespoons fresh orange juice

1 Check the manufacturer's
instructions for your ice cream maker,
if using one, to find out its capacity. If
necessary, halve the recipe.

2 ▲ Pick over and wash the
cranberries. Discard any that are
blemished or soft.

3 ▼ Place the cranberries in a non-
reactive saucepan with the water and
bring to a boil. Reduce the heat and
simmer until the cranberries are soft,
about 15 minutes.

4 Push the cranberry mixture through
a fine-mesh nylon strainer set in a
bowl. Return the purée to the pan,
add the sugar, and stir to dissolve. Boil
5 minutes. Stir in the orange rind and
juice. Remove from the heat and let
the cranberry mixture cool to room
temperature.

5 To freeze in an ice cream maker,
pour the cranberry mixture into the
machine and freeze following the
manufacturer's instructions.

6 ▲ If you do not have an ice cream
maker, pour the mixture into a metal
or plastic freezer container and freeze
until softly set, about 3 hours.
Remove the frozen cranberry mixture
from the container and chop roughly
into 3-inch pieces. Place in a food
processor and process until smooth.
Return the mixture to the freezer
container and freeze again until firm.
Repeat this freezing and chopping
process 2 or 3 times, then leave to
freeze until firm.

Vermont Baked Maple Custard (top), Cranberry Ice

THE SOUTH

RICH AND DIVERSE CULINARY
INFLUENCES – FRENCH, SPANISH,
NATIVE AMERICAN, AND AFRICAN –
HAVE BROUGHT ABOUT SEVERAL
DISTINCT CUISINES, CAJUN BEING
PERHAPS THE MOST WELL KNOWN.
ALL HAVE CAPITALIZED ON THE
BOUNTY OF FIELD AND FOREST,
THE PROXIMITY OF WATER
THROUGHOUT MUCH OF THE
REGION, AND A WARM CLIMATE.

Miami Chilled Avocado Soup

SERVES 4

2 large or 3 medium-size ripe avocados

1 tablespoon fresh lemon juice

¼ cup coarsely chopped peeled
    cucumber

2 tablespoons dry sherry wine

¼ cup coarsely chopped scallions, with
    some of the green stems

2 cups mild-flavored chicken stock

1 teaspoon salt

hot pepper sauce (optional)

plain yogurt or cream, for serving

1 ▼ Halve the avocados, pull out the pits, and peel. Roughly chop the flesh and place in a food processor or blender. Add the lemon juice, and process until very smooth.

2 ▲ Add the cucumber, sherry, and most of the scallions. Process again until smooth.

3 ▲ In a large bowl, combine the avocado mixture with the chicken stock. Whisk until well blended. Season with the salt and a few drops of hot pepper sauce, if desired. Cover the bowl and chill well.

4 ▲ To serve, fill individual bowls with the soup. Place a spoonful of yogurt or cream in the center of each bowl and swirl with a spoon. Sprinkle with the reserved scallions.

Shrimp and Corn Bisque

SERVES 4

2 tablespoons olive oil

1 onion, minced

4 tablespoons butter or margarine

¼ cup flour

3 cups fish or chicken stock, or clam juice

1 cup milk

1 cup peeled cooked small shrimp, deveined if necessary

1½ cups corn kernels (fresh, frozen, or canned)

½ teaspoon minced fresh dill or thyme

salt

hot pepper sauce

½ cup light cream

1 Heat the olive oil in a large heavy saucepan. Add the onion and cook over low heat until softened, 8–10 minutes.

2 Meanwhile, melt the butter or margarine in a medium-size saucepan. Add the flour and stir with a wire whisk until blended. Cook 1–2 minutes. Pour in the stock and milk and stir to blend. Bring to a boil over medium heat and cook 5–8 minutes, stirring frequently.

3 ▲ Cut each shrimp into 2 or 3 pieces and add to the onion with the corn and dill or thyme. Cook 2–3 minutes, stirring occasionally. Remove the pan from the heat.

4 ▼ Add the sauce mixture to the shrimp and corn mixture and mix well. Remove 3 cups of the soup and purée in a blender or food processor. Return it to the rest of the soup in the pan and stir well. Season with salt and hot pepper sauce to taste.

5 ▲ Add the cream and stir to blend. Heat the soup almost to boiling point, stirring frequently. Serve hot.

Palm Beach Papaya and Avocado Salad

SERVES 4

2 ripe avocados

1 ripe papaya

1 large sweet orange

1 small red onion

2 cups small arugula leaves, washed
and spun dry

FOR THE DRESSING

¼ cup olive oil

2 tablespoons fresh lemon or lime juice

salt and pepper

1 ▼ Halve the avocados and remove the pits. Carefully peel off the skin. Cut each avocado half lengthwise into 4 thick slices.

2 ▲ Peel the papaya. Cut it in half lengthwise and scoop out the seeds with a spoon. Set aside 1 teaspoon of the seeds for the dressing. Cut each papaya half lengthwise into 8 slices.

3 ▲ Peel the orange. Using a sharp paring knife, cut out the sections, cutting on either side of the dividing membranes. Cut the onion into very thin slices and separate into rings.

4 ▲ Combine the dressing ingredients in a bowl and mix well. Stir in the reserved papaya seeds.

5 Assemble the salad on 4 individual serving plates. Alternate slices of papaya and avocado and add the orange sections and a small mound of arugula topped with onion rings. Spoon on the dressing.

Warm Salad of Black-Eyed Peas

SERVES 4

2 small red bell peppers

½ teaspoon Dijon-style mustard

2 tablespoons wine vinegar

¼ teaspoon salt

⅛ teaspoon pepper

6 tablespoons olive oil

2 tablespoons minced fresh chives

3 cups fresh black-eyed peas

1 bay leaf

8 lean bacon slices

1 Preheat the broiler.

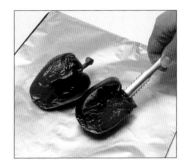

2 ▲ Broil the bell peppers until the skin blackens and blisters, turning the peppers so that all sides are charred. Remove from the broiler and place the peppers in a paper or plastic bag to steam. Let cool 10 minutes.

3 Peel off the skin. Cut the peppers in half, discard the seeds, white membranes, and stem, and slice into ½- × 2-inch strips. Set aside.

~ COOK'S TIP ~

If preferred, chop the roasted red peppers rather than cutting them into strips and mix into the warm black-eyed peas.

4 ▼ Combine the mustard and vinegar in a small bowl. Add the salt and pepper. Beat in the oil until well blended. Add the chives.

5 Add the black-eyed peas to a pan of boiling salted water, with the bay leaf. Boil until just tender, 13–15 minutes.

6 Meanwhile, cook the bacon until crisp. Drain on paper towels. Cut or break into small pieces.

7 ▲ When the black-eyed peas are done, drain them and discard the bay leaf. While they are still warm, toss them with the chive dressing.

8 Make a mound of peas on a serving dish. Sprinkle with the bacon pieces and garnish with the strips of red pepper. Serve warm.

Fromajardis

MAKES ABOUT 40

2 cups flour

¼ teaspoon grated nutmeg

½ teaspoon salt

10 tablespoons cold butter or
    shortening, or a combination of both

4–5 tablespoons ice water

FOR THE FILLING

2 eggs

¼ pound sharp cheddar cheese,
    shredded (about 1 cup)

hot pepper sauce

1 tablespoon minced mixed fresh herbs,
    such as thyme, chives, and sage

1 For the pastry, sift the flour,
nutmeg, and salt into a bowl. Using a
pastry blender or 2 knives, cut the
butter or shortening into the dry
ingredients as quickly as possible until
the mixture is crumbly and resembles
coarse meal.

2 ▲ Sprinkle 4 tablespoons of the ice
water over the flour mixture.
Combine with a fork until the dough
holds together. If the dough is too
crumbly, add a little more water,
1 teaspoon at a time. Gather the
dough into a ball.

3 ▲ Divide the dough in half and pat
each portion into a disk. Wrap the
disks in wax paper and refrigerate
them at least 20 minutes.

4 Preheat the oven to 425°F.

5 ▲ For the filling, put the eggs in a
mixing bowl and beat well with a fork.
Add the cheese, hot pepper sauce to
taste, and the herbs.

6 ▲ On a lightly floured surface, roll
out the dough to a thickness of ⅛ inch
or less. Cut out rounds using a 3-inch
cookie cutter or drinking glass.

7 ▲ Place 1 teaspoon of filling in the
center of each pastry round. Fold over
to make half-moon shapes, and press
the edges together with the tines of a
fork. A bit of filling may ooze through
the seam.

8 ▲ Cut a few small slashes in the
top of each pastry with the point of a
sharp knife. Place on ungreased
baking sheets. Bake until the pastries
start to darken slightly, 18–20
minutes. To test for doneness, cut one
in half; the pastry should be cooked
through. Serve warm with drinks.

~ COOK'S TIP ~

The fromajardis may be made
ahead of time. Let them cool on a
wire rack and then store in an
airtight container. Just before
serving, reheat the pastries in a
preheated 375°F oven for
5–10 minutes.

Crab Bayou

SERVES 6

1 pound fresh lump crab meat

3 hard-cooked egg yolks

1 teaspoon Dijon-style mustard

6 tablespoons butter or margarine,
   at room temperature

¼ teaspoon cayenne

3 tablespoons sherry wine

2 tablespoons minced fresh parsley

½ cup whipping cream

½ cup thinly sliced scallions, including
   some of the green stems

salt and black pepper

½ cup dry bread crumbs

1 Preheat the oven to 350°F.

2 ▼ Pick over the crab meat and remove any shell or cartilage, keeping the pieces of crab as big as possible.

3 ▲ In a medium bowl, crumble the egg yolks with a fork. Add the mustard, 4 tablespoons of the butter or margarine, and the cayenne, and mash together to form a paste. Mash in the sherry and parsley.

4 ▲ Mix in the cream and scallions. Stir in the crab meat. Season with salt and pepper.

5 ▲ Divide the mixture equally among 6 greased scallop shells or other individual baking dishes. Sprinkle with the bread crumbs and dot with the remaining butter or margarine.

6 Bake until bubbling hot and golden brown, about 20 minutes.

Cajun "Popcorn" with Basil Mayonnaise

SERVES 8

2 pounds raw crawfish tails, peeled, or small shrimp, peeled and deveined

2 eggs

1 cup dry white wine

½ cup fine cornmeal (or all-purpose flour, if not available)

½ cup all-purpose flour

1 tablespoon minced fresh chives

1 garlic clove, minced

½ teaspoon fresh thyme leaves

¼ teaspoon salt

¼ teaspoon cayenne

¼ teaspoon black pepper

oil for deep-frying

FOR THE MAYONNAISE

1 egg yolk

2 teaspoons Dijon-style mustard

1 tablespoon white wine vinegar

salt and pepper

1 cup olive or vegetable oil

½ cup fresh basil leaves, minced

1 ▲ Rinse the crawfish tails or shrimp in cool water. Drain well and set aside in a cool place.

2 Mix together the eggs and wine in a small bowl.

3 ▼ In a mixing bowl, combine the cornmeal and/or flour, chives, garlic, thyme, salt, cayenne, and pepper. Gradually whisk in the egg mixture, blending well. Cover the batter and let stand 1 hour at room temperature.

4 For the mayonnaise, combine the egg yolk, mustard, and vinegar in a mixing bowl. Add salt and pepper to taste. Add the oil in a thin stream, beating vigorously with a wire whisk. When the mixture is thick and smooth, stir in the basil. Cover and refrigerate until ready to serve.

5 Heat 2–3 inches of oil in a large skillet or deep-fryer to 365–370°F. Dip the seafood into the batter and fry in small batches until golden brown, 2–3 minutes. Turn as necessary for even coloring. Remove with a slotted spoon and drain on paper towels. Serve hot, with the basil mayonnaise.

Crawfish or Shrimp Etouffée

SERVES 6

2½ pounds raw crawfish or shrimp in shell, with heads

3 cups water

⅓ cup vegetable oil or lard

⅓ cup flour

¾ cup minced onions

¼ cup minced green bell pepper

¼ cup minced celery

1 garlic clove, minced

½ cup dry white wine

2 tablespoons butter or margarine

½ cup minced fresh parsley

¼ cup minced fresh chives

salt

hot pepper sauce

rice, for serving

1 Peel and devein the crawfish or shrimp; reserve the heads and shells. Keep the seafood in a covered bowl in the refrigerator.

2 ▲ Put the heads and shells in a large pot with the water. Bring to a boil, cover, and simmer 15 minutes. Strain and reserve 1½ cups of this stock. Set aside.

3 To make the Cajun roux, heat the oil or lard in a heavy castiron skillet or steel saucepan. (Do not use a nonstick pan.)

4 ▲ When the oil is hot, add the flour, a little at a time, and blend to a smooth paste using a long-handled flat-bottomed wooden spoon.

5 ▲ Cook over medium-low heat, stirring constantly, until the Cajun roux reaches the desired color, 25–40 minutes. It will gradually deepen in color from light beige to tan, to a deeper, redder brown. When it reaches the color of peanut butter, remove the pan from the heat and immediately mix in the onions, bell pepper, and celery. Continue stirring to prevent further darkening.

6 ▲ Return the pan to low heat. Add the garlic and cook 1–2 minutes, stirring. Add the seafood stock and blend well with a wire whisk. Whisk in the white wine.

7 ▲ Bring to a boil, stirring, and simmer until the sauce is thick, 3–4 minutes. Remove from the heat.

8 ▲ In a large heavy saucepan, melt the butter or margarine. Add the crawfish or shrimp, stir, and cook until pink, 2–3 minutes. Stir in the parsley and chives.

9 Add the sauce and stir well to combine. Season with salt and hot pepper sauce to taste. Simmer over medium heat 3–4 minutes more. Serve hot with rice.

~ COOK'S TIP ~

When making the Cajun roux, take great care not to burn the flour. If the mixture starts to smoke, immediately remove the pan from the heat and stir until the mixture cools slightly. If the flour mixture should burn, or if black specks appear, throw it away and start again, or the étouffée will have a bitter burned taste.

Shrimp-Stuffed Eggplant

SERVES 4

2 large firm eggplants, of equal size
2 tablespoons fresh lemon juice
3 tablespoons butter or margarine
½ pound raw shrimp, peeled and deveined
½ cup thinly sliced scallions, including some green stems
1½ cups chopped fresh tomatoes
1 garlic clove, minced
¼ cup chopped fresh parsley
¼ cup chopped fresh basil
⅛ teaspoon grated nutmeg
salt and pepper
hot pepper sauce
½ cup dry bread crumbs
rice, for serving

1 Preheat the oven to 375°F.

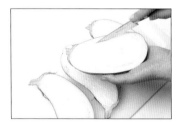

2 ▲ Cut the eggplants in half lengthwise. With a small sharp knife, cut around the inside edge of each eggplant half, about ½ inch from the skin. Carefully scoop out the flesh, leaving a shell ½ inch thick.

3 Immerse the shells, skin side up, in cold water to prevent them from discoloring.

~ COOK'S TIP ~

This can also be served cold for an unusual summer dish.

4 ▲ Chop the scooped-out eggplant flesh coarsely, toss with the lemon juice, and set aside.

5 ▲ Melt 2 tablespoons of the butter or margarine in a skillet. Add the shrimp and sauté until pink, 2–3 minutes, turning so they cook evenly. Remove the shrimp with a slotted spoon and set aside.

6 ▲ Add the scallions to the skillet and cook over medium heat about 2 minutes, stirring constantly. Add the tomatoes, garlic, and parsley and cook 5 minutes more.

7 Add the chopped eggplant, basil, and nutmeg. If necessary, add a little water to prevent the vegetables sticking. Mix well. Cover and simmer 8–10 minutes. Remove from the heat.

8 ▲ Cut each shrimp into 2 or 3 pieces. Stir into the vegetable mixture. Season with salt, pepper, and hot sauce to taste.

9 Lightly oil a shallow baking pan large enough to hold the eggplant halves in one layer. Drain and dry the eggplant shells and arrange in the pan.

10 ▲ Sprinkle a layer of bread crumbs into each shell. Spoon in a layer of the shrimp mixture. Repeat, finishing with a layer of crumbs.

11 ▲ Dot with the remaining butter or margarine. Bake until bubbling hot and golden brown on top, 20–25 minutes. Serve immediately, accompanied by rice, if desired.

Shrimp Creole

SERVES 4

1½ pounds raw shrimp in shell, with heads, if available

2 cups water

3 tablespoons olive or vegetable oil

1½ cups minced onions

½ cup minced celery

½ cup minced green bell pepper

½ cup chopped fresh parsley

1 garlic clove, minced

1 tablespoon Worcestershire sauce

¼ teaspoon cayenne

½ cup dry white wine

1 cup chopped peeled plum tomatoes

1 teaspoon salt

1 bay leaf

1 teaspoon sugar

rice, for serving

1 ▲ Peel and devein the shrimp; reserve the heads and shells. Keep the shrimp in a covered bowl in the refrigerator while you make the sauce.

2 Put the shrimp heads and shells in a saucepan with the water. Bring to a boil and simmer 15 minutes. Strain and reserve 1½ cups of this stock. Set the stock aside.

3 ▲ Heat the oil in a heavy saucepan. Add the onions and cook over low heat until softened, 8–10 minutes. Add the celery and bell pepper and cook 5 minutes more. Stir in the parsley, garlic, Worcestershire sauce, and cayenne. Cook another 5 minutes, stirring occasionally.

4 Raise the heat to medium. Stir in the wine and simmer 3–4 minutes. Add the tomatoes, shrimp stock, salt, bay leaf, and sugar and bring to a boil. Stir well, then reduce the heat to low and simmer until the tomatoes have fallen apart and the sauce has reduced slightly, about 30 minutes. Remove from the heat and let cool slightly.

5 Discard the bay leaf. Pour the sauce into a food processor or blender and purée until quite smooth. Taste and adjust the seasoning.

6 ▲ Return the sauce to the pan and bring to a boil. Add the shrimp and simmer until they turn pink, 4–5 minutes only. Serve with rice.

Fried Catfish Fillets with Piquant Sauce

SERVES 4

1 egg

¼ cup olive oil

squeeze of lemon juice

½ teaspoon minced fresh dill or parsley

salt and pepper

4 catfish fillets

½ cup flour

2 tablespoons butter or margarine

FOR THE SAUCE

1 egg yolk

2 tablespoons Dijon-style mustard

2 tablespoons white wine vinegar

2 teaspoons paprika

1¼ cups olive or vegetable oil

2 tablespoons prepared horseradish

½ teaspoon minced garlic

¼ cup minced celery

2 tablespoons catsup

½ teaspoon pepper

½ teaspoon salt

1 ▲ For the sauce, combine the egg yolk, mustard, vinegar, and paprika in a mixing bowl. Add the oil in a thin stream, beating vigorously with a wire whisk to blend it in.

~ **VARIATION** ~

If preferred, serve the catfish fillets with lime or lemon wedges.

2 ▲ When the mixture is smooth and thick, beat in all the other sauce ingredients. Cover and refrigerate until ready to serve.

3 ▲ Combine the egg, 1 tablespoon olive oil, the lemon juice, herbs, and a little salt and pepper in a shallow dish. Beat until well combined.

4 ▼ Dip both sides of each catfish fillet in the egg and herb mixture, then coat lightly with flour, shaking off the excess.

5 Heat the butter or margarine with the remaining olive oil in a large heavy skillet or frying pan. Add the fillets and fry until golden brown on both sides and cooked, 8–10 minutes. To test for doneness, insert the point of a sharp knife into the fish: it should still be opaque in the center.

6 Serve the catfish fillets hot, with the piquant sauce.

Seafood and Sausage Gumbo

SERVES 10–12

3 pounds raw shrimp in shell, with heads, if available

7 cups water

1 onion, quartered

4 bay leaves

¼ cup vegetable oil

1 cup flour

4 tablespoons margarine or butter

3 cups minced onions

2 cups minced green bell pepper

2 cups minced celery

1½ pounds kielbasa (Polish) or andouille sausage, cut in ½-inch rounds

1 pound fresh okra, cut in ½-inch slices

3 garlic cloves, minced

½ teaspoon fresh or dried thyme leaves

2 teaspoons salt

½ teaspoon black pepper

½ teaspoon white pepper

1 teaspoon cayenne

hot pepper sauce (optional)

2 cups chopped peeled fresh or canned plum tomatoes

1 pound fresh lump crab meat

rice, for serving

1 Peel and devein the shrimp; reserve the heads and shells. Keep the shrimp in a covered bowl in the refrigerator while you make the sauce.

2 Put the shrimp heads and shells in a saucepan with the water, quartered onion, and 1 bay leaf. Bring to a boil, then partly cover and simmer 20 minutes. Strain and set aside.

3 Heat the oil in a heavy castiron or steel pan. (Do not use a nonstick pan.) When the oil is hot, add the flour, a little at a time, and blend to a smooth paste using a long-handled flat-bottomed wooden spoon.

4 ▲ Cook over medium-low heat, stirring constantly, until the Cajun roux reaches the desired color, 25–40 minutes. The roux will gradually deepen in color from light beige to tan, to a deeper, redder brown. When it reaches the color of peanut butter, remove the pan from the heat and continue stirring until the roux has cooled and stopped cooking.

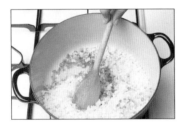

5 ▲ Melt the margarine or butter in a large heavy saucepan or Dutch oven. Add the minced onions, bell pepper, and celery. Cook over medium-low heat until the onions are softened, 6–8 minutes, stirring occasionally.

6 ▲ Add the sausage and mix well. Cook 5 minutes more. Add the okra and garlic, stir, and cook until the okra stops producing white "threads."

7 ▲ Add the remaining bay leaves, the thyme, salt, black and white peppers, cayenne, and hot pepper sauce to taste, if desired. Mix well. Stir in 6 cups of the shrimp stock and the tomatoes. Bring to a boil, then partly cover the pan, lower the heat, and simmer about 20 minutes.

8 Whisk in the Cajun roux. Raise the heat and bring to a boil, whisking well. Lower the heat again and simmer, uncovered, 40–50 minutes more, stirring occasionally.

9 ▲ Gently stir in the shrimp and crabmeat. Cook until the shrimp turn pink, 3–4 minutes. To serve, put a mound of hot rice in each serving bowl and ladle on the gumbo, making sure each person gets some seafood and some sausage.

~ COOK'S TIP ~

Heavy pans retain their heat. When making a Cajun roux, do not let it get too dark, as the roux will continue cooking off the heat.

Smothered Rabbit

SERVES 4

6 tablespoons soy sauce

hot pepper sauce

½ teaspoon white pepper

1 teaspoon sweet paprika

1 teaspoon dried basil

2- to 3-pound rabbit, cut in pieces

3 tablespoons peanut or olive oil

¾ cup flour

2 cups finely sliced onions

1 cup dry white wine

1 cup chicken or meat stock

1 teaspoon salt

1 teaspoon minced garlic

½ cup minced fresh parsley

mashed potatoes or rice, for serving

1 ▼ Combine the soy sauce, hot pepper sauce to taste, white pepper, paprika, and basil in a medium-size bowl. Add the rabbit pieces and rub them with the mixture. Let marinate at least 1 hour.

2 ▲ Heat the oil in a high-sided ovenproof skillet or Dutch oven. Coat the rabbit pieces lightly in the flour, shaking off the excess. Brown the rabbit in the hot oil, turning frequently, 5–6 minutes. Remove with tongs and set aside.

3 Preheat the oven to 350°F.

4 ▲ Add the onions to the skillet and cook over low heat until softened, 8–10 minutes. Raise the heat to medium, add the wine, and stir well to mix in all the cooking juices.

5 Return the rabbit to the skillet. Add the stock, salt, garlic, and parsley. Mix well and turn the rabbit to coat with the sauce.

6 Cover the skillet and place it in the oven. Cook until the rabbit is tender, about 1 hour, stirring occasionally. Serve with mashed potatoes or rice.

Pork Jambalaya

SERVES 6

2½ pounds boneless pork shoulder butt

¼ cup peanut or olive oil

1½ cups minced onions

1 cup minced celery

1½ cups minced green or red bell
 peppers

1½ cups tasso or other smoked ham,
 cut in ½-inch cubes

1 teaspoon black pepper

1 teaspoon white pepper

½ teaspoon cayenne

1 teaspoon salt

1 garlic clove, minced

1½ cups chopped peeled fresh or
 canned tomatoes

1 bay leaf

½ teaspoon fresh or dried thyme leaves

hot pepper sauce

1 cup dry white wine

2 cups long-grain rice

3–4 cups chicken stock, heated

1 Remove any visible fat or gristle
from the pork, and cut the meat into
½-inch cubes.

2 ▲ Heat the oil in a large pot or
Dutch oven. Brown the cubes of pork,
in batches, stirring to color evenly.
Remove the pork with a slotted spoon
and set aside.

3 ▼ Add the onions, celery, and bell
peppers to the pot and cook, stirring,
3–4 minutes. Add the ham, black and
white peppers, cayenne, and salt.
Cook over medium heat, stirring
frequently, until the onions are soft
and golden, about 12 minutes.

4 Add the garlic, tomatoes, herbs,
and hot pepper sauce to taste. Cook 5
minutes more. Add the pork and wine
and mix well, then cover the pot and
cook gently over low heat for about
45 minutes.

5 Add the rice and stir well. Cook
3–4 minutes.

6 Pour in 3 cups of the chicken stock
and stir to blend. Bring to a boil.
Cover, reduce the heat to low, and
simmer until the rice is tender, about
15 minutes. Stir the mixture
occasionally and add more chicken
stock if necessary. The rice should be
moist, not dry and fluffy. Serve from
the casserole or in a large heated
 serving dish.

Pecan-Stuffed Pork Chops

4 pork chops, at least 1 inch thick, trimmed of almost all fat

½ cup fresh bread crumbs

½ cup minced scallions

½ cup minced apple

½ cup chopped pecans

1 garlic clove, minced

¼ cup minced fresh parsley

¼ teaspoon cayenne

¼ teaspoon black pepper

½ teaspoon dry mustard

⅛ teaspoon ground cumin

2 tablespoons olive oil

½ cup meat or chicken stock

½ cup dry white wine

1 bay leaf

1 Preheat the oven to 350°F.

2 ▲ Make a pocket in each chop by cutting horizontally from the fatty side straight to the bone.

3 ▲ Combine all the other ingredients except the stock, wine, and bay leaf. Mix well. Divide the mixture among the chops, filling each pocket with as much stuffing as it will comfortably hold.

4 ▲ Place the chops in a greased baking dish large enough to hold them in one layer.

5 ▲ Pour the stock and wine over them and add the bay leaf and any leftover stuffing. Cover tightly. Bake until tender, about 1 hour, basting occasionally with pan juices. Serve with cooking juices spooned over.

Ham with Red-Eye Gravy

1 tablespoon butter or margarine

1 slice of ham, ¼–½ inch thick, preferably uncooked country-style ham, with some fat left on it

½ cup strong brewed coffee, heated

mashed potatoes for serving

~ COOK'S TIP ~

Try ham cooked this way for breakfast, accompanied by grits.

1 ▼ Melt the butter or margarine in a small skillet. Add the ham and sauté until golden brown on both sides. Remove to a warm plate.

2 ▲ Pour the coffee into the skillet and stir to mix with the cooking juices. When the gravy is boiling, pour it over the ham. Serve the ham with mashed potatoes, if desired.

Pecan-Stuffed Pork Chops (top), Ham with Red-Eye Gravy

Oven "Fried" Chicken

SERVES 4

4 large chicken pieces

½ cup flour

½ teaspoon salt

¼ teaspoon pepper

1 egg

2 tablespoons water

2 tablespoons minced mixed fresh herbs,
   such as parsley, basil, and thyme

1 cup dry bread crumbs

¼ cup freshly grated Parmesan cheese

lemon wedges, for serving

1 Preheat the oven to 400°F.

2 Rinse the chicken pieces in cool
water. Pat dry with paper towels.

3 ▼ Combine the flour, salt, and
pepper on a plate and stir with a fork
to mix. Coat the chicken pieces on
both sides with the seasoned flour and
shake off the excess.

4 Sprinkle a little water onto the
chicken pieces, and coat again lightly
with the seasoned flour.

5 ▲ Beat the egg with the water in a
shallow dish. Stir in the herbs. Dip
the chicken pieces into the egg
mixture, turning to coat them evenly.

6 ▲ Combine the bread crumbs and
grated Parmesan cheese on a plate.
Roll the chicken pieces in the crumbs,
patting with your fingers to help them
to adhere.

7 ▲ Place the chicken pieces in a
greased shallow pan large enough to
hold them in one layer. Bake until
thoroughly cooked and golden brown,
20–30 minutes. To test for doneness,
prick with a fork; the juices that run
out should be clear, not pink. Serve
hot, with lemon wedges.

Blackened Chicken Breasts

SERVES 6

6 medium-size skinless boneless chicken
  breast halves

6 tablespoons butter or margarine

1 teaspoon garlic powder

2 teaspoons onion powder

1 teaspoon cayenne

2 teaspoons sweet paprika

1½ teaspoons salt

½ teaspoon white pepper

1 teaspoon black pepper

¼ teaspoon ground cumin

1 teaspoon dried thyme leaves

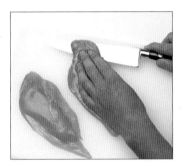

1 ▲ Slice each chicken breast piece
in half horizontally, making 2 pieces
of about the same thickness. Flatten
slightly with the heel of the hand.

2 Melt the butter or margarine in a
small saucepan.

3 ▼ Combine all the remaining
ingredients in a shallow bowl and stir
to blend well. Brush the chicken
pieces on both sides with melted
butter or margarine, then sprinkle
evenly with the seasoning mixture.

4 Heat a large heavy skillet over high
heat until a drop of water sprinkled on
the surface sizzles. This will take 5–8
minutes.

5 ▲ Drizzle a teaspoon of melted
butter on each chicken piece. Place
them in the skillet in an even layer,
2 or 3 at a time. Cook until the
underside begins to blacken, 2–3
minutes. Turn and cook the other side
2–3 minutes more. Serve hot.

~ **VARIATION** ~

For Blackened Catfish Fillets,
substitute 6 medium catfish fillets
for the chicken. Do not slice them
in half, but season as chicken and
cook 2 minutes on the first side
and 1½–2 minutes on the other,
or until the fish flakes easily.

Corn Maque Choux

SERVES 4

2 tablespoons peanut or olive oil

½ cup minced onion

⅓ cup minced celery

⅓ cup minced red bell pepper

3 cups corn kernels (fresh, frozen, or canned)

½ teaspoon cayenne

½ cup dry white wine or water

1 medium tomato, diced

1 teaspoon salt

black pepper

3 tablespoons whipping cream

2 tablespoons shredded fresh basil

1 Heat the oil in a heavy saucepan or skillet. Add the onion and cook over low heat until softened, 8–10 minutes, stirring occasionally.

2 ▲ Raise the heat to medium, add the celery and bell pepper, and cook 5 minutes more, stirring.

3 ▲ Stir in the corn kernels and the cayenne and cook until the corn begins to stick to the bottom of the pan, about 10 minutes.

4 ▲ Pour in the wine or water and scrape up the corn from the bottom of the pan. Add the tomato, salt, and pepper to taste. Mix well. Cover and cook over low heat until the tomato has softened, 8–10 minutes.

5 ▲ Remove from the heat, stir in the cream and basil, and serve.

Collards and Rice

SERVES 4

2 cups chicken or meat stock

1 cup long-grain rice

1 tablespoon butter or margarine

½ teaspoon salt

3 cups chopped collard leaves, loosely packed

pepper

1 ▼ Bring the stock to a boil in a medium-size saucepan. Add the rice, butter or margarine, and salt. Stir.

2 ▲ Add the collards, a handful at a time, stirring well after each addition.

3 Bring back to a boil, then cover, reduce the heat, and cook until the rice is tender, 15–20 minutes. Season with pepper before serving.

Corn Maque Choux (top), Collards and Rice

Dirty Rice

SERVES 4

6 tablespoons olive or vegetable oil

1 cup minced onion

½ pound ground pork

1 garlic clove, minced

½ pound chicken gizzards, chopped

½ cup minced celery

½ cup minced red or green bell pepper

½ teaspoon white pepper

1 teaspoon cayenne

1 bay leaf

½ teaspoon fresh or dried thyme leaves

1 teaspoon salt

3 cups chicken stock

½ pound chicken livers, chopped

1 cup long-grain rice

3 tablespoons chopped fresh parsley

1 Heat the oil in a large skillet over low heat. Add the onion and cook until softened, 8–10 minutes.

2 ▼ Add the ground pork. Raise the heat to medium-high and stir with a fork or wooden spoon to break up the lumps. When the meat has lost its pink, raw color, add the garlic and gizzards. Stir well. Cover the pan, lower the heat to medium, and cook 10 minutes, stirring occasionally.

3 ▲ Add the celery and bell pepper and cook 5 minutes more. Stir in the white pepper, cayenne, bay leaf, thyme, and salt. Add the chicken stock, stirring to scrape up the cooking juices in the bottom of the skillet. Cook about 10 minutes, stirring occasionally.

4 ▲ Add the chicken livers and cook 2 minutes, stirring.

5 ▲ Stir in the rice. Reduce the heat to low, cover the pan, and cook until the rice is tender, 15–20 minutes. Stir in the parsley before serving.

Spoonbread

SERVES 4

2½ cups milk

1 cup yellow cornmeal

6 tablespoons butter or margarine

1 teaspoon salt

1½ teaspoons baking powder

3 eggs, separated

1 Preheat the oven to 375°F.

2 ▲ Heat the milk in a heavy saucepan. Just before it boils, beat in the cornmeal with a wire whisk. Cook over low heat about 10 minutes, stirring constantly.

3 ▲ Remove from the heat and beat in the butter or margarine, salt, and baking powder.

4 ▼ Add the egg yolks and beat until the mixture is smooth.

~ COOK'S TIP ~

The beaten eggs whites give a light texture a bit like a soufflé.

5 ▲ In a large bowl, beat the egg whites until they form stiff peaks. Fold them into the cornmeal mixture.

6 Pour into a well greased 6-cup baking dish. Bake until puffed and brown, 30–40 minutes. Serve with a spoon from the baking dish, and pass butter on the side.

Charleston Cheese Corn Bread

SERVES 8

¾ cup yellow cornmeal

¾ cup flour

2 teaspoons baking powder

1 teaspoon salt

3 eggs

¾ cup buttermilk

¾ cup chopped corn kernels (fresh, frozen, or canned)

⅓ cup melted shortening or vegetable oil

1 cup shredded sharp cheddar cheese

2 tablespoons butter or margarine

1 Preheat the oven to 400°F.

~ VARIATION ~

For a spicier version, add 1 mild chili pepper, seeded and finely chopped, to the mixture.

2 ▲ In a large bowl, combine the cornmeal, flour, baking powder, and salt. Stir to mix.

3 ▲ In a medium-size bowl, beat the eggs until blended. Stir in the buttermilk, corn, shortening or oil, and ½ cup of the cheese.

4 Put the butter or margarine in an 8- or 9-inch skillet (with a heatproof handle) and place in the oven. Heat until melted. Remove from the oven and swirl the fat around to coat the bottom and sides of the skillet.

5 ▲ Add the liquid ingredients to the dry ones and mix until just blended. Pour the batter into the hot skillet and sprinkle with the remaining cheese.

6 Bake until the bread is golden brown and shrinks slightly from the edges of the skillet, 25–30 minutes. Cut into wedges and serve hot, with butter or margarine.

Hush Puppies

SERVES 6

1 cup flour

2 teaspoons baking powder

1 teaspoon salt

1 cup cornmeal, preferably stone-ground

½ cup minced scallions

1 egg, beaten

1 cup buttermilk

oil for deep-frying

1 Sift the flour, baking powder, and salt into a medium-size bowl. Stir in the cornmeal and the scallions.

2 ▲ In a separate bowl, beat the egg and buttermilk together. Stir rapidly into the dry ingredients. Let the batter rest 20–30 minutes.

3 Heat oil in a deep-fryer or large, heavy saucepan to 375°F (or when a cube of bread browns in 40 seconds).

4 ▼ Drop the cornmeal mixture by tablespoonfuls into the hot oil. If the mixture seems too thick, add a little more buttermilk. Fry until golden brown. Drain on paper towels. Serve the hush puppies hot.

Charleston Cheese Corn Bread (top), Hush Puppies

Cornmeal Biscuits

MAKES ABOUT 12

1¼ cups flour

2½ teaspoons baking powder

¼ teaspoon salt

½ cup cornmeal, plus more for sprinkling

⅓ cup shortening or cold butter

¾ cup milk

1 Preheat the oven to 450°F.

2 ▼ Sift the flour, baking powder, and salt into a bowl. Stir in the cornmeal. Using a pastry blender or 2 knives scissor-fashion, cut the shortening or cold butter into the dry ingredients until the mixture is the consistency of coarse meal.

3 ▲ Make a well in the center and pour in the milk. Stir in quickly with a wooden spoon until the dough begins to pull away from the sides of the bowl, about 1 minute.

4 ▲ Turn the dough onto a lightly floured surface and knead lightly 8–10 times only. Roll out to a thickness of ½ inch. Cut into rounds with a floured 2-inch cookie cutter. Do not twist the cutter.

5 ▲ Sprinkle an ungreased cookie sheet lightly with cornmeal. Arrange the biscuits on the sheet, about 1 inch apart. Sprinkle the tops of the biscuits with more cornmeal.

6 Bake until golden brown, 10–12 minutes. Serve the biscuits hot, with butter or margarine.

French Quarter Beignets

MAKES ABOUT 20

2 cups flour
1 teaspoon salt
1 tablespoon baking powder
1 teaspoon ground cinnamon
2 eggs
¼ cup granulated sugar
¼ cup milk
½ teaspoon vanilla extract
oil for deep-frying
confectioners' sugar, for sprinkling

1 ▲ To make the dough, sift the flour, salt, baking powder, and ground cinnamon into a medium-size mixing bowl.

2 ▲ In a separate bowl, beat together the eggs, granulated sugar, milk, and vanilla. Pour the egg mixture into the dry ingredients and mix together quickly to form a dough.

3 Turn the dough onto a lightly floured surface and knead until smooth and elastic.

4 Heat oil in a deep-fryer or large, heavy saucepan to 375°F.

5 ▼ Roll out the dough to a round ¼ inch thick. Slice diagonally into diamonds about 3 inches long.

6 ▲ Fry in the hot oil, turning once, until golden brown on both sides. Remove with tongs or a slotted spoon and drain well on paper towels. Sprinkle the beignets with confectioners' sugar before serving.

Georgia Peanut Butter Pie

SERVES 8

2 cups fine graham-cracker crumbs

¼ cup light brown sugar, firmly packed

6 tablespoons butter or margarine, melted

whipped cream or ice cream, for serving

FOR THE FILLING

3 egg yolks

½ cup granulated sugar

¼ cup light brown sugar, firmly packed

¼ cup cornstarch

⅛ teaspoon salt

2½ cups evaporated milk

2 tablespoons unsalted butter or margarine

1½ teaspoons vanilla extract

½ cup chunky peanut butter, preferably made from freshly ground peanuts

¾ cup confectioners' sugar

1 Preheat the oven to 350°F.

2 ▲ Combine the crumbs, sugar, and butter or margarine in a bowl and blend well. Spread the mixture in a well-greased 9-inch pie pan, pressing evenly over the bottom and sides with your fingertips.

3 Bake the crumb crust 10 minutes. Remove from the oven and let cool. Leave the oven on.

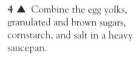

4 ▲ Combine the egg yolks, granulated and brown sugars, cornstarch, and salt in a heavy saucepan.

5 Slowly whisk in the milk. Cook over medium heat, stirring constantly, until the mixture thickens, about 8–10 minutes. Reduce the heat to very low and cook until very thick, 3–4 minutes more.

6 ▲ Beat in the butter or margarine. Stir in the vanilla. Remove from the heat. Cover the surface closely with plastic wrap and let cool.

~ VARIATIONS ~

If preferred, use an equal amount of finely crushed vanilla wafers or ginger snaps in place of graham crackers for the crumb crust. Or make the pie with a ready-to-use graham cracker crust.

7 ▲ In a small bowl combine the peanut butter with the confectioners' sugar, working with your fingers to blend the ingredients to the consistency of small crumbs.

8 ▲ Sprinkle all but 3 tablespoons of the peanut butter crumbs evenly over the bottom of the crumb crust.

9 ▲ Pour in the filling, spreading it into an even layer. Sprinkle with the remaining crumbs. Bake 15 minutes.

10 Let the pie cool 1 hour. Serve with whipped cream or ice cream.

Mississippi Mud Cake

SERVES 8–10

2 cups flour

⅛ teaspoon salt

1 teaspoon baking powder

1¼ cups strong brewed coffee

¼ cup bourbon or brandy

5 1-ounce squares unsweetened
  chocolate

1 cup (2 sticks) butter or margarine

2 cups sugar

2 eggs, at room temperature

1½ teaspoons vanilla extract

unsweetened cocoa powder

sweetened whipped cream or ice cream,
  for serving

1 Preheat the oven to 275°F.

2 Sift the flour, salt, and baking powder together.

3 ▼ Combine the coffee, bourbon or brandy, chocolate, and butter or margarine in the top of a double boiler. Heat until the chocolate and butter have melted and the mixture is smooth, stirring occasionally.

4 ▲ Pour the chocolate mixture into a large bowl. Using an electric mixer on low speed, gradually beat in the sugar. Continue beating until the sugar has dissolved.

5 Raise the speed to medium and add the sifted dry ingredients. Mix well, then beat in the eggs and vanilla until thoroughly blended.

6 Pour the batter into a well-greased 3-quart bundt pan that has been dusted lightly with cocoa powder. Bake until a cake tester inserted in the cake comes out clean, about 1 hour 20 minutes.

7 ▲ Let cool in the pan for 15 minutes, then unmold onto a wire rack. Let cool completely.

8 When the cake is cold, dust it lightly with cocoa powder. Serve with sweetened whipped cream or ice cream, if desired.

Banana Lemon Layer Cake

SERVES 8–10

2¼ cups cake flour
1¼ teaspoons baking powder
½ teaspoon salt
½ cup (1 stick) butter, at room temperature
1 cup granulated sugar
½ cup light brown sugar, firmly packed
2 eggs
½ teaspoon grated lemon rind
1 cup mashed very ripe bananas
1 teaspoon vanilla extract
¼ cup milk
¼ cup chopped walnuts
FOR THE FROSTING
½ cup (1 stick) butter, at room temperature
4½ cups confectioners' sugar
¼ teaspoon grated lemon rind
3–5 tablespoons fresh lemon juice

1 Preheat the oven to 350°F. Grease 2 9-inch round cake pans, and line the bottom of each with a disk of greased wax paper.

2 Sift the flour with the baking powder and salt.

3 ▲ In a large mixing bowl, cream the butter with the sugars until light and fluffy. Beat in the eggs, one at a time. Stir in the lemon rind.

4 ▲ In a small bowl mix the mashed bananas with the vanilla and milk. Add the banana mixture and the dry ingredients to the butter mixture alternately in 2 or 3 batches and stir until just blended. Fold in the nuts.

5 Divide the batter between the cake pans and spread it out evenly. Bake until a cake tester inserted in the center comes out clean, 30–35 minutes. Let stand 5 minutes before unmolding onto a wire rack. Peel off the wax paper.

6 For the frosting, cream the butter until smooth, then gradually beat in the sugar. Stir in the lemon rind and enough juice to make a spreadable consistency.

7 ▼ Set one of the cake layers on a serving plate. Cover with about one-third of the frosting. Top with the second cake layer. Spread the remaining frosting evenly over the top and sides of the cake.

Southern Ambrosia

SERVES 6

4 large sweet oranges

1 fresh ripe pineapple

1 coconut

confectioners' sugar (optional)

strips of fresh coconut or lime wedges,
for garnishing

1 Using a sharp knife, cut the peel
and pith off the oranges, working over
a bowl to catch the juices. Slice each
orange into very thin rounds and place
in the bowl with the juice.

2 ▲ Peel the pineapple. Cut into
quarters lengthwise, and cut away the
core. Cut into thin slices.

3 Pierce the "eyes" of the coconut
with a screwdriver or ice pick. Drain
off the liquid. Using a heavy hammer,
crack the shell until it can be opened.
Prise out the white meat with a blunt
knife. Peel the dark brown skin from
the coconut meat and shred the meat
using the coarse blade of a grater or
food processor.

4 To assemble the dessert, layer the
fruits and coconut alternately in a
glass serving bowl. Sprinkle the layers
occasionally with a small amount of
confectioners' sugar, if desired, to
increase the sweetness. Serve
immediately or chill before eating.
Garnish with strips of fresh coconut
or lime wedges before serving.

Pecan Pralines

MAKES ABOUT 30

1½ cups light brown sugar, firmly
packed

1½ cups dark brown sugar, firmly
packed

¼ teaspoon salt

½ cup milk

½ cup light cream

2 tablespoons butter or margarine

1 teaspoon vanilla extract

1 cup pecan pieces or halves

~ COOK'S TIP ~

To test for the soft ball stage
without a candy thermometer,
drop a small amount of the
caramel into ice water. It should
form a ball that will hold its shape
and flatten readily when picked up
between the fingers.

1 ▲ In a heavy saucepan mix
together the sugars, salt, milk, and
cream. Stir constantly until the
mixture comes to a boil. Cover the
pan and cook, without stirring, until
crystals no longer form on the sides of
the pan, about 3 minutes.

2 Uncover the pan and cook over
medium heat, without stirring, to the
soft ball stage, 238°F on a candy
thermometer.

3 Remove from the heat and beat in
the butter or margarine with a wooden
spoon. Continue beating until the
mixture is smooth and creamy and the
temperature of the mixture comes
down to 110°F. Beat in the vanilla
and the nuts.

4 ▼ Using 2 spoons, drop the candy
by the spoonful onto a baking sheet
lined with buttered wax paper. When
cool, store the pralines in an airtight
container with wax paper between
each of the layers.

Southern Ambrosia (top), Pecan Pralines

Pink Grapefruit Sherbet

SERVES 8

¾ cup granulated sugar

½ cup water

4 cups strained freshly squeezed pink
grapefruit juice

1–2 tablespoons fresh lemon juice

confectioners' sugar, to taste

1 In a small heavy saucepan, dissolve
the granulated sugar in the water over
medium heat, without stirring. When
the sugar has dissolved, boil 3–4
minutes. Remove from the heat and
let cool.

2 ▼ Pour the cooled sugar syrup into
the grapefruit juice. Stir well. Taste
the mixture and adjust the flavor by
adding some lemon juice or a little
confectioners' sugar, if necessary, but
do not over-sweeten.

3 ▲ Pour the mixture into a metal or
plastic freezer container and freeze
until softly set, about 3 hours.

4 ▲ Remove from the container and
chop roughly into 3-inch pieces. Place
in a food processor and process until
smooth. Return the mixture to the
freezer container and freeze again until
set. Repeat this freezing and chopping
process 2 or 3 times, until a smooth
consistency is obtained.

5 Alternatively, freeze the sherbet in
an ice cream maker, following the
manufacturer's instructions.

~ **VARIATION** ~

For Orange Sherbet, substitute an
equal amount of orange juice for
the grapefruit juice and increase
the lemon juice to 3–4 tablespoons,
or to taste. For additional flavor,
add 1 tablespoon finely grated
orange rind. If blood oranges are
available, their deep red color gives
a dramatic effect, and the flavor
is exciting as well.

Key Lime Sherbet

SERVES 4

1¼ cups granulated sugar

2½ cups water

grated rind of 1 lime

¾ cup freshly squeezed key lime juice

1–2 tablespoons fresh lemon juice

confectioners' sugar, to taste

1 ▲ In a small heavy saucepan, dissolve the granulated sugar in the water, without stirring, over medium heat. When the sugar has dissolved, boil 5–6 minutes. Remove from the heat and let cool.

2 ▲ Combine the cooled sugar syrup and lime rind and juice in a measure or bowl. Stir well. Taste and adjust the flavor by adding lemon juice or some confectioners' sugar, if necessary. Do not over-sweeten.

3 ▲ Freeze the mixture in an ice cream maker, following the manufacturer's instructions.

4 If you do not have an ice cream maker, pour the mixture into a metal or plastic freezer container and freeze until softly set, about 3 hours.

5 Remove from the container and chop roughly into 3-inch pieces. Place in a food processor and process until smooth. Return the mixture to the freezer container and freeze again until set. Repeat this freezing and chopping process 2 or 3 times, until a smooth consistency is obtained.

~ COOK'S TIP ~

If using an ice cream maker for these sherbets, check the manufacturer's instructions to find out the freezing capacity. If necessary, halve the recipe quantities.

THE MIDWEST

THE HEARTLAND OF AMERICA
CONTRIBUTES SIGNIFICANTLY TO
THE FOOD SUPPLY OF THE ENTIRE
COUNTRY, WITH GREAT FIELDS OF
WHEAT AND CORN, ORCHARDS AND
VERDANT FARMLAND. THE SYSTEM
OF WATERWAYS, INCLUDING THE
GREAT LAKES AND THE MISSISSIPPI,
HAS HISTORICALLY MOVED
PRODUCE TO OTHER REGIONS
WHILE PROVIDING A RICH SOURCE
OF FOOD AND BEAUTY.

Onion Rivel Soup

SERVES 6

4 tablespoons butter or margarine

2 tablespoons olive oil

1½ pounds onions, finely sliced (about 6 cups)

1 tablespoon brown sugar

1 teaspoon salt

2 quarts good beef stock or bouillon, homemade if possible

1 cup dry white wine

FOR THE RIVELS

1 egg

¼–1 cup flour

½ teaspoon salt

pepper

1 Heat the butter or margarine with the oil in a large heavy saucepan. Add the onions and stir to coat well with the fats. Cover the pan and cook over low heat about 15 minutes, stirring occasionally.

2 ▲ Uncover the pan, add the sugar and salt, and continue cooking until the onions turn a rich brown color. Stir often or the onions may burn.

3 ▲ Stir in the stock or bouillon and wine and bring to a boil. Lower the heat and let simmer, partly covered, while you prepare the rivels.

4 ▲ Beat the egg in a medium-size bowl. Add the flour, salt, and pepper to taste and mix with a wooden spoon. Finish mixing with your fingers, rubbing to blend the egg and flour together. The pieces of dough should be pea-size or smaller.

5 ▲ Bring the soup back to a boil. Sprinkle in the pieces of dough, stirring gently. Reduce the heat and simmer about 6 minutes, until the rivels are slightly swollen and cooked through. Serve immediately.

Split Pea Soup

Serves 8

1 pound dried green split peas
2 quarts water
1 ham bone with some meat left on it, or 1 ham hock
1 cup minced onion
1 cup sliced leeks
½ cup finely sliced celery
¼ cup fresh parsley sprigs
1 teaspoon salt
6 black peppercorns
2 bay leaves

1 ▲ Rinse the split peas under cold running water. Discard any discolored peas. Place the peas in a large kettle and add water to cover. Bring to a boil and boil 2 minutes. Remove from the heat and let soak 1 hour. Drain.

2 ▲ Put the peas back in the kettle and add the measured water, ham bone or hock, onion, leeks, celery, parsley, salt, peppercorns, and bay leaves. Bring to a boil. Reduce the heat, cover, and simmer gently until the peas are tender, 1–1½ hours. Skim occasionally.

3 ▼ Remove the bay leaves and the ham bone or hock from the soup. Cut the meat off the bone, discarding any fat, and chop the meat finely. Set aside. Discard the ham bone and the bay leaves.

4 ▲ Purée the soup in batches in a food processor or blender. Pour into a clean saucepan and add the chopped ham. Check the seasoning. Simmer the soup 3–4 minutes to heat through before serving.

Spiced Pumpkin Soup

SERVES 6

3 tablespoons olive oil

½ cup sliced onion

6 medium-size scallions, bulbs and
   greens sliced separately

⅛ teaspoon cayenne

¼ teaspoon ground cumin

⅛ teaspoon ground nutmeg or mace

5 cups chicken stock

2½ cups pumpkin purée

½ teaspoon salt

1 cup light cream

1 Heat the oil in a large heavy
saucepan. Add the onion and scallion
bulbs and cook over low heat until
softened, 8–10 minutes.

2 ▲ Add the spices and stir well to
coat the onions. Cook 3–4 minutes.
Add the pumpkin purée, stock, and
salt. Raise the heat to medium; cook
15 minutes, stirring occasionally.

3 Let the soup cool slightly. Purée it
in a food processor or blender.

4 ▼ Return the soup to the pan.
Taste and add more cayenne if
desired. Heat to simmering. Stir in
most of the cream and simmer
2–3 minutes more. Serve hot, with a
swirl of cream and some sliced
scallion greens.

Indian Beef and Berry Soup

SERVES 4

2 tablespoons vegetable oil

1 pound tender steak of beef or buffalo

1½ cups finely sliced onions

2 tablespoons butter

4 cups good beef stock or bouillon

½ teaspoon salt

1 cup fresh huckleberries, blueberries, or
   blackberries, lightly mashed

1 tablespoon honey

1 Heat the oil in a heavy saucepan
until almost smoking. Add the steak
and brown on both sides over
medium-high heat. Remove the steak
and set aside.

2 Reduce the heat to low and add the
onions and butter to the pan. Stir
well, scraping up the meat juices.
Cook over low heat until the onions
are softened, 8–10 minutes.

3 ▲ Add the stock or bouillon and
salt and bring to a boil, stirring well.
Mix in the berries and honey. Simmer
20 minutes.

4 Meanwhile, cut the steak into thin,
bite-size slivers.

5 ▼ Taste the soup and add more salt
or honey if necessary. Add the steak
and its juices to the pan. Stir, cook 30
seconds, and serve.

Spiced Pumpkin Soup (top), Indian Beef and Berry Soup

Dandelion Salad with Hot Bacon Dressing

SERVES 6

¼ pound young tender dandelion leaves
  or other sharp-flavored leaves such as
  arugula or rocket (about 2½ cups)

1 head of Boston or leaf lettuce

4 scallions, thinly sliced

8 bacon slices, cut across in thin strips

¼ cup fresh lemon juice

2 tablespoons sugar

1 teaspoon Dijon-style mustard

pepper

1 Carefully pick over the dandelion leaves and wash thoroughly in several changes of water. Pat or spin dry. Wash and dry the lettuce leaves.

2 ▼ Tear each lettuce and dandelion leaf into 2 or 3 pieces. Arrange a mixture of leaves on individual serving plates. Sprinkle with the sliced scallions.

3 ▲ In a small frying pan, cook the bacon until crisp. Remove the bacon pieces with a slotted spoon and drain on paper towels.

4 ▲ Add the lemon juice, sugar, and mustard to the bacon fat in the pan. Heat the mixture gently 3–4 minutes, scraping up the browned bits in the cooking juices and blending in the mustard with a wooden spoon.

5 Spoon the hot dressing over the salads and sprinkle with the bacon pieces and freshly ground black pepper. Serve immediately.

~ COOK'S TIP ~

Commercially grown dandelion leaves are sometimes available from specialist grocers. If picking your own, choose leaves from spring plants that have not yet flowered, and use them fresh. After flowering the leaves of dandelions become bitter and tough.

Vegetable Chili

SERVES 8

¼ cup olive or vegetable oil

2 cups chopped onions

½ cup finely sliced celery

1 cup carrots, cut in ½-inch cubes

2 garlic cloves, minced

½ teaspoon celery seed

¼ teaspoon cayenne

1 teaspoon ground cumin

3 tablespoons chili powder

2 cups canned crushed plum tomatoes with their juice

1 cup vegetable stock or water

1½ teaspoons salt

½ teaspoon fresh or dried thyme leaves

1 bay leaf

2 cups cauliflower florets

2 cups zucchini, cut in ½-inch cubes

kernels from 1 ear of corn

2 cups cooked or canned kidney or pinto beans

hot pepper sauce (optional)

2 Stir in the celery seed, cayenne, cumin, and chili powder. Mix well. Add the tomatoes, stock or water, salt, thyme, and bay leaf. Stir. Cook 15 minutes, uncovered.

3 ▼ Add the cauliflower, zucchini, and corn kernels. Cover and cook a further 15 minutes.

4 ▲ Add the kidney or pinto beans, stir well, and cook 10 minutes more, uncovered. Check the seasoning, and add a dash of hot pepper sauce if desired. Good with freshly boiled rice or baked potatoes.

1 ▲ Heat the oil in a large flameproof casserole or heavy saucepan and add the onions, celery, carrots, and garlic. Cover the casserole and cook over low heat, stirring from time to time, until the onions are softened, 8–10 minutes.

Stuffed Deviled Eggs

SERVES 6

6 hard-cooked eggs, peeled

¼ cup minced cooked ham

6 walnut halves, minced

1 tablespoon minced scallion

1 tablespoon Dijon-style mustard

1 tablespoon mayonnaise

2 teaspoons vinegar

¼ teaspoon salt

¼ teaspoon black pepper

¼ teaspoon cayenne (optional)

paprika and a few slices of dill pickle, for garnishing

1 Cut each egg in half lengthwise. Place the yolks in a bowl and set the whites aside.

2 ▲ Mash the yolks well with a fork, or push them through a strainer. Add all the remaining ingredients and mix well with the yolks. Taste and adjust the seasoning if necessary.

3 ▼ Spoon the filling into the egg white halves, or pipe it in with a pastry bag and nozzle. Garnish the top of each stuffed egg with a little paprika and a small star or other shape cut from the pickle slices. Serve the stuffed eggs at room temperature.

Stuffed Celery Sticks

SERVES 4–6

12 crisp, tender celery stalks

¼ cup crumbled blue cheese

½ cup cream cheese

3 tablespoons sour cream

½ cup chopped walnuts

2 ▼ In a small bowl, combine the crumbled blue cheese, cream cheese, and sour cream. Stir together with a wooden spoon until smoothly blended. Fold in all but 1 tablespoon of the chopped walnuts.

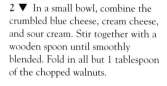

3 ▲ Fill the celery pieces with the cheese mixture. Chill before serving, garnished with the reserved walnuts.

~ **VARIATION** ~

Use the same filling to stuff scooped out cherry tomatoes.

1 ▲ Trim the celery stalks and cut into 4-inch pieces.

Stuffed Deviled Eggs, Stuffed Celery Sticks

Chicago Deep-Pan Pizza

MAKES A 14-INCH PIZZA

| 1½ packages active dry yeast |
| 1 cup lukewarm water |
| 1 tablespoon sugar |
| 3¾ cups flour |
| 1 teaspoon salt |
| 3 tablespoons olive oil |
| FOR THE TOPPING |
| 3 tablespoons olive oil |
| 2½ cups diced mozzarella cheese |
| 2½ cups peeled and chopped tomatoes, preferably plum-type |
| ½ cup freshly grated Parmesan cheese |
| salt and pepper |
| ½ cup fresh basil leaves, loosely packed |

1 In a small bowl, mix the yeast with ½ cup of the warm water. Stir in the sugar. Let stand 10 minutes.

2 Put the flour in a food processor fitted with the steel blade. Add the salt. Pour in the yeast mixture, olive oil, and the remaining warm water. Process until the dough begins to form a ball. If the dough is too sticky, add a little more flour. If it will not mass together, add a little more warm water and process again.

3 Turn the dough onto a lightly floured surface. Knead until smooth, about 5 minutes. Form into a ball and place in a lightly oiled large bowl. Cover with a damp dishtowel. Let rise in a warm place until the dough doubles its volume, about 1½ hours.

4 Preheat the oven to 475°F.

5 ▲ Punch the dough down and knead it lightly, 2–3 minutes. Set it in the center of an oiled 14-inch diameter pizza pan. Using your fingertips, stretch and pat out the dough to line the pan evenly.

6 ▲ Prick the dough evenly all over with a fork. Bake 5 minutes.

7 ▲ Brush the pizza dough base with 1 tablespoon olive oil. Sprinkle with the mozzarella, leaving the rim clear. Spoon the tomatoes over the mozzarella and sprinkle with the Parmesan. Season and drizzle over the remaining olive oil.

8 Bake until the crust is golden brown and the topping is bubbling hot, 25–30 minutes. Scatter over the basil leaves and serve.

Pirozhki with Ham Filling

MAKES 12

2 tablespoons butter or margarine

¼ cup minced onions

1½ cups minced cooked ham (about 6 ounces)

½ cup whipping cream

2 tablespoons minced fresh parsley

1 tablespoon Worcestershire sauce

salt and pepper

FOR THE DOUGH

2 cups flour

1 teaspoon salt

2½ teaspoons baking powder

½ cup cold butter or shortening, or a combination of both

3–4 tablespoons milk, plus more for brushing

1 ▲ Melt the butter or margarine in a small skillet. Add the onions and cook over low heat until soft and golden, 10–12 minutes. Add the ham and cook 2–3 minutes more, stirring.

2 ▲ Turn the onion and ham mixture into a bowl. Let cool slightly, then stir in the cream, parsley, and Worcestershire sauce. Season with salt and pepper.

3 Preheat the oven to 450°F.

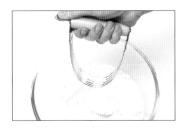

4 ▲ For the dough, sift the flour, salt, and baking powder into a bowl. With a pastry blender or 2 knives used scissor-fashion, cut the butter or shortening into the flour until the mixture resembles coarse meal.

5 Make a well in the center and add the milk. Stir with a fork until the dough begins to pull away from the sides of the bowl, no more than 1 minute. (If overmixed, the pastry will not be as light and tender.)

6 Turn the dough onto a lightly floured surface and knead lightly, less than 1 minute. Roll out to ¼-inch thickness. Cut into 3-inch squares.

7 ▲ Place a spoonful of the ham filling in the center of each dough square. Brush the edges with milk and fold the dough over to form a triangular shape. Press the edges together with a fork to seal.

8 Arrange the triangles on a baking sheet and brush them with milk. Bake until the pastry is golden and cooked, about 30 minutes.

Pan-Fried Honey Chicken Drumsticks

SERVES 4

½ cup honey

juice of 1 lemon

2 tablespoons soy sauce

1 tablespoon sesame seeds

½ teaspoon fresh or dried thyme leaves

12 chicken drumsticks

½ teaspoon salt

½ teaspoon pepper

¾ cup flour

3 tablespoons butter or margarine

3 tablespoons vegetable oil

½ cup white wine

½ cup chicken stock

1 In a large bowl, combine the honey, lemon juice, soy sauce, sesame seeds, and thyme. Add the drumsticks and mix to coat them well. Let marinate in a cool place 2 hours or more, turning occasionally.

2 ▲ Mix the salt, pepper, and flour in a shallow bowl. Drain the drumsticks, reserving the marinade. Roll them in the seasoned flour to coat all over.

3 Heat the butter or margarine with the oil in a large heavy skillet. When hot and sizzling, add the drumsticks. Brown on all sides. Reduce the heat to medium-low and cook until the chicken is done, 12–15 minutes.

4 Test for doneness with a fork; the juices should be clear. Remove the drumsticks to a serving platter and keep hot.

5 ▲ Pour off most of the fat from the pan. Add the wine, stock, and reserved marinade and stir well to mix in the cooking juices on the bottom of the pan. Bring to a boil and simmer until reduced by half. Check for seasoning, then spoon this sauce over the drumsticks and serve.

Oatmeal Pan-Fried Trout

SERVES 4

1½ cups rolled oats

salt and pepper

4 medium-size brook trout, cleaned, heads and tails left on if desired

6 tablespoons butter or margarine

lemon halves, for serving

1 Grind the oats in a food processor or blender until they are the texture of fine meal. Turn into a shallow dish and spread out evenly. Season with salt and pepper.

2 Rinse the trout and dry well with paper towels.

3 Melt the butter or margarine in a large skillet over low heat.

4 ▲ Dip both sides of each trout in the butter or margarine, then roll in the ground oats, patting with your fingers to help the oats stick.

5 ▼ Put the fish in the skillet in one layer. Increase the heat to medium and cook until golden brown, 3–4 minutes on each side. (Cook in batches, if necessary, using more butter or margarine.) Serve hot, with lemon halves on the side.

Pan-fried Honey Chicken Drumsticks (top), Oatmeal Pan-Fried Trout

Sausage Gravy on Biscuits

SERVES 4

1¼ cups flour

1 teaspoon salt

2½ teaspoons baking powder

4 tablespoons cold butter or shortening

¾ cup plus 3 tablespoons milk

FOR THE GRAVY

3 tablespoons butter or margarine

3 tablespoons minced onion

¾ pound lean bulk pork sausage

¼ cup flour

2 cups milk, warmed

¼ teaspoon paprika

1 tablespoon chopped fresh parsley

1 Preheat the oven to 450°F.

2 For the biscuits, sift the flour, salt, and baking powder into a mixing bowl. Using a pastry blender or 2 knives, cut the butter or shortening into the flour until the mixture resembles coarse meal.

3 Make a well in the center and add ¾ cup of the milk. Stir with a wooden spoon until the dough begins to come away from the sides of the bowl, less than 1 minute. (Do not overmix the dough or the biscuits will not be as light and tender.)

4 Turn the dough onto a lightly floured surface and knead gently about ½ minute, making 8–10 folds only. Roll out to about ¾-inch thickness. Cut out rounds using a 2½-inch cookie cutter. Do not twist the cutter.

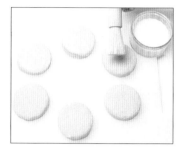

5 ▲ Brush the tops of the rounds with the 3 tablespoons of milk. Arrange on a lightly greased cookie sheet. Bake until puffed and lightly golden, 12–15 minutes.

6 While the biscuits are baking, make the gravy. Melt the butter or margarine in a heavy saucepan. Add the onion and cook 3–4 minutes. Add the sausage and cook over medium-low heat until lightly browned and crumbly. Do not overcook. Drain off the excess fat in the pan, leaving about 2–3 tablespoons.

7 ▲ Sprinkle the flour over the sausage mixture in the pan. Stir well to blend thoroughly.

8 Slowly add the warmed milk, blending it in well and scraping up the pan juices. Simmer until thickened. Add the paprika and parsley.

9 Split the biscuits and place on individual serving plates. Spoon the gravy on top and serve immediately.

Twin Cities Meatballs

SERVES 6

2 tablespoons butter or margarine

¼ cup minced onion

¾ pound ground round

¼ pound ground veal

½ pound lean ground pork

1 egg

½ cup mashed potatoes

2 tablespoons minced fresh dill or
  parsley

1 garlic clove, minced

1 teaspoon salt

½ teaspoon pepper

½ teaspoon ground allspice

¼ teaspoon ground nutmeg

¾ cup fresh bread crumbs

¾ cup milk

¼ cup plus 1 tablespoon flour

2 tablespoons olive oil

¾ cup half and half or evaporated milk

buttered noodles, for serving

1 Melt the butter or margarine in a
large skillet. Add the onion and cook
over low heat until softened, 8–10
minutes. Remove from the heat.
Using a slotted spoon, transfer the
onion to a large mixing bowl.

2 ▲ Add the ground meats, egg,
mashed potatoes, dill or parsley,
garlic, salt, pepper, allspice, and
nutmeg to the bowl.

3 Put the breadcrumbs in a small
bowl and add the milk. Stir until well
moistened, then add to the other
ingredients. Mix well.

4 ▲ Shape the mixture into balls
about 1 inch in diameter. Roll them
in ¼ cup of the flour to coat all over.

5 Add the olive oil to the skillet and
heat over medium heat. Add the
meatballs and brown on all sides, 8–10
minutes. Shake the pan occasionally
to roll the balls so they color evenly.
With a slotted spoon, remove the
meatballs to a serving dish. Cover
with foil and keep warm.

6 ▲ Stir the 1 tablespoon of flour
into the fat in the skillet. Add the half
and half or evaporated milk and mix
in with a small whisk. Simmer 3–4
minutes. Check the seasoning.

7 Pour the gravy over the meatballs.
Serve hot with noodles.

~ COOK'S TIP ~

The meatballs are also good for
a buffet or cocktail party.
To serve with drinks,
omit the gravy.

Country Meat Loaf

SERVES 6

2 tablespoons butter or margarine

½ cup minced onion

2 garlic cloves, minced

½ cup minced celery

1 pound lean ground beef

½ pound ground veal

½ pound lean ground pork

2 eggs

1 cup fine fresh bread crumbs

½ cup chopped fresh parsley

2 tablespoons chopped fresh basil

½ teaspoon fresh or dried thyme leaves

½ teaspoon salt

½ teaspoon pepper

2 tablespoons Worcestershire sauce

¼ cup chili sauce or catsup

6 bacon slices

1 Preheat the oven to 350°F.

2 ▼ Melt the butter or margarine in a small skillet over low heat. Add the onion, garlic, and celery and cook until softened, 8–10 minutes. Remove from the heat and let cool slightly.

3 ▲ In a large mixing bowl combine the onion, garlic, and celery with all the other ingredients except the bacon. Mix together lightly, using a fork or your fingers. Do not overwork or the meat loaf will be too compact.

4 ▲ Form the meat mixture into an oval loaf. Carefully transfer it to a shallow baking pan.

5 ▲ Lay the bacon slices across the meat loaf. Bake 1¼ hours, basting occasionally with the juices and bacon fat in the pan.

6 Remove from the oven and drain off the fat. Let the meat loaf stand 10 minutes before serving.

Spareribs with Sauerkraut

SERVES 4

3–4 pounds spareribs, cut in individual portions

¼ cup minced onion

¼ cup Worcestershire sauce

1 tablespoon dry mustard

½ teaspoon paprika

1 teaspoon salt

3 cups flat beer

3 tablespoons olive or vegetable oil

1½ quarts sauerkraut, canned or bulk

1 tart-sweet apple, peeled, cored, and sliced

1 teaspoon caraway seeds

parsley, for garnishing

1 Arrange the ribs in a single layer in a large baking dish.

2 ▲ In a large measure, combine the onion, Worcestershire sauce, mustard, paprika, salt, and beer. Mix well. Pour the mixture evenly over the ribs. Let marinate at least 2 hours, basting occasionally.

3 Preheat the oven to 375°F.

4 Remove the ribs from the dish and pat dry with paper towels. Reserve the marinade.

5 ▲ Heat the oil in a flameproof casserole or Dutch oven. Brown the ribs, turning to sear them on all sides. Work in batches, if necessary. Pour in the marinade. Transfer the casserole to the oven. Bake 35–40 minutes, turning the ribs occasionally.

6 Rinse the sauerkraut, if desired, and drain well. Mix with the apple and caraway seeds.

7 ▼ Remove the pot from the oven. Holding the ribs to one side, distribute the sauerkraut mixture evenly in the bottom of the casserole. Arrange the ribs on top of the kraut, pushing them down evenly.

8 Return to the oven and bake until the meat on the ribs is tender, ¼–1 hour more. Serve the ribs on a large heated platter, on a bed of sauerkraut, garnished with parsley.

Baked Pork Loin with Red Cabbage and Apples

SERVES 8

4½-pound boned loin of pork

½ teaspoon ground ginger

salt and pepper

4 tablespoons butter, melted

about 1½ cups sweet apple cider or dry
  white wine

FOR THE CABBAGE

3 tablespoons butter or margarine

1½ cups finely sliced onions

1 teaspoon caraway seeds

3 tart-sweet apples, quartered, cored,
  and sliced

1 tablespoon dark brown sugar

3½-pound head of red cabbage, cored
  and shredded

6 tablespoons cider vinegar, or ¼ cup
  wine vinegar and 2 tablespoons water

½ cup beef stock

½ cup sweet apple cider or white wine

1 teaspoon salt

¼ teaspoon fresh or dried thyme leaves

1 Preheat the oven to 350°F.

2 ▲ Trim any excess fat from the
pork roast. Tie it into a neat shape, if
necessary. Sprinkle with the ginger,
salt, and pepper.

3 ▲ Place the pork, fat side down,
in a large Dutch oven. Cook over
medium heat, turning frequently,
until browned on all sides, about
15 minutes. Add a little of the melted
butter if the roast starts to stick.

4 Cover, transfer to the oven, and
roast for 1 hour, basting frequently
with the pan drippings, melted butter,
and cider or wine.

5 ▲ Meanwhile, to prepare the
cabbage, melt the butter or margarine
in a large skillet and add the onions
and caraway seeds. Cook over low
heat until softened, 8–10 minutes.
Stir in the apple slices and brown
sugar. Cover the pan and cook 4–5
minutes more.

6 Stir in the cabbage. Add the
vinegar. Cover and cook 10 minutes.
Pour in the stock and cider or wine,
add the salt and thyme leaves, and stir
well. Cover again and cook over
medium-low heat 30 minutes.

7 ▲ After this time, remove the pot
from the oven. Transfer the roast to a
plate and keep hot. Tilt the pot and
spoon off and discard all but 2
tablespoons of the fat.

8 ▲ Transfer the cabbage mixture
from the skillet to the Dutch oven and
stir well to mix thoroughly with the
roasting juices.

9 ▲ Place the pork roast on top of the
layer of cabbage. Cover and return to
the oven. Cook another hour, basting
occasionally with cider or wine.

Spicy Sauerbraten with Gingersnap Gravy

SERVES 8

4-pound beef chuck roast or boneless
    venison shoulder roast

2 teaspoons salt

pepper

1 cup sliced onions

½ cup sliced carrots

2 bay leaves

1 teaspoon black peppercorns

12 juniper berries

6 whole cloves

1 teaspoon dry mustard

a few blades of mace

2 cups wine vinegar

2 cups boiling water

¼ cup vegetable oil or butter

1 tablespoon dark brown sugar

¼ cup crushed gingersnap cookies

noodles, for serving

1 ▲ Rub the roast with the salt and some freshly ground black pepper.

~ COOK'S TIP ~

In braising, meat is browned or seared in hot fat on all sides to seal in the juices before being cooked slowly in liquid. Check the sauerbraten after about 30 minutes of baking to make sure that the cooking liquid is simmering slowly, not boiling. If necessary, lower the oven temperature slightly.

2 ▲ In a deep earthenware crock or non-reactive bowl, combine the onions, carrots, bay leaves, peppercorns, juniper berries, cloves, mustard, mace, and vinegar. Mix well. Stir in the boiling water.

3 ▲ Set the meat in the crock and add more water if necessary: the meat should be at least half covered. Cover tightly and marinate in the refrigerator at least 48 hours and up to 4 days. Turn the meat once a day.

4 Preheat the oven to 350°F.

5 ▲ Remove the meat, reserving the marinade. Pat it dry with paper towels. Heat the oil or butter in a large flameproof casserole and brown the meat on all sides. This will take about 15 minutes.

6 ▲ Add the onions and carrots from the marinade, as well as 2 cups of the liquid. Reserve the remaining marinade. Cover the casserole and transfer to the oven. Cook 4 hours.

7 ▲ Remove the meat to a hot serving platter. Press the vegetables and liquids from the casserole through a fine strainer. There should be about 2½ cups strained liquid; if necessary, add a little more of the marinade liquid. Pour into a saucepan.

8 ▲ Boil until slightly reduced and thickened, about 5 minutes. Stir in the brown sugar and gingersnap crumbs. Adjust the seasoning if necessary.

9 Slice the meat. Serve with the hot gingersnap gravy and boiled noodles, if desired.

Mashed Carrots and Parsnips

SERVES 6

1 pound parsnips, cut in ½-inch slices (about 2½ cups)

1 pound carrots, cut in ½-inch slices (about 2½ cups)

½ cup chopped onion

1 bay leaf

2 teaspoons sugar

¼ teaspoon salt

1 cup water

2 tablespoons butter or olive oil

minced fresh chives, for garnishing

1 Put the parsnip and carrot slices in a medium-size saucepan with the chopped onion, bay leaf, sugar, and salt. Add the water.

2 ▼ Cover the pan tightly and cook over medium heat, stirring occasionally, until the vegetables are just tender, about 20 minutes. Check from time to time to be sure the water has not evaporated, adding a little more if necessary.

3 ▲ Drain most of the water from the vegetables and discard the bay leaf. Purée the vegetables in a food processor or food mill. Beat in the butter or oil and turn into a warmed serving dish. Sprinkle with the chives, and serve immediately.

Baked Acorn Squash with Herbs

SERVES 4

2 medium-size acorn squash

6 tablespoons mixed minced fresh chives, thyme, basil, and parsley

4 tablespoons butter or margarine

salt and pepper

1 ▲ Cut each squash in half crosswise and scoop out the seeds and stringy fibers. If necessary, cut a small slice off the base of each squash half so it sits level.

2 Preheat the oven to 375°F.

3 ▼ Divide the herbs in 4, and spoon into the hollows in the squash halves.

~ VARIATION ~

For Caramel-Baked Acorn Squash, replace the herbs with 3 tablespoons dark brown sugar. Melt the butter or margarine, dissolve the brown sugar in it and fill squashes.

4 ▲ Top each half with 1 tablespoon butter or margarine and season with salt and pepper.

5 Arrange the squash halves in a shallow baking dish large enough to hold them in one layer. Pour boiling water into the bottom of the dish, to a depth of about 1 inch. Cover the squash loosely with a piece of foil.

6 Bake until the squash is tender when tested with a fork, ¾–1 hour. Serve hot, keeping the halves upright.

Mashed Carrots and Parsnips (top), Baked Acorn Squash with Herbs

Wisconsin Cheddar and Chive Biscuits

MAKES ABOUT 20

1¼ cups flour

2 teaspoons baking powder

½ teaspoon baking soda

¼ teaspoon salt

¼ teaspoon pepper

5 tablespoons cold unsalted butter

½ cup grated sharp cheddar cheese

2 tablespoons minced fresh chives

¾ cup buttermilk

~ VARIATION ~

For Cheddar and Bacon Biscuits, substitute 3 tablespoons crumbled cooked bacon for the chives.

1 Preheat the oven to 400°F.

2 ▲ Sift the flour, baking powder, baking soda, salt, and pepper into a large bowl. Using a pastry blender or 2 knives, cut the butter into the dry ingredients until the mixture resembles coarse meal. Add the cheese and chives and stir to blend.

3 Make a well in the center of the mixture. Add the buttermilk and stir vigorously until the batter comes away from the sides of the bowl, 1 minute.

4 ▼ Drop in 2-tablespoon mounds spaced 2–3 inches apart on a lightly greased cookie sheet. Bake until golden brown, 12–15 minutes.

Corn Oysters

MAKES ABOUT 8

1 cup grated fresh corn

1 egg, separated

2 tablespoons flour

¼ teaspoon salt

¼ teaspoon pepper

2–4 tablespoons butter or margarine

2–4 tablespoons vegetable oil

1 Combine the corn, egg yolk, and flour in a bowl. Mix well. Add the salt and pepper.

~ COOK'S TIP ~

Thawed frozen or canned corn kernels can also be used. Drain them well and chop.

2 ▲ In a separate bowl, beat the egg white until it forms stiff peaks. Fold it carefully into the corn mixture.

3 Heat 2 tablespoons of butter or margarine with 2 tablespoons of oil in a skillet. When the fats are very hot and almost smoking, drop tablespoonfuls of the corn mixture into the pan. Fry until crisp and brown on the bases.

4 ▼ Turn the "oysters" over and cook 1–2 minutes on the other side. Drain on paper towels and keep hot. Continue frying the "oysters," adding more fat as necessary.

5 Serve hot as an accompaniment to meat or chicken dishes, or by themselves as a light dish with a mixed salad.

Wisconsin Cheddar and Chive Biscuits (top), Corn Oysters

Milwaukee Onion Shortcake

SERVES 6

2 tablespoons butter or olive oil

2½ cups thinly sliced onions

½ teaspoon salt

½ teaspoon fresh or dried thyme leaves

¼ teaspoon pepper

1 egg

½ cup sour cream or plain yogurt

2 teaspoons poppy seeds

¼ teaspoon ground mace or nutmeg

FOR THE SHORTCAKE DOUGH

1 cup flour

1¼ teaspoons baking powder

½ teaspoon salt

3 tablespoons cold butter or shortening

2–3 tablespoons milk

1 ▲ Heat the butter or oil in a medium-size skillet. Add the onions and cook over low heat until soft and golden, 10–12 minutes. Season with the salt, thyme, and pepper. Remove from the heat and let cool.

2 Preheat the oven to 425°F.

3 ▲ For the shortcake dough, sift the flour, baking powder, and salt into a bowl. Using a pastry blender or 2 knives, cut the butter or shortening into the dry ingredients until the mixture resembles coarse meal. Add the milk and stir in lightly with a wooden spoon to make a dough.

4 Turn the dough onto a floured surface and knead lightly, ½ minute.

5 Pat out the dough into a disk about 8 inches in diameter. Transfer to an 8-inch baking pan that is at least 2 inches deep. Press the dough into an even layer. Cover with the onions.

6 ▲ Beat together the egg and sour cream or yogurt. Spread evenly over the onions. Sprinkle with the poppy seeds and mace or nutmeg. Bake until the egg topping is puffed and golden, 25–30 minutes.

7 Let cool in the pan 10 minutes. Slip a knife between the shortcake and the pan to loosen, then unmold onto a plate. Cut the shortcake into wedges and serve warm.

Huckleberry Coffee Cake

SERVES 10

2 cups flour

1 tablespoon baking powder

1 teaspoon salt

⅓ cup butter or margarine, at room
temperature

¾ cup granulated sugar

1 egg

1 cup milk

½ teaspoon grated lemon rind

2 cups fresh or frozen huckleberries,
well drained

1 cup confectioners' sugar

2 tablespoons fresh lemon juice

1 Preheat the oven to 350°F.

2 ▲ Sift the flour with the baking
powder and salt.

3 ▲ In a large bowl, beat the butter
or margarine with the granulated sugar
until light and fluffy. Beat in the egg
and milk. Fold in the flour mixture,
mixing well until evenly blended to a
batter. Mix in the lemon rind.

4 ▼ Spread half of the batter in a
greased 13- × 9- × 2-inch baking
pan. Sprinkle with 1 cup of the
berries. Top with the remaining batter
and sprinkle with the rest of the
berries. Bake until golden brown and a
cake tester inserted in the center
comes out clean, 35–45 minutes.

5 ▲ Mix the confectioners' sugar
gradually into the lemon juice to make
a smooth glaze with a pourable
consistency. Drizzle the glaze over the
top of the warm coffee cake and allow
it to set before serving, still warm or at
room temperature.

Pickled Eggs and Beets

SERVES 8

2 pounds small beets, cooked and peeled

1½ cups cider vinegar

1½ cups beet cooking liquid or water

½ cup sugar

1 bay leaf

1 teaspoon salt

1 tablespoon whole allspice berries

1 teaspoon whole cloves

½ teaspoon ground ginger

½ teaspoon caraway seeds

8 hard-cooked eggs, shelled

1 ▲ Place the beets in a very large glass jar, or in several smaller jars.

2 Combine the vinegar, beet liquid or water, sugar, bay leaf, salt, and spices in a saucepan. Heat, stirring to dissolve the sugar. Simmer 5 minutes.

3 Pour the mixture over the beets. Let cool completely.

4 ▼ Add the eggs to the jar of beets. Cover and refrigerate 2 or 3 days before serving. The pickle will keep up to a week in the refrigerator.

Bread and Butter Pickles

MAKES ABOUT 4 CUPS

2 pounds cucumbers, scrubbed and cut in ¼-inch slices

2 cups very thinly sliced onions

2 tablespoons salt

1½ cups cider vinegar

1½ cups sugar

2 tablespoons mustard seeds

2 tablespoons celery seeds

¼ teaspoon turmeric

¼ teaspoon cayenne

1 ▲ Put the sliced cucumbers and onions in a large bowl and sprinkle with the salt. Mix well. Cover loosely and let stand 3 hours.

2 Drain the vegetables. Rinse well under cold water and drain again.

3 Prepare some heatproof glass jars (such as canning jars). Wash them well in warm soapy water and rinse thoroughly in clean warm water. Put them in a 300°F oven and heat 30 minutes to sterilize them. Keep the jars hot until ready to use.

4 ▼ Combine the remaining ingredients in a large non-reactive saucepan and bring to a boil. Add the cucumbers and onions. Reduce the heat and simmer 2–3 minutes. Do not boil or the pickles will be limp.

5 ▲ Spoon the hot vegetables into the hot jars. Add enough of the hot liquid to come to ½ inch from the top. Carefully wipe the jar rims with a clean damp cloth.

6 To seal, cover the surface of the pickles with a waxed disc, wax side down, then put on the jar lid. The pickles should be sealed immediately. If the lid does not have a rubber gasket, first cover the top of the jar with plastic wrap or cellophane and then screw a plastic top down over it. Avoid using metal, as it may rust. Store in a cool dark place at least 4 weeks before serving.

Pickled Eggs and Beets (center), Bread and Butter Pickles

Rhubarb Pie

SERVES 6

1½ cups flour

½ teaspoon salt

2 teaspoons sugar

6 tablespoons cold butter or shortening

2–3 tablespoons ice water

2 tablespoons whipping cream

FOR THE FILLING

3½ cups fresh rhubarb, cut in ½- to 1-inch slices (about 2 pounds)

2 tablespoons cornstarch

1 egg

1½ cups sugar

1 tablespoon grated orange rind

1 ▲ For the pastry, sift the flour, salt, and sugar into a bowl. Using a pastry blender or 2 knives, cut the butter or shortening into the dry ingredients as quickly as possible until the mixture resembles coarse meal.

2 Sprinkle with 2 tablespoons of the ice water and mix until the dough holds together. If the dough is too crumbly, add a little more water, 1 teaspoon at a time.

~ COOK'S TIP ~

Be sure to cut off and discard the green rhubarb leaves from the pink stalks, as they are toxic and not edible.

3 ▲ Gather the dough into a ball, flatten into a disk, wrap in wax paper, and refrigerate at least 20 minutes.

4 ▲ Roll out the dough between 2 sheets of wax paper to a thickness of about ⅛ inch. Use to line a 9-inch pie pan. Trim all around, leaving a ½-inch overhang. Fold the overhang under the edge and flute. Refrigerate the pie shell and dough trimmings 30 minutes.

5 ▲ For the filling, put the rhubarb in a bowl and sprinkle with the cornstarch. Toss to coat.

6 Preheat the oven to 425°F.

7 In a small bowl beat the egg with the sugar. Mix in the orange rind.

8 ▲ Stir the sugar mixture into the rhubarb and mix well. Spoon the fruit into the pie shell.

9 ▲ Roll out the dough trimmings. Stamp out decorative shapes with a cookie cutter or cut shapes with a small knife, using a cardboard template as a guide, if wished.

10 Arrange the shapes on top of the pie. Brush the trimmings and the edge of the pie shell with cream.

11 Bake 30 minutes. Reduce the heat to 325°F and continue baking until the pastry is golden brown and the rhubarb is tender, about 15–20 minutes more.

Brown Sugar Pie

SERVES 8

1½ cups flour

½ teaspoon salt

2 teaspoons granulated sugar

6 tablespoons cold butter

2–3 tablespoons ice water

FOR THE FILLING

¼ cup flour, sifted

1 cup light brown sugar

½ teaspoon vanilla extract

1½ cups whipping cream

3 tablespoons butter, cut in tiny pieces

⅛ teaspoon grated nutmeg

1 Sift the flour, salt, and sugar into a bowl. Using a pastry blender or 2 knives, cut in the butter until it resembles coarse meal.

2 ▲ Sprinkle with 2 tablespoons of the water and mix until the dough holds together. If it is too crumbly, add more water, 1 teaspoon at a time. Gather into a ball and flatten. Wrap in wax paper and refrigerate at least 20 minutes.

3 Roll out the dough about ⅛ inch thick and line a 9-inch pie pan. Trim all around, leaving a ½-inch overhang. Fold it under and flute the edge. Refrigerate for 30 minutes.

4 Preheat the oven to 425°F.

5 Line the pie shell with a piece of wax paper that is 2 inches larger all around than the diameter of the pan. Fill the shell with dried beans. Bake until the pastry has just set, 8–10 minutes. Remove from the oven and carefully lift out the paper and beans. Prick the bottom of the pie shell all over with a fork. Return to the oven and bake 5 minutes more. Let the pie shell cool slightly before filling. Turn the oven down to 375°F.

6 ▲ In a small bowl, mix together the flour and sugar using a fork. Spread this mixture in an even layer on the bottom of the pie shell.

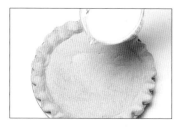

7 ▲ Stir the vanilla into the cream. Pour the flavored cream over the flour and sugar mixture and gently swirl with a fork to mix. Dot with the butter. Sprinkle the nutmeg on top.

8 Cover the edge of the pie with foil strips to prevent overbrowning. Set on a cookie sheet and bake until the filling is golden brown and set to the touch, about 45 minutes. Serve the pie at room temperature.

Apple Maple Dumplings

SERVES 8

4½ cups flour
2 teaspoons salt
1½ cups shortening
6–7 tablespoons ice water
8 firm, tart-sweet apples
1 egg white
⅔ cup sugar
3 tablespoons whipping cream
½ teaspoon vanilla extract
1 cup maple syrup
whipped cream, for serving

1 Sift the flour and salt into a large bowl. Using a pastry blender or 2 knives, cut in the shortening until the mixture resembles coarse meal. Sprinkle with 6 tablespoons of the water and mix until the dough holds together. If it is too crumbly, add a little more water, 1 teaspoon at a time. Gather into a ball. Wrap in wax paper and refrigerate at least 20 minutes. Preheat the oven to 425°F.

2 Peel the apples. Remove the cores, cutting from the stem end, without cutting through the base.

3 ▲ Roll out the dough thinly. Cut squares almost large enough to enclose the apples. Brush the squares with egg white. Set an apple in the center of each square of dough.

4 Combine the sugar, cream, and vanilla in a small bowl. Spoon some into the hollow in each apple.

5 ▼ Pull the points of the dough squares up around the apples and moisten the edges where they overlap. Mold the dough around the apples, pleating the top. Do not cover the center hollows. Crimp the edges tightly to seal.

6 Set the apples in a large greased baking dish, at least ¼ inch apart. Bake 30 minutes. Lower the oven temperature to 350°F and continue baking until the pastry is golden brown and the apples are tender, about 20 minutes more.

7 Transfer the dumplings to a serving dish. Mix the maple syrup with the juices in the baking dish and drizzle over the dumplings.

8 Serve the dumplings hot with whipped cream.

Apple Fritters

<u>SERVES 4–6</u>

1⅓ cups flour
2 teaspoons baking powder
¼ teaspoon salt
⅔ cup milk
1 egg, beaten
oil for deep-frying
¾ cup granulated sugar
1 teaspoon ground cinnamon
2 large tart-sweet apples, peeled, cored, and cut in ¼-inch slices
confectioners' sugar, for dusting

1 Sift the flour, baking powder, and salt into a bowl. Beat in the milk and egg with a wire whisk.

2 Heat at least 3 inches of oil in a heavy frying pan to 360°F.

3 ▲ Mix the granulated sugar and cinnamon in a shallow bowl or plate. Toss the apple slices in the sugar mixture to coat all over.

4 Dip the apple slices in the batter, using a fork or slotted spoon. Drain off excess batter. Fry, in batches, in the hot oil until golden brown on both sides, about 4–5 minutes. Drain the fritters on paper towels.

5 ▼ Sprinkle with confectioners' sugar, and serve hot.

Cherry Compote

<u>SERVES 6</u>

½ cup water
½ cup red wine
¼ cup light brown sugar, firmly packed
¼ cup granulated sugar
1 tablespoon honey
2 1-inch strips of orange rind
¼ teaspoon almond extract
1½ pounds sweet fresh cherries, pitted
ice cream or whipped cream, for serving

~ VARIATION ~

Sour cherries may be used for the compote instead of sweet. If using sour cherries, increase the amount of the sugars to ⅓ cup each, or to taste.

1 ▼ Combine all the ingredients except the cherries in a saucepan. Stir over medium heat until the sugar dissolves. Raise the heat and boil until the liquid reduces slightly.

2 ▲ Add the cherries. Bring back to a boil. Reduce the heat slightly and simmer 8–10 minutes. If necessary, skim off any foam.

3 Let cool to lukewarm. Spoon warm over vanilla ice cream, or refrigerate and serve cold with whipped cream, if desired.

Apple Fritters (top), Cherry Compote

Black Walnut Layer Cake

SERVES 8

2 cups cake flour

1 tablespoon baking powder

½ teaspoon salt

½ cup (1 stick) butter or margarine,
at room temperature

1 cup granulated sugar

2 eggs

1 teaspoon grated orange rind

1 teaspoon vanilla extract

1 cup minced black walnut pieces

¾ cup milk

black walnut halves, for decoration

FOR THE FROSTING

½ cup (1 stick) butter

¾ cup light brown sugar, firmly packed

3 tablespoons maple syrup

¼ cup milk

1¼–2 cups confectioners' sugar, sifted

1 ▲ Grease 2 8- × 2-inch cake pans and line the bottoms of each with a disk of greased wax paper. Preheat the oven to 375°F.

2 Sift together the flour, baking powder, and salt.

~ **VARIATION** ~

If black walnuts are unavailable, substitute regular walnuts, or use pecans instead.

3 ▲ Beat the butter or margarine to soften, then gradually beat in the granulated sugar until light and fluffy. Beat in the eggs, one at a time. Add the orange rind and vanilla and beat to mix well.

4 ▲ Stir in the minced walnuts. Add the flour alternately with the milk, stirring only enough to blend after each addition.

5 ▲ Divide the batter between the prepared cake pans. Bake until a cake tester inserted in the center comes out clean, about 25 minutes. Cool in the cake pans for 5 minutes before unmolding onto a wire rack.

6 ▲ For the frosting, melt the butter in a medium-size saucepan. Add the brown sugar and maple syrup and boil 2 minutes, stirring constantly.

7 ▲ Add the milk. Bring back to a boil and stir in ¼ cup of the confectioners' sugar. Remove from the heat and let cool to lukewarm. Gradually beat in the remaining confectioners' sugar. Set the pan in a bowl of ice water and stir until the frosting is thick enough to spread.

8 ▲ Spread some of the frosting on one of the cake layers. Set the other layer on top. Spread the remaining frosting over the top and sides of the cake. Decorate with walnut halves.

Applesauce Cookies

MAKES 3 DOZEN

½ cup sugar

4 tablespoons butter or shortening, at room temperature

¼ cup thick applesauce

⅛ teaspoon grated lemon rind

1 cup flour

½ teaspoon baking powder

¼ teaspoon baking soda

¼ teaspoon salt

½ teaspoon ground cinnamon

½ cup chopped walnuts

~ COOK'S TIP ~

If the applesauce is runny, put it in a strainer over a bowl and let it drain for 10 minutes.

1 Preheat the oven to 375°F.

2 In a medium-size bowl, beat together the sugar and butter or shortening until well mixed. Beat in the applesauce and lemon rind.

3 ▲ Sift the flour, baking powder, baking soda, salt, and cinnamon into the mixture, and stir to blend. Fold in the chopped walnuts.

4 ▲ Drop teaspoonfuls of the dough on a lightly greased cookie sheet, spacing them about 2 inches apart.

5 Bake the cookies in the center of the oven until they are golden brown, 8–10 minutes. Transfer the cookies to a wire rack to cool.

Toffee Bars

MAKES 32

2 cups light brown sugar, firmly packed

2 cups (4 sticks) butter or margarine, at room temperature

2 egg yolks

1½ teaspoons vanilla extract

4 cups all-purpose or whole-wheat flour

½ teaspoon salt

2 4-ounce bars of milk chocolate, broken in pieces

1 cup chopped walnuts or pecans

1 Preheat the oven to 350°F.

2 Beat together the sugar and butter or margarine until light and fluffy. Beat in the egg yolks and vanilla. Stir in the flour and salt.

3 ▼ Spread the dough in a greased 13- × 9- × 2-inch baking pan. Bake until lightly browned, 25–30 minutes. The texture will be soft.

4 ▲ Remove from the oven and immediately place the chocolate pieces on the hot cookie base. Let stand until the chocolate softens, then spread it evenly with a spatula. Sprinkle with the nuts.

5 While still warm, cut into bars about 2 × 1½ inches.

Applesauce Cookies (top), Toffee Bars

THE SOUTHWEST

THE POPULAR TASTE FOR "TEX-MEX" HAS SPREAD FAR AND WIDE, BUT THE ROOTS OF THIS CUISINE ARE IN OUR NATIVE AMERICAN HERITAGE. THE FOOD OF THIS REGION FEATURES PRODUCTS CULTIVATED BY THE ORIGINAL AMERICANS — CORN IN MANY FORMS, TOMATOES, BEANS — COMBINED WITH INFLUENCES FROM SOUTH OF THE BORDER AND FROM THE RIGORS OF FARMING IN A DESERT.

Tortilla Soup

SERVES 4–6

1 tablespoon vegetable oil

1 onion, minced

1 large garlic clove, minced

2 medium tomatoes, peeled, seeded, and chopped

½ teaspoon salt

2 quarts chicken stock

1 carrot, diced

1 small zucchini, diced

1 skinless boneless chicken breast half, cooked and shredded

¼ cup canned green chilies, chopped

FOR GARNISHING

4 corn tortillas

oil for frying

1 small ripe avocado

2 scallions, chopped

chopped fresh coriander (cilantro)

shredded Monterey Jack cheese (optional)

1 ▲ Heat the oil in a saucepan. Add the onion and garlic and cook over medium heat until just softened, 5–8 minutes. Add the tomatoes and salt and cook 5 minutes more.

2 Stir in the stock. Bring to a boil, then lower the heat and simmer, covered, about 15 minutes.

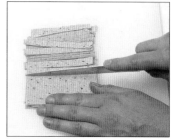

3 ▲ Meanwhile, for the garnish, trim the tortillas into squares, then cut them into strips.

4 ▲ Put a ½-inch layer of oil in a skillet and heat until hot but not smoking. Add the tortilla strips, in batches, and fry until just beginning to brown, turning occasionally. Remove with a slotted spoon and drain on paper towels.

5 Add the carrot to the soup. Cook, covered, 10 minutes. Add the zucchini, chicken, and chilies and continue cooking, uncovered, until the vegetables are just tender, about 5 minutes more.

6 Meanwhile, peel and pit the avocado. Chop into a fine dice.

7 Divide the tortilla strips among 4 soup bowls. Sprinkle with the avocado. Ladle in the soup, then scatter scallions and coriander on top. Serve immediately, with shredded Monterey Jack cheese if desired.

Spicy Bean Soup

SERVES 6–8

1 cup dried black beans, soaked
   overnight and drained

1 cup dried kidney beans, soaked
   overnight and drained

2 bay leaves

6 tablespoons coarse salt

2 tablespoons olive or vegetable oil

3 carrots, chopped

1 onion, chopped

1 celery stal

1 garlic clove, minced

1 teaspoon ground cumin

¼–½ teaspoon cayenne

½ teaspoon dried oregano

salt and pepper

⅓ cup red wine

1 quart beef stock

1 cup water

FOR GARNISHING

sour cream

chopped fresh coriander (cilantro)

3 Heat the oil in a large flameproof casserole. Add the carrots, onion, celery, and garlic and cook over low heat, stirring, until softened, 8–10 minutes. Stir in the cumin, cayenne, oregano, and salt to taste.

4 ▼ Add the wine, stock, and water and stir to mix. Add the beans. Bring to a boil, reduce the heat, then cover and simmer about 20 minutes, stirring occasionally.

5 ▲ Transfer half of the soup (including most of the solids) to a food processor or blender. Process until smooth. Return to the pan and stir to combine well.

6 Reheat the soup if necessary and taste for seasoning. Serve hot, garnished with sour cream and chopped fresh coriander.

1 ▲ Put the black beans and kidney beans in two separate pots. To each, add fresh cold water to cover and a bay leaf. Bring to a boil, then cover, and simmer 30 minutes.

2 Add 3 tablespoons coarse salt to each pot and continue simmering until the beans are tender, about 30 minutes more. Drain and let cool slightly. Discard the bay leaves.

Desert Nachos

1 6-ounce bag blue corn tortilla chips or ordinary tortilla chips

2–4 tablespoons chopped pickled jalapeños, according to taste

⅓ cup sliced black olives

2 cups shredded Monterey Jack cheese

FOR SERVING

guacamole

tomato salsa

sour cream

1 Preheat the oven to 350°F.

2 ▲ Put the tortilla chips in a 13- × 9-inch baking dish and spread them out evenly. Sprinkle the jalapeños, olives, and cheese evenly over the tortilla chips.

3 ▼ Place in the top of the oven and bake until the cheese melts, 10–15 minutes. Serve the nachos at once, with the guacamole, tomato salsa, and sour cream for dipping.

Huevos Rancheros

1 17-ounce can refried beans

1¼ cups enchilada sauce

oil for frying

4 corn tortillas

4 eggs

salt and pepper

1¼ cups shredded Monterey Jack or cheddar cheese

1 ▼ Heat the beans in a saucepan. Cover and set aside.

2 Heat the enchilada sauce in a small saucepan. Cover and set aside.

3 Preheat the oven to 160°F.

4 ▲ Put a ¼-inch layer of oil in a small nonstick skillet and heat. When hot, add the tortillas, one at a time, and fry until just crisp, about 30 seconds per side. Drain the tortillas on paper towels and keep them warm on a baking sheet in the oven. Discard the oil used for frying.

5 Let the skillet cool slightly, then wipe it with a paper towel to remove all but a film of oil. Heat the skillet over low heat. Break in 2 eggs and cook until the whites are just set. Season with salt and pepper, then transfer to the oven to keep warm. Repeat to cook the remaining eggs.

6 ▼ To serve, place a tortilla on each of 4 plates. Spread a layer of refried beans over each tortilla, then top each with an egg. Spoon over the warm enchilada sauce, then sprinkle with the cheese. Serve hot.

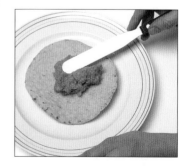

Desert Nachos (top), Huevos Rancheros

Arizona Jalapeño-Onion Quiche

SERVES 6

1 tablespoon butter
2 onions, sliced
4 scallions, cut in ½-inch pieces
½ teaspoon ground cumin
1–2 tablespoons chopped canned jalapeños
4 eggs
1¼ cups milk
½ teaspoon salt
⅔ cup shredded Monterey Jack or cheddar cheese

FOR THE CRUST

1½ cups flour
¼ teaspoon salt
¼ teaspoon cayenne
6 tablespoons cold butter
6 tablespoons cold margarine
2–3 tablespoons ice water

1 For the crust, sift the flour, salt, and cayenne into a bowl. Using a pastry blender or 2 knives, cut in the butter and margarine until the mixture resembles coarse meal. Sprinkle with 2 tablespoons ice water and mix until the dough holds together. If the dough is too crumbly, add a little more water, 1 teaspoon at a time. Gather the dough into a ball and flatten into a disk. Wrap the dough in wax paper and refrigerate at least 30 minutes.

2 Preheat the oven to 375°F.

3 Roll out the dough to a thickness of about ⅛ inch. Use to line a 9-inch fluted tart pan that has a removable base. Line the shell with wax paper and fill with dried beans.

4 Bake until the pastry has just set, 12–15 minutes. Remove from the oven and carefully lift out the paper and beans. Prick the bottom of the pastry shell all over. Return to the oven and bake until golden, 5–8 minutes more. Leave the oven on.

5 ▲ Melt the butter in a nonstick skillet. Add the onions and cook over medium heat until softened, about 5 minutes. Add the scallions and cook 1 minute more. Stir in the cumin and jalapeños and set aside.

6 In a mixing bowl, combine the eggs, milk, and salt and whisk until thoroughly blended.

7 ▲ Spoon the onion mixture into the pastry shell. Sprinkle with the cheese, then pour in the egg mixture.

8 Bake until the filling is golden and set, 30–40 minutes. Serve hot or at room temperature.

San Antonio Tortilla

1 tablespoon vegetable oil

½ onion, sliced

1 small green bell pepper, seeded and sliced

1 garlic clove, minced

1 tomato, chopped

6 black olives, chopped

3 small potatoes (about 10 ounces total), cooked and sliced

2 ounces sliced chorizo, cut in strips

1 tablespoon chopped canned jalapeños, or to taste

½ cup shredded cheddar cheese

6 extra large eggs

3 tablespoons milk

½–¾ teaspoon salt

¼ teaspoon ground cumin

¼ teaspoon dried oregano

¼ teaspoon paprika

black pepper

1 Preheat the oven to 375°F.

2 ▲ Heat the oil in a nonstick skillet. Add the onion, bell pepper, and garlic and cook over medium heat until softened, 5–8 minutes.

3 Transfer the vegetables to a 9-inch round nonstick springform pan. Add the tomato, olives, potatoes, chorizo, and jalapeños. Sprinkle with the cheese and set aside.

4 ▲ In a bowl, combine the eggs and milk and whisk until frothy. Add the salt, cumin, oregano, paprika, and pepper to taste. Whisk to blend.

5 Pour the egg mixture into the vegetable mixture, tilting the pan to spread it evenly.

6 ▲ Bake until set and lightly golden, about 30 minutes. Serve hot or cold.

Santa Fe Shrimp Salad

SERVES 4

1 pound cooked peeled shrimp

2 scallions, chopped

2 tablespoons fresh lemon juice

2 tablespoons extra-virgin olive oil

1 teaspoon salt

6 cups shredded lettuce

1 large ripe avocado

1 cup tomato salsa

FOR GARNISHING

fresh coriander (cilantro) sprigs

lime slices

1 ▲ In a bowl, combine the shrimp, scallions, lemon juice, oil, and salt. Mix well and set aside.

2 ▲ Line 4 plates (or a large platter) with the shredded lettuce.

3 ▲ Halve the avocado and remove the pit. With a small melon baller, scoop out balls of avocado and add to the shrimp mixture. Scrape the remaining avocado flesh into the salsa and stir. Add the salsa to the shrimp mixture and stir gently to blend.

4 ▲ Divide the shrimp mixture among the plates, piling it in the center. Garnish each salad with fresh coriander sprigs and slices of lime, and serve immediately.

Pinto Bean Salad

SERVES 4

1½ cups dried pinto beans, soaked overnight and drained

1 bay leaf

3 tablespoons coarse salt

2 ripe tomatoes, diced

4 scallions, minced

FOR THE DRESSING

¼ cup fresh lemon juice

salt and pepper

6 tablespoons olive oil

1 garlic clove, minced

3 tablespoons chopped fresh coriander (cilantro)

1 ▲ Put the beans in a large pot. Add fresh cold water to cover and the bay leaf. Bring to a boil, then cover, and simmer 30 minutes. Add the salt and continue simmering until tender, about 30 minutes more. Drain and let cool slightly. Discard the bay leaf.

2 ▲ For the dressing, mix the lemon juice and 1 teaspoon salt with a fork until dissolved. Gradually stir in the oil until thick. Add the garlic, coriander, and pepper to taste.

3 ▲ While the beans are still warm, place them in a large bowl. Add the dressing and toss to coat. Let the beans cool completely.

4 ▼ Add the tomatoes and scallions and toss to coat evenly. Let stand at least 30 minutes before serving.

Chiles Rellenos

SERVES 4

8 large green bell peppers or fresh green chilies such as poblano

1–2 tablespoons vegetable oil, plus more for frying

4 cups shredded Monterey Jack cheese

4 eggs, separated

⅔ cup flour

FOR THE SAUCE

1 tablespoon vegetable oil

1 small onion, minced

¼ teaspoon salt

1–2 teaspoons red pepper flakes

½ teaspoon ground cumin

1 cup beef or chicken stock

3 cups canned peeled tomatoes

1 ▲ For the sauce, heat the oil in a skillet. Add the onion and cook over low heat until just soft, about 8 minutes. Stir in the salt, pepper flakes, cumin, stock, and tomatoes. Cover and simmer gently 5 minutes, stirring occasionally.

2 Transfer to a food processor or blender and process until smooth. Strain into a clean pan. Taste for seasoning, and set aside.

~ COOK'S TIP ~

If necessary, work in batches, but do not coat the peppers until you are ready to fry them.

3 Preheat the broiler.

4 ▲ Brush the bell peppers or chilies lightly all over with oil. Lay them on a baking sheet. Broil as close to the heat as possible until blackened all over, 5–8 minutes. Cover with a clean dishtowel and set aside.

5 ▲ When cool enough to handle, remove the charred skin. Carefully slit the peppers or chilies and scoop out the seeds. If using chilies, wear rubber gloves. For less chili-heat, gently remove the white veins.

6 ▲ With your hands, form the cheese into 8 cylinders that are slightly shorter than the peppers. Place the cheese cylinders inside the peppers. Secure the slits with wooden toothpicks. Set aside.

7 ▲ Beat the egg whites until just stiff. Add the egg yolks, one at a time, beating on low speed just to incorporate them. Beat in 1 tablespoon of the flour.

8 Put a 1-inch layer of oil in a skillet or frying pan. Heat until hot but not smoking (to test, drop a scrap of batter in the oil: if the oil sizzles, it is hot enough for frying).

9 ▲ Coat the peppers lightly in flour all over; shake off any excess. Dip into the egg batter, then place in the hot oil. Fry until brown on one side, about 2 minutes. Turn carefully and brown the other side.

10 Reheat the sauce and serve with the chiles rellenos.

~ VARIATION ~

If using bell peppers instead of green chillies, mix the grated cheese with ½–1 tablespoon hot chili powder for a more authentic Southwest taste.

Black Bean Burritos

SERVES 4

1 cup dried black beans, soaked overnight and drained

1 bay leaf

3 tablespoons coarse salt

1 small red onion, minced

2 cups shredded Monterey Jack cheese

1–3 tablespoons chopped pickled jalapeños

1 tablespoon chopped fresh coriander (cilantro)

3½ cups tomato salsa

8 flour tortillas

diced avocado, for serving

1 ▲ Place the beans in a large pot. Add fresh cold water to cover and the bay leaf. Bring to a boil, then cover, and simmer 30 minutes. Add the salt and continue simmering until tender, about 30 minutes more. Drain and let cool slightly. Discard the bay leaf.

2 Preheat the oven to 350°F. Grease a rectangular baking dish.

3 ▲ In a bowl, combine the beans, onion, half the cheese, the jalapeños, coriander, and 1 cup of the salsa. Stir to blend and taste for seasoning.

4 ▲ Place 1 tortilla on a work surface. Spread a large spoonful of the filling down the middle, then roll up to enclose the filling. Place the burrito in the prepared dish, seam side down. Repeat with the remaining tortillas.

5 ▲ Sprinkle the remaining cheese over the burritos, in a line down the middle. Bake until the cheese melts, about 15 minutes.

6 Serve the burritos immediately, with avocado and the remaining salsa.

Black Bean Chili

SERVES 6

2 cups dried black beans, soaked overnight and drained

2 tablespoons coarse salt

2 tablespoons vegetable oil

2 onions, chopped

1 green bell pepper, seeded and chopped

4 garlic cloves, minced

2 pounds ground chuck

1½ tablespoons ground cumin

½ teaspoon cayenne, or to taste

2½ teaspoons paprika

2 tablespoons dried oregano

1 teaspoon salt

3 tablespoons tomato paste

3 cups chopped peeled fresh or canned tomatoes

½ cup red wine

1 bay leaf

FOR SERVING

chopped fresh coriander (cilantro)

sour cream

shredded Monterey Jack or cheddar cheese

1 Put the beans in a large pot. Add fresh cold water to cover. Bring to a boil, then cover and simmer 30 minutes. Add the coarse salt and continue simmering until the beans are tender, about 30 minutes or longer. Drain and set aside.

2 Heat the oil in a large saucepan or flameproof casserole. Add the onions and bell pepper. Cook the vegetables over medium heat until just softened, about 5 minutes, stirring occasionally. Stir in the garlic and continue cooking 1 minute more.

3 Add the beef and cook over high heat, stirring frequently, until browned and crumbly. Reduce the heat and stir in the cumin, cayenne, paprika, oregano, and salt.

4 ▼ Add the tomato paste, tomatoes, drained black beans, wine, and bay leaf and stir well. Simmer 20 minutes, stirring occasionally.

5 ▲ Taste for seasoning. Remove the bay leaf and serve immediately, with chopped fresh coriander, sour cream, and shredded cheese.

Red Snapper with Cilantro Salsa

SERVES 4

4 red snapper fillets, about 6 ounces each

salt and pepper

1½ tablespoons vegetable oil

1 tablespoon butter

FOR THE SALSA

2 cups fresh coriander (cilantro) leaves

1 cup olive oil

2 garlic cloves, chopped

2 tomatoes, cored and chopped

2 tablespoons fresh orange juice

1 tablespoon sherry vinegar

1 teaspoon salt

1 ▲ For the salsa, place the coriander, oil, and garlic in a food processor or blender. Process until almost smooth. Add the tomatoes and pulse on and off several times; the mixture should be slightly chunky.

2 ▲ Transfer to a bowl. Stir in the orange juice, vinegar, and salt. Set the salsa aside.

3 ▲ Rinse the fish fillets and pat dry. Sprinkle on both sides with salt and pepper. Heat the oil and butter in a large nonstick skillet. When hot, add the fish and cook until opaque throughout, 2–3 minutes on each side. Work in batches, if necessary.

4 ▲ Carefully transfer the fillets to warmed dinner plates. Top each with a spoonful of salsa. Serve additional salsa on the side.

Cornmeal-Coated Gulf Shrimp

SERVES 4

¼ cup cornmeal

1–2 teaspoons cayenne

½ teaspoon ground cumin

1 teaspoon salt

2 tablespoons chopped fresh coriander (cilantro) or parsley

2 pounds large raw Gulf shrimp, peeled and deveined

flour, for dredging

¼ cup vegetable oil

1 cup shredded Monterey Jack or cheddar cheese

FOR SERVING

lime wedges

tomato salsa

1 Preheat the broiler.

2 ▲ In a bowl, combine the cornmeal, cayenne, cumin, salt, and coriander or parsley.

3 ▲ Coat the shrimp lightly in flour, then dip in water and roll in the cornmeal mixture to coat.

4 ▼ Heat the oil in a nonstick skillet. When hot, add the shrimp, in batches if necessary. Cook until they are opaque throughout, 2–3 minutes on each side. Drain on paper towels.

5 ▲ Place the shrimp in a large baking dish, or individual dishes. Sprinkle the cheese evenly over the top. Broil about 3 inches from the heat until the cheese melts, 2–3 minutes. Serve immediately, with lime wedges and salsa.

Galveston Chicken

SERVES 4

3½-pound chicken

juice of 1 lemon

4 garlic cloves, minced

1 tablespoon cayenne

1 tablespoon paprika

1 tablespoon dried oregano

½ teaspoon coarse black pepper

2 teaspoons olive oil

1 teaspoon salt

~ COOK'S TIP ~

Roasting chicken in an oven that
has not been preheated produces
a particularly crispy skin.

1 ▼ With a sharp knife or poultry
shears, remove the backbone from the
chicken. Turn it breast side up. With
the heel of your hand, press down to
break the breastbone, and open the
chicken flat like a book. Insert a
skewer through the chicken, at the
thighs, to keep it flat during cooking.

2 ▲ Place the chicken in a shallow
dish and pour over the lemon juice.

3 ▲ In a small bowl, combine the
garlic, cayenne, paprika, oregano,
pepper, and oil. Mix well. Rub evenly
over the surface of the chicken.

4 Cover and let marinate 2–3 hours
at room temperature, or refrigerate
overnight (return to room
temperature before roasting).

5 Season the chicken with salt on
both sides. Transfer it to a shallow
roasting pan.

6 Put the pan in a cold oven and set
the temperature to 400°F. Roast until
the chicken is done, about 1 hour,
turning occasionally and basting with
the pan juices. To test for doneness,
prick with a skewer: the juices that
run out should be clear.

Turkey Breasts with Tomato-Corn Salsa

SERVES 4

4 skinless boneless turkey breast halves, about 6 ounces each

2 tablespoons fresh lemon juice

2 tablespoons olive oil

½ teaspoon ground cumin

½ teaspoon dried oregano

1 teaspoon coarse black pepper

salt

FOR THE SALSA

1 fresh hot green chili pepper

1 pound tomatoes, seeded and chopped

1½ cups corn kernels, freshly cooked or thawed frozen

3 scallions, chopped

1 tablespoon chopped fresh parsley

2 tablespoons chopped fresh coriander (cilantro)

2 tablespoons fresh lemon juice

3 tablespoons olive oil

1 teaspoon salt

1 ▲ With a meat mallet, pound the turkey breasts between 2 sheets of wax paper until thin.

~ VARIATION ~

Use the cooked turkey, thinly sliced and combined with the salsa, as a filling for warmed flour tortillas.

2 ▲ In a shallow dish, combine the lemon juice, oil, cumin, oregano, and pepper. Add the turkey and turn to coat. Cover and let stand at least 2 hours, or refrigerate overnight.

3 For the salsa, roast the chili over a gas flame, holding it with tongs, until charred on all sides. (Alternatively, char the skin under the broiler.) Let cool 5 minutes. Wearing rubber gloves, carefully rub off the charred skin. For a less hot flavor, discard the seeds. Chop the chili finely and place in a bowl.

4 ▲ Add the remaining salsa ingredients to the chili and toss well to blend. Set aside.

5 Remove the turkey from the marinade. Season lightly on both sides with salt to taste.

6 Heat a ridged grill pan. When hot, add the turkey breasts and cook until browned, about 3 minutes. Turn and cook the meat on the other side until it is cooked through, 3–4 minutes more. Serve the turkey immediately, accompanied by salsa.

Spicy New Mexico Pork Stew

SERVES 6

1 cup water

1 tablespoon tomato paste

4 garlic cloves, minced

2 teaspoons dried oregano

2½ teaspoons ground cumin

2 teaspoons salt

1–3 tablespoons red pepper flakes

4 pounds boneless pork shoulder, cubed

2 onions, thickly sliced

warm flour tortillas, for serving

1 In a large casserole, combine the water, tomato paste, garlic, oregano, cumin, and salt. Add red pepper flakes to taste and stir to mix.

2 ▲ Add the pork cubes and toss to coat them evenly. Cover and allow to marinate 6–8 hours, or overnight, in the refrigerator.

3 Preheat the oven to 300°F.

4 ▼ Cover the casserole and put it in the oven. Cook for 1½ hours. Add the onions and cook 1½ hours more. Serve with flour tortillas.

Turkey-Chorizo Tacos

SERVES 4

1 tablespoon vegetable oil

1 pound ground turkey

1 teaspoon salt

1 teaspoon ground cumin

12 taco shells

3 ounces chorizo, minced

3 scallions, chopped

2 tomatoes, chopped

2 ½ cups shredded lettuce

2 cups shredded Monterey Jack cheese

FOR SERVING

tomato salsa

guacamole

1 Preheat the oven to 350°F.

2 ▲ Heat the oil in a nonstick skillet. Add the turkey, salt, and cumin and sauté over medium heat until the turkey is cooked through, 5–8 minutes. Stir frequently to prevent large lumps from forming.

3 Meanwhile, arrange the taco shells in one layer on a large baking sheet and heat in the oven about 10 minutes, or according to the directions on the package.

4 Add the chorizo and scallions to the turkey and stir to mix. Cook until just warmed through, stirring the mixture occasionally.

5 ▲ To assemble each taco, place 1–2 spoonfuls of the turkey mixture in the bottom of a warmed taco shell. Top with a generous sprinkling of chopped tomato, shredded lettuce, and shredded cheese.

6 Serve immediately, with tomato salsa and guacamole.

~ VARIATION ~

For Chicken Tacos, use minced chicken instead of the turkey.

Spicy New Mexico Pork Stew (top), Turkey-Chorizo Tacos

Pork Chops with Sour Green Chili Salsa

SERVES 4

2 tablespoons vegetable oil

1 tablespoon fresh lemon juice

2 teaspoons ground cumin

1 teaspoon dried oregano

salt and pepper

8 pork loin chops, about ¾ inch thick

FOR THE SALSA

2 fresh hot green chili peppers

2 green bell peppers, seeded and
  chopped

1 tomato, peeled and seeded

½ onion, coarsely chopped

4 scallions

1 pickled jalapeño, stem removed

2 tablespoons olive oil

2 tablespoons fresh lime juice

3 tablespoons cider vinegar

1 teaspoon salt

1 In a small bowl, combine the vegetable oil, lemon juice, cumin, and oregano. Add pepper to taste and stir to blend.

2 ▼ Arrange the pork chops in one layer in a shallow dish. Brush each with the oil mixture on both sides. Cover and let stand 2–3 hours, or refrigerate overnight.

3 ▲ For the salsa, roast the chilies over a gas flame, holding them with tongs, until charred on all sides. (Alternatively, char the skins under the broiler.) Let cool 5 minutes. Wearing rubber gloves, remove the charred skin. For a less hot flavor, discard the seeds.

4 Place the chilies in a food processor or blender. Add the remaining salsa ingredients. Process until finely chopped; do not purée.

5 Transfer the salsa to a heavy saucepan and simmer 15 minutes, stirring occasionally. Set aside.

6 ▲ Season the pork chops. Heat a ridged grill pan. (Alternatively, preheat the broiler.) When hot, add the pork chops and cook until browned, about 5 minutes. Turn and continue cooking until done, 5–7 minutes more. Work in batches, if necessary.

7 Serve immediately, with the sour green chili salsa.

Pork Fajitas

SERVES 6

juice of 3 limes

6 tablespoons olive oil

1 teaspoon dried oregano

1 teaspoon ground cumin

½ teaspoon red pepper flakes

1½ pounds pork tenderloin, cut across
  in 3-inch pieces

salt and pepper

2 large onions, halved and thinly sliced

1 large green bell pepper, seeded and
  thinly sliced lengthwise

FOR SERVING

12–15 flour tortillas, warmed

tomato salsa

guacamole

sour cream

1 ▲ In a shallow dish, combine the lime juice, 3 tablespoons of the oil, the oregano, cumin, and red pepper flakes and mix well. Add the pork pieces and turn to coat. Cover and let stand 1 hour, or refrigerate overnight.

2 Remove the pieces of pork from the marinade. Pat them dry and season with salt and pepper.

3 Heat a ridged grill pan. When hot, add the pork and cook over high heat, turning occasionally, until browned on all sides and cooked through, about 10–12 minutes.

4 ▼ Meanwhile, heat the remaining oil in a large skillet. Add the onions and bell pepper. Stir in ½ teaspoon salt and cook until the vegetables are very soft, about 15 minutes. Stir occasionally. Remove from the heat and set aside.

5 ▲ Slice the pork pieces into thin strips. Add to the onion mixture and reheat briefly if necessary.

6 Spoon a little of the pork mixture onto each tortilla. Garnish with salsa, guacamole, and sour cream, and roll up. Alternatively, the fajitas may be assembled at the table.

Lamb Stew with Cornmeal Dumplings

SERVES 6

1 tablespoon vegetable oil

1 large onion, chopped

1 large celery stalk, chopped

1 red bell pepper, seeded and chopped

1½ pounds boneless lamb, cubed

1 teaspoon salt, or to taste

3 medium tomatoes, cored and chopped

1 teaspoon ground cumin

⅛ teaspoon ground cinnamon

¼ teaspoon cayenne, or to taste

5 cups beef stock

2 zucchini (about ½ pound), quartered
   and chopped

FOR THE DUMPLINGS

1 cup cornmeal

2 tablespoons flour

2 teaspoons baking powder

½ teaspoon salt

1 extra large egg, beaten

2 tablespoons butter, melted

⅓ cup milk

1 Heat the oil in a large flameproof casserole. Add the onion and celery and cook over medium heat until just soft, about 5 minutes.

2 ▲ Add the bell pepper, lamb, and salt. Cook until the cubes of lamb are browned, 5–7 minutes more. Stir to brown them evenly.

3 Stir in the tomatoes, spices, and stock. Bring to a boil, skimming off any foam that rises to the surface. Reduce the heat, cover, and simmer gently 25 minutes. From time to time, skim off any surface fat.

4 Meanwhile, for the dumplings, heat about 2 inches of water in the bottom of a steamer.

5 ▲ Combine the cornmeal, flour, baking powder, and salt in a bowl. Make a well in the center and add the egg, butter, and milk. Stir with a fork until blended.

6 With your hands, shape the mixture into 6 balls, each about 2 inches in diameter.

7 ▲ When the water in the steamer is hot, place the dumplings in the steamer basket. Cover and steam about 20 minutes. (If necessary, add boiling water to replenish the bottom of the steamer.)

8 About 5 minutes before the stew has finished cooking, add the zucchini and stir to mix.

9 Ladle the stew into shallow bowls. Place a dumpling in the center of each and serve immediately.

Tamale Pie

SERVES 8

4 ounces bacon, chopped

1 onion, minced

1 pound lean ground beef

2–3 teaspoons chili powder

1 teaspoon salt

2 cups peeled fresh or canned
  tomatoes

⅓ cup chopped black olives

1 cup corn kernels, freshly cooked or
  thawed frozen

½ cup sour cream

1 cup shredded Monterey Jack cheese

FOR THE TAMALE CRUST

1–1¼ cups chicken stock

salt and pepper

1½ cups masa harina or cornmeal

6 tablespoons margarine or shortening

½ teaspoon baking powder

¼ cup milk

1 Preheat the oven to 375°F.

2 Cook the bacon in a large skillet
until the fat is rendered, 2–3 minutes.
Pour off excess fat, leaving 1–2
tablespoons. Add the onion and cook
until just softened, about 5 minutes.

3 ▲ Add the beef, chili powder, and
salt and cook 5 minutes, stirring to
break up the meat. Stir in the
tomatoes and cook 5 minutes more,
breaking them up with a spoon.

4 ▲ Add the olives, corn, and sour
cream, and mix well. Transfer to a
15-inch-long rectangular or oval
baking dish. Set aside.

5 For the crust, bring the stock to a
boil in a saucepan; season it with salt
and pepper if necessary.

6 In a food processor, combine the
masa harina or cornmeal, margarine
or shortening, baking powder, and
milk. Process until combined. With
the machine on, gradually pour in the
hot stock until a smooth, thick batter
is obtained. If the batter is too thick
to spread, add additional hot stock or
water, a little at a time.

7 Pour the batter over the top of the
beef mixture, spreading it evenly with
a metal spatula.

8 Bake until the top is just browned,
about 20 minutes. Sprinkle the surface
evenly with the shredded cheese and
continue baking until melted and
bubbling, 10–15 minutes more.
Serve immediately.

Beef Enchiladas

SERVES 4

2 pounds chuck steak

1 tablespoon vegetable oil, plus more for frying

1 teaspoon salt

1 teaspoon dried oregano

½ teaspoon ground cumin

1 onion, quartered

2 garlic cloves, crushed

4 cups enchilada sauce

12 corn tortillas

1 cup shredded Monterey Jack cheese

chopped scallions, for serving

sour cream, for serving

1 Preheat the oven to 325°F.

2 ▲ Place the meat on a sheet of foil. Rub all over with the oil. Sprinkle both sides with the salt, oregano, and cumin and rub in well. Add the onion and garlic. Top with another sheet of foil and roll up to seal the edges, leaving room for some steam expansion during cooking.

~ COOK'S TIP ~

Allow extra tortillas because some will break when dipping in the oil or sauce.

3 ▲ Place in a baking dish. Bake until the meat is tender enough to shred, about 3 hours. Remove the meat from the foil and shred with a fork. (This can be prepared 1–2 days in advance.)

4 ▲ Add ½ cup of the enchilada sauce to the beef. Stir well. Spoon a thin layer of enchilada sauce on the bottom of a rectangular baking dish, or in 4 individual baking dishes.

5 ▲ Place the remaining enchilada sauce in a skillet and warm gently.

6 ▲ Put a ½-inch layer of vegetable oil in a second skillet and heat until hot but not smoking. With tongs, lower a tortilla into the oil; the temperature is correct if it just sizzles. Cook 2 seconds, then turn and cook the other side 2 seconds. Lift out, drain over the skillet, and then transfer to the skillet of sauce. Dip in the sauce just to coat both sides.

7 ▲ Transfer the softened tortilla immediately to a plate. Spread 2–3 spoonfuls of the beef mixture down the center of the tortilla. Roll up and place seam-side down in the prepared dish. Repeat the process for the remaining tortillas.

8 Spoon the remaining sauce from the skillet over the enchiladas, spreading it to the ends. Sprinkle the cheese down the center.

9 Bake until the cheese just melts, 10–15 minutes. Sprinkle with chopped scallions and serve at once, with sour cream on the side.

Lone Star Steak and Potato Dinner

SERVES 4

3 tablespoons olive oil

5 large garlic cloves, minced

1 teaspoon coarse black pepper

½ teaspoon ground allspice

1 teaspoon ground cumin

½ teaspoon chili powder

2 teaspoons dried oregano

1 tablespoon cider vinegar

4 boneless sirloin steaks, about ¾ inch thick

salt

tomato salsa, for serving

freshly cooked corn-on-the-cob, for serving (optional)

FOR THE POTATOES

¼ cup vegetable oil

1 onion, chopped

1 teaspoon salt

2 pounds potatoes, boiled and diced

2–5 tablespoons chopped canned green chilies, according to taste

1 ▲ Heat the olive oil in a heavy skillet. When hot, add the garlic and cook, stirring often, until tender and just brown, about 3 minutes; do not let the garlic burn.

2 Transfer the garlic and oil to a shallow dish large enough to hold the steaks in one layer.

3 ▲ Add the pepper, spices, herbs, and vinegar to the garlic and stir to blend thoroughly. If necessary, add just enough water to obtain a moderately thick paste.

4 ▲ Add the steaks to the dish and turn to coat evenly on both sides with the spice mixture. Cover and let stand 2 hours, or refrigerate the steaks overnight. (Bring them to room temperature before cooking.)

~ VARIATION ~

The steaks can also be cooked on a charcoal grill. Prepare the fire, and when the coals are glowing red and covered with grey ash, spread them in a single layer. Cook the steaks in the center of an oiled grill rack set about 5 inches above the coals for 1 minute per side to sear them. Move them away from the center and cook 10–12 minutes longer for medium rare, turning once.

5 ▲ For the potatoes, heat the oil in a large nonstick skillet. Add the onion and salt. Cook over medium heat until softened, about 5 minutes. Add the potatoes and chilies. Cook, stirring occasionally, until well browned, 15–20 minutes.

6 ▲ Season the steaks on both sides with salt to taste. Heat a ridged grill pan. When hot, add the steaks and cook, turning once, until done to your taste. Allow about 2 minutes on each side for medium-rare, and 3–4 minutes for well done.

7 ▲ If necessary, briefly reheat the potatoes. Serve immediately, with the tomato salsa and corn, if using.

Guacamole

MAKES 2 CUPS

3 large ripe avocados

3 scallions, minced

1 garlic clove, minced

1 tablespoon olive oil

1 tablespoon sour cream

½ teaspoon salt

2 tablespoons fresh lemon or lime juice

1 ▲ Halve the avocados and remove the pits. Peel the halves. Put the avocado flesh in a large bowl.

2 ▲ With a fork, mash the avocado flesh coarsely.

3 Add the scallions, garlic, olive oil, sour cream, salt, and lemon or lime juice. Mash until well blended, but do not overwork the mixture. Small chunks of avocado should still remain. Taste the guacamole and adjust the seasoning if necessary, with more salt or lemon or lime juice.

4 ▼ Transfer to a serving bowl. Serve immediately.

~ COOK'S TIP ~

Guacamole does not keep well, but, if necessary, it can be stored in the refrigerator a few hours. Cover the surface with plastic wrap to prevent discoloring.

Tomato Salsa

MAKES 3½ CUPS

1 fresh hot green chili pepper, seeded if desired, chopped

1 garlic clove

½ red onion, coarsely chopped

3 scallions, chopped

¼ cup fresh coriander (cilantro) leaves

1½ pounds ripe tomatoes, seeded and coarsely chopped

1–3 canned green chilies

1 tablespoon olive oil

2 tablespoons fresh lime or lemon juice

½ teaspoon salt, or to taste

2–3 tablespoons tomato juice or cold water

1 In a food processor or blender, combine the fresh green chili, garlic, red onion, scallions, and coriander. Process until finely chopped.

2 ▼ Add the tomatoes, canned chilies, olive oil, lime or lemon juice, salt, and tomato juice or water. Pulse on and off until just chopped; the salsa should be chunky.

3 ▲ Transfer to a bowl and taste for seasoning. Let stand at least 30 minutes before serving. This salsa is best served the day it is made.

~ COOK'S TIP ~

For less heat, remove the seeds from fresh and canned chilies.

Guacamole (top), Tomato Salsa

Tomato Rice

<u>SERVES 4</u>

2 cups unsalted chicken or beef stock

1½ tablespoons vegetable oil

1 small onion, minced

1 cup long-grain rice

1 teaspoon salt

½ teaspoon ground cumin

1 medium-size tomato, peeled, seeded, and chopped

1 tablespoon tomato paste

1 tablespoon chopped fresh coriander (cilantro)

1 Place the stock in a saucepan and heat until just simmering. Remove from the heat, cover, and set aside.

2 ▼ Heat the oil in a large heavy saucepan. Add the onion and rice and cook over medium heat until the onion is just softened, about 5 minutes. Stir in the salt, cumin, tomato, and tomato paste and cook 1 minute more, stirring.

3 ▲ Gradually add the warm stock, stirring to blend. Bring to a boil, then lower the heat, cover, and cook until the rice is tender and all the liquid is absorbed, 30–40 minutes.

4 Fluff the rice with a fork and stir in the coriander. Serve immediately.

Enchilada Sauce

<u>MAKES ABOUT 6 CUPS</u>

4 16-ounce cans peeled plum tomatoes, drained

3 garlic cloves, coarsely chopped

1 onion, coarsely chopped

2–4 tablespoons ground red chili

1 teaspoon cayenne, or to taste

1 teaspoon ground cumin

½ teaspoon dried oregano

½ teaspoon salt

1 ▼ In a food processor or blender, combine the tomatoes, garlic, and onion. Process until smooth.

2 Pour and scrape the mixture into a heavy saucepan.

3 ▲ Add the remaining ingredients and stir to blend. Bring to a boil, stirring occasionally. Boil 2–3 minutes. Reduce the heat, cover, and simmer 15 minutes.

4 Dilute with ½–1 cup water, as necessary, to obtain a pouring consistency. Taste for seasoning; if a hotter sauce is desired, add more cayenne, not ground chili.

~ COOK'S TIP ~

Ground red chili is not the same thing as chili powder. If ground red chili is unavailable, use hot red pepper flakes and strain the sauce before using.

Tomato Rice (top), Enchilada Sauce

Navajo Fry Bread

MAKES 8 BREAD ROUNDS

2 cups flour

2 teaspoons baking powder

½ teaspoon salt

1 cup lukewarm water

oil for frying

1 Sift the flour, baking powder, and salt into a bowl. Pour in the water and stir quickly with a fork until the dough gathers into a ball.

2 ▼ With floured hands, gently knead the dough by rolling it around the bowl. Do not overknead; the dough should be very soft.

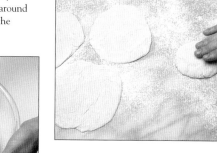

3 ▲ Divide the dough into 8 pieces. With floured hands, pat each piece into a round about 5 inches in diameter. Place the rounds on a floured baking sheet.

4 Put a 1-inch layer of oil in a heavy skillet and heat until hot but not smoking. To test the temperature, drop in a small piece of dough; if it bubbles immediately, the oil is ready.

5 ▲ Add the dough rounds to the hot oil and press down with a slotted spoon to submerge them. Release the dough and cook until puffed and golden on both sides, 3–5 minutes total, turning for even browning. Fry in batches, if necessary.

6 Drain the bread on paper towels and serve immediately. Good as an accompaniment for chili or with shredded cheese and an assortment of southwestern salsas. (Fry bread will not keep.)

Bean Dip

MAKES 3 CUPS

1½ cups dried pinto beans, soaked overnight and drained

1 bay leaf

3 tablespoons coarse salt

1 tablespoon vegetable oil

1 small onion, sliced

1 garlic clove, minced

2–4 canned hot green chilies (optional)

⅓ cup sour cream, plus more for garnishing

½ teaspoon ground cumin

hot pepper sauce

1 tablespoon chopped fresh coriander (cilantro)

tortilla chips, for serving

1 ▲ Place the beans in a large pot. Add fresh cold water to cover and the bay leaf. Bring to a boil, then cover, and simmer 30 minutes.

2 Add the coarse salt and continue simmering until the beans are tender, about 30 minutes or more.

3 Drain the beans, reserving ½ cup of the cooking liquid. Let cool slightly. Discard the bay leaf.

4 Heat the oil in a nonstick skillet. Add the onion and garlic and cook over low heat until just softened, 8–10 minutes, stirring occasionally.

5 ▲ In a food processor or blender, combine the beans, onion mixture, chilies if using, and the reserved cooking liquid. Process until the mixture resembles a coarse purée.

6 ▼ Transfer to a bowl and stir in the sour cream, cumin, and hot pepper sauce to taste. Stir in the coriander, garnish with sour cream, and serve warm, with tortilla chips.

Chocolate Cinnamon Cake with Banana Sauce

SERVES 6

4 1-ounce squares semisweet chocolate, finely chopped

½ cup (1 stick) unsalted butter, at room temperature

1 tablespoon instant coffee powder

5 eggs, separated

1 cup granulated sugar

1 cup flour

2 teaspoons ground cinnamon

FOR THE SAUCE

4 ripe bananas

¼ cup light brown sugar, firmly packed

1 tablespoon fresh lemon juice

¾ cup whipping cream

1 tablespoon rum (optional)

1 Preheat the oven to 350°F. Grease an 8-inch round cake pan.

2 ▲ Combine the chocolate and butter in the top of a double boiler or in a heatproof bowl set over hot water. Stir until melted. Remove from the heat and stir in the coffee. Set aside.

3 Beat the egg yolks with the granulated sugar until thick and lemon-colored. Add the chocolate mixture and beat on low speed just to blend the mixtures evenly.

4 Sift together the flour and cinnamon into a bowl.

5 ▲ In another bowl, beat the egg whites until they hold stiff peaks.

6 ▲ Fold a dollop of whites into the chocolate mixture to lighten it. Fold in the remaining whites in 3 batches, alternating with the shifted flour.

7 ▲ Pour the batter into the prepared pan. Bake until a cake tester inserted in the center comes out clean, 40–50 minutes. Unmold the cake onto a wire rack.

8 Preheat the broiler.

9 ▲ For the sauce, slice the bananas into a shallow, heatproof dish. Add the brown sugar and lemon juice and stir to blend. Place under the broiler and cook, stirring occasionally, until the sugar is caramelized and bubbling, about 8 minutes.

10 ▲ Transfer the bananas to a bowl and mash with a fork until almost smooth. Stir in the cream and rum, if using. Serve the cake and sauce warm.

~ VARIATION ~

For a special occasion, top the cake slices with a scoop of ice cream (rum-raisin, chocolate, or vanilla) before adding the banana sauce. With this addition, the dessert will make at least 8 portions.

Mexican Hot Fudge Sundaes

SERVES 4

1 pint vanilla ice cream

1 pint coffee ice cream

2 large ripe bananas, sliced

whipped cream

toasted sliced almonds

FOR THE SAUCE

¼ cup light brown sugar, firmly packed

½ cup light corn syrup

3 tablespoons strong black coffee

1 teaspoon ground cinnamon

5 1-ounce squares bittersweet chocolate, broken up

⅓ cup whipping cream

3 tablespoons coffee liqueur (optional)

1 ▼ For the sauce, combine the brown sugar, corn syrup, coffee, and cinnamon in a heavy saucepan. Bring to a boil. Boil the mixture, stirring constantly, about 5 minutes.

2 ▲ Remove from the heat and stir in the chocolate. When melted and smooth, stir in the cream and liqueur, if using. Let the sauce cool just to lukewarm, or if made ahead, reheat gently while assembling the sundaes.

3 ▲ Fill sundae dishes with 1 scoop each of vanilla and coffee ice cream.

4 ▲ Arrange the bananas on the top of each dish. Pour the warm sauce over the bananas, then top each sundae with a generous rosette of whipped cream. Top with toasted almonds and serve immediately.

New Mexico Christmas Biscochitos

MAKES 24

1½ cups flour

1 teaspoon baking powder

⅛ teaspoon salt

½ cup (1 stick) unsalted butter, at room temperature

½ cup sugar

1 egg

1 teaspoon whole aniseed

1 tablespoon brandy

¼ cup sugar mixed with ½ teaspoon ground cinnamon, for sprinkling

1 Sift together the flour, baking powder, and salt. Set aside.

2 ▲ Beat the butter with the sugar until soft and fluffy. Add the egg, aniseed, and brandy and beat until incorporated. Fold in the dry ingredients just until blended to a dough. Refrigerate 30 minutes.

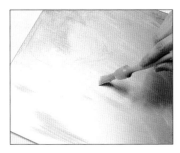

3 ▲ Preheat the oven to 350°F. Grease 2 cookie sheets.

4 On a lightly floured surface, roll out the chilled cookie dough to about ⅛-inch thickness.

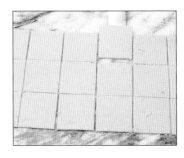

5 ▲ With a cutter, pastry wheel, or knife, cut out the cookies into squares, diamonds, or other shapes. The traditional shape for biscochitos is a fleur-de-lis.

6 ▲ Place on the prepared cookie sheets and sprinkle lightly with the cinnamon sugar.

7 Bake until just barely golden, about 10 minutes. Cool on the sheet 5 minutes before transferring to a wire rack to cool completely. The cookies can be kept in an airtight container up to 1 week.

Pueblo Pastelitos

MAKES 16

2 cups dried fruit, such as apricots
  or prunes

½ cup light brown sugar, firmly packed

½ cup raisins

½ cup pine nuts or chopped almonds

½ teaspoon ground cinnamon

oil for frying

3 tablespoons granulated sugar mixed
  with 1 teaspoon ground cinnamon,
  for sprinkling

FOR THE PASTRY DOUGH

2 cups flour

¼ teaspoon baking powder

¼ teaspoon salt

2 teaspoons granulated sugar

4 tablespoons unsalted butter, chilled

2 tablespoons shortening

4–5 tablespoons ice water

1 ▲ For the pastry dough, sift the flour, baking powder, salt, and sugar into a bowl. With a plastry blender or 2 knives, cut in the butter and shortening until the mixture resembles coarse meal. Sprinkle with 4 tablespoons of the ice water and mix until the dough holds together. If the dough is too crumbly, add a little more water, 1 teaspoon at a time.

2 Gather the dough into a ball and flatten into a disk. Wrap the dough in wax paper and refrigerate it at least 30 minutes.

3 ▲ Place the dried fruit in a saucepan and add cold water to cover. Bring to a boil, then simmer gently until the fruit is soft enough to purée, about 30 minutes.

4 ▲ Drain the fruit and place in a food processor or blender. Process until smooth. Return the fruit purée to the saucepan. Add the brown sugar and cook, stirring constantly, until thick, about 5 minutes. Remove from the heat and stir in the raisins, pine nuts or almonds, and cinnamon. Allow the mixture to cool.

5 Roll out the chilled dough to about ⅛-inch thickness. Stamp out rounds with a 4-inch cookie cutter. (Roll and cut out in 2 batches if it is more convenient.)

~ COOK'S TIP ~

If desired, the pastry and the filling can both be made up to 2 days in advance and refrigerated.

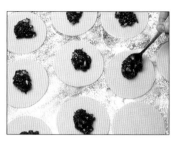

6 ▲ Place a spoonful of the fruit filling in the center of each round.

7 ▲ Moisten the edge with a brush dipped in water, then fold over the dough to form a half-moon shape. With a fork, crimp the rounded edge.

8 ▲ Put a ½-inch layer of oil in a heavy skillet and heat until hot but not smoking (to test, drop a scrap of dough in the oil; if the oil sizzles, it is hot enough). Add the turnovers, a few at a time, and fry until golden on both sides, about 1½ minutes per side.

9 Drain briefly on paper towels, then sprinkle with the cinnamon sugar. Serve the pastelitos warm.

Flan

SERVES 8–10

3½ cups milk
½ cup whipping cream
1 cup sugar
1 cinnamon stick
8 extra large eggs
1 teaspoon vanilla extract
FOR THE CARAMEL
⅔ cup sugar
¼ cup water

1 In a saucepan, combine the milk, cream, sugar, and cinnamon. Scald over medium heat, stirring. Remove, cover, and let stand 30 minutes.

2 For the caramel, combine the sugar and water in a small, heavy saucepan over medium-high heat.

3 Bring to a boil, then simmer until the syrup begins to color; do not stir. When the syrup is a deep golden brown, dip the base of the pan in cold water to stop the cooking.

4 ▲ Quickly pour the caramel syrup into a 2½-quart mold and tilt the mold to coat the bottom evenly.

5 Preheat the oven to 350°F.

6 ▲ Reheat the milk mixture just to warm. Remove the cinnamon stick.

7 In a large bowl, combine the eggs and vanilla and mix together. Pour the milk mixture over the egg mixture, stirring constantly.

8 ▲ Place the caramel-coated mold in a large baking dish and add just enough hot water to come about 2 inches up the side of the mold. Pour the egg mixture through a strainer into the mold. Cover with foil.

9 Bake until the custard is just set, 40–50 minutes. Let cool in the water bath, then refrigerate at least 4 hours.

10 To unmold, run a knife around the inside of the mold. Place an inverted plate on top and flip over to release the flan. Scrape any remaining caramel onto the flan. Serve cold.

Southwestern Rice Pudding

SERVES 4–6

¼ cup raisins
2 cups water
1 cup short-grain rice
1 cinnamon stick
2 tablespoons sugar
2 cups milk
1 cup canned sweetened coconut cream
½ teaspoon vanilla extract
1 tablespoon butter
⅓ cup shredded coconut
ground cinnamon, for sprinkling

1 ▲ Put the raisins in a small bowl and add water to cover. Let soak.

2 ▲ In a medium-size saucepan, bring the water to a boil. Add the rice, cinnamon stick, and sugar and stir. Return to a boil, then lower the heat, cover, and simmer gently until the liquid is absorbed, 15–20 minutes.

3 ▼ Meanwhile, combine the milk, coconut cream, and vanilla in a bowl. Drain the raisins.

4 Remove the cinnamon stick from the pan. Add the milk mixture and drained raisins to the rice and stir to mix. Continue cooking, covered and stirring often, until the mixture is just thick, about 20 minutes. Do not overcook the rice.

5 Preheat the broiler.

6 Transfer the mixture to a heatproof serving dish. Dot with the butter and sprinkle coconut evenly over the surface. Broil about 5 inches from the heat until the top is just browned, 3–5 minutes. Sprinkle with cinnamon. Serve warm or cold.

CALIFORNIA

TRENDS, CULINARY AND
OTHERWISE, SEEM TO BEGIN HERE.
LIFESTYLE – WEST COAST
INFORMALITY, WITH ITS EMPHASIS
ON OUTDOOR LIVING AND DINING –
DICTATES A UNIQUE CUISINE. FOOD
GURUS AND THEIR BOUTIQUE FARMS
BRING DIVERSE AGRICULTURAL
PRODUCTS INCLUDING FRUIT,
BERRIES, NUTS, AVOCADOS, AND
ARTICHOKES TO OUR TABLES YEAR
ROUND, AND CALIFORNIA WINE IS
APPRECIATED WORLDWIDE.

Tomato Sandwiches with Olive Mayonnaise

SERVES 6

1 garlic clove, minced

2 tablespoons olive oil

1 teaspoon red wine vinegar

2 beefsteak tomatoes

½ cup fresh basil leaves or parsley, chopped

¼ teaspoon salt

black pepper

7 brine-cured black olives, pitted and minced

6 tablespoons mayonnaise

12 slices of sourdough bread, lightly toasted

6 large lettuce leaves

1 ▼ Combine the garlic, oil, and vinegar in a small bowl and mix together. Or, shake the ingredients in a screwtop jar until blended. Set this dressing aside.

2 ▲ Core the tomatoes. With a sharp knife, cut 6 shallow lengthwise slits in the skin of each to make the tomatoes easier to eat; do not cut too deeply into the flesh. Cut the tomatoes crosswise into thin slices.

3 Place the tomato slices in a shallow dish. Add the oil and vinegar dressing, basil or parsley, salt, and pepper to taste. Let marinate at least 30 minutes.

4 ▲ In another bowl, stir together the olives and mayonnaise.

5 ▲ Spread 6 slices of bread with the olive mayonnaise. Arrange the tomato slices on top and drizzle over any remaining dressing from the bowl. Top each with a lettuce leaf. Cover with the remaining bread and serve.

Gazpacho

Serves 4

½ hothouse cucumber (about 8 ounces), coarsely chopped

½ green bell pepper, seeded and coarsely chopped

½ red bell pepper, seeded and coarsely chopped

1 large tomato, coarsely chopped

2 scallions, chopped

hot pepper sauce (optional)

3 tablespoons chopped fresh parsley or coriander (cilantro)

croutons, for serving

For the soup base

1 pound ripe tomatoes, peeled, seeded, and chopped

1 tablespoon ketchup

2 tablespoons tomato paste

¼ teaspoon sugar

¾ teaspoon salt

1 teaspoon pepper

¼ cup sherry vinegar

¼ cup olive oil

1½ cups tomato juice

2 Add the ketchup, tomato paste, sugar, salt, pepper, vinegar, and oil and pulse on and off 3–4 times, just to blend. Transfer to a large bowl. Stir in the tomato juice.

3 ▼ Place the cucumber and bell peppers in the food processor or blender and pulse on and off until finely chopped; do not overmix.

4 ▲ Reserve about 2 tablespoons of the chopped vegetables for garnishing; stir the remainder into the soup base. Taste for seasoning. Mix in the chopped tomato, scallions, and a dash of hot pepper sauce if desired. Chill well.

5 To serve, ladle into bowls and sprinkle with the reserved chopped vegetables, chopped fresh parsley or coriander, and croutons.

1 ▲ For the soup base, put the tomatoes in a food processor or blender and pulse on and off until just smooth, scraping the sides of the container occasionally.

Individual Goat Cheese Tarts

SERVES 6

6–8 sheets phyllo pastry (about 4 ounces)

4 tablespoons butter, melted

12 ounces firm log-shaped goat cheese, rind removed

9 cherry tomatoes, quartered

½ cup milk

2 eggs

2 tablespoons whipping cream

⅛ teaspoon ground white pepper

~ COOK'S TIP ~

Keep the phyllo pastry under a damp cloth while working to prevent the sheets from drying out.

1 Preheat the oven to 375°F. Grease 6 4-inch tartlet pans.

2 ▲ For one pan, cut out 4 circles of phyllo pastry, each about 4½ inches in diameter. Place one circle in the pan and brush with butter. Top with another phyllo circle and brush with butter. Continue until there are 4 layers of phyllo; do not butter the last layer. Repeat the procedure for the remaining pans.

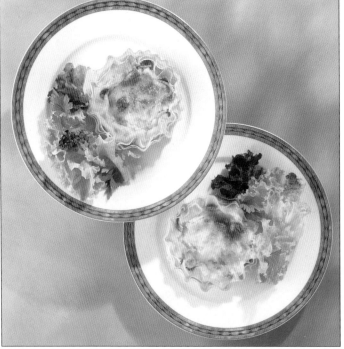

3 ▲ Place the pastry-lined pans on a baking sheet. Cut the goat cheese log into 6 slices. Place a slice in each of the pastry shells.

4 ▲ Arrange the tomato quarters around the cheese slices.

5 ▲ Combine the milk, eggs, cream, and pepper in a measure or bowl and whisk to mix. Pour into the pastry shells, filling them almost to the top.

6 Bake until puffed and golden, 30–40 minutes. Serve hot or warm, with a mixed green salad if desired.

Turkey and Avocado Pita Pizzas

SERVES 4

8 plum tomatoes, quartered

3–4 tablespoons olive oil

salt and pepper

1 large ripe avocado

8 pita bread rounds

6–7 slices of cooked turkey, chopped

1 onion, thinly sliced

2½ cups shredded Monterey Jack cheese

2 tablespoons chopped fresh coriander
  (cilantro)

1 Preheat the oven to 450°F.

2 ▲ Place the tomatoes in a baking dish. Drizzle over 1 tablespoon of the oil and season with salt and pepper. Bake 30 minutes; do not stir.

3 Remove the baking dish from the oven and mash the tomatoes with a fork, removing the skins as you mash. Set aside.

4 ▲ Peel and pit the avocado. Cut into 16 thin slices.

5 Brush the edges of the pita breads with oil. Arrange the breads on 2 baking sheets.

6 ▼ Spread each pita with mashed tomato, almost to the edges.

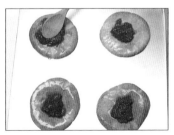

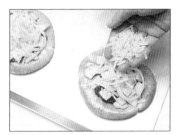

7 ▲ Top each with 2 avocado slices. Sprinkle with the turkey, then add a few onion slices. Season with salt and pepper. Sprinkle on the cheese.

8 Place one sheet in the middle of the oven and bake until the cheese begins to melt, 15–20 minutes. Sprinkle with half the coriander and serve. Meanwhile, bake the second batch of pizzas to serve them hot.

Crab Louis

SERVES 4

4 cups Boston or Bibb lettuce leaves

2 cups fresh lump crab meat

4 hard-cooked eggs, sliced

4 tomatoes, quartered

½ green bell pepper, seeded and thinly
  sliced

½ cup pitted black olives, sliced

FOR THE DRESSING

1 cup mayonnaise

2 teaspoons fresh lemon juice

¼ cup chili sauce

½ green bell pepper, seeded and minced

1 teaspoon prepared horseradish

1 teaspoon Worcestershire sauce

1 ▲ For the dressing, combine all
the ingredients in a bowl and mix
well. Set aside.

2 Line 4 salad plates with the lettuce
leaves. Mound the crab meat in the
center. Arrange hard-cooked eggs and
tomatoes around the outside.

3 ▼ Spoon some of the dressing over
the crab. Arrange the green pepper
slices on top and sprinkle with the
olives. Serve immediately, with the
remaining dressing.

Poolside Tuna Salad

SERVES 4–6

6 ounces radishes

1 hothouse cucumber

3 celery stalks

1 yellow bell pepper

6 ounces cherry tomatoes, halved

4 scallions, thinly sliced

½ teaspoon salt, or to taste

¼ cup fresh lemon juice

¼ cup olive oil

black pepper

2 7-ounce cans tuna, drained

2 tablespoons chopped fresh parsley

lettuce leaves, for serving

twisted lemon peel, for garnishing

1 Cut the radishes, cucumber, celery,
and bell pepper into pea-sized dice.
Place in a large, shallow dish. Add the
tomatoes and scallions.

2 ▼ In a small bowl, stir together the
salt and lemon juice with a fork until
dissolved. Pour this over the vegetable
mixture. Add the oil and pepper to
taste. Stir to blend. Cover and let
stand 1 hour.

3 Add the tuna and parsley and toss
gently until combined.

4 ▲ Arrange lettuce leaves on a
platter and mound the salad in the
center. Garnish with the lemon peel.

~ VARIATION ~

Prepare the vegetables as above
and add the parsley. Arrange
lettuce leaves on individual plates
and divide the vegetable mixture
among them. Place a mound of
tuna on top of each and finish
with a dollop of mayonnaise.

Crab Louis (top), Poolside Tuna Salad

Goat Cheese Salad

SERVES 4

2 tablespoons olive oil

4 slices of French bread, ½ inch thick

8 cups mixed salad greens, such as curly endive, radicchio, and red oak leaf, torn in small pieces

4 firm goat cheese rounds, about 2 ounces each, rind removed

1 yellow or red bell pepper, seeded and finely diced

1 small red onion, thinly sliced

3 tablespoons chopped fresh parsley

2 tablespoons chopped fresh chives

FOR THE DRESSING

2 tablespoons wine vinegar

¼ teaspoon salt

1 teaspoon whole-grain mustard

5 tablespoons olive oil

black pepper

1 For the dressing, mix the vinegar and salt with a fork until dissolved. Stir in the mustard. Gradually stir in the oil until blended. Season with pepper and set aside.

2 Preheat the broiler.

3 ▲ Heat the oil in a skillet. When hot, add the bread slices and cook until golden, about 1 minute. Turn and cook the other side, about 30 seconds more. Drain on paper towels and set aside.

4 ▲ Place the salad greens in a bowl. Add 3 tablespoons of the dressing and toss to coat. Divide the dressed leaves among 4 salad plates.

5 ▲ Put the goat cheeses, cut side up, on a baking sheet and broil until bubbling and golden, 1–2 minutes.

6 Set 1 goat cheese on each slice of bread and place in the center of each plate. Scatter the diced bell pepper, red onion, parsley, and chives over the salad. Drizzle with the remaining dressing and serve.

~ VARIATION ~

For a more substantial main course salad, increase the amount of greens and make double the quantity of dressing. Add 2 cups sliced cooked green beans and 2 cups slivered or diced ham to the greens, and toss with half of the dressing. Top with broiled goat cheeses and remaining dressing.

Three-Bean and Lentil Salad

SERVES 6

1 cup dried garbanzo beans (chick peas), soaked overnight and drained

1 cup dried red kidney beans, soaked overnight and drained

3 bay leaves

2 tablespoons coarse salt

½ cup lentils

8 ounces fresh green beans, cut in 1-inch slices and cooked

1 small red onion, minced

3 scallions, chopped

1 tablespoon chopped fresh parsley

FOR THE DRESSING

5–6 tablespoons red wine vinegar

1 teaspoon salt

2 teaspoons Dijon-style mustard

6 tablespoons olive oil

1 garlic clove, minced

black pepper

3 Halfway through the beans' cooking time, put the lentils in a large pot and add cold water to cover and the remaining bay leaf. Bring to a boil, then cover and simmer until just tender, 30–40 minutes.

4 ▼ As the lentils and the beans finish cooking, drain thoroughly in a colander and place them in a large bowl. Discard the bay leaves.

5 ▲ Add the green beans, red onion, scallions, and parsley to the bowl. Add the dressing and toss well.

6 Taste the salad and adjust the seasoning, adding more vinegar, salt, and pepper if desired. Serve at room temperature.

1 ▲ For the dressing, in a bowl mix 4 tablespoons of the vinegar and the salt with a fork until dissolved. Stir in the mustard. Gradually stir in the oil until blended. Add the garlic and pepper to taste. Set aside.

2 Put the garbanzo beans and kidney beans in separate large pots. To each, add fresh cold water to cover and 1 bay leaf. Bring to a boil, then cover and simmer 30 minutes. Add 1 tablespoon coarse salt to each pot and continue simmering until tender, 30 minutes–1½ hours more.

Artichoke Pasta Salad

SERVES 4

7 tablespoons olive oil

1 red bell pepper, quartered, seeded, and thinly sliced

1 onion, halved and thinly sliced

1 teaspoon dried thyme

salt and pepper

3 tablespoons sherry vinegar

1 pound pasta shapes, such as penne or fusilli

2 6-ounce jars marinated artichoke hearts, drained and thinly sliced

5 ounces cooked broccoli, chopped

20–25 salt-cured black olives, pitted and chopped

2 tablespoons chopped fresh parsley

1 ▼ Heat 2 tablespoons of the oil in a nonstick skillet. Add the red bell pepper and onion and cook over low heat until just soft, 8–10 minutes, stirring occasionally.

2 ▲ Stir in the thyme, ¼ teaspoon salt, and the vinegar. Cook, stirring, 30 seconds more, then set aside.

3 ▲ Bring a large pot of salted water to a boil. Add the pasta and cook until just tender (check package directions for timing). Drain, rinse with hot water, then drain again well. Transfer to a large bowl. Add 2 tablespoons of the oil and toss well to coat.

4 ▲ Add the artichokes, broccoli, olives, parsley, onion mixture, and remaining oil to the pasta. Season with salt and pepper. Stir to blend. Let stand at least 1 hour before serving, or refrigerate overnight. Serve at room temperature.

Asparagus with Creamy Raspberry Vinaigrette

SERVES 4

1½ pounds thin asparagus spears

2 tablespoons raspberry vinegar

½ teaspoon salt

1 teaspoon Dijon-style mustard

5 tablespoons sunflower oil

2 tablespoons sour cream or plain yogurt

white pepper

1 cup fresh raspberries

1 Fill a large wide pot, frying pan, or wok with water about 4 inches deep and bring to a boil.

2 ▲ Trim the tough ends of the asparagus spears. If desired, remove the "scales" using a vegetable peeler.

4 ▼ With a slotted spatula, carefully remove the asparagus bundles from the boiling water and immerse in cold water to stop the cooking. Drain and untie the bundles. Pat dry with paper towels. Refrigerate the asparagus at least 1 hour.

3 ▲ Tie the spears into 2 bundles. Lower into the boiling water and cook, keeping the bundles upright, until just tender, about 2 minutes.

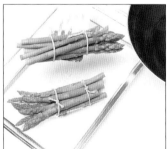

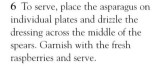

5 ▲ Combine the vinegar and salt in a bowl and stir with a fork until dissolved. Stir in the mustard. Gradually stir in the oil until blended. Add the sour cream or yogurt and pepper to taste.

6 To serve, place the asparagus on individual plates and drizzle the dressing across the middle of the spears. Garnish with the fresh raspberries and serve.

California Taco Salad with Beef

SERVES 4

2 teaspoons vegetable oil

1 pound lean ground beef

1 small onion, chopped

½ teaspoon salt

¼ teaspoon cayenne, or to taste

1 cup corn kernels (fresh, frozen, or canned)

1 cup cooked or canned kidney beans

1 tablespoon chopped fresh coriander (cilantro), plus more coriander leaves for garnishing

1 small head of romaine lettuce

3 tomatoes, quartered

2 cups shredded Monterey Jack or cheddar cheese

1 avocado

⅓ cup pitted black olives, sliced

4 scallions, chopped

tortilla chips, for serving

FOR THE DRESSING

3 tablespoons white wine vinegar

½ teaspoon salt

1 teaspoon Dijon-style mustard

2 tablespoons buttermilk

⅔ cup vegetable oil

1 small garlic clove, minced

1 teaspoon ground cumin

1 teaspoon dried oregano

¼ teaspoon pepper

~ VARIATIONS ~

For California Taco Salad with Chicken, substitute 1 pound boneless, skinless chicken breast, finely diced, for the ground beef. Garbanzo beans (chick peas) may be used in place of kidney beans. Although frozen or canned corn is convenient, freshly cooked corn kernels scraped from the cob give added moisture and extra flavor.

1 ▲ For the dressing, mix the vinegar and salt with a fork until dissolved. Stir in the mustard and buttermilk. Gradually stir in the oil until blended. Add the garlic, cumin, oregano, and pepper and set aside.

2 ▲ Heat the oil in a nonstick skillet. Add the beef, onion, salt, and cayenne and cook until just browned, 5–7 minutes. Stir frequently to break up lumps. Drain and let cool.

3 ▲ In a large bowl, combine the beef, corn, kidney beans, and chopped coriander and toss to blend.

4 ▲ Stack the lettuce leaves on top of one another and slice thinly, crosswise, into shreds. Place in another bowl and toss with ¼ cup of the dressing. Divide the lettuce among 4 dinner plates.

5 ▲ Mound the meat mixture in the center of each plate. Arrange the tomatoes at the edge. Sprinkle with the shredded cheese.

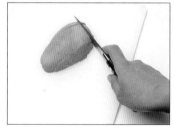

6 ▲ Peel, pit, and dice the avocado. Scatter on top of the salad together with the olives and scallions.

7 Pour the remaining dressing over the salads. Garnish with coriander. Serve with tortilla chips.

Zucchini-Cheese Casserole

SERVES 4

1 garlic clove, crushed with a knife

2 tablespoons olive oil or melted butter

2 pounds zucchini

salt and pepper

2 cups shredded Monterey Jack cheese

2 eggs

1½ cups milk

~ VARIATIONS ~

For a spicier version, replace the cheese with Jalapeño Jack cheese, and toss the zucchini with 2 teaspoons chili powder.

1 Preheat the oven to 375°F.

2 ▼ Rub the garlic clove around the inside of a baking dish, pressing hard to extract the juice; discard the garlic. Grease the dish with half the oil or melted butter.

3 ▲ Cut the zucchini across into ¼-inch slices. Place them in a bowl and toss with the remaining oil or melted butter and salt to taste.

4 ▲ Arrange half the zucchini slices in an even layer in the baking dish. Sprinkle with half the cheese. Add the remaining zucchini, spreading it evenly on the top.

5 ▲ Combine the eggs, milk, ½ teaspoon salt, and pepper to taste in a bowl and whisk together. Pour over the zucchini. Sprinkle with the remaining cheese.

6 Cover with foil and bake about 30 minutes. Remove the foil and continue baking until the top is browned, 30–40 minutes more. Serve hot, warm, or cold.

San Francisco Chicken Wings

SERVES 4

⅓ cup soy sauce
1 tablespoon light brown sugar
1 tablespoon rice vinegar
2 tablespoons dry sherry wine
juice of 1 orange
2-inch strip of orange peel
1 star anise
1 teaspoon cornstarch
¼ cup water
1 tablespoon minced fresh gingerroot
¼–1 teaspoon Oriental chili-garlic sauce, to taste
3½ pounds chicken wings (22–24), tips removed

1 Preheat the oven to 400°F.

2 ▲ Combine the soy sauce, brown sugar, vinegar, sherry, orange juice and peel, and star anise in a saucepan. Bring to a boil over medium heat.

3 ▲ Combine the cornstarch and water in a small bowl and stir until blended. Add to the boiling soy sauce mixture, stirring well. Boil 1 minute more, stirring constantly.

4 ▼ Remove the soy sauce mixture from the heat and stir in the minced ginger and chili-garlic sauce.

5 ▲ Arrange the chicken wings, in one layer, in a large baking dish. Pour over the soy sauce mixture and stir to coat the wings evenly.

6 Bake until tender and browned, 30–40 minutes, basting occasionally. Serve the wings hot or warm.

Swordfish with Bell Pepper-Orange Relish

SERVES 4

5 tablespoons olive oil

1 large fennel bulb, cut in ¼-inch dice

1 red bell pepper, seeded and cut in ¼-inch dice

1 yellow bell pepper, seeded and cut in ¼-inch dice

1 orange or green bell pepper, seeded and cut in ¼-inch dice

1 small onion, cut in ¼-inch dice

1 teaspoon grated orange rind

¼ cup fresh orange juice

salt

4 pieces of swordfish steak, about 5 ounces each

1 ▼ Heat 3 tablespoons of the oil in a large nonstick skillet. Add the fennel, bell peppers, and onion and cook over medium heat until just tender, about 5 minutes (they should retain some crunch).

2 ▲ Stir in the orange rind and juice and cook 1 minute more. Stir in ½ teaspoon salt. Cover and set aside.

3 Bring some water to a boil in the bottom of a steamer.

4 ▲ Meanwhile, brush the fish steaks on both sides with the remaining oil and season with salt.

5 ▲ Place the fish steaks in the top part of the steamer. Cover the pan and steam until the steaks are opaque throughout, about 5 minutes.

6 Transfer the fish to dinner plates. Serve immediately, accompanied by the bell pepper relish.

Tangerine-Soy Marinated Salmon

SERVES 4

1 cup soy sauce

1½ teaspoons firmly packed brown sugar

¼ cup rice vinegar

1 tablespoon minced fresh gingerroot

2 garlic cloves, minced

grated rind and juice of 1 tangerine

½ cup water

4 pieces of salmon fillet, about 6 ounces
each

1 ▲ Combine the soy sauce, sugar,
vinegar, ginger, garlic, orange rind
and juice, and water in a bowl. Stir
until well blended.

2 ▲ Arrange the fish, in one layer,
in a large shallow dish. Pour over the
soy sauce mixture and turn the fish so
that both sides are coated. Cover and
let marinate at room temperature 1
hour, or refrigerate overnight.

3 Preheat the oven to 350°F.

4 ▼ Remove the fish from the
marinade, leaving on any pieces of
ginger that cling to the fish. Place in a
baking dish, in one layer.

5 ▲ Cover the dish with foil. Bake
until the fish is opaque throughout,
20–30 minutes. Transfer to dinner
plates and serve immediately. Good
served with steamed broccoli.

Cioppino

SERVES 4

1½ tablespoons olive oil

1 onion, halved and thinly sliced

several saffron threads, crushed

1 teaspoon dried thyme

⅛ teaspoon cayenne

salt and pepper

2 garlic cloves, minced

1 28-ounce can peeled tomatoes,
   drained and chopped

¾ cup dry white wine

2 quarts fish stock

12 ounces skinless fish fillets, cut into
   pieces

1 pound monkfish, membrane removed,
   cut into pieces

1 pound mussels in shell, thoroughly
   scrubbed

½ pound small squid bodies, cleaned
   and cut in rings

2 tablespoons chopped fresh parsley

thickly sliced sourdough bread, for
   serving

1 ▼ Heat the oil in a large, heavy pot. Add the onion, saffron, thyme, cayenne, and ½ teaspoon salt. Stir well and cook over low heat until soft, 8–10 minutes. Add the garlic and cook 1 minute more.

~ COOK'S TIP ~

Do not prepare mussels more than a few hours in advance of cooking or they will spoil and die.

2 ▲ Stir in the tomatoes, wine, and fish stock. Bring to a boil and boil 1 minute, then reduce the heat to medium-low and simmer 15 minutes.

3 ▲ Add the fish fillet and monkfish pieces to the pot and simmer gently 3 minutes.

4 ▲ Add the mussels and squid and simmer until the mussel shells open, about 2 minutes more. Stir in the parsley. Season with salt and pepper.

5 Ladle into warmed soup bowls and serve immediately, with bread.

Shrimp Kabobs with Plum Sauce

SERVES 6

1 tablespoon vegetable oil
1 onion, minced
1 garlic clove, minced
1 pound purple plums, pitted and chopped
1 tablespoon rice vinegar
2 tablespoons fresh orange juice
1 teaspoon Dijon-style mustard
2 tablespoons soy sauce
1 tablespoon firmly packed light brown sugar
1 point of a star anise
½ cup water
1½ pounds medium-size raw shrimp, peeled (tails left on if desired) and deveined
boiled rice, for serving

1 ▲ Heat the oil in a saucepan. Add the onion, garlic, and plums and cook over low heat, stirring occasionally, until softened, about 10 minutes.

2 Stir in the vinegar, orange juice, mustard, soy sauce, sugar, star anise, and water. Bring to a boil. Lower the heat, cover, and simmer, stirring occasionally, 20 minutes.

3 Uncover the pan and simmer the sauce 10 minutes more to thicken, stirring frequently.

4 ▼ Remove the star anise. Transfer to a food processor or blender and purée until smooth.

5 Press the sauce through a fine strainer to remove all the fibers and plum skins.

6 Preheat the broiler.

7 ▲ Thread the shrimp, flat, onto 6 skewers. Brush them all over with three-quarters of the plum sauce.

8 Place the shrimp kabobs on the foil-lined broiler pan. Broil until opaque throughout, 5–6 minutes. Turn the kabobs once.

9 Meanwhile, reheat the remaining plum sauce. Serve the kabobs with rice and the sauce.

Lemon Chicken with Guacamole Sauce

SERVES 4

juice of 2 lemons

3 tablespoons olive oil

2 garlic cloves, minced

salt and pepper

4 chicken breast halves, about 7 ounces each

2 beefsteak tomatoes, cored and cut in half

chopped fresh coriander (cilantro), for garnishing

FOR THE SAUCE

1 ripe avocado

¼ cup sour cream

3 tablespoons fresh lemon juice

½ teaspoon salt

¼ cup water

1 ▲ Combine the lemon juice, oil, garlic, ½ teaspoon salt, and a little pepper in a bowl. Stir to mix.

~ VARIATION ~

To grill the chicken, prepare the fire, and when the coals are glowing red and covered with grey ash, spread them in a single layer. Set an oiled grill rack about 5 inches above the coals and cook the chicken breasts until lightly charred and cooked through, about 15–20 minutes. Allow extra olive oil for basting.

2 ▲ Arrange the chicken breasts, in one layer, in a shallow glass or ceramic dish. Pour over the lemon mixture and turn to coat evenly. Cover and let stand at least 1 hour at room temperature, or refrigerate overnight.

3 ▲ For the sauce, cut the avocado in half, remove the pit, and scrape the flesh into a food processor or blender.

4 ▲ Add the sour cream, lemon juice, and salt and process until smooth. Add the water and process just to blend. If necessary, add more water to thin the sauce. Transfer to a bowl, taste and adjust the seasoning, if necessary. Set aside.

5 ▲ Preheat the broiler. Heat a ridged grill pan. Remove the chicken from the marinade and pat dry.

6 ▲ When the grill pan is hot, add the chicken breasts and cook, turning often, until they are cooked through, about 10 minutes.

7 ▲ Meanwhile, arrange the tomato halves, cut-sides up, on a baking sheet and season lightly with salt and pepper. Broil until hot and bubbling, about 5 minutes.

8 To serve, place a chicken breast, tomato half, and a dollop of avocado sauce on each plate. Sprinkle with coriander and serve.

Cornish Hens with Raisin-Walnut Stuffing

SERVES 4

1 cup Port wine

⅔ cup raisins

1 tablespoon walnut oil

3 ounces mushrooms, minced

1 large celery stalk, minced

1 small onion, chopped

salt and pepper

1 cup fresh bread crumbs

½ cup chopped walnuts

1 tablespoon each chopped fresh basil
and parsley, or 2 tablespoons
chopped parsley

½ teaspoon dried thyme

6 tablespoons butter, melted

4 Cornish hens

1 Preheat the oven to 350°F.

2 In a small bowl, combine the Port wine and raisins and let soak about 20 minutes.

3 ▲ Meanwhile, heat the oil in a nonstick skillet. Add the mushrooms, celery, onion, and ¼ teaspoon salt and cook over low heat until softened, 8–10 minutes. Let cool slightly.

4 ▲ Drain the raisins, reserving the Port. Combine the raisins, bread crumbs, walnuts, basil, parsley, and thyme in a bowl. Stir in the onion mixture and 4 tablespoons of the butter. Add ½ teaspoon salt and pepper to taste.

5 ▲ Fill the cavity of each hen with the stuffing mixture. Do not pack down. Tie the legs together, looping the tail with the string to enclose the stuffing securely.

6 Brush the hens with the remaining butter and place in a baking dish just large enough to hold the birds comfortably. Pour over the reserved Port wine.

7 Roast, basting occasionally, about 1 hour. To test for doneness, pierce the thigh with a skewer; the juices should run clear. Serve immediately, pouring some of the pan juices over each bird.

Fusilli with Turkey, Tomatoes, and Broccoli

SERVES 4

1½ pounds ripe but firm plum tomatoes, quartered

6 tablespoons olive oil

1 teaspoon dried oregano

salt and pepper

12 ounces broccoli florets

1 small onion, sliced

1 teaspoon dried thyme

1 pound skinless boneless turkey breast, cubed

3 garlic cloves, minced

1 tablespoon fresh lemon juice

1 pound fusilli

1 Preheat the oven to 400°F.

2 ▲ Place the tomatoes in a baking dish. Add 1 tablespoon oil, the oregano, and ½ teaspoon salt and stir to blend.

3 Bake until the tomatoes are just browned, 30–40 minutes; do not stir.

4 Meanwhile, bring a large pot of salted water to a boil. Add the broccoli and cook until just tender, about 5 minutes. Drain and set aside. (Alternatively, steam the broccoli until tender.)

5 ▲ Heat 2 tablespoons of the oil in a large nonstick skillet. Add the onion, thyme, cubes of turkey, and ½ teaspoon salt. Cook over high heat, stirring often, until the meat is cooked and beginning to brown, 5–7 minutes. Add the garlic and cook 1 minute more, stirring frequently.

6 Remove from the heat. Stir in the lemon juice and season with pepper. Set aside and keep warm.

7 Bring another large pot of salted water to a boil. Add the fusilli and cook until just tender (check package directions for timing). Drain and place in a large bowl. Toss with the remaining oil.

8 ▼ Add the broccoli to the turkey mixture. Add to the fusilli. Add the tomatoes and stir gently to blend. Serve immediately.

Chicken with White Wine, Olives, and Garlic

SERVES 4

3½-pound chicken, cut in serving
  pieces

1 onion, sliced

salt and pepper

3–6 garlic cloves, to taste, minced

1 teaspoon dried thyme

2 cups dry white California wine

1 cup green olives (16–18), pitted

1 bay leaf

1 tablespoon lemon juice

1–2 tablespoons butter

1 Heat a deep, heavy castiron skillet. When hot, add the chicken pieces, skin side down, and cook over medium heat until browned, about 10 minutes. Turn and brown the other side, 5–8 minutes more. (Work in batches if necessary.)

2 Transfer the chicken pieces to a platter and set aside.

3 Drain the excess fat from the skillet, leaving about 1 tablespoon. Add the onion and ½ teaspoon salt and cook until just soft, about 5 minutes. Add the garlic and thyme and cook 1 minute more.

4 ▼ Add the wine and stir, scraping up any bits that cling to the pan. Bring to a boil and boil 1 minute. Stir in the green olives.

5 ▲ Return the chicken pieces to the pan. Add the bay leaf and season lightly with pepper. Lower the heat, cover, and simmer until the chicken is cooked through, 20–30 minutes.

6 Transfer the chicken pieces to a warmed platter. Stir the lemon juice into the sauce. Whisk in the butter to thicken the sauce slightly. Spoon over the chicken and serve immediately.

Turkey Meat Loaf

SERVES 4

1 tablespoon olive oil

1 onion, chopped

1 green bell pepper, seeded and minced

1 garlic clove, minced

1 pound ground turkey

1 cup fresh bread crumbs

1 egg, beaten

½ cup pine nuts

12 sun-dried tomatoes in oil, drained
  and chopped

⅓ cup milk

2 teaspoons chopped fresh rosemary, or
  ½ teaspoon dried rosemary

1 teaspoon ground fennel

½ teaspoon dried oregano

½ teaspoon salt

1 Preheat the oven to 375°F.

2 ▼ Heat the oil in a skillet. Add the onion, bell pepper, and garlic and cook over low heat, stirring often, until just softened, 8–10 minutes. Remove from the heat and let cool.

3 Place the turkey in a large bowl. Add the onion mixture and the remaining ingredients and mix thoroughly together.

4 ▲ Transfer to an 8½- × 4½-inch loaf pan, packing the mixture down firmly. Bake until golden brown, about 1 hour. Serve hot or cold.

Chicken with White Wine, Olives, and Garlic (top), Turkey Meat Loaf

Pork Chops with Chili-Nectarine Relish

SERVES 4

1 cup fresh orange juice	
3 tablespoons olive oil	
2 garlic cloves, minced	
1 teaspoon ground cumin	
1 tablespoon coarsely ground black pepper	
8 pork loin chops, about ¼ inch thick, well trimmed	
salt	

FOR THE RELISH

1 small fresh green chili pepper	
2 tablespoons honey	
juice of ½ lemon	
1 cup chicken stock	
2 nectarines, pitted and chopped	
1 garlic clove, minced	
½ onion, minced	
1 teaspoon minced fresh gingerroot	
¼ teaspoon salt	
1 tablespoon chopped fresh coriander (cilantro)	

1 For the relish, roast the chili over a gas flame, holding it with tongs, until charred on all sides. (Alternatively, char the skin under the broiler.) Let cool 5 minutes.

2 ▼ Wearing rubber gloves, carefully remove the charred skin of the chili. Discard seeds if a less hot flavor is desired. Mince the chili and place in a heavy saucepan.

3 ▲ Add the honey, lemon juice, chicken stock, nectarines, garlic, onion, ginger, and salt. Bring to a boil, then simmer, stirring occasionally, about 30 minutes. Stir in the coriander and set aside.

4 In a small bowl, combine the orange juice, oil, garlic, cumin, and pepper. Stir to mix.

5 ▲ Arrange the pork chops, in one layer, in a shallow dish. Pour over the orange juice mixture and turn to coat. Cover and let stand at least 1 hour, or refrigerate overnight.

6 Remove the pork from the marinade and pat dry with paper towels. Season lightly with salt.

7 Heat a ridged grill pan. When hot, add the pork chops and cook until browned, about 5 minutes. Turn and cook on the other side until done, about 10 minutes more. (Work in batches if necessary.) Serve immediately, with the relish.

Roast Leg of Lamb with Pesto

SERVES 6

2 cups fresh basil leaves

4 garlic cloves, coarsely chopped

3 tablespoons pine nuts

⅔ cup olive oil

⅔ cup freshly grated Parmesan cheese

1 teaspoon salt, or to taste

5- to 6-pound leg of lamb

5 ▲ Continue patting on the pesto in a thick, even layer. Cover and let stand 2 hours at room temperature, or refrigerate overnight.

6 Preheat the oven to 350°F.

7 Place the lamb in the oven and roast, allowing about 20 minutes per pound for rare meat, 25 minutes per pound for medium-rare. Turn the lamb occasionally during roasting.

8 Remove the leg of lamb from the oven, cover it loosely with foil, and let rest about 15 minutes before carving and serving.

1 ▲ To make the pesto, combine the basil, garlic, and pine nuts in a food processor, and process until finely chopped. With the motor running, slowly add the oil in a steady stream.

2 Scrape the mixture into a bowl. Stir in the Parmesan and salt.

3 ▲ Set the lamb in a roasting pan. Make several slits in the meat with a sharp knife and spoon some pesto into each slit.

4 Rub more pesto over the surface of the lamb.

Beef and Eggplant Stir-Fry with Ginger

SERVES 4–6

1⅓ pounds boneless beef, such as flank
   steak, thinly sliced

2 tablespoons soy sauce, plus extra for
   serving

1 pound eggplant

3 tablespoons water

2 tablespoons rice vinegar

1 tablespoon dry sherry wine

1 teaspoon honey

1 teaspoon red pepper flakes

¼ cup vegetable oil

3 teaspoons sesame oil

1 garlic clove, minced

1 tablespoon minced fresh gingerroot

boiled rice, for serving

1 ▲ Combine the beef and soy sauce in a shallow dish. Stir to coat evenly. Cover and let marinate 1 hour, or refrigerate overnight.

~ VARIATIONS ~

For Turkey and Eggplant Stir-Fry, substitute thinly sliced turkey breast for the beef. If time is short, it is not essential to precook the eggplant, but microwaving or steaming the eggplant before stir-frying helps to eliminate any bitterness and also prevents the eggplant from soaking up too much oil.

2 ▲ Cut the eggplant into eighths lengthwise. Trim away the inner part with the seeds, leaving a flat edge. Cut the eggplant slices on the diagonal into diamond shapes that are about 1 inch wide.

3 ▲ Place the eggplant in a large microwaveable dish. Stir in the water. Cover and microwave on high (650 watt) 3 minutes. Stir gently, then microwave 3 minutes more. Set aside, still covered. (Alternatively, steam the eggplant over boiling water until tender, if preferred.)

4 ▲ In a small bowl, combine the vinegar, sherry, honey, and pepper flakes. Stir to mix. Set aside.

5 ▲ Heat 1 tablespoon vegetable oil and 1 teaspoon sesame oil in a large nonstick skillet or wok. Add half of the beef, garlic, and ginger. Cook over high heat, stirring frequently, until the beef is just cooked through, 2–3 minutes. Remove to a bowl. Cook the remaining beef, garlic, and ginger in the same way. Add to the bowl and set aside.

6 ▲ Heat the remaining vegetable and sesame oils in the skillet or wok. Add the eggplant and cook over moderate heat until just browned and tender, about 5 minutes. (Work in 2 batches if necessary.)

7 Return the beef to the skillet or wok. Stir in the vinegar mixture and cook just until the liquid is absorbed, 2–3 minutes more. Taste for seasoning. Serve immediately, with rice and extra soy sauce.

Berry Salsa

MAKES 3 CUPS

1 fresh jalapeño pepper

½ red onion, minced

2 scallions, chopped

1 tomato, finely diced

1 small yellow bell pepper, seeded and minced

¼ cup chopped fresh coriander (cilantro)

¼ teaspoon salt

1 tablespoon raspberry vinegar

1 tablespoon fresh orange juice

1 teaspoon honey

1 tablespoon olive oil

½ pint strawberries, hulled

½ pint blueberries or blackberries

½ pint raspberries

1 ▼ Wearing rubber gloves, finely mince the jalapeño pepper (discard the seeds and membrane if a less hot flavor is desired. Place the pepper in a medium-size bowl.

2 ▲ Add the red onion, scallions, tomato, bell pepper, and coriander and stir to blend.

3 ▲ In a small bowl, whisk together the salt, vinegar, orange juice, honey, and oil. Pour over the jalapeño mixture and stir well.

4 ▲ Coarsely chop the strawberries. Add to the jalapeño mixture with the other berries and stir to blend. Let stand at room temperature 3 hours.

5 Serve the salsa at room temperature, with grilled fish or poultry.

Fresh Pineapple-Mint Chutney

MAKES 3 CUPS

1 cup raspberry vinegar
1 cup dry white wine
2 cups chopped fresh pineapple (about 1 small pineapple)
1 cup chopped fresh orange flesh (2 medium-size oranges)
1 cup chopped peeled apple
1 red bell pepper, seeded and diced
1½ onions, minced
¼ cup honey
⅛ teaspoon salt
1 whole clove
4 black peppercorns
2 tablespoons chopped fresh mint

1 ▲ In a saucepan, combine the vinegar and wine and bring to a boil. Boil 3 minutes.

2 ▲ Add the remaining ingredients, except the mint, and stir to blend. Simmer gently about 30 minutes, stirring occasionally.

3 Transfer to a strainer set over a bowl and drain, pressing down to extract the liquid. Remove and discard the clove and peppercorns. Set the fruit mixture aside.

4 ▼ Return the strained juice to the pan and boil until reduced by two-thirds. Pour over the fruit mixture.

5 ▲ Stir in the mint. Let the chutney stand 6–8 hours before serving, with pork or lamb dishes.

~ COOK'S TIP ~

The chutney will keep about 1 week in the refrigerator.

Eggplant Ratatouille

SERVES 6

3½ pounds eggplants (about 4)

3 tablespoons olive oil

1 large onion, sliced

salt and pepper

3 garlic cloves, minced

1 28-ounce can peeled plum tomatoes, drained and chopped

2 tablespoons chopped fresh basil, or 1 teaspoon dried basil

fresh basil leaves, for garnishing

1 Cut the eggplants into large cubes. Bring a large pot of salted water to a boil. Add the eggplant and cook 3–4 minutes. Drain thoroughly.

2 ▼ Heat 2 tablespoons of the oil in a large skillet. Add the onion and ¼ teaspoon salt and cook over low heat until just soft, 8–10 minutes.

3 Add the garlic, eggplant, and remaining oil and stir to mix. Cook gently about 5 minutes.

4 ▲ Stir in the tomatoes and basil. Season with salt and pepper. Cover and cook over low heat until the eggplant is very tender, about 30 minutes, stirring occasionally.

5 Sprinkle the ratatouille with fresh basil leaves and serve.

Garlicky Sautéed Zucchini

SERVES 4

6 medium-size zucchini

2 tablespoons olive oil

½ teaspoon salt

4–6 garlic cloves, minced

1 teaspoon dried thyme

1 tablespoon fresh lemon juice

black pepper

~ **VARIATION** ~

For Pasta with Zucchini Sauce, add 1 large (28-ounce) can of tomatoes packed in juice, roughly chopped, to the browned zucchini instead of the lemon juice. Simmer until thickened, 5–10 minutes longer. Serve with boiled pasta shapes and sprinkle with grated Parmesan cheese, if desired.

1 ▼ Trim the ends of the zucchini, then halve and quarter them lengthwise. Cut into slices about ¼ inch thick.

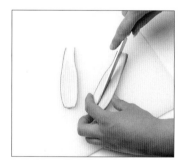

2 Heat the oil in a large nonstick skillet. Add the zucchini and toss to coat evenly. Add the salt and stir, then leave to cook until browned on one side, about 5 minutes.

3 ▲ Add the garlic and thyme. Shake the pan and turn the zucchini with the aid of a wooden spatula. Continue cooking until golden brown on both sides and tender, about 5 minutes more. Do not let the garlic burn; if necessary, reduce the heat and increase the cooking time slightly.

4 Stir in the lemon juice, season liberally with black pepper, and serve.

Eggplant Ratatouille (top), Garlicky Sautéed Zucchini

Herbed Goat Cheese Dip

MAKES ABOUT 2 CUPS

10 ounces soft mild goat cheese

½ cup light cream or half and half

2 teaspoons fresh lemon juice

1 tablespoon chopped fresh chives

1 tablespoons chopped fresh parsley

2 tablespoons chopped fresh basil

black pepper

raw or briefly cooked cold vegetables,
  potato chips, or crackers, for serving

1 ▼ In a food processor or blender, combine the goat cheese and cream and process to blend. Add the lemon juice and process until smooth.

2 ▲ Scrape into a bowl. Stir in the chives, parsley, basil, and pepper to taste. Serve cold, as a dip for vegetables, potato chips, or crackers.

Avocado Dressing

MAKES ABOUT 1½ CUPS

2 tablespoons wine vinegar

½ teaspoon salt, or to taste

¾ teaspoon white pepper

½ red onion, coarsely chopped

3 tablespoons olive oil

1 large ripe avocado, halved and pit
  removed

1 tablespoon fresh lemon juice

3 tablespoons plain yogurt

3 tablespoons water, or as needed

2 tablespoons chopped fresh coriander
  (cilantro)

raw or briefly cooked cold vegetables,
  for serving

1 ▲ In a bowl, combine the vinegar and salt and stir with a fork to dissolve. Stir in the pepper, chopped red onion, and olive oil.

3 ▲ Add the yogurt and water and process until smooth. If desired, add more water to thin. Taste and adjust the seasoning if necessary.

2 ▲ Scoop the avocado flesh into a food processor or blender. Add the lemon juice and onion dressing and process just to blend.

4 ▲ Scrape into a bowl. Stir in the coriander. Serve immediately, as a dressing for salads, or use as a dip for raw or briefly cooked cold vegetables.

~ COOK'S TIP ~

This versatile dressing need not be limited to serving with salads and crudités. Serve it as a sauce with grilled chicken or fish, or use it on sandwiches in place of mayonnaise or mustard, or to provide a cool contrast to any sort of spicy food.

Herbed Goat Cheese Dip (top), Avocado Dressing

Zinfandel Poached Pears

SERVES 4

1 bottle of red Zinfandel wine

¼ cup sugar

3 tablespoons honey

juice of ½ lemon

1 cinnamon stick

1 vanilla bean, split open lengthwise

2-inch piece of orange peel

1 whole clove

1 black peppercorn

4 firm, ripe pears

whipped cream or sour cream, for serving

1 ▼ In a saucepan just large enough to hold the pears standing upright, combine the wine, sugar, honey, lemon juice, cinnamon, vanilla bean, orange peel, clove, and peppercorn. Heat gently, stirring occasionally until the sugar has dissolved.

2 ▲ Meanwhile, peel the pears, leaving the core and stem intact. Slice a small piece off the base of each pear so it will stand upright.

3 ▲ Gently place the pears in the wine mixture. Simmer, uncovered, until the pears are just tender, 20–35 minutes depending on size and ripeness; do not overcook.

4 ▲ With a slotted spoon, gently transfer the pears to a bowl. Continue to boil the poaching liquid until reduced by about half. Let cool.

5 Strain the cooled liquid over the pears and refrigerate at least 3 hours.

6 Place the pears in serving dishes and spoon over the liquid. Serve with whipped cream or sour cream.

Baked Peaches with Raspberry Sauce

SERVES 6

3 tablespoons unsalted butter, at room
  temperature

¼ cup sugar

1 egg, beaten

½ cup ground almonds

6 ripe peaches

FOR THE SAUCE

1 cup raspberries

1 tablespoon confectioners' sugar

1 tablespoon fruit-flavored brandy
  (optional)

1 Preheat the oven to 350°F.

2 ▲ Beat the butter with the sugar until soft and fluffy. Beat in the egg. Add the ground almonds and beat just to blend well together.

3 ▲ Halve the peaches and remove the pits. With a spoon, scrape out some of the flesh from each peach half, slightly enlarging the hollow left by the pit. Reserve the excess peach flesh to use in the sauce.

4 ▼ Place the peach halves on a baking sheet (if necessary, secure with crumpled foil to keep them steady). Fill the hollow in each peach half with the almond mixture.

5 Bake until the almond filling is puffed and golden and the peaches are very tender, about 30 minutes.

6 ▲ Meanwhile, for the sauce, combine all the ingredients in a food processor or blender. Add the reserved peach flesh. Process until smooth. Press through a strainer set over a bowl to remove fibers and seeds.

7 Let the peaches cool slightly. Place 2 peach halves on each plate and spoon over some of the sauce. Serve immediately.

Chocolate, Coconut, and Macadamia Parfait

SERVES 10

8 ounces white chocolate, chopped

2½ cups whipping cream

½ cup milk

10 egg yolks

1 tablespoon sugar

½ cup shredded coconut, plus more for garnishing

½ cup canned sweetened coconut cream

5 ounces unsalted macadamia nuts

FOR THE GLAZE

8 1-ounce squares bittersweet chocolate

6 tablespoons butter

1 generous tablespoon light corn syrup

¼ cup whipping cream

1 ▲ Line the bottom and sides of a 6-cup terrine mold (10 × 4 inches) with plastic wrap or wax paper.

2 ▲ Combine the white chocolate and ¼ cup of the cream in the top of a double boiler or in a heatproof bowl set over hot water. Stir until melted and smooth. Set aside.

3 Put 1 cup of the cream and the milk in a heavy saucepan and scald over medium heat.

4 ▲ Meanwhile, in a large bowl, beat the egg yolks and sugar together until thick and pale.

5 ▲ Add the hot cream mixture to the yolks, beating constantly. Pour back into the saucepan and cook over low heat until thickened, 2–3 minutes. Stir constantly and do not boil. Remove from the heat.

6 Stir in the melted chocolate, shredded coconut, and coconut cream until blended. Let cool.

7 Whip the remaining cream until thick. Fold into the chocolate and coconut mixture.

8 Put 2 cups of the parfait mixture in the prepared mold and spread evenly. Cover and freeze until just firm, about 2 hours. Cover the remaining mixture and refrigerate.

9 ▲ Arrange the macadamia nuts evenly over the frozen parfait layer. Pour in the remaining parfait mixture. Cover the mold and freeze until the parfait is firm, 6–8 hours or overnight.

10 ▲ For the glaze, combine the bittersweet chocolate, butter, and corn syrup in the top of a double boiler and stir occasionally until melted.

11 In a saucepan, heat the cream until just simmering. Stir into the chocolate mixture. Remove from the heat and let cool to lukewarm.

12 To unmold the parfait, wrap the mold in a hot towel and set it upside down on a plate. Peel off the plastic wrap or wax paper. Set the parfait on a rack over a baking sheet. Pour the glaze evenly over the top. Working quickly, smooth the glaze down the sides with a metal spatula. Let set slightly, then sprinkle with shredded coconut. Freeze 3–4 hours more.

13 To serve the parfait, slice it with a knife dipped in hot water.

Lemon Pound Cake

SERVES 8–10

1¼ cups (2½ sticks) unsalted butter, at
  room temperature

1¼ cups granulated sugar

6 eggs

grated rind and juice of 1 large lemon

2⅓ cups sifted cake flour

½ teaspoon salt

confectioners' sugar, for dusting

1 Preheat the oven to 350°F. Grease
a 9-cup bundt pan.

2 Beat the butter until it is soft and
creamy. Gradually add the sugar and
continue beating until fluffy.

3 ▼ Beat in the eggs, one at a time,
beating well after each addition. Beat
in the lemon rind and juice. Fold in
the flour and salt in 3 batches.

4 Pour the batter into the prepared
pan and smooth the surface.

5 ▲ Bake until a cake tester inserted
in the center comes out clean, 40–50
minutes. Let cool 10 minutes before
unmolding onto a wire rack.

6 When the cake is cold, dust it with
confectioners' sugar.

Piña Colada Fruit Salad

SERVES 4

1 large pineapple

2 kiwi fruits

¼ cup slivered fresh coconut

2 tablespoons fresh lime juice

1 teaspoon sugar

1–2 tablespoons rum

8 large strawberries, halved

1 ▲ Cut a thick slice off one long
side of the pineapple, not cutting into
the crown of leaves.

2 ▼ Using a sharp spoon or a
grapefruit knife, scoop out the flesh,
taking care not to puncture the skin.
Cut out and discard the core. Set the
pineapple boat aside.

3 Chop the scooped-out flesh into
bite-size pieces, keeping any juice,
and place in a bowl.

4 Peel the kiwis and chop into bite-
size pieces. Add the kiwis and coconut
to the pineapple pieces.

5 ▲ In a small bowl, combine the
lime juice, sugar, and rum to taste.
Stir to blend, then pour over the fruit.
Toss well. Cover and refrigerate the
fruit salad 1 hour.

6 To serve, spoon the fruit mixture
into the pineapple boat. Garnish with
the strawberries and serve
immediately.

Lemon Pound Cake (top), Pine Colada Fruit Salad

THE NORTHWEST & MOUNTAIN STATES

AN AREA THAT ENCOMPASSES SOME
OF THE MOST MODERN CITIES AND
WILDEST TERRAIN ALSO PROVIDES
CULINARY CONTRASTS. MUCH
OF IT OFFERS GOOD HUNTING AND
FISHING TERRITORY, WHICH ARE
COMPLIMENTED BY ORCHARDS AND
AGRICULTURAL CULTIVATION, AS
WELL AS ARTISANAL WINE AND
CHEESEMAKING.

Salmon Chowder

SERVES 4

1½ tablespoons butter or margarine

1 onion, minced

1 leek, minced

½ cup minced bulb fennel

¼ cup flour

1½ quarts fish stock

2 cups potatoes, cut in ½-inch cubes
(about 2 medium-size potatoes)

salt and pepper

1 pound boneless, skinless salmon, cut
in ¾-inch cubes

¾ cup milk

½ cup whipping cream

2 tablespoons chopped fresh dill

1 ▲ Melt the butter or margarine in a large saucepan. Add the onion, leek, and fennel and cook over medium heat until softened, 5–8 minutes, stirring occasionally.

2 Stir in the flour. Reduce the heat to low and cook, stirring occasionally, 3 minutes.

3 ▲ Add the stock and potatoes. Season with salt and pepper. Bring to a boil, then reduce the heat, cover, and simmer until the potatoes are tender, about 20 minutes.

4 ▲ Add the salmon and simmer until just cooked, 3–5 minutes.

5 ▲ Stir in the milk, cream, and dill. Cook just until warmed through; do not boil. Taste and adjust the seasoning, if necessary, then serve.

Smoked Turkey and Lentil Soup

SERVES 4

2 tablespoons butter
1 large carrot, chopped
1 onion, chopped
1 celery stalk, chopped
1 leek, white part only, chopped
4 ounces mushrooms, chopped
¼ cup dry white wine
4½ cups chicken stock
2 teaspoons dried thyme
1 bay leaf
½ cup lentils
8 ounces smoked turkey meat, diced
salt and pepper
chopped fresh parsley, for garnishing

1 ▲ Melt the butter in a large saucepan. Add the carrot, onion, leek, celery, and mushrooms. Cook until golden, 3–5 minutes.

2 ▲ Stir in the wine and chicken stock. Bring to a boil and skim any foam that rises to the surface. Add the thyme and bay leaf. Lower the heat, cover, and simmer gently 30 minutes.

3 ▼ Add the lentils and continue cooking, covered, until they are just tender, 30–40 minutes more. Stir the soup from time to time.

4 ▲ Stir in the turkey and season to taste with salt and pepper. Cook until just heated through. Ladle into bowls and garnish with parsley.

Tomato-Blue Cheese Soup with Bacon

SERVES 4

3 pounds ripe tomatoes, peeled, quartered, and seeded

2 garlic cloves, minced

salt and pepper

2 tablespoons vegetable oil or butter

1 leek, chopped

1 carrot, chopped

1 quart unsalted chicken stock

4 ounces Oregon Blue cheese, crumbled

3 tablespoons whipping cream

several large fresh basil leaves, or 1–2 fresh parsley sprigs

6 ounces bacon, cooked and crumbled

1 Preheat the oven to 400°F.

2 ▲ Spread the tomatoes in a baking dish. Sprinkle with the garlic and some salt and pepper. Place in the oven and bake 35 minutes.

3 ▲ Heat the oil or butter in a large saucepan. Add the leek and carrot and season lightly with salt and pepper. Cook over low heat, stirring often, until softened, about 10 minutes.

4 ▲ Stir in the stock and tomatoes. Bring to a boil, then lower the heat, cover, and simmer 20 minutes.

5 ▲ Add the blue cheese, cream, and basil or parsley. Transfer to a food processor or blender and process until smooth (work in batches if necessary). Taste for seasoning.

6 If necessary, reheat the soup, but do not boil. Ladle into bowls and sprinkle with crumbled bacon.

Macaroni and Blue Cheese

SERVES 6

1 pound macaroni

1 quart milk

4 tablespoons butter

6 tablespoons flour

¼ teaspoon salt

8 ounces Oregon Blue cheese, crumbled

black pepper, for serving

1 Preheat the oven to 350°F. Grease a 13- × 9-inch baking dish.

2 ▲ Bring a large pot of water to a boil. Salt to taste and add the macaroni. Cook until just tender (check package directions for cooking times). Drain and rinse under cold water. Place in a large bowl. Set aside.

3 In another pan, bring the milk to a boil and set aside.

4 ▲ Melt the butter in a heavy saucepan over low heat. Whisk in the flour and cook 5 minutes, whisking constantly; do not let the mixture become brown.

5 ▼ Remove from the heat and whisk the hot milk into the butter and flour mixture. When the mixture is smoothly blended, return to medium heat and continue cooking, whisking constantly, until the sauce is thick, about 5 minutes. Add the salt.

6 Add the sauce to the macaroni. Add three-quarters of the crumbled blue cheese and stir well. Transfer the macaroni mixture to the prepared baking dish and spread in an even layer.

7 Sprinkle the remaining cheese evenly over the surface. Bake until bubbling hot, about 25 minutes.

8 If desired, lightly brown the top of the macaroni and cheese under the broiler, 3–4 minutes. Serve hot, sprinkled with freshly ground black pepper.

Smoked Trout Pasta Salad

SERVES 6

1 tablespoon butter

1 cup minced bulb fennel

6 scallions, 2 minced and 4 thinly sliced

salt and pepper

8 ounces skinless smoked trout fillets, flaked

3 tablespoons chopped fresh dill

½ cup mayonnaise

2 teaspoons fresh lemon juice

2 tablespoons whipping cream

1 pound small pasta shapes, such as shells

fresh dill sprigs, for garnishing

1 ▼ Melt the butter in a small nonstick skillet. Add the fennel and minced scallions and season lightly with salt and pepper. Cook over medium heat until just softened, 3–5 minutes. Transfer to a large bowl and let cool slightly.

2 ▲ Add the sliced scallions, trout, dill, mayonnaise, lemon juice, and cream. Mix gently until well blended.

3 ▲ Bring a large pot of water to a boil. Salt to taste and add the pasta. Cook until just tender (check package directions for cooking times). Drain thoroughly and let cool.

4 ▲ Add the pasta to the vegetable and trout mixture and toss to coat evenly. Taste for seasoning. Serve the salad lightly chilled or at room temperature, garnished with dill, if desired.

Trout and Bacon Hash

SERVES 2

3 cups potatoes, cut in ½-inch cubes
    (3–4 medium-size potatoes)

salt and pepper

3 tablespoons unsalted butter

½ onion, minced

½ green bell pepper, seeded and minced

1 garlic clove, minced

2 ounces Canadian bacon, chopped

7 ounces skinless trout fillets, cut in
    ½-inch pieces

1 teaspoon dried oregano

1 tablespoon chopped fresh parsley
    (optional)

3 ▼ Add the remaining butter and the potatoes to the skillet. Cook over high heat, stirring occasionally, until the potatoes are lightly browned, about 5 minutes longer.

4 ▲ Add the trout, oregano, and parsley if using. Season with salt and pepper. Continue cooking, smashing down with a wooden spatula, until the trout is cooked through, 3–4 minutes more. Serve immediately.

1 ▲ Put the potatoes in a saucepan, add cold water to cover, and bring to a boil. Add 1 tablespoon salt and simmer until just tender, 8–10 minutes. Drain and set aside.

2 ▲ Melt 2 tablespoons of the butter in a large nonstick skillet. Add the onion, bell pepper, garlic, and bacon and cook over medium heat until the onion is just softened, 5–8 minutes.

Seattle Fish Fritters

SERVES 4

½ fennel bulb, cut in pieces

1 medium leek, cut in pieces

1 green bell pepper, seeded and cut in pieces

2 garlic cloves

1 tablespoon butter

⅛ teaspoon red pepper flakes

salt and pepper

6 ounces skinless boneless salmon, cut in pieces

3½ ounces skinless boneless rockfish or ling cod, cut in pieces

3 ounces cooked peeled shrimp

1 cup flour

6 eggs, beaten

1½–2 cups milk

1 tablespoon chopped fresh basil

4–6 tablespoons oil, for greasing

sour cream, for serving

1 ▲ Combine the fennel, leek, bell pepper, and garlic in a food processor and process until finely chopped.

~ VARIATION ~

For Seattle Salmon Fritters, increase the amount of salmon to ¼ pound, and omit the rockfish or ling cod and shrimp. Use dill in place of the basil. Serve with a tossed green salad, if desired.

2 ▲ Melt the butter in a skillet until sizzling. Add the vegetable mixture and red pepper flakes. Season with salt and pepper. Cook over low heat until softened, 8–10 minutes. Remove from the heat and set aside.

3 ▲ Combine the salmon, rockfish or ling cod, and shrimp in the food processor. Process, using the pulse button and scraping the sides of the container several times, until the mixture is coarsely chopped. Scrape into a large bowl and set aside.

4 ▲ Sift the flour into another bowl and make a well in the center.

5 ▲ Gradually whisk in the eggs alternately with 1½ cups milk to make a smooth batter. If necessary, strain the batter to remove lumps.

6 ▲ Stir the seafood, vegetables, and basil into the batter. If it seems too thick, add a little more milk.

7 ▲ Lightly oil a griddle or nonstick skillet and heat over medium heat. Spoon in the batter by ⅓-cupfuls. Cook until the fritters are golden around the edges, 2–3 minutes. Turn them over and cook the other side, 2–3 minutes more. Work in batches, keeping the cooked fritters warm.

8 Serve hot, with sour cream.

Scalloped Oysters

SERVES 4

7 tablespoons butter

1 shallot, minced

4 ounces mushrooms, minced

½ teaspoon flour

⅛ teaspoon hot pepper sauce

salt and pepper

24 oysters, shucked and drained

⅓ cup dry white wine

⅔ cup whipping cream

2 tablespoons chopped fresh parsley

6 tablespoons fresh bread crumbs

1 Preheat the oven to 375°F. Grease a 6- × 8-inch baking dish.

2 Melt the butter in a large skillet. Add the shallot and mushrooms and cook until softened, about 3 minutes.

3 ▼ Add the flour and hot pepper sauce. Season with salt and pepper. Cook, stirring constantly, 1 minute.

4 ▲ Stir in the oysters and wine, scraping the bottom of the skillet. Add the cream. Transfer the mixture to the prepared baking dish.

5 ▲ In a small bowl, combine the chopped parsley, fresh bread crumbs, and salt to taste. Stir to mix.

6 ▲ Sprinkle the crumbs evenly over the oyster mixture. Bake until the top is golden and the sauce bubbling, 15–20 minutes. Serve immediately.

Penn Cove Steamed Mussels

SERVES 2

1½ pounds mussels in shell
½ fennel bulb, minced
1 shallot, minced
3 tablespoons dry white wine
3 tablespoons whipping cream
2 tablespoons chopped fresh parsley
black pepper

1 ▲ Scrub the mussels under cold running water. Remove any barnacles with a small knife, and remove the beards. Rinse once more.

2 ▲ Place the mussels in a large skillet with a lid. Sprinkle them with the fennel, shallot, and wine. Cover the skillet and place over medium-high heat. Steam until the mussels open, 3–5 minutes.

3 Lift out the mussels with a slotted spoon and remove the top shells. Discard any mussels that did not open. Arrange the mussels, on their bottom shells, in one layer in a shallow serving dish. Keep warm.

4 ▼ Place a double layer of dampened cheesecloth in a strainer set over a bowl. Strain the mussel cooking liquid through the cheesecloth. Return the liquid to a clean saucepan and bring to a boil.

5 ▲ Add the cream, stir well, and boil 3 minutes to reduce slightly. Stir in the parsley. Spoon the sauce over the mussels and sprinkle with freshly ground black pepper. Serve the mussels immediately.

Stuffed Potato Skins

SERVES 6

3 baking potatoes, about 12 ounces
  each, scrubbed and patted dry

1 tablespoon vegetable oil

3 tablespoons butter

1 onion, chopped

salt and pepper

1 green bell pepper, seeded and coarsely
  chopped

1 teaspoon paprika

1 cup shredded Monterey Jack or
  cheddar cheese

1 Preheat the oven to 450°F.

2 ▲ Brush the potatoes all over with
the oil. Prick them in several places
on all sides with a fork.

3 ▲ Place in a baking dish. Bake
until tender, about 1½ hours.

4 ▲ Meanwhile, heat the butter in a
large nonstick skillet. Add the onion
and a little salt and cook over medium
heat until softened, about 5 minutes.
Add the bell pepper and continue
cooking until just tender but still
crunchy, 2–3 minutes more. Stir in
the paprika and set aside.

5 ▲ When the potatoes are done,
halve them lengthwise. Scoop out the
flesh, keeping the pieces coarse. Keep
the potato skins warm.

6 Preheat the broiler.

~ VARIATION ~

For Bacon-Stuffed Potato Skins,
add ¾ cup chopped cooked bacon
to the cooked potato flesh and
vegetables. Stuff as above.

7 ▲ Add the potato flesh to the
skillet and cook over high heat,
stirring, until the potato is lightly
browned. Season with pepper.

8 ▲ Divide the vegetable mixture
among the potato skins.

9 ▲ Sprinkle the cheese on top.
Broil until the cheese just melts,
3–5 minutes. Serve immediately.

Pasta with Scallops

SERVES 4

1 pound pasta, such as fettucine or linguine

2 tablespoons olive oil

2 garlic cloves, minced

1 pound sea scallops, sliced in half horizontally

salt and pepper

FOR THE SAUCE

2 tablespoons olive oil

½ onion, minced

1 garlic clove, minced

½ teaspoon salt

1 28-ounce can peeled tomatoes

2 tablespoons chopped fresh basil

1 For the sauce, heat the oil in a nonstick skillet. Add the onion, garlic, and a little salt, and cook over medium heat until just softened, about 5 minutes, stirring occasionally.

2 ▲ Add the tomatoes, with their juice, and crush with the tines of a fork. Bring to a boil, then reduce the heat and simmer gently 15 minutes. Remove from the heat and set aside.

3 ▲ Bring a large pot of salted water to a boil. Add the pasta and cook until just tender to the bite (check package directions for timing).

4 ▲ Meanwhile, combine the oil and garlic in another nonstick skillet and cook until just sizzling, about 30 seconds. Add the scallops and ½ teaspoon salt and cook over high heat, tossing, until the scallops are cooked through, about 3 minutes.

5 ▲ Add the scallops to the tomato sauce. Season with salt and pepper, stir, and keep warm.

6 Drain the pasta, rinse under hot water, and drain again. Place in a large warmed serving bowl. Add the scallop sauce and the basil and toss thoroughly. Serve immediately.

Clam and Sausage Chili

SERVES 4

1 cup dried black beans, soaked
    overnight and drained

1 bay leaf

2 teaspoons coarse salt

½ pound lean bulk pork sausage meat

1 tablespoon vegetable oil

1 onion, minced

1 garlic clove, minced

1 teaspoon fennel seeds

1 teaspoon dried oregano

¼ teaspoon red pepper flakes, or to taste

2–3 teaspoons chili powder, or to taste

1 teaspoon ground cumin

2 16-ounce cans chopped tomatoes in
    purée

½ cup dry white wine

1½ cups drained canned clams
    (approximately 2 10-ounce cans),
    liquid reserved

salt and pepper

1 Put the beans in a large pot. Add fresh cold water to cover and the bay leaf. Bring to a boil, then cover, and simmer 30 minutes. Add the coarse salt and continue simmering until tender, about 30 minutes more. Drain and discard the bay leaf.

2 ▲ Put the sausage meat in a large flameproof casserole. Cook over medium heat until just beginning to brown, 2–3 minutes. Stir frequently to break up lumps. Add the oil, onion, and garlic.

3 Continue cooking until the vegetables are softened, about 5 minutes more, stirring occasionally.

4 ▼ Stir in the herbs and spices, tomatoes, wine, and ⅔ cup of the reserved clam juice. Bring to a boil, then lower the heat and cook, stirring occasionally, 15 minutes.

5 ▲ Add the black beans and clams and stir to combine. Taste and adjust the seasoning if necessary. Continue cooking just until the clams are heated through. Serve immediately.

Pan-Fried Trout with Horseradish Sauce

SERVES 4

4 whole rainbow trout, about 6 ounces
   each, cleaned

salt and pepper

¼ cup flour

2 tablespoons butter

1 tablespoon vegetable oil

FOR THE SAUCE

½ cup mayonnaise

½ cup sour cream

¾ teaspoon grated horseradish

¼ teaspoon paprika

2 tablespoons tomato or lemon juice

1 tablespoon chopped fresh herbs, such
   as chives, parsley, or basil

1 ▼ For the sauce, combine the mayonnaise, sour cream, horseradish, paprika, tomato or lemon juice, and herbs. Season with salt and pepper and mix well. Set the sauce aside.

2 ▲ Rinse the trout and pat dry. Season the cavities in the fish generously with salt and pepper.

3 ▲ Combine the flour, ½ teaspoon salt, and a little pepper in a shallow dish. Coat the trout on both sides with the seasoned flour, shaking off any excess.

4 ▲ Heat the butter and oil in a large nonstick skillet over medium-high heat. When sizzling, add the trout and cook until opaque throughout, 4–5 minutes on each side. Serve immediately, with the sauce.

Salmon with Sizzling Herbs

SERVES 4

4 salmon steaks, 6–7 ounces each

salt and pepper

⅓ cup olive oil

½ cup chopped fresh coriander
(cilantro)

3 tablespoons minced fresh gingerroot

½ cup chopped scallions

¼ cup soy sauce, plus extra for serving

1 Bring some water to a boil in the bottom of a steamer.

2 ▲ Season the fish steaks on both sides with salt and pepper.

3 ▲ Place the fish steaks in the top part of the steamer. Cover the pan and steam until the fish is opaque throughout, 7–8 minutes.

4 ▼ Meanwhile, heat the oil in a small heavy saucepan until very hot. (To test the temperature, drop in a piece of chopped scallion; if it sizzles, the oil is hot enough.)

5 Place the steamed salmon steaks on warmed plates.

6 ▲ Divide the chopped coriander among the salmon steaks, mounding it on top of the fish. Sprinkle with the ginger and then the scallions. Drizzle 1 tablespoon of soy sauce over each salmon steak.

7 Spoon the hot oil over each salmon steak and serve immediately, with additional soy sauce.

Pork Chops with Cider and Apples

1 pound tart cooking apples (3–4), peeled, quartered, and cored

4 pork chops, about 1 inch thick

1 teaspoon dried thyme

¼ teaspoon ground allspice

salt and pepper

1 tablespoon butter

1 tablespoon vegetable oil

1 bay leaf

½ cup apple cider

2 tablespoons whipping cream

potato pancakes, for serving

1 Preheat the oven to 375°F. Grease a casserole large enough to hold the pork chops in one layer.

2 ▲ Spread the apples in an even layer in the prepared dish. Set aside.

3 Sprinkle the pork chops on both sides with the thyme, ground allspice, and a little salt and pepper.

4 Heat the butter and oil in a skillet. When hot, add the pork chops and cook over medium-high heat until browned, 2–3 minutes. Turn and cook the other side, 2–3 minutes more. Remove from the heat.

5 ▲ Arrange the pork chops on top of the apples. Add the bay leaf and pour over the cider. Cover and bake for 15 minutes.

6 ▲ Turn the chops over. Continue baking until they are cooked through, about 15 minutes more.

7 Transfer the pork chops to warmed plates. Remove the apple quarters with a slotted spoon and divide them equally among the plates.

8 Stir the cream into the sauce and heat just until warmed through. Taste for seasoning. Spoon the sauce over the pork chops and serve immediately, with potato pancakes.

Pork Braised in Beer

SERVES 6

4–5-pound loin of pork, boned, trimmed of excess fat, and tied into a neat shape

salt and pepper

1 tablespoon butter

1 tablespoon vegetable oil

3 large onions, halved and thinly sliced

1 garlic clove, minced

3 cups beer

1 bay leaf

1 tablespoon flour blended with 2 tablespoons water

3 ▲ Stir in the beer, scraping to remove any bits on the bottom of the pan. Add the bay leaf.

4 Return the pork roast to the casserole. Cover and cook over low heat about 2 hours, turning the roast halfway through the cooking time.

5 ▼ Remove the pork roast. Cut it into serving slices and arrange on a platter. Cover and keep warm.

6 Discard the bay leaf. Add the flour to the cooking juices and cook over high heat, stirring constantly, until thickened. Taste for seasoning. Pour the sauce over the pork slices and serve immediately.

1 ▲ Season the pork roast on all sides with salt and pepper. Heat the butter and oil in a flameproof casserole just large enough to hold the pork loin. When hot, add the roast and brown on all sides, 5–7 minutes, turning it to color evenly. Remove from the pot and set aside.

2 ▲ Drain excess fat from the pot, leaving about 1 tablespoon. Add the onions and garlic and cook just until softened, about 5 minutes.

Chicken-Mushroom Pie

SERVES 6

½ ounce dried porcini mushrooms

4 tablespoons butter

2 tablespoons flour

1 cup chicken stock, warmed

¼ cup whipping cream or milk

salt and pepper

1 onion, coarsely chopped

2 carrots, sliced

2 celery stalks, coarsely chopped

2 ounces fresh mushrooms, quartered

1 pound cooked chicken meat, cubed

½ cup shelled fresh or frozen peas

beaten egg, for glazing

FOR THE CRUST

2 cups flour

¼ teaspoon salt

6 tablespoons cold butter, cut
in pieces

2 tablespoons shortening

3–4 tablespoons ice water

1 ▲ For the crust, sift the flour and salt into a bowl. With a pastry blender or 2 knives, cut in the butter and shortening until the mixture resembles coarse meal. Sprinkle with 3 tablespoons of the ice water and mix until the dough holds together. If the dough is too crumbly, add a little more water, 1 teaspoon at a time. Gather the dough into a ball and flatten into a disk. Wrap in wax paper and refrigerate at least 30 minutes.

2 Place the porcini mushrooms in a small bowl. Add hot water to cover and soak until soft, about 30 minutes. Lift out of the water with a slotted spoon to leave any grit behind and drain. Discard the soaking water.

3 Preheat the oven to 375°F.

4 ▲ Melt 2 tablespoons of the butter in a heavy saucepan. Whisk in the flour and cook until bubbling, whisking constantly. Add the warm stock and cook over medium heat, whisking, until the mixture boils. Cook 2–3 minutes more. Whisk in the cream or milk. Season with salt and pepper. Set aside.

5 ▲ Heat the remaining butter in a large nonstick skillet until foamy. Add the onion and carrots and cook until softened, about 5 minutes. Add the celery and fresh mushrooms and cook 5 minutes more. Stir in the chicken, peas, and drained porcini mushrooms.

6 Add the chicken mixture to the cream sauce and stir to mix. Taste for seasoning. Transfer to a 10-cup rectangular baking dish.

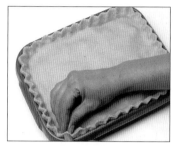

7 ▲ Roll out the dough to about ⅛-inch thickness. Cut out a rectangle about 1 inch larger all around than the dish. Lay the rectangle of dough over the filling. Make a decorative edge, crimping the dough by pushing the index finger of one hand between the thumb and index finger of the other.

8 Cut several vents in the top crust to allow steam to escape. Brush with the egg glaze.

9 ▲ Press together the dough trimmings, then roll out again. Cut into strips and lay them over the top crust. Glaze again. If desired, roll small balls of dough and set them in the "windows" in the lattice.

10 Bake until the top crust is browned, about 30 minutes. Serve the pie hot from the dish.

Oregon Blue Cheese Burgers

SERVES 4

2 pounds lean ground beef

1 garlic clove, minced

2 tablespoons chopped fresh parsley

2 tablespoons chopped fresh chives

½ teaspoon salt

pepper

8 ounces Oregon Blue cheese, crumbled

4 hamburger buns, split and toasted

tomato slices and lettuce, for serving

mustard or catsup, for serving

1 ▼ In a bowl, combine the beef, garlic, parsley, chives, salt, and a little pepper. Mix lightly together, then form into 4 thick patties.

2 ▲ Make a slit in the side of each patty, poking well into the beef to form a pocket. Fill each pocket with 2 ounces of the blue cheese.

3 ▲ Close the holes to seal the blue cheese inside the patties.

4 Heat a ridged grill pan (or preheat the broiler).

5 Cook the burgers 4–5 minutes on each side for medium-rare, 6–7 minutes for well-done.

6 ▲ Place the burgers in the split hamburger buns. Serve immediately, with sliced tomatoes and lettuce leaves, and mustard or catsup if desired.

Steak with Mushrooms and Leeks in Red Wine

SERVES 4

6–8 leeks (about 1¼ pounds), white and light green parts only

¼ cup olive oil

1½ pounds mushrooms, quartered

2 cups dry red wine, such as an Oregon Pinot Noir or a Washington State Merlot

salt and pepper

4 8-ounce boneless sirloin steaks, about ¾ inch thick

1 tablespoon chopped fresh parsley

1 ▲ Trim the leeks and cut into 1-inch slices on the diagonal.

2 ▲ Heat 3 tablespoons of the oil in a large skillet. When hot, add the leeks and mushrooms and cook over medium heat, stirring often, until lightly browned.

3 Stir in the wine, scraping the bottom of the pan. Season with salt and pepper. Bring to a boil and boil 1 minute. Reduce the heat to low, then cover and cook 5 minutes.

4 Remove the lid, raise the heat, and cook until the wine has reduced slightly, about 5 minutes. Set aside.

5 ▼ Brush the steaks with the remaining 1 tablespoon oil and sprinkle generously on both sides with salt and pepper.

6 Heat a ridged grill pan (or preheat the broiler). When hot, add the steaks and cook 3–4 minutes on each side for medium-rare.

7 Meanwhile, stir the parsley into the leek mixture and reheat.

8 Place the steaks on 4 warmed plates. Mound the leek mixture on top and serve.

~ **VARIATION** ~

If available, use fresh wild mushrooms for extra flavor.

Idaho Beef Stew

SERVES 6

¼ cup vegetable oil

2 onions, chopped

4 large carrots, thickly sliced

3 pounds chuck steak, cubed

salt and pepper

3 tablespoons flour

3 cups unsalted beef stock

1 cup strong black coffee

2 teaspoons dried oregano

1 bay leaf

1 cup shelled fresh or frozen peas

mashed potatoes, for serving

1 ▼ Heat 2 tablespoons of the oil in a large flameproof casserole. Add the onions and carrots and cook over medium heat until lightly browned, about 8 minutes. Remove them with a slotted spoon, transfer to a plate or dish, and reserve.

2 ▲ Add another tablespoon of oil to the casserole and then add the beef cubes. Raise the heat to medium-high and cook until browned all over. (Work in batches if necessary.) Season with salt and pepper.

3 ▲ Return the vegetables to the casserole. Add the flour and the remaining tablespoon of oil. Cook, stirring constantly, 1 minute. Add the stock, coffee, oregano, and bay leaf. Bring to a boil and cook, stirring often, until thickened. Reduce the heat to low, then cover the casserole and simmer gently until the beef is tender, about 45 minutes.

4 ▲ Add the peas and simmer 5–10 minutes more. Discard the bay leaf, and taste for seasoning. Serve hot, with mashed potatoes.

Pot-Roasted Veal Chops with Carrots

SERVES 4

1 tablespoon vegetable oil
1 tablespoon butter
4 veal chops, about ¾ inch thick
salt and pepper
1 onion, halved and thinly sliced
½ cup dry white wine
1½ pounds carrots, cut in ½-inch slices
1 bay leaf
½ cup whipping cream

1 Preheat the oven to 350°F.

2 ▲ Heat the oil and butter in a flameproof casserole large enough to hold the veal chops in one layer. Add the chops and cook over medium heat until well browned on both sides, 6–8 minutes. Transfer to a plate, season with salt and pepper, and set aside.

3 ▲ Add the onion to the pot and cook until it is just softened, about 5 minutes. Stir in the wine.

4 ▼ Return the veal chops to the pot. Add the carrots. Season with salt and pepper and add the bay leaf.

5 Cover the casserole and transfer it to the oven. Cook until the chops are tender, about 30 minutes.

6 Remove the chops and carrots to warm plates and keep warm. Discard the bay leaf. Stir the cream into the cooking liquid and bring to a boil. Simmer until the sauce is slightly thickened, 2–3 minutes.

7 Taste the sauce and adjust the seasoning if necessary, then spoon it over the chops. Serve immediately.

Cauliflower au Gratin

SERVES 4

2½ pounds cauliflower florets (about 1 large head)

3 tablespoons butter

3 tablespoons flour

2 cups milk

½ cup shredded sharp cheddar cheese

salt and pepper

3 bay leaves

1 ▲ Preheat the oven to 350°F. Grease a 12-inch round baking dish.

2 Bring a large pot of salted water to a boil. Add the cauliflower and cook until just tender but still firm, 7–8 minutes. Drain well.

3 ▲ Melt the butter in a heavy saucepan. Whisk in the flour until thoroughly blended and cook until bubbling. Gradually add the milk. Bring to a boil and continue cooking, stirring constantly, until thick.

4 ▲ Remove from the heat and stir in the shredded cheese. Season the sauce with salt and pepper.

5 ▲ Place the bay leaves on the bottom of the prepared dish. Arrange the cauliflower florets on top in an even layer. Pour the cheese sauce evenly over the cauliflower.

6 Bake until browned, 20–25 minutes. Serve immediately.

Wild Rice Pilaf

SERVES 6

1 cup wild rice
salt and pepper
3 tablespoons butter
½ onion, minced
1 cup long-grain rice
2 cups chicken stock
⅔ cup sliced or slivered almonds
⅔ cup golden raisins
2 tablespoons chopped fresh parsley

3 Stir in the stock and bring to a boil. Cover and simmer gently until the rice is tender and the liquid has been absorbed, 30–40 minutes.

4 ▼ Melt the remaining butter in a small skillet. Add the almonds and cook until they are just golden, 2–3 minutes, stirring. Set aside.

5 ▲ In a large bowl, combine the wild rice, long-grain rice, raisins, almonds, and parsley. Stir to mix. Taste and adjust the seasoning if necessary. Transfer to a warmed serving dish and serve immediately.

1 ▲ Bring a large saucepan of water to a boil. Add the wild rice and 1 teaspoon salt. Cover and simmer gently until the rice is tender, 45–60 minutes. When done, drain well.

2 ▲ Meanwhile, melt 1 tablespoon of the butter in another saucepan. Add the onion and cook over medium heat until it is just softened, about 5 minutes. Stir in the long-grain rice and cook 1 minute more.

Blue Cheese-Chive Pennies

MAKES 4 DOZEN

8 ounces Oregon Blue cheese, crumbled

½ cup (1 stick) unsalted butter, at room
   temperature

1 egg

1 egg yolk

3 tablespoons chopped fresh chives

black pepper

2 cups flour, sifted

1 ▼ The day before serving, beat the
cheese and butter together until well
blended. Add the egg, egg yolk,
chives, and a little pepper and beat
just until blended.

2 ▲ Add the flour in 3 batches,
folding in well, between each addition.

3 ▲ Divide the dough in half and
shape each half into a log about
2 inches in diameter. Wrap in wax
paper and refrigerate overnight.

4 Preheat the oven to 375°F. Lightly
grease 2 baking sheets.

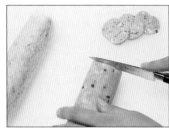

5 ▲ Cut the dough logs across into
slices about ⅛ inch thick. Place on
the prepared sheets.

6 Bake until just golden around the
edges, about 10 minutes. Transfer to a
wire rack to cool.

~ COOK'S TIP ~

The cheese pennies will keep up to
10 days in an airtight container.

Dilled Smoked Salmon Spread

MAKES 3 CUPS

1 cup ricotta cheese

1 cup cream cheese, at room
   temperature

6 ounces smoked salmon, finely
   chopped

4 ounces cooked salmon, flaked

¼ cup chopped fresh dill

3–4 tablespoons fresh lemon juice

salt and pepper

vegetables, such as cucumber slices,
   Belgian endive leaves, bell pepper
   strips, or small toasts, for serving

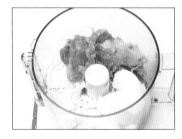

1 ▲ In a food processor or blender,
combine the ricotta cheese, cream
cheese, and smoked salmon. Process
until light and fluffy. Scrape the
mixture into a bowl.

2 ▼ Stir in the cooked salmon, dill,
and 3 tablespoons of the lemon juice.
Season with salt and pepper. Taste
and add the remaining lemon juice if
desired. Serve the spread cold.

Blue Cheese-Chive Pennies (top), Dilled Smoked Salmon Spread

Winter Warmer (Hot White Chocolate)

SERVES 4

6 ounces white chocolate

1½ quarts milk

1 teaspoon coffee extract, or 2 teaspoons instant coffee powder

2 teaspoons orange-flavored liqueur (optional)

FOR SERVING

whipped cream

ground cinnamon

~ COOK'S TIP ~

If preferred, use milk chocolate or semisweet dark chocolate instead of white chocolate, but taste before serving in case a little sugar is needed.

---

1 ▼ With a sharp knife, finely chop the white chocolate. (Try not to handle it too much or it will soften and stick together.)

2 Pour the milk into a medium-sized heavy saucepan and bring just to a boil (bubbles will form around the edge of the pan).

3 ▲ Add the chopped white chocolate, coffee extract or powder, and orange-flavored liqueur if using. Stir until the chocolate has melted.

4 Divide the hot chocolate among 4 coffee mugs. Top each with a rosette or spoonful of whipped cream and a sprinkling of ground cinnamon. Serve immediately.

Easy Hazelnut Fudge

MAKES 16 SQUARES

⅔ cup evaporated milk

1¾ cups sugar

⅛ teaspoon salt

½ cup halved hazelnuts

2 cups semisweet chocolate chips

1 teaspoon hazelnut liqueur (optional)

1 Generously grease an 8-inch square cake pan.

~ VARIATION ~

For Easy Peanut Butter Fudge, substitute peanut butter chips for the chocolate chips and replace the hazelnuts with peanuts.

---

2 Combine the evaporated milk, sugar, and salt in a heavy saucepan. Bring to a boil over medium heat, stirring constantly. Simmer gently, stirring, about 5 minutes.

3 ▼ Remove from the heat and add the hazelnuts, chocolate chips, and liqueur if using. Stir until the chocolate has completely melted.

4 ▲ Quickly pour the fudge mixture into the prepared pan and spread it out evenly. Let cool.

5 When the fudge is set, cut into 1-inch squares. Store in an airtight container, separating the layers with wax paper.

Winter Warmer (top), Easy Hazelnut Fudge

Northwestern Brown Betty

SERVES 6

2¼ pounds pears (about 8)

¼ cup lemon juice

3 cups fresh bread crumbs, preferably from egg bread

6 tablespoons butter, melted

⅔ cup dried cherries

⅔ cup coarsely chopped hazelnuts

½ cup brown sugar, firmly packed

1–2 tablespoons butter, cut in small pieces

whipped cream, for serving

1 Preheat the oven to 375°F. Grease an 8-inch square cake pan.

2 ▼ Peel, core, and dice the pears. Sprinkle them with the lemon juice to prevent discoloration.

3 ▲ Combine the bread crumbs and melted butter in a bowl. Spread a scant one-third of the crumb mixture on the bottom of the prepared dish.

4 ▲ Top with half of the pears. Sprinkle over half of the dried cherries, half of the hazelnuts, and half of the sugar. Repeat the layers, then finish with a layer of crumbs.

5 ▲ Dot with the pieces of butter. Bake until golden, 30–35 minutes. Serve hot, with whipped cream.

Rhubarb-Strawberry Crisp

SERVES 4

8 ounces strawberries, hulled
1 pound rhubarb, diced
½ cup granulated sugar
1 tablespoon cornstarch
⅓ cup fresh orange juice
1 cup flour
1 cup rolled oats
½ cup light brown sugar, firmly packed
½ teaspoon ground cinnamon
½ cup ground almonds
10 tablespoons (1¼ sticks) cold butter
1 egg, lightly beaten

1 Preheat the oven to 350°F.

2 ▲ If the strawberries are large, cut them in half. Combine the strawberries, rhubarb, and granulated sugar in a 2-quart baking dish.

4 ▼ In a bowl, toss together the flour, oats, brown sugar, cinnamon, and almonds. With a pastry blender or 2 knives, cut in the butter until the mixture resembles coarse crumbs. Stir in the beaten egg.

3 ▲ In a small bowl, blend the cornstarch with the orange juice. Pour this mixture over the fruit and stir gently to coat. Set the baking dish aside while making the topping.

5 ▲ Spoon the oat mixture evenly over the fruit and press down gently. Bake until browned, 50–60 minutes. Serve the crisp warm.

Blackberry Cobbler

SERVES 8

6 cups blackberries (about 1¼ pounds)

1 cup sugar

3 tablespoons flour

grated rind of 1 lemon

2 tablespoons sugar mixed with
¼ teaspoon grated nutmeg

FOR THE TOPPING

2 cups flour

1 cup sugar

1 tablespoon baking powder

⅛ teaspoon salt

1 cup milk

½ cup (1 stick) butter, melted

1 Preheat the oven to 350°F.

2 ▼ In a bowl, combine the blackberries, sugar, flour, and lemon rind. Stir gently to blend. Transfer to a 2-quart baking dish.

3 ▲ For the topping, sift the flour, sugar, baking powder, and salt into a large bowl. Set aside. In a large measure, combine the milk and butter.

4 ▲ Gradually stir the milk mixture into the dry ingredients and stir until the batter is just smooth.

5 ▲ Spoon the batter over the berries, spreading to the edges.

6 Sprinkle the surface with the sugar-nutmeg mixture. Bake until the batter topping is set and lightly browned, about 50 minutes. Serve hot.

Baked Apples

SERVES 6

½ cup chopped dried apricots

½ cup chopped walnuts

1 teaspoon grated lemon rind

¼ teaspoon ground cinnamon

½ cup light brown sugar, firmly packed

2 tablespoons butter, at room temperature

6 baking apples

1 tablespoon melted butter

1 Preheat the oven to 375°F.

2 ▲ In a bowl, combine the apricots, walnuts, lemon rind, and cinnamon. Add the sugar and butter and stir until thoroughly combined.

3 ▲ Core the apples, without cutting all the way through to the base. With a small knife, slightly widen the top of each opening by about 1½ inches to make room for the filling.

4 Spoon the apricot and walnut filling into the opening in the apples, packing it down lightly.

5 ▼ Place the apples in a baking dish just large enough to hold them comfortably side by side.

6 ▲ Brush the apples with the melted butter. Bake until they are tender, 40–45 minutes. Serve hot.

Blueberry-Hazelnut Cheesecake

12 ounces blueberries

1 tablespoon honey

6 tablespoons granulated sugar

1 teaspoon plus 1 tablespoon fresh lemon juice

6 ounces cream cheese, at room temperature

1 egg

1 teaspoon hazelnut liqueur (optional)

½ cup whipping cream

FOR THE CRUST

1⅔ cups ground hazelnuts

⅔ cup flour

⅛ teaspoon salt

4 tablespoons butter, at room temperature

⅓ cup light brown sugar, firmly packed

1 egg yolk

1 ▲ For the crust, put the hazelnuts in a large bowl. Sift in the flour and salt, and stir to mix. Set aside.

~ COOK'S TIP ~

The cheesecake can be prepared 1 day in advance, but add the fruit shortly before serving. Instead of covering the top completely, leave spaces to make a design, if wished.

2 Beat the butter with the brown sugar until light and fluffy. Beat in the egg yolk. Gradually fold in the nut mixture, in 3 batches.

3 ▲ Press the dough into a greased 9-inch pie pan, spreading it evenly against the sides. Form a rim around the top edge that is slightly thicker than the sides. Cover and refrigerate at least 30 minutes.

4 Preheat the oven to 350°F.

5 ▲ Meanwhile, for the topping, combine the blueberries, honey, 1 tablespoon of the granulated sugar, and 1 teaspoon lemon juice in a heavy saucepan. Cook the mixture over low heat, stirring occasionally, until the berries have given off some liquid but still retain their shape, 5–7 minutes. Remove from the heat and set aside.

6 Place the crust in the oven and bake 15 minutes. Remove and let cool while making the filling.

7 ▲ Beat together the cream cheese and remaining granulated sugar until light and fluffy. Add the egg, remaining lemon juice, the liqueur, if using, and the cream and beat until thoroughly incorporated.

8 ▲ Pour the cheese mixture into the crust and spread evenly. Bake until just set, 20–25 minutes.

9 Let the cheesecake cool completely on a wire rack, then cover and refrigerate at least 1 hour.

10 Spread the blueberry mixture evenly over the top of the cheesecake. Serve at cool room temperature.

Chocolate-Coffee-Vanilla Pudding Cups

SERVES 6

1½ cups sugar

6 tablespoons cornstarch

4 cups milk

3 egg yolks

6 tablespoons unsalted butter, at room temperature

1 generous tablespoon instant coffee powder

2 teaspoons vanilla extract

2 tablespoons unsweetened cocoa powder

whipped cream, for serving

1 ▲ For the coffee layer, combine ½ cup of the sugar and 2 tablespoons of the cornstarch in a heavy saucepan. Gradually add 1⅓ cups of the milk, whisking until well blended. Over medium heat, whisk in 1 egg yolk and bring to a boil, whisking constantly. Boil 1 minute, still whisking.

2 ▲ Remove from the heat. Stir in 2 tablespoons of the butter and the coffee powder. Let cool slightly.

3 ▲ Divide the coffee mixture among 6 wine glasses. Smooth the tops before the mixture sets.

4 ▲ Wipe any dribbles on the insides and outsides of the glasses with a damp paper towel.

5 ▲ For the vanilla layer, combine ½ cup of the sugar and 2 tablespoons of the cornstarch in a heavy saucepan. Gradually whisk in 1⅓ cups of the milk until well blended. Over medium heat, whisk in 1 egg yolk and bring to a boil, whisking. Boil 1 minute.

6 Remove from the heat and stir in 2 tablespoons of the butter and the vanilla. Let cool slightly, then spoon into the glasses on top of the coffee layer. Smooth the tops and wipe the glasses with paper towel.

7 ▲ For the chocolate layer, combine the remaining sugar and cornstarch in a heavy saucepan. Gradually whisk in the remaining milk until well blended. Over moderate heat, whisk in the last egg yolk and bring to a boil, whisking constantly. Boil 1 minute. Off the heat, stir in the remaining butter and the cocoa powder. Let cool slightly, then spoon into the glasses on top of the vanilla layer. Chill until set.

8 ▲ Pipe or spoon whipped cream on top of each pudding before serving.

~ COOK'S TIP ~

For a special occasion, prepare the vanilla layer using a fresh vanilla bean. Choose a plump, supple bean and split it down the center with a sharp knife. Add to the mixture with the milk and discard the bean before spooning into the glasses. The flavor will be more pronounced and the pudding will have pretty brown speckles from the vanilla seeds.

GREAT AMERICAN BAKING

Nothing equals the satisfaction of home baking. No commercial cake mix or store-bought cookie can match one that is made from the best fresh ingredients with all the added enjoyment that baking at home provides – the enticing aromas that fill the house and stimulate appetites, the delicious straight-from-the-oven flavor, as well as the pride of having created such wonderful goodies yourself.

This section of the book is filled with familiar favorites from our melting-pot heritage as well as many other lesser known, but equally good recipes. Explore the wealth of cookies, muffins, quick breads, yeast breads, pies, tarts, and cakes within these pages. Even if you are a novice baker, the easy-to-follow and clear step-by-step photographs will help you achieve good results. For the more experienced home baker, this book will provide many new recipes to add to your repertoire.

Baking is an exact science and needs to be approached in an ordered way. First read through the recipe from beginning to end. Set out all the required ingredients before you begin. In this book, granulated sugar, all-purpose flour, and size "large" eggs are assumed unless specified otherwise. Eggs should be at room temperature for best results. All the recipes use the scoop and then level method of measuring flour: scoop up flour with the measuring cup and level it off with the back of a knife. Sift the flour after you have measured it, and incorporate other dry ingredients as specified in the individual recipes. If you sift the flour from a fair height, it will have more chance to aerate and lighten.

When a recipe calls for folding one ingredient into another, it should be done in a way that incorporates as much air as possible into the batter. Use either a large metal spoon or a long rubber or plastic spatula. Gently plunge the spoon or spatula deep into the center of the batter and, scooping up a large amount of the batter, fold it over. Turn the bowl slightly so each scoop folds over another part of the batter.

No two ovens are alike. Buy a reliable oven thermometer and test the temperature of your oven. When possible, bake in the center of the oven where the heat is more likely to be constant. If using a fan-assisted oven, follow the manufacturer's guidelines for baking. Good quality baking pans can improve your results, as they conduct heat more efficiently.

Practice, patience, and enthusiasm are the keys to confident and successful baking. The recipes that follow will inspire you to start sifting flour, breaking eggs and stirring up all sorts of delectable homemade treats – all guaranteed to bring great satisfaction to both the baker and those lucky enough to enjoy the results.

COOKIES
& BARS

KEEP THE COOKIE JAR FILLED WITH
THIS WONDERFUL ARRAY OF
COOKIES AND BARS – SOME SOFT
AND CHEWY, SOME CRUNCHY AND
NUTTY, SOME RICH AND SINFUL,
AND SOME PLAIN AND WHOLESOME.
ALL ARE IRRESISTIBLE.

Farmhouse Cookies

Makes 18

¹/₂ cup (1 stick) butter or margarine, at room temperature

generous 1 cup light brown sugar

¹/₄ cup crunchy peanut butter

1 egg

¹/₂ cup flour

¹/₂ teaspoon baking powder

¹/₂ teaspoon ground cinnamon

pinch of salt

1¹/₂ cups granola cereal

¹/₃ cup raisins

¹/₂ cup chopped walnuts

1 Preheat the oven to 350°F. Grease a cookie sheet.

2 With an electric mixer, cream the butter or margarine and sugar until light and fluffy. Beat in the peanut butter. Beat in the egg.

3 ▲ Sift the flour, baking powder, cinnamon, and salt over the peanut butter mixture and stir to blend. Stir in the granola, raisins, and walnuts. Taste the mixture to see if it needs more sugar, as granolas vary.

4 ▲ Drop rounded tablespoonfuls of the batter onto the prepared cookie sheet about 1 inch apart. Press gently with the back of a spoon to spread each mound into a circle.

5 Bake until lightly colored, about 15 minutes. With a metal spatula, transfer to a rack to cool. Store in an airtight container.

Crunchy Oatmeal Cookies

MAKES 14

³/₄ cup (1¹/₂ sticks) butter or margarine, at room temperature

scant 1 cup superfine sugar

1 egg yolk

1¹/₂ cups flour

1 teaspoon baking soda

¹/₂ teaspoon salt

¹/₂ cup rolled oats

¹/₂ cup small crunchy nugget cereal

1 ▲ With an electric mixer, cream the butter or margarine and sugar together until light and fluffy. Mix in the egg yolk.

2 Sift over the flour, baking soda, and salt, then stir into the butter mixture. Add the oats and cereal and stir to blend. Chill for at least 20 minutes. Meanwhile, preheat the oven to 375°F. Grease a cookie sheet.

3 ▼ Roll the mixture into balls. Place them on the sheet and flatten with the bottom of a floured glass.

4 Bake until golden, 10–12 minutes. With a metal spatula, transfer to a rack to cool completely. Store in an airtight container.

~ VARIATION ~

For Nutty Oatmeal Cookies, substitute an equal quantity of chopped walnuts or pecans for the cereal, and prepare as described.

Farmhouse Cookies (top), Crunchy Oatmeal Cookies

Oaty Coconut Cookies

MAKES 48

1¾ cups quick-cooking oats
1 cup dry unsweetened shredded coconut
1 cup (2 sticks) butter or margarine, at room temperature
generous ½ cup superfine sugar, plus 2 tablespoons for dipping
¼ cup soft dark brown sugar
2 eggs
4 tablespoons milk
1½ teaspoons vanilla extract
1 cup flour
½ teaspoon baking soda
½ teaspoon salt
1 teaspoon ground cinnamon

1 Preheat the oven to 400°F. Lightly grease 2 cookie sheets.

2 ▲ Spread the oats and coconut on an ungreased cookie sheet. Bake until golden brown, 8–10 minutes, stirring occasionally.

3 With an electric mixer, cream the butter or margarine and both sugars until light and fluffy. Beat in the eggs, 1 at a time, then the milk and vanilla. Sift over the dry ingredients and fold in. Stir in the oats and coconut.

4 ▼ Drop spoonfuls of the mixture 1–2 inches apart on the prepared sheets and flatten with the bottom of a greased glass dipped in sugar. Bake until golden, 8–10 minutes. Transfer to a rack to cool.

Crunchy Jumbles

MAKES 36

½ cup (1 stick) butter or margarine, at room temperature
generous 1 cup superfine sugar
1 egg
1 teaspoon vanilla extract
¾ cup flour
½ teaspoon baking soda
pinch of salt
2 ounces crisped rice cereal
6 ounces chocolate chips

~ VARIATION ~

For even crunchier cookies, add ⅓ cup walnuts, coarsely chopped, with the cereal and chocolate chips.

1 Preheat the oven to 350°F. Lightly grease 2 cookie sheets.

2 ▲ With an electric mixer, cream the butter or margarine and sugar until light and fluffy. Beat in the egg and vanilla. Sift over the flour, baking soda, and salt and fold in carefully.

3 ▼ Add the cereal and chocolate chips. Stir to mix thoroughly.

4 Drop spoonfuls of the mixture 1–2 inches apart on the sheets. Bake until golden, 10–12 minutes. Transfer to a rack to cool.

Oaty Coconut Cookies (top), Crunchy Jumbles

Ginger Cookies

MAKES 36

generous 1 cup superfine sugar

generous 1 cup soft light brown sugar

1/2 cup (1 stick) butter,
    at room temperature

1/2 cup (1 stick) margarine,
    at room temperature

1 egg

6 tablespoons molasses

2 1/4 cups flour

2 teaspoons ground ginger

1/2 teaspoon freshly grated nutmeg

1 teaspoon ground cinnamon

2 teaspoons baking soda

1/2 teaspoon salt

1 Preheat the oven to 325°F. Line 2–3 cookie sheets with wax paper; grease the paper lightly.

2 ▲ With an electric mixer, cream half the superfine sugar, the brown sugar, butter, and margarine until light and fluffy. Add the egg and continue beating to blend well. Add the molasses.

3 ▲ Sift the flour, spices, and baking soda 3 times, then stir them into the butter mixture. Refrigerate for about 30 minutes.

4 ▲ Place the remaining sugar in a shallow dish. Roll tablespoonfuls of the dough into balls, then roll the balls in the sugar to coat.

5 Place the balls 2 inches apart on the prepared sheets and flatten slightly. Bake until golden around the edges but soft in the middle, about 12–15 minutes. Let stand for 5 minutes before transferring to a rack to cool.

~ VARIATION ~

To make Gingerbread Men, increase the amount of flour by 1/4 cup. Roll out the mixture and cut out shapes with a special cutter. Decorate with icing, if you like.

Orange Cookies

MAKES 30

¹/₂ cup (1 stick) butter, at room temperature
1 cup superfine sugar
2 egg yolks
1 tablespoon fresh orange juice
grated rind of 1 large orange
scant 2 cups flour
1 tablespoon cornstarch
¹/₂ teaspoon salt
1 teaspoon baking powder

1 ▲ With an electric mixer, cream the butter and sugar until light and fluffy. Add the yolks, orange juice, and rind, and continue beating to blend. Set aside.

2 In another bowl, sift together the flour, cornstarch, salt, and baking powder. Add to the butter mixture and stir until it forms a dough.

4 Preheat the oven to 375°F. Grease 2 cookie sheets.

6 ▼ Press down with a fork to flatten. Bake until golden brown, 8–10 minutes. With a metal spatula transfer to a rack to cool.

3 ▲ Wrap the dough in wax paper and refrigerate for 2 hours.

5 ▲ Roll spoonfuls of the dough into balls and place 1–2 inches apart on the prepared sheets.

Cinnamon-coated Cookies

MAKES 30

$^1/2$ cup (1 stick) butter,
    at room temperature

$1^3/4$ cups superfine sugar

1 teaspoon vanilla extract

2 eggs

$^1/4$ cup milk

$3^1/2$ cups flour

1 teaspoon baking soda

$^1/2$ cup finely chopped walnuts

FOR THE COATING

5 tablespoons sugar

2 tablespoons ground cinnamon

1 Preheat the oven to 375°F. Grease 2 cookie sheets.

2 With an electric mixer, cream the butter until light. Add the sugar and vanilla and continue mixing until fluffy. Beat in the eggs, then the milk.

3 ▲ Sift the flour and baking soda over the butter mixture and stir to blend. Stir in the nuts. Refrigerate for 15 minutes.

4 ▲ For the coating, mix the sugar and cinnamon. Roll tablespoonfuls of the dough into walnut-size balls. Roll the balls in the sugar mixture. You may need to work in batches.

5 Place 2 inches apart on the prepared sheets and flatten slightly. Bake until golden, about 10 minutes. Transfer to a rack to cool.

Chewy Chocolate Cookies

MAKES 18

4 egg whites

scant $2^1/2$ cups confectioners' sugar

1 cup unsweetened cocoa powder

2 tablespoons flour

1 teaspoon instant coffee

1 tablespoon water

$^1/2$ cup finely chopped walnuts

1 Preheat the oven to 350°F. Line 2 cookie sheets with wax paper and grease the paper.

> **~ VARIATION ~**
>
> If wished, add 3 ounces chocolate chips to the mixture with the nuts.

2 With an electric mixer, beat the egg whites until frothy.

3 ▼ Sift the sugar, cocoa, flour, and coffee into the whites. Add the water and continue beating on low speed to blend, then on high for a few minutes until the mixture thickens. With a rubber spatula, fold in the walnuts.

4 ▲ Place generous spoonfuls of the mixture 1 inch apart on the prepared sheets. Bake until firm and cracked on top but soft on the inside, about 12–15 minutes. With a metal spatula, transfer to a rack to cool.

Cinnamon-coated Cookies (top), Chewy Chocolate Cookies

Chocolate Pretzels

Makes 28

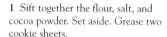

1¼ cups flour

pinch of salt

1 tablespoon unsweetened cocoa powder

½ cup (1 stick) butter,
    at room temperature

scant ¾ cup superfine sugar

1 egg

1 egg white, lightly beaten, for glazing

sugar crystals, for sprinkling

1 Sift together the flour, salt, and cocoa powder. Set aside. Grease two cookie sheets.

2 ▲ With an electric mixer, cream the butter until light. Add the sugar and continue beating until light and fluffy. Beat in the egg. Add the dry ingredients and stir to blend. Gather the dough into a ball, wrap in clear film (plastic wrap), and refrigerate for 1 hour or freeze for 30 minutes.

3 ▲ Roll the dough into 28 small balls. Refrigerate the balls until they are needed. Preheat the oven to 375°F.

4 ▲ Roll each ball into a rope about 10 inches long. With each rope, form a loop with the two ends facing you. Twist the ends and fold back onto the circle, pressing in to make a pretzel shape. Place on the prepared sheets.

5 ▲ Brush the pretzels with the egg white. Sprinkle sugar crystals over the tops and bake until firm, about 10–12 minutes. Transfer to a rack to cool.

Cream Cheese Spirals

MAKES 32

1 cup (2 sticks) butter,
  at room temperature

1 cup cream cheese

2 teaspoons superfine sugar

2 cups flour

1 egg white beaten with 1 tablespoon
  water, for glazing

sugar, for sprinkling

FOR THE FILLING

1 cup finely chopped walnuts

¹/₂ cup soft light brown sugar

1 teaspoon ground cinnamon

1 With an electric mixer, cream the butter, cream cheese, and sugar until soft. Sift over the flour and mix until combined. Gather into a ball and divide in half. Flatten each half, wrap in wax paper and refrigerate for at least 30 minutes.

2 Meanwhile, make the filling. Mix together the chopped walnuts, the brown sugar, and the cinnamon, and set aside.

3 Preheat the oven to 375°F. Grease 2 cookie sheets.

4 ▲ Working with one half of the mixture at a time, roll out thinly into a circle about 28cm/11in in diameter. Trim the edges with a knife, using a dinner plate as a guide.

5 ▼ Brush the surface with the egg white glaze and then sprinkle evenly with half the filling.

6 Cut the circle into quarters, and each quarter into 4 sections, to form 16 triangles.

7 ▲ Starting from the base of the triangles, roll up to form spirals.

8 Place on the sheets and brush with the remaining glaze. Sprinkle with superfine sugar. Bake until golden, 15–20 minutes. Cool on a rack.

Vanilla Crescents

1 cup unblanched almonds

1 cup flour

pinch of salt

1 cup (2 sticks) unsalted butter,
   at room temperature

generous $^1/_2$ cup sugar

1 teaspoon vanilla extract

confectioners' sugar, for dusting

1 Grind the almonds with a few tablespoons of the flour in a food processor, blender, or nut grinder.

2 Sift the remaining flour with the salt into a bowl. Set aside.

3 With an electric mixer, cream together the butter and sugar until light and fluffy.

4 ▼ Add the almonds, vanilla essence, and the flour mixture. Stir to mix well. Gather the dough into a ball, wrap in wax paper, and refrigerate for at least 30 minutes.

5 Preheat the oven to 325°F. Lightly grease 2 cookie sheets.

6 ▲ Break off walnut-size pieces of dough and roll into small cylinders about $^1/_2$ inch in diameter. Bend into small crescents and place on the prepared cookie sheets.

7 Bake until dry but not brown, about 20 minutes. Transfer to a wire rack to cool only slightly. Set the rack over a cookie sheet and dust with an even layer of confectioners' sugar. Let cool completely.

Walnut Crescents

$^2/_3$ cup walnuts

1 cup (2 sticks) unsalted butter,
   at room temperature

generous $^1/_2$ cup sugar

$^1/_2$ teaspoon vanilla extract

2 cups flour

$^1/_4$ teaspoon salt

confectioners' sugar, for dusting

1 Preheat the oven to 350°F.

2 Grind the walnuts in a food processor, blender, or nut grinder until they are almost a paste. Transfer to a bowl.

3 Add the butter to the walnuts and mix with a wooden spoon until blended. Add the sugar and vanilla, and stir to blend.

4 ▼ Sift the flour and salt into the walnut mixture. Work into a dough.

5 Shape the dough into small cylinders about $1^1/_2$ inches long. Bend into crescents and place evenly spaced on an ungreased cookie sheet.

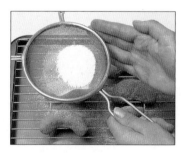

6 ▲ Bake until lightly browned, about 15 minutes. Transfer to a rack to cool only slightly. Set the rack over a cookie sheet and dust lightly with confectioners' sugar.

Vanilla Crescents (top), Walnut Crescents

Pecan Puffs

Makes 24

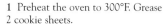

1/2 cup (1 stick) unsalted butter

2 tablespoons sugar

pinch of salt

1 teaspoon vanilla extract

2/3 cup pecans

1 cup cake flour, sifted

confectioners' sugar, for dusting

1 Preheat the oven to 300°F. Grease 2 cookie sheets.

2 ▲ With an electric mixer, cream the butter and sugar until light and fluffy. Stir in the salt and vanilla.

3 Grind the nuts in a food processor, blender, or nut grinder. Stir several times to prevent them becoming oily. If necessary, grind in batches.

4 ▲ Force the ground nuts through a strainer set over a bowl to aerate them. Pieces too large to go through the sieve can be ground again.

5 ▲ Stir the nuts and flour into the butter mixture to make a firm, springy dough.

6 Roll the dough into marble-size balls. Place on the prepared cookie sheets and bake for about 30 minutes, until lightly golden.

7 ▲ While the puffs are still hot, roll them in confectioners' sugar. Leave to cool completely, then roll once more in confectioners' sugar.

Pecan Tassies

MAKES 24

$^1/_2$ cup cream cheese
$^1/_2$ cup (1 stick) butter, at room temperature
1 cup flour
FOR THE FILLING
2 eggs
$^1/_2$ cup soft dark brown sugar
1 teaspoon vanilla extract
pinch of salt
2 tablespoons butter, melted
$^2/_3$ cup pecans

1 Place a cookie sheet in the oven and preheat to 350°F. Grease 24 mini-muffin tins.

2 Chop the cream cheese and butter into cubes. Put them in a mixing bowl. Sift over half the flour and mix. Add the remaining flour and continue mixing to form a dough.

3 ▲ Roll the dough out thinly. With a floured, fluted pastry cutter, stamp out 24 2$^1/_2$-inch rounds. Line the muffin cups with the rounds and refrigerate while making the filling.

4 To make the filling, lightly whisk the eggs in a bowl. Gradually whisk in the brown sugar, and add the vanilla extract, salt, and butter. Set aside until required.

5 ▼ Reserve 24 undamaged pecan halves and chop the rest coarsely with a sharp knife.

6 ▲ Place a spoonful of chopped nuts in each muffin tin and cover with the filling. Set a pecan half on the top of each.

7 Bake on the hot cookie sheet for about 20 minutes, until puffed and set. Transfer to a wire rack to cool. Serve at room temperature.

> **~ VARIATION ~**
>
> To make Jam Tassies, fill the cream cheese pastry shells with raspberry or blackberry jam, or other fruit jams. Bake as described.

Lady Fingers

MAKES 18

³/4 cup flour

pinch of salt

4 eggs, separated

generous ¹/2 cup sugar

¹/2 teaspoon vanilla extract

confectioners' sugar, for sprinkling

1 Preheat the oven to 300°F. Grease 2 cookie sheets, then coat lightly with flour, and shake off the excess.

2 Sift the flour and salt together twice in a bowl.

~ COOK'S TIP ~

To make the biscuits all the same length, mark parallel lines 4 inches apart on the cookie sheets and pipe between them.

3 With an electric mixer, beat the egg yolks with half the sugar until thick enough to leave a ribbon trail when the beaters are lifted.

4 ▲ In another bowl, beat the egg whites until stiff. Beat in the remaining sugar until glossy.

5 Sift the flour over the yolks and spoon a large dollop of egg whites over the flour. Carefully fold in with a large metal spoon, adding the vanilla extract. Gently fold in the remaining whites.

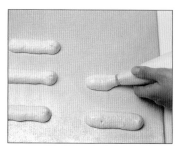

6 ▲ Spoon the mixture into a pastry bag fitted with a large plain nozzle. Pipe 4-inch long lines on the prepared cookie sheets about 1 inch apart. Sift over a layer of confectioners' sugar. Turn the sheet upside down to dislodge any excess sugar.

7 Bake for about 20 minutes until crusty on the outside but soft in the center. Cool slightly on the cookie sheets before transferring to a wire rack to cool completely.

Walnut Cookies

MAKES 60

¹/2 cup (1 stick) butter or margarine, at room temperature

scant 1 cup superfine sugar

1 cup flour

2 teaspoons vanilla extract

²/3 cup walnuts, finely chopped

~ VARIATION ~

To make Almond Cookies, use an equal amount of finely chopped unblanched almonds instead of walnuts. Replace half the vanilla with ¹/2 teaspoon almond essence.

1 Preheat the oven to 300°F. Grease 2 cookie sheets.

2 ▲ With an electric mixer, cream the butter or margarine until soft. Add ¹/3 cup of the sugar and continue beating until light and fluffy. Stir in the flour, vanilla extract, and walnuts.

3 Drop teaspoonfuls of the batter 1–2 inches apart on the prepared cookie sheets and flatten slightly with a fork. Bake for about 25 minutes.

4 ▼ Transfer to a wire rack set over a cookie sheet and sprinkle with the remaining sugar.

Lady Fingers (top), Walnut Cookies

Italian Almond Biscotti

MAKES 48

generous 1 cup whole unblanched almonds

scant 2 cups flour

$1/2$ cup superfine sugar

pinch of salt

pinch of saffron threads

$1/2$ teaspoon baking soda

2 eggs

1 egg white, lightly beaten

~ COOK'S TIP ~

Dunk biscotti in sweet white wine, such as an Italian Vin Santo or a French Muscat de Beaumes-de-Venise.

1 Preheat the oven to 375°F. Grease and flour 2 cookie sheets.

2 ▲ Spread the almonds in a baking tray and bake until lightly browned, about 15 minutes. When cool, grind $1/3$ cup of the almonds in a food processor, blender, or nut grinder until pulverized. Coarsely chop the remaining almonds in 2 or 3 pieces each. Set aside.

3 ▲ Combine the flour, sugar, salt, saffron, baking soda, and ground almonds in a bowl and mix to blend. Make a well in the centre and add the eggs. Stir to form a rough dough. Transfer to a floured surface and knead until well blended. Knead in the chopped almonds.

4 ▲ Divide the dough into 3 equal parts. Roll into logs about 1 inch in diameter. Place on one of the prepared sheets, leaving room to spread, brush with the egg white, and bake for 20 minutes. Remove from the oven.

5 ▲ With a very sharp knife, cut into each log at an angle making $1/2$-inch slices. Return the slices on the cookie sheets to a 275°F oven and bake for 25 minutes more. Transfer to a rack to cool.

Christmas Cookies

MAKES 30

³/₄ cup (1¹/₂ sticks) unsalted butter,
   at room temperature

scant 1¹/₂ cups superfine sugar

1 egg

1 egg yolk

1 teaspoon vanilla extract

grated rind of 1 lemon

¹/₄ teaspoon salt

2¹/₂ cups flour

FOR DECORATING (OPTIONAL)

colored icing and small decorations

1 Preheat the oven to 350°F.

2 ▲ With an electric mixer, cream
the butter until soft. Add the sugar
gradually and continue beating until
light and fluffy.

3 ▲ Using a wooden spoon, slowly
mix in the whole egg and the egg yolk.
Add the vanilla, lemon rind and salt.
Stir to mix well.

4 Add the flour and stir until blended.
Gather the mixture into a ball, wrap
in wax paper, and refrigerate for at
least 30 minutes.

5 ▼ On a floured surface, roll out the
dough to about ¹/₈ inch thick.

6 ▲ Stamp out shapes or rounds with
cookie cutters.

7 Bake until lightly colored, about
8 minutes. Transfer to a rack and
leave to cool completely before icing
and decorating, if wished.

Toasted Oat Meringues

MAKES 12

1/2 cup rolled oats

2 egg whites

pinch of salt

1 1/2 teaspoons cornstarch

scant 1 cup superfine sugar

1 Preheat the oven to 275°F. Spread the oats on a cookie sheet and toast in the oven until golden, about 10 minutes. Lower the heat to 250°F. Grease and flour a cookie sheet.

+--+
| **~ VARIATION ~** |
| |
| Add 1/2 teaspoon ground cinnamon |
| with the oats, and fold in gently. |
+--+

2 ▼ With an electric mixer, beat the egg whites and salt until they start to form soft peaks.

3 Sift over the cornstarch and continue beating until the whites hold stiff peaks. Add half the sugar and whisk until glossy.

4 ▲ Add the remaining sugar and fold in, then fold in the oats.

5 Gently spoon the mixture onto the prepared sheet and bake for 2 hours.

6 When done, turn off the oven. Lift the meringues from the sheet, turn over, and set in another place on the sheet to prevent sticking. Leave in the oven as it cools down.

Meringues

MAKES 24

4 egg whites

pinch of salt

scant 1 1/2 cups superfine sugar

1/2 teaspoon vanilla or almond extract (optional)

1 cup whipped cream (optional)

1 Preheat the oven to 225°F. Grease and flour 2 large cookie sheets.

2 With an electric mixer, beat the egg whites and salt in a very clean metal bowl on low speed. When they start to form soft peaks, add half the sugar and continue beating until the mixture holds stiff peaks.

3 ▲ With a large metal spoon, fold in the remaining sugar and vanilla or almond extract, if using.

4 ▼ Pipe the meringue mixture or spoon it on the prepared sheet.

5 Bake for 2 hours then turn off the oven. Loosen the meringues, invert, and set in another place on the sheets to prevent sticking. Leave in the oven as it cools. Serve sandwiched with whipped cream, if you wish.

Toasted Oat Meringues (top), Meringues

Chocolate Macaroons

MAKES 24

2 1-ounce squares semisweet chocolate
1 cup blanched almonds
generous 1 cup superfine sugar
$^1/_3$ cup egg whites (about 2 eggs)
$^1/_2$ teaspoon vanilla extract
$^1/_4$ teaspoon almond extract
confectioners' sugar, for dusting

1 Preheat the oven to 300°F. Line 2 cookie sheets with wax paper and grease the paper.

2 ▼ Melt the chocolate in the top of a double boiler, or in a heatproof bowl set over a pan of hot water.

3 ▲ Grind the almonds finely in a food processor, blender, or nut grinder. Transfer to a mixing bowl.

4 ▲ In a mixing bowl, whisk the egg whites until they form soft peaks. Fold in the sugar, vanilla and almond extracts, ground almonds, and melted chocolate. Refrigerate for 15 minutes.

5 ▲ Use a teaspoon and your hands to shape the mixture into walnut-size balls. Place on the sheets and flatten slightly. Brush each ball with a little water and sift over a thin layer of confectioners' sugar. Bake until just firm, 20–25 minutes. With a metal spatula, transfer to a rack to cool.

~ VARIATION ~

For Chocolate Pine Nut Macaroons, spread $^3/_4$ cup pine nuts in a shallow dish. Press the chocolate macaroon balls into the nuts to cover one side and bake as described, nut-side up.

Coconut Macaroons

MAKES 24

$^1/_3$ cup flour
pinch of salt
scant 3 cups dry unsweetened shredded coconut
$^3/_4$ cup sweetened condensed milk
1 teaspoon vanilla extract

1 Preheat the oven to 350°F. Grease 2 cookie sheets.

2 Sift the flour and salt into a bowl. Stir in the coconut.

3 ▲ Pour in the milk. Add the vanilla and stir from the center to make a very thick batter.

4 Drop heaped tablespoonfuls of batter 1 inch apart on the prepared sheets. Bake until golden brown, about 20 minutes. Cool on a rack.

Chocolate Macaroons (top), Coconut Macaroons

Almond Tuiles

MAKES 40

$^1/_3$ cup blanched almonds
generous $^1/_2$ cup superfine sugar
$^1/_4$ cup unsalted butter
2 egg whites
$^1/_3$ cup flour
$^1/_2$ teaspoon vanilla extract
1 cup sliced almonds

1 Grind the blanched almonds with 30ml/2 tablespoons of the sugar in a food processor, blender, or nut grinder. If necessary, grind in batches.

2 Preheat the oven to 425°F. Grease 2 cookie sheets.

3 ▲ Put the butter in a large bowl and mix in the remaining sugar, using a metal spoon. With an electric mixer, cream them together until light and fluffy.

4 Add the egg whites and stir until blended. Sift over the flour and fold in with a metal spoon. Fold in the ground almonds and vanilla extract.

5 ▲ Working in small batches, drop tablespoonfuls of the batter 3 inches apart on one of the prepared sheets. With the back of a spoon, spread out into thin, almost transparent circles about 2$^1/_2$ inches in diameter. Sprinkle each circle with some of the sliced almonds.

6 Bake until the outer edges have browned slightly, about 4 minutes.

7 ▲ Remove from the oven. With a metal spatula, quickly drape the biscuits over a rolling pin to form a curved shape. Transfer to a rack when firm. If the biscuits harden too quickly to shape, reheat them briefly. Repeat the baking and shaping process until the batter is used up. Store in an airtight container.

Florentines

MAKES 36

3 tablespoons butter

¹/₂ cup whipping cream

scant ³/₄ cup superfine sugar

generous 1 cup sliced almonds

¹/₃ cup candied orange peel,
   finely chopped

¹/₄ cup candied cherries, chopped

¹/₂ cup flour, sifted

8 1-ounce squares semisweet chocolate

1 teaspoon vegetable oil

5 Melt the chocolate in the top of a double boiler or in a heatproof bowl set over a pan of hot water. Add the oil and stir to blend.

6 ▲ With a palette knife or metal spatula, spread the smooth underside of the cooled florentines with a thin coating of the melted chocolate.

7 ▼ When the chocolate is about to set, draw a serrated knife across the surface with a slight sawing motion to make wavy lines. Store in an airtight container in a cool place.

1 ▲ Preheat the oven to 350°F. Grease 2 cookie sheets. Melt the butter, cream, and sugar together and slowly bring to a boil. Take off the heat and stir in the almonds, orange peel, cherries, and flour until blended.

3 Drop teaspoonfuls of the batter 1–2 inches apart on the prepared sheets and flatten with a fork.

4 Bake for about 10 minutes until brown at the edges. Remove from the oven and correct the shape while they are hot by quickly pushing in any uneven edges with a knife or a round cookie cutter. If necessary, return to the oven for a few moments to soften. While still hot, use a metal spatula to transfer the florentines to a clean, flat surface.

Nut Lace Wafers

MAKES 18

1/2 cup blanched almonds

1/4 cup (1/2 stick) butter

1/3 cup flour

1/2 cup superfine sugar

2 tablespoons heavy cream

1/2 teaspoon vanilla extract

1 Preheat the oven to 375°F. Grease 1–2 cookie sheets.

2 With a sharp knife, chop the almonds as finely as possible. Alternatively, use a food processor, blender, or nut grinder to chop the nuts very finely.

3 ▼ Melt the butter in a saucepan over low heat. Remove from the heat and stir in the remaining ingredients and the almonds.

4 Drop teaspoonfuls 2½ inches apart on the prepared sheets. Bake until golden, about 5 minutes. Cool on the cookie sheets briefly, just until the wafers are stiff enough to remove.

5 ▲ With a metal spatula, transfer to a rack to cool completely.

~ VARIATION ~

Add 1/4 cup finely chopped candied orange peel to the batter.

Oatmeal Lace Rounds

MAKES 36

11 tablespoons butter or margarine

1¼ cups rolled oats

scant 1 cup soft dark brown sugar

3/4 cup superfine sugar ·

1/3 cup flour

1/4 teaspoon salt

1 egg, lightly beaten

1 teaspoon vanilla extract

1/2 cup pecans or walnuts, finely chopped

1 Preheat the oven to 350°F. Grease 2 cookie sheets.

2 Melt the butter or margarine in a saucepan over low heat. Set aside.

3 In a mixing bowl, combine the oats, brown sugar, superfine sugar, flour, and salt.

4 ▲ Make a well in the center and add the butter or margarine, the egg, and vanilla.

5 ▼ Mix until blended, then stir in the chopped nuts.

6 Drop rounded teaspoonfuls of the mixture about 2 inches apart on the prepared sheets. Bake until lightly browned on the edges and bubbling, 5–8 minutes. Let cool on the sheet for 2 minutes, then transfer to a rack to cool completely.

Nut Lace Wafers (top), Oatmeal Lace Rounds

Raspberry Sandwich Cookies

MAKES 32

1 cup blanched almonds

1½ cups flour

¾ cup (1½ sticks) butter,
  at room temperature

generous ½ cup superfine sugar

grated rind of 1 lemon

1 teaspoon vanilla extract

1 egg white

pinch of salt

¼ cup slivered almonds

1 cup raspberry jam

1 tablespoon fresh lemon juice

1 Place the blanched almonds and 3 tablespoons of the flour in a food processor, blender, or nut grinder and process until finely ground. Set aside.

2 With an electric mixer, cream the butter and sugar together until light and fluffy. Stir in the lemon rind and vanilla. Add the ground almonds and remaining flour, and mix well to form a dough. Gather into a ball, wrap in wax paper, and refrigerate for at least 1 hour.

3 Preheat the oven to 325°F. Line 2 cookie sheets with wax paper.

4 Divide the dough into 4 equal parts. Working with one section of the dough at a time, roll out to a thickness of ⅛ inch on a lightly floured surface. With a 2½-inch fluted pastry cutter, stamp out circles. Gather the dough scraps, roll out, and stamp out more circles. Repeat with the remaining dough.

5 ▲ Using a ¾-inch piping tip or pastry cutter, stamp out the centers from half the circles. Place the dough rings and circles 1 inch apart on the prepared sheets.

6 ▲ Whisk the egg white with the salt until just frothy. Chop the slivered almonds. Brush only the cookie rings with the egg white, then sprinkle over the almonds. Bake until very lightly browned, 12–15 minutes. Let cool for a few minutes on the sheets before transferring to a rack.

7 ▲ In a saucepan, melt the jam with the lemon juice until it comes to a simmer. Brush the jam over the cookie circles and sandwich together with the rings. Store in an airtight container with sheets of wax paper between the layers.

Brandy Snaps

Makes 18

$^1/_4$ cup butter, at room temperature
$^3/_4$ cup superfine sugar
1 tablespoon light corn syrup
$^1/_3$ cup flour
$^1/_2$ teaspoon ground ginger
For the filling
1 cup whipping cream
2 tablespoons brandy

1 With an electric mixer, cream together the butter and sugar until light and fluffy, then beat in the corn syrup. Sift over the flour and ginger and mix to a rough dough.

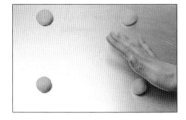

2 ▲ Transfer the dough to a work surface and knead until smooth. Cover and refrigerate for 30 minutes.

3 Preheat the oven to 375°F. Grease a cookie sheet.

4 ▲ Working in batches of 4, form the dough into walnut-size balls. Place far apart on the prepared sheet and flatten slightly. Bake until golden and bubbling, about 10 minutes.

5 ▼ Remove from the oven and let cool a few moments. Working quickly, slide a metal spatula under each one, turn over, and wrap around the handle of a wooden spoon (have four spoons ready). If they firm up too quickly, reheat for a few seconds to soften. When firm, slide the snaps off and place on a rack to cool.

6 ▲ When all the brandy snaps are cool, prepare the filling. Whip the cream and brandy until soft peaks form. Fill a pastry bag with the brandy cream. Pipe into each end of the brandy snaps just before serving.

Shortbread

MAKES 8

11 tablespoons unsalted butter,
   at room temperature

$^{1}/_{2}$ cup superfine sugar

$1^{2}/_{3}$ cups flour

$^{1}/_{2}$ cup rice flour

$^{1}/_{4}$ teaspoon baking powder

pinch of salt

1 Preheat the oven to 325°F. Grease a shallow 8-inch cake pan, preferably with a removable base.

2 With an electric mixer, cream the butter and sugar together until light and fluffy. Sift over the flours, baking powder, and salt and mix well.

3 ▲ Press the dough neatly into the prepared pan, smoothing the surface with the back of a spoon.

4 Prick all over with a fork, then score into 8 equal wedges.

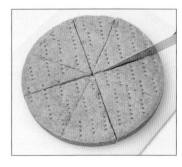

5 ▲ Bake until golden, 40–45 minutes. Leave in the pan until cool enough to handle, then unmold and recut the wedges while still hot. Let cool. Store in an airtight container.

Oatmeal Wedges

MAKES 8

$^{1}/_{4}$ cup butter

1 tablespoon dark corn syrup

$^{1}/_{3}$ cup soft dark brown sugar

1 cup quick-cooking oats

pinch of salt

1 ▲ Preheat the oven to 350°F. Line an 8-inch shallow cake pan with wax paper and grease the paper.

2 ▼ Place the butter, corn syrup, and sugar in a saucepan over low heat. Cook, stirring, until melted and combined.

~ VARIATION ~

If wished, add 1 teaspoon ground ginger to the melted butter.

3 ▲ Remove from the heat and add the oats and salt. Stir to blend.

4 Spoon into the prepared pan and smooth the surface. Place in the center of the oven and bake until golden brown, 20–25 minutes. Leave in the pan until cool enough to handle, then unmold and cut into wedges while still hot.

Shortbread (top), Oatmeal Wedges

Chocolate Delights

MAKES 50

1 1-ounce square semisweet chocolate
1 1-ounce square bittersweet cooking chocolate
2 cups flour
1/2 teaspoon salt
1 cup (2 sticks) unsalted butter, at room temperature
generous 1 cup superfine sugar
2 eggs
1 teaspoon vanilla extract
1 cup finely chopped walnuts

1 Melt the chocolates in the top of a double boiler, or in a heatproof bowl set over a saucepan of gently simmering water. Set aside.

2 ▼ In a small bowl, sift together the flour and salt. Set aside.

3 With an electric mixer, cream the butter until soft. Add the sugar and continue beating until the mixture is light and fluffy.

4 Mix the eggs and vanilla, then gradually stir into the butter mixture.

5 ▲ Stir in the chocolate, then the flour. Stir in the nuts.

6 ▲ Divide the dough into 4 equal parts, and roll each into 2-inch diameter logs. Wrap tightly in foil and refrigerate or freeze until firm.

7 Preheat the oven to 375°F. Grease 2 cookie sheets.

8 With a sharp knife, cut the logs into 1/4-inch slices. Place the rounds on the prepared sheets and bake until lightly colored, about 10 minutes. Transfer to a rack to cool.

~ VARIATION ~

For two-tone cookies, melt only half the chocolate. Combine all the ingredients, except the chocolate, as above. Divide the mixture in half. Add the chocolate to one half. Roll out the plain dough on a flat sheet. Roll out the chocolate mixture, place on top of the plain one and roll up. Wrap, slice, and bake as described.

Cinnamon Treats

MAKES 50

2¹/₄ cups flour
¹/₂ teaspoon salt
2 teaspoons ground cinnamon
1 cup (2 sticks) unsalted butter, at room temperature
generous 1 cup superfine sugar
2 eggs
1 teaspoon vanilla extract

1 In a bowl, sift together the flour, salt, and cinnamon. Set aside.

2 ▲ With an electric mixer, cream the butter until soft. Add the sugar and continue beating until the mixture is light and fluffy.

3 Beat the eggs and vanilla, then gradually stir into the butter mixture.

4 ▲ Stir in the dry ingredients.

5 ▲ Divide the dough into 4 equal parts, then roll each into 2-inch diameter logs. Wrap tightly in foil and refrigerate or freeze until firm.

6 Preheat the oven to 375°F. Grease 2 cookie sheets.

7 ▼ With a sharp knife, cut the logs into ¹/₄-inch slices. Place the rounds on the prepared sheets and bake until lightly colored, about 10 minutes. With a metal spatula, transfer to a rack to cool.

Peanut Butter Cookies

MAKES 24

1¹/₄ cups flour
¹/₂ teaspoon baking soda
¹/₂ teaspoon salt
¹/₂ cup (1 stick) butter, at room temperature
³/₄ cup soft light brown sugar
1 egg
1 teaspoon vanilla extract
1¹/₄ cups crunchy peanut butter

1 Sift together the flour, baking soda, and salt and set aside.

2 With an electric mixer, cream the butter and sugar together until light and fluffy.

3 In another bowl, mix together the egg and vanilla, then gradually beat into the butter mixture.

4 ▲ Stir in the peanut butter and blend thoroughly. Stir in the dry ingredients. Refrigerate for at least 30 minutes, or until firm.

5 Preheat the oven to 350°F. Grease 2 cookie sheets.

6 Spoon out rounded teaspoonfuls of the dough and roll into balls.

7 ▲ Place the balls on the prepared sheets and press flat with a fork into circles about 2¹/₂ inches in diameter, making a criss-cross pattern. Bake until lightly colored, 12–15 minutes. Transfer to a rack to cool.

~ VARIATION ~

Add ¹/₂ cup peanuts, coarsely chopped, with the peanut butter.

Chocolate Chip Cookies

MAKES 24

¹/₂ cup (1 stick) butter or margarine, at room temperature
¹/₄ cup superfine sugar
scant ¹/₂ cup soft dark brown sugar
1 egg
¹/₂ teaspoon vanilla extract
1¹/₂ cups flour
¹/₂ teaspoon baking soda
pinch of salt
6 ounces chocolate chips
¹/₃ cup walnuts, chopped

1 Preheat the oven to 350°F. Grease 2 large cookie sheets.

2 ▼ With an electric mixer, cream the butter or margarine and two sugars together until light and fluffy.

3 In another bowl, mix the egg and vanilla, then gradually beat into the butter mixture. Sift over the flour, baking soda, and salt. Stir to blend.

4 ▲ Add the chocolate chips and walnuts, and mix to combine well.

5 Place heaped teaspoonfuls of the dough 2 inches apart on the prepared sheets. Bake until lightly colored, 10–15 minutes. With a metal spatula, transfer to a rack to cool.

Peanut Butter Cookies (top), Chocolate Chip Cookies

Salted Peanut Cookies

Makes 70

3 cups flour

¹/₂ teaspoon baking soda

¹/₂ cup (1 stick) butter,
    at room temperature

¹/₂ cup (1 stick) margarine,
    at room temperature

generous 1 cup soft light brown sugar

2 eggs

2 teaspoons vanilla extract

1¹/₃ cups salted peanuts

1 Preheat the oven to 375°F. Lightly
grease 2 cookie sheets.

2 Sift together the flour and baking
soda. Set aside.

3 ▲ Cream the butter, margarine,
and sugar until fluffy. Beat in the eggs
and vanilla. Fold in the flour mixture.

4 ▲ Stir the peanuts into the butter
mixture until evenly combined.

5 ▲ Drop teaspoonfuls 2 inches apart
on the sheets. Flatten with the greased
bottom of a glass dipped in sugar.

6 Bake for about 10 minutes, until
lightly colored. With a metal spatula,
transfer to a wire rack to cool.

> **~ VARIATION ~**
>
> To make Cashew Cookies,
> substitute an equal amount of
> salted cashew nuts for the
> peanuts, and add as above.

Cheddar Pennies

Makes 20

¹/₄ cup (¹/₂ stick) butter,
    at room temperature

1¹/₃ cups grated Cheddar cheese

¹/₃ cup flour

pinch of salt

pinch of chilli powder

1 Put the butter in a large bowl and
cut into 1-inch cubes. With an
electric mixer, cream the butter until
soft and fluffy.

2 ▲ Stir in the cheese, flour, salt,
and chilli. Gather to form a dough.

3 Transfer to a lightly flored surface.
Shape into a cylinder about 1¹/₄ inches
in diameter. Wrap in wax paper and
refrigerate for 1–2 hours.

4 Preheat the oven to 350°F. Grease
1–2 cookie sheets.

5 ▲ Slice the dough into ¹/₄-inch
thick rounds and place on the sheets.
Bake until golden, about 15 minutes.
Transfer to a wire rack to cool.

Salted Peanut Cookies (top), Cheddar Pennies

Chocolate Chip Brownies

MAKES 24

4 1-ounce squares semisweet chocolate

$^1/_2$ cup (1 stick) butter

3 eggs

1 cup superfine sugar

$^1/_2$ teaspoon vanilla extract

pinch of salt

1$^1/_4$ cups flour

6 ounces chocolate chips

1 ▼ Preheat the oven to 350°F. Line the bottom and sides of a 13- × 9-inch pan with wax paper and grease.

2 ▲ Melt the chocolate and butter in the top of a double boiler, or in a heatproof bowl set over a pan of gently simmering water.

3 ▲ Beat together the eggs, sugar, vanilla, and salt. Stir in the chocolate mixture. Sift over the flour and fold in. Add the chocolate chips.

4 ▲ Pour the batter into the prepared pan and spread evenly. Bake until just set, about 30 minutes. Do not overbake; the brownies should be slightly moist inside. Cool in the pan.

5 To unmold, run a knife all around the edge and invert onto a cookie sheet. Remove the paper. Place another sheet on top and invert again so the brownies are right-side up. Cut into squares for serving.

Marbled Brownies

MAKES 24

8 1-ounce squares semisweet chocolate
6 tablespoons butter
4 eggs
generous 1^1/$_2$ cups superfine sugar
1^1/$_4$ cups flour
^{1}/$_2$ teaspoon salt
1 teaspoon baking powder
2 teaspoons vanilla extract
^{2}/$_3$ cups walnuts, chopped
FOR THE PLAIN BATTER
^{1}/$_4$ cup (^{1}/$_2$ stick) butter, at room temperature
^{3}/$_4$ cup cream cheese
^{1}/$_2$ cup superfine sugar
2 eggs
^{1}/$_4$ cup flour
1 teaspoon vanilla extract

1 Preheat the oven to 350°F. Line the bottom and sides of a 13- × 9-inch pan with wax paper and grease.

2 Melt the chocolate and butter over very low heat, stirring constantly. Set aside to cool.

3 Meanwhile, beat the eggs until light and fluffy. Gradually add the sugar and continue beating until blended. Sift over the flour, salt, and baking powder and fold to combine.

4 ▲ Stir in the cooled chocolate mixture. Add the vanilla and walnuts. Measure and set aside 2 cups of the chocolate batter.

5 ▲ For the plain batter, cream the butter and cream cheese with an electric mixer.

6 Add the sugar and continue beating until blended. Beat in the eggs, flour, and vanilla.

7 Spread the unmeasured chocolate batter in the pan. Pour over the plain batter. Drop spoonfuls of the reserved chocolate batter on top.

8 ▲ With a metal spatula, swirl the batters to marble. Do not blend completely. Bake until just set, about 35–40 minutes. Unmold when cool and cut into squares for serving.

Nutty Chocolate Squares

2 eggs

2 teaspoons vanilla extract

pinch of salt

1 cup pecans, coarsely chopped

1/2 cup flour

1/4 cup superfine sugar

1/2 cup dark corn syrup

3 1-ounce squares semisweet chocolate, finely chopped

3 tablespoons butter

16 pecan halves, for decorating

1 Preheat the oven to 325°F. Line the bottom and sides of an 8-inch square baking pan with wax paper and grease lightly.

2 ▼ Whisk together the eggs, vanilla, and salt. In another bowl, mix together the pecans and flour. Set both aside.

3 In a saucepan, bring the sugar and corn syrup to a boil. Remove from the heat and stir in the chocolate and butter and blend thoroughly with a wooden spoon.

4 ▲ Mix in the beaten eggs, then fold in the pecan mixture.

5 Pour the batter into the prepared pan and bake until set, about 35 minutes. Cool in the tin for 10 minutes before unmolding. Cut into 2-inch squares and press pecan halves into the tops while warm. Cool completely on a rack.

Raisin Brownies

1/2 cup (1 stick) butter or margarine

1/2 cup unsweetened cocoa powder

2 eggs

generous 1 cup superfine sugar

1 teaspoon vanilla extract

1/3 cup flour

3/4 cup chopped walnuts

2/3 cup raisins

1 Preheat the oven to 350°F. Line the bottom and sides of an 8-inch square baking pan with wax paper and grease the paper.

2 ▼ Gently melt the butter or margarine in a small saucepan. Remove from the heat and stir in the cocoa powder.

3 With an electric mixer, beat the eggs, sugar, and vanilla together until light. Add the cocoa mixture and stir to blend.

4 ▲ Sift the flour over the cocoa mixture and gently fold in. Add the walnuts and raisins and scrape the batter into the prepared tin.

5 Bake in the center of the oven for 30 minutes. Do not overbake. Leave in the tin to cool before cutting into 2-inch squares and removing. The brownies should be soft and moist.

Nutty Chocolate Squares (top), Raisin Brownies

Chocolate Walnut Bars

MAKES 24

$^1/_3$ cup walnuts

$^1/_4$ cup superfine sugar

1 cup flour, sifted

6 tablespoons cold unsalted butter, cut into pieces

FOR THE TOPPING

2 tablespoons unsalted butter

6 tablespoons water

$^1/_4$ cup unsweetened cocoa powder

$^1/_2$ cup superfine sugar

1 teaspoon vanilla extract

pinch of salt

2 eggs

confectioners' sugar, for dusting

1 Preheat the oven to 350°F. Grease the bottom and sides of an 8-inch square baking pan.

2 ▼ Grind the walnuts with a few tablespoons of the sugar in a food processor, blender, or nut grinder.

3 In a bowl, combine the ground walnuts, remaining sugar, and flour. With a pastry blender, rub in the butter until the mixture resembles coarse crumbs. Alternatively, combine all the ingredients in a food processor and process until the mixture resembles coarse crumbs.

4 ▲ Pat the walnut mixture into the base of the prepared pan in an even layer. Bake for 25 minutes.

5 ▲ Meanwhile, for the topping, melt the butter with the water. Whisk in the cocoa and sugar. Remove the pan from the heat, stir in the vanilla and salt and let cool for 5 minutes. Whisk in the eggs until blended.

6 ▲ Pour the topping over the crust when baked.

7 Return to the oven and bake until set, about 20 minutes. Set the tin on a rack to cool. Cut into $2^1/_2$- × 1-inch bars and dust with confectioners' sugar. Store in the refrigerator.

Pecan Squares

MAKES 36

2 cups flour
pinch of salt
generous $^1/_2$ cup sugar
1 cup (2 sticks) cold butter or margarine, cut into pieces
1 egg
finely grated rind of 1 lemon
FOR THE TOPPING
$^3/_4$ cup (1$^1/_2$ sticks) butter
scant $^1/_3$ cup honey
$^1/_4$ cup sugar
$^1/_2$ cup soft dark brown sugar
5 tablespoons whipping cream
2$^2/_3$ cups pecan halves

1 Preheat the oven to 375°F. Lightly grease a 15$^1/_2$- × 10$^1/_2$- × 1-inch jelly-roll pan.

2 ▲ Sift the flour and salt into a mixing bowl. Stir in the sugar. With a pastry blender, cut in the butter or margarine until the mixture resembles coarse crumbs. Add the egg and lemon rind and blend with a fork until the mixture just holds together.

3 ▼ Spoon the mixture into the prepared pan. With floured fingertips, press into an even layer. Prick the pastry all over with a fork and refrigerate for 10 minutes.

4 Bake the pastry crust for 15 minutes. Remove the pan from the oven, but keep the oven on while making the topping.

5 ▲ To make the topping, melt the butter, honey, and both sugars. Bring to a boil. Boil, without stirring, for 2 minutes. Off the heat, stir in the cream and pecan halves. Pour over the crust, return to the oven and bake for 25 minutes. Let cool.

6 When cool, run a knife around the edge. Invert onto a baking sheet, place another sheet on top and invert again. Dip a sharp knife into very hot water and cut into squares for serving.

Fig Bars

Makes 48

2 cups dried figs

3 eggs

scant 1 cup superfine sugar

²/₃ cup flour

1 teaspoon baking powder

¹/₂ teaspoon ground cinnamon

¹/₄ teaspoon ground cloves

¹/₄ teaspoon freshly grated nutmeg

¹/₄ teaspoon salt

³/₄ cup finely chopped walnuts

2 tablespoons brandy or cognac

confectioners' sugar, for dusting

1 Preheat the oven to 325°F. Line a 12- × 8- × 1¹/₂-inch pan with wax paper and grease the paper.

2 ▲ With a sharp knife, chop the figs roughly. Set aside.

3 In a bowl, whisk the eggs and sugar until well blended. In another bowl, sift together the dry ingredients, then fold into the egg mixture in several batches.

4 ▼ Stir in the figs, walnuts, and brandy or cognac.

5 Scrape the mixture into the prepared pan and bake until the top is firm and brown, 35–40 minutes. It should still be soft underneath.

6 Cool in the pan for 5 minutes, then unmold and transfer to a sheet of wax paper lightly sprinkled with confectioners' sugar. Cut into bars.

Lemon Bars

Makes 36

¹/₂ cup confectioners' sugar

1¹/₂ cups flour

¹/₂ teaspoon salt

³/₄ cup (1¹/₂ sticks) butter, cut in small pieces

For the topping

4 eggs

1³/₄ cups superfine sugar

grated rind of 1 lemon

¹/₂ cup fresh lemon juice

³/₄ cup whipping cream

confectioners' sugar, for dusting

1 Preheat the oven to 325°F.

2 Grease a 13- × 9-inch baking pan.

3 Sift the sugar, flour, and salt into a bowl. With a pastry blender, cut in the butter until the mixture resembles coarse crumbs.

4 ▲ Press the mixture into the base of the prepared pan. Bake until golden brown, about 20 minutes.

5 Meanwhile, for the topping, whisk the eggs and sugar together until blended. Add the lemon rind and juice and mix well.

6 ▲ Lightly whip the cream and fold into the egg mixture. Pour over the still-warm crust, return to the oven, and bake until set, about 40 minutes.

7 Cool completely before cutting into bars. Dust with confectioners' sugar.

Fig Bars (top), Lemon Bars

Apricot Specials

generous ⅓ cup soft light brown sugar

⅔ cup flour

6 tablespoons cold unsalted butter,
  cut in pieces

For the topping

generous ½ cup dried apricots

1 cup water

grated rind of 1 lemon

5 tablespoons superfine sugar

2 teaspoons cornstarch

½ cup chopped walnuts

1 Preheat the oven to 350°F.

2 ▲ In a bowl, combine the brown sugar and flour. With a pastry blender, cut in the butter until the mixture resembles coarse crumbs.

3 ▲ Transfer to an 8-inch square baking pan and press level. Bake for 15 minutes. Remove from the oven but leave the oven on.

4 Meanwhile, for the topping, combine the apricots and water in a saucepan and simmer until soft, about 10 minutes. Strain the liquid and reserve. Chop the apricots.

5 ▲ Return the apricots to the saucepan and add the lemon rind, superfine sugar, cornstarch, and 4 tablespoons of the soaking liquid. Cook for 1 minute.

6 ▲ Cool slightly before spreading the topping over the base. Sprinkle over the walnuts and continue baking for 20 minutes more. Leave to cool in the pan before cutting into bars.

Almond-topped Squares

MAKES 18

²/₃ cup butter, at room temperature

¹/₄ cup sugar

1 egg yolk

grated rind and juice of ¹/₂ lemon

¹/₂ teaspoon vanilla extract

2 tablespoons whipping cream

1 cup flour

FOR THE TOPPING

generous 1 cup sugar

³/₄ cup sliced almonds

4 egg whites

¹/₂ teaspoon ground ginger

¹/₂ teaspoon ground cinnamon

1 ▲ Preheat the oven to 375°F. Line a 13- × 9-inch jelly-roll pan with wax paper and grease the paper.

2 With an electric mixer, cream the butter and sugar until light and fluffy. Beat in the egg yolk, lemon rind and juice, vanilla extract, and cream.

3 ▲ Gradually stir in the flour until mixed. Gather into a ball of dough.

4 With lightly floured fingers, press the dough into the pan in a thin even layer. Bake for 15 minutes. Remove from the oven but leave the oven on.

5 ▲ To make the topping, combine all the ingredients in a heavy saucepan. Cook, stirring until the mixture comes to a boil.

6 Continue boiling until just golden, about 1 minute. Pour over the dough, spreading it evenly.

7 ▲ Return to the oven and bake until golden, about 45 minutes. Remove and score into bars or squares. Cool completely before cutting into squares and serving.

Spiced Raisin Bars

MAKES 30

1 cup flour

1¹/₂ teaspoons baking powder

1 teaspoon ground cinnamon

¹/₂ teaspoon freshly grated nutmeg

¹/₄ teaspoon ground cloves

¹/₄ teaspoon ground allspice

1¹/₂ cups raisins

¹/₂ cup (1 stick) butter or margarine,
    at room temperature

¹/₂ cup sugar

2 eggs

scant ¹/₂ cup molasses

¹/₃ cup walnuts, chopped

1 Preheat the oven to 350°F. Line the bottom and sides of a 13- × 9-inch pan with wax paper and grease.

2 Sift together the flour, baking powder, and spices.

3 ▲ Place the raisins in another bowl and toss with a few tablespoons of the flour mixture.

4 ▲ With an electric mixer, cream the butter or margarine and sugar together until light and fluffy. Beat in the eggs, 1 at a time, then the molasses. Stir in the flour mixture, raisins, and walnuts.

5 Spread evenly in the pan. Bake until just set, 15–18 minutes. Let cool in the pan before cutting into squares.

Toffee Meringue Bars

MAKES 12

¹/₄ cup (¹/₂ stick) butter

scant 1 cup soft dark brown sugar

1 egg

¹/₂ teaspoon vanilla extract

9 tablespoons flour

¹/₂ teaspoon salt

¹/₄ teaspoon freshly grated nutmeg

FOR THE TOPPING

1 egg white

pinch of salt

1 tablespoon light corn syrup

¹/₂ cup superfine sugar

¹/₃ cup walnuts, finely chopped

1 ▲ Combine the butter and brown sugar in a saucepan and heat until bubbling. Set aside to cool.

2 Preheat the oven to 350°F. Line the bottom and sides of an 8-inch square cake pan with wax paper and grease.

3 Beat the egg and vanilla into the cooled sugar mixture. Sift over the flour, salt, and nutmeg, and fold in. Spread in the bottom of the tin.

4 ▲ For the topping, beat the egg white with the salt until it holds soft peaks. Beat in the corn syrup, then the sugar and continue beating until the mixture holds stiff peaks. Fold in the nuts and spread on top. Bake for 30 minutes. Cut into bars when cool.

Spiced Raisin Bars (top), Toffee Meringue Bars

MUFFINS & QUICK BREADS

EASY TO MAKE AND SATISFYING TO EAT, THESE MUFFINS AND QUICK BREADS WILL FILL THE HOUSE WITH HOMEY SCENTS AND LURE YOUR FAMILY AND FRIENDS TO LINGER OVER BREAKFAST, COFFEE, OR TEA – AND THEY ARE GREAT FOR SNACKS OR LUNCH.

Blueberry Muffins

MAKES 12

1²/³ cups flour

5 tablespoons superfine sugar

2 teaspoons baking powder

¹/₄ teaspoon salt

2 eggs

¹/₄ cup (¹/₂ stick) butter, melted

³/₄ cup milk

1 teaspoon vanilla extract

1 teaspoon grated lemon rind

1¹/₂ cups fresh blueberries

1 Preheat the oven to 400°F/.

2 ▼ Grease a 12-cup muffin pan or use paper liners.

3 ▲ Sift the flour, sugar, baking powder, and salt into a bowl.

4 In another bowl, whisk the eggs until blended. Add the melted butter, milk, vanilla, and lemon rind and stir to combine.

5 Make a well in the dry ingredients and pour in the egg mixture. With a large metal spoon, stir just until the flour is moistened, not until smooth.

6 ▲ Fold in the blueberries.

7 ▲ Spoon the batter into the cups, leaving room for the muffins to rise.

8 Bake until the tops spring back when touched lightly, 20–25 minutes. Let cool in the pan for 5 minutes before unmolding.

Apple and Cranberry Muffins

MAKES 12

1/4 cup (1/2 stick) butter or margarine
1 egg
1/2 cup superfine sugar
grated rind of 1 large orange
1/2 cup freshly squeezed orange juice
1 1/4 cups flour
1 teaspoon baking powder
1/2 teaspoon baking soda
1 teaspoon ground cinnamon
1/2 teaspoon freshly grated nutmeg
1/2 teaspoon ground allspice
1/4 teaspoon ground ginger
1/4 teaspoon salt
1–2 eating apples
1 1/2 cups cranberries
1/3 cup walnuts, chopped
confectioners' sugar, for dusting (optional)

1 Preheat the oven to 350°F. Grease a 12-cup muffin pan or use paper cases.

2 Melt the butter or margarine over gentle heat. Set aside to cool.

3 ▲ Place the egg in a mixing bowl and whisk lightly. Add the melted butter or margarine and whisk to combine.

4 Add the sugar, orange rind, and juice. Whisk to blend, then set aside.

5 In a large bowl, sift together the flour, baking powder, baking soda, cinnamon, nutmeg, allspice, ginger, and salt. Set aside.

6 ▲ Quarter, core, and peel the apples. With a sharp knife, chop in a coarse dice to obtain 1½ cups.

7 Make a well in the dry ingredients and pour in the egg mixture. With a spoon, stir until just blended.

8 ▲ Add the apples, cranberries, and walnuts and stir to blend.

9 Fill the cups three-quarters full and bake until the tops spring back when touched lightly, 25–30 minutes. Transfer to a rack to cool. Dust with confectioners' sugar, if desired.

Chocolate Chip Muffins

MAKES 10

1/2 cup (1 stick) butter or margarine, at room temperature
5 tablespoons superfine sugar
2 tablespoons soft dark brown sugar
2 eggs, at room temperature
scant 2 cups flour
1 teaspoon baking powder
1/2 cup milk
6 ounces semisweet chocolate chips

1 Preheat the oven to 375°F. Grease 10 muffin cups or use paper liners.

2 ▼ With an electric mixer, cream the butter or margarine until soft. Add both sugars and beat until light and fluffy. Beat in the eggs, 1 at a time.

3 Sift together the flour and baking powder, twice. Fold into the butter mixture, alternating with the milk.

4 ▲ Divide half the mixture between the muffin cups. Sprinkle several chocolate chips on top, then cover with a spoonful of the batter. To ensure even baking, half-fill any empty cups with water.

5 Bake until lightly colored, about 25 minutes. Let stand 5 minutes before unmolding.

Chocolate Walnut Muffins

MAKES 12

3/4 cup (1 1/2 sticks) unsalted butter
5 1-ounce squares semisweet chocolate
1 cup superfine sugar
1/4 cup soft dark brown sugar
4 eggs
1 teaspoon vanilla extract
1/4 teaspoon almond extract
3/4 cup flour
1 tablespoon unsweetened cocoa powder
2/3 cup walnuts, chopped

1 Preheat the oven to 350°F. Grease a 12-cup muffin pan or use paper liners.

2 ▼ Melt the butter with the chocolate in the top of a double boiler or in a heatproof bowl set over a saucepan of hot water. Transfer to a large mixing bowl.

3 Stir both the sugars into the chocolate mixture. Mix in the eggs, 1 at a time, then add the vanilla and almond extracts.

4 Sift over the flour and cocoa.

5 ▲ Fold in and stir in the walnuts.

6 Fill the prepared cups almost to the top and bake until a cake tester inserted in the center barely comes out clean, 30–35 minutes. Let stand 5 minutes before unmolding onto a rack to cool completely.

Chocolate Chip Muffins (top), Chocolate Walnut Muffins

Raisin Bran Muffins

MAKES 15

¹/₄ cup (¹/₂ stick) butter or margarine

¹/₃ cup flour

¹/₂ cup whole-wheat flour

1¹/₂ teaspoons baking soda

pinch of salt

1 teaspoon ground cinnamon

¹/₄ cup bran

generous ¹/₂ cup raisins

5 tablespoons soft dark brown sugar

¹/₄ cup superfine sugar

1 egg

1 cup buttermilk

juice of ¹/₂ lemon

1 Preheat the oven to 400°F. Grease 15 muffin cups or use paper liners.

2 ▲ Place the butter or margarine in a saucepan and melt over gentle heat. Set aside.

3 In a mixing bowl, sift together the flours, baking soda, salt, and cinnamon.

4 ▲ Add the bran, raisins, and sugars and stir until blended.

5 In another bowl, mix together the egg, buttermilk, lemon juice, and melted butter.

6 ▲ Add the buttermilk mixture to the dry ingredients and stir lightly and quickly until just moistened; do not mix until smooth.

7 ▲ Spoon the batter into the prepared muffin cups, filling them almost to the top. For even baking, half-fill any empty cups with water.

8 Bake until golden, 15–20 minutes. Serve warm or at room temperature.

Raspberry Crumble Muffins

MAKES 12

1¹/₂ cups flour
¹/₄ cup superfine sugar
¹/₄ cup soft light brown sugar
2 teaspoons baking powder
pinch of salt
1 teaspoon ground cinnamon
¹/₂ cup (1 stick) butter, melted
1 egg
¹/₂ cup milk
scant 1 cup fresh raspberries
grated rind of 1 lemon
FOR THE CRUMBLE TOPPING
¹/₄ cup finely chopped pecans or walnuts
¹/₄ cup soft dark brown sugar
3 tablespoons flour
1 teaspoon ground cinnamon
3 tablespoons butter, melted

1 Preheat the oven to 350°F. Lightly grease a 12-cup muffin pan or use paper liners.

2 Sift the flour into a bowl. Add the sugars, baking powder, salt, and cinnamon and stir to blend.

3 ▲ Make a well in the center. Place the butter, egg, and milk in the well and mix until just combined. Stir in the raspberries and lemon rind. Spoon the batter into the prepared muffin cups, filling them almost to the top. Half-fill any empty cups with water.

4 ▼ For the crumble topping, mix the nuts, dark brown sugar, flour, and cinnamon in a bowl. Add the melted butter and stir to blend.

5 ▲ Spoon some of the crumble over each muffin. Bake until browned, about 25 minutes. Transfer to a rack to cool slightly. Serve warm.

Carrot Muffins

MAKES 12

³/4 cup margarine, at room temperature

generous ¹/3 cup soft dark brown sugar

1 egg, at room temperature

1 tablespoon water

1 cup grated carrots

1¹/4 cups flour

1 teaspoon baking powder

¹/2 teaspoon baking soda

1 teaspoon ground cinnamon

¹/4 teaspoon freshly grated nutmeg

¹/2 teaspoon salt

1 Preheat the oven to 350°F. Grease a 12-cup muffin pan or use paper liners.

2 With an electric mixer, cream the margarine and sugar until light and fluffy. Beat in the egg and water.

3 ▲ Stir in the carrots.

4 Sift over the flour, baking powder, baking soda, cinnamon, nutmeg, and salt. Stir to blend.

5 ▼ Spoon the batter into the prepared muffin cups, filling them almost to the top. Bake until the tops spring back when touched lightly, about 35 minutes. Let stand about 10 minutes before transferring to a rack.

Dried Cherry Muffins

MAKES 16

1 cup plain yogurt

³/4 cup dried cherries

¹/2 cup (¹/4 stick) butter, at room temperature

scant 1 cup superfine sugar

2 eggs, at room temperature

1 teaspoon vanilla extract

1³/4 cups flour

2 teaspoons baking powder

1 teaspoon baking soda

pinch of salt

1 In a mixing bowl, combine the yogurt and cherries. Cover and let stand 30 minutes.

2 Preheat the oven to 350°F. Grease 16 muffin cups or use paper liners.

3 With an electric mixer, cream the butter and sugar together until light and fluffy.

4 ▼ Add the eggs, 1 at a time, beating well after each addition. Add the vanilla and the cherry mixture and stir to blend. Set aside.

5 ▲ In another bowl, sift together the flour, baking powder, baking soda, and salt. Fold into the cherry mixture in 3 batches; do not overmix

6 Fill the prepared cups two-thirds full. For even baking, half-fill any empty cups with water. Bake until the tops spring back when touched lightly, about 20 minutes. Transfer to a rack to cool.

Carrot Muffins (top), Dried Cherry Muffins

Oatmeal Buttermilk Muffins

Makes 12

scant 1 cup rolled oats

1 cup buttermilk

¹/₂ cup (1 stick) butter,
  at room temperature

generous ¹/₃ cup soft dark brown sugar

1 egg, at room temperature

1 cup flour

1 teaspoon baking powder

¹/₂ teaspoon baking soda

¹/₄ teaspoon salt

2 tablespoons raisins

1 ▲ In a bowl, combine the oats and buttermilk and let soak for 1 hour.

2 ▲ Lightly grease a 12-cup muffin pan or use paper liners.

3 ▲ Preheat the oven to 400°F. With an electric mixer, cream the butter and sugar until light and fluffy. Beat in the egg.

4 In another bowl, sift together the flour, baking powder, baking soda, and salt. Stir into the butter mixture, alternating with the oat mixture. Fold in the raisins. Do not overmix.

5 Fill the prepared cups two-thirds full. Bake until a cake tester inserted in the center comes out clean, 20–25 minutes. Transfer to a rack to cool.

> **~ COOK'S TIP ~**
>
> If buttermilk is not available, add 1 teaspoon lemon juice or vinegar to 1 cup milk. Let the mixture stand for a few minutes to curdle.

Pumpkin Muffins

Makes 14

¹/₂ cup (1 stick) butter or margarine,
  at room temperature

²/₃ cup soft dark brown sugar

4 tablespoons molasses

1 egg, at room temperature, beaten

1 cup cooked or canned pumpkin (about
  8 ounces)

2 cups flour

¹/₄ teaspoon salt

1 teaspoon baking soda

1¹/₂ teaspoons ground cinnamon

1 teaspoon freshly grated nutmeg

2 tablespoons currants or raisins

1 Preheat the oven to 400°F. Grease 14 muffin cups or use paper liners.

2 With an electric mixer, cream the butter or margarine until soft. Add the sugar and molasses and beat until light and fluffy.

3 ▲ Add the egg and pumpkin and stir until well blended.

4 Sift over the flour, salt, baking soda, cinnamon, and nutmeg. Fold just enough to blend; do not overmix.

5 ▼ Fold in the currants or raisins.

6 Spoon the batter into the prepared muffin cups, filling them three-quarters full. For even baking, half-fill any empty cups with water.

7 Bake until the tops spring back when touched lightly, 12–15 minutes. Serve warm or cold.

Oatmeal Buttermilk Muffins (top), Pumpkin Muffins

Prune Muffins

MAKES 12

1 egg

1 cup milk

$^1\!/_2$ cup vegetable oil

$^1\!/_4$ cup superfine sugar

2 tablespoons soft dark brown sugar

$2^1\!/_2$ cups flour

2 teaspoons baking powder

$^1\!/_2$ teaspoon salt

$^1\!/_4$ teaspoon grated nutmeg

$^1\!/_2$ cup cooked pitted prunes, chopped

1 Preheat the oven to 400°F. Grease a 12-cup muffin pan or use paper liners.

2 Break the egg into a mixing bowl and beat with a fork. Beat in the milk and oil.

3 ▼ Stir in the sugars. Set aside.

4 Sift the flour, baking powder, salt, and nutmeg into a mixing bowl. Make a well in the center, pour in the egg mixture and stir until moistened. Do not overmix; the batter should be slightly lumpy.

5 ▲ Fold in the prunes.

6 Fill the prepared cups two-thirds full. For even baking, half-fill any empty cups with water. Bake the muffins until golden brown, about 20 minutes. Let stand 10 minutes before unmolding. Serve warm or at room temperature.

Yogurt and Honey Muffins

MAKES 12

$^1\!/_4$ cup ($^1\!/_2$ stick) butter

5 tablespoons thin honey

1 cup plain yogurt

1 large egg, at room temperature

grated rind of 1 lemon

$^1\!/_4$ cup fresh lemon juice

$1^1\!/_4$ cups flour

$1^2\!/_3$ cups whole-wheat flour

$1^1\!/_2$ teaspoons baking soda

pinch of freshly grated nutmeg

~ VARIATION ~

For Walnut Yogurt Honey Muffins, add $^1\!/_2$ cup chopped walnuts, folded in with the flour. This makes a more substantial muffin.

1 Preheat the oven to 375°F. Grease a 12-cup muffin pan or, if you prefer, use paper liners.

2 In a saucepan, melt the butter and honey. Remove from the heat and set aside to cool slightly.

3 ▲ In a bowl, whisk together the yogurt, egg, lemon rind, and juice. Add the butter and honey mixture. Set aside.

4 ▲ In another bowl, sift together the dry ingredients.

5 Fold the dry ingredients into the yogurt mixture just to blend.

6 Fill the prepared cups two-thirds full. Bake until the tops spring back when touched lightly, 20–25 minutes. Let cool in the pan for 5 minutes before unmolding. Serve warm or at room temperature.

Prune Muffins (top), Yogurt and Honey Muffins

Banana Muffins

MAKES 10

2¼ cups flour

1 teaspoon baking powder

1 teaspoon baking soda

¼ teaspoon salt

½ teaspoon ground cinnamon

¼ teaspoon freshly grated nutmeg

3 large ripe bananas

1 egg

scant ⅓ cup soft dark brown sugar

¼ cup vegetable oil

2 tablespoons raisins

1 ▼ Preheat the oven to 375°F. Lightly grease 10 muffin cups or line them with paper liners.

2 Sift together the flour, baking powder, baking soda, salt, cinnamon, and nutmeg. Set aside.

3 ▲ With an electric mixer, beat the peeled bananas at moderate speed until mashed.

4 ▲ Beat in the egg, sugar, and oil.

5 Add the dry ingredients and beat in gradually, on low speed. Mix just until blended. With a wooden spoon, stir in the raisins.

6 Fill the prepared cups two-thirds full. For even baking, half-fill any empty cups with water.

7 ▲ Bake until the tops spring back when touched lightly, 20–25 minutes. Transfer to a rack to cool.

Maple Pecan Muffins

MAKES 20

1 cup pecans

3 cups flour

1 teaspoon baking powder

1 teaspoon baking soda

1/4 teaspoon salt

1/4 teaspoon ground cinnamon

1/2 cup superfine sugar

scant 1/3 cup soft light brown sugar

3 tablespoons maple syrup

10 tablespoons butter, at room temperature

3 eggs, at room temperature

1 1/4 cups buttermilk

60 pecan halves, for decorating

1 Preheat the oven to 350°F. Grease 20 muffin cups or use paper liners.

2 ▲ Spread the pecans on a baking sheet and toast in the oven for 5 minutes. When cool, chop coarsely and set aside.

~ VARIATION ~

For Pecan Spice Muffins, substitute an equal quantity of molasses for the maple syrup. Increase the cinnamon to 1/2 teaspoon, and add 1 teaspoon ground ginger and 1/2 teaspoon freshly grated nutmeg, sifted with the dry ingredients.

3 In a bowl, sift together the flour, baking powder, baking soda, salt, and cinnamon. Set aside.

4 ▲ In a large mixing bowl, combine the caster sugar, light brown sugar, maple syrup, and butter. Beat with an electric mixer until light and fluffy.

5 Add the eggs, 1 at a time, beating to incorporate thoroughly after each addition.

6 ▲ Pour half the buttermilk and half the dry ingredients into the butter mixture, then stir until blended. Repeat with the remaining buttermilk and dry ingredients.

7 Fold in the chopped pecans. Fill the prepared cups two-thirds full. Top with the pecan halves. For even baking, half-fill any empty cups with water.

8 Bake until puffed up and golden, 20–25 minutes. Let stand 5 minutes before unmolding onto a rack.

Cheese Muffins

MAKES 9

1/4 cup (1/2 stick) butter
1 3/4 cups flour
2 teaspoons baking powder
2 tablespoons sugar
1/4 teaspoon salt
1 teaspoon paprika
2 eggs
1/2 cup milk
1 teaspoon dried thyme
1/2 cup sharp Cheddar cheese, cut into 1/2-inch dice

1 Preheat the oven to 375°F. Thickly grease 9 muffin cups or use paper liners.

2 Melt the butter and set aside.

3 ▼ In a mixing bowl, sift together the flour, baking powder, sugar, salt, and paprika.

4 ▲ In another bowl, combine the eggs, milk, melted butter, and thyme, and whisk to blend.

5 Add the milk mixture to the dry ingredients and stir until just moistened; do not mix until smooth.

6 ▲ Place a heaped spoonful of batter into the prepared cups. Drop a few pieces of cheese over each, then top with another spoonful of batter. For even baking, half-fill any empty muffin cups with water.

7 ▲ Bake until puffed and golden, about 25 minutes. Let stand 5 minutes before unmolding onto a rack. Serve warm or at room temperature.

Bacon and Cornmeal Muffins

MAKES 14

8 slices bacon
1/4 cup butter
1/4 cup margarine
1 cup flour
1 tablespoon baking powder
1 teaspoon sugar
1/4 teaspoon salt
2 cups cornmeal
1/2 cup milk
2 eggs

1 Preheat the oven to 400°F. Lightly grease 14 muffin cups or use paper liners.

2 ▲ Fry the bacon until crisp. Drain on paper towels, then chop into small pieces. Set aside.

3 Gently melt the butter and margarine, and set aside.

4 ▲ Sift the flour, baking powder, sugar, and salt into a large mixing bowl. Stir in the cornmeal, then make a well in the center.

5 In a saucepan, heat the milk to lukewarm. In a small bowl, lightly whisk the eggs, then add to the milk. Stir in the melted fats.

6 ▼ Pour the milk mixture into the center of the well and stir until smooth and well blended.

7 ▲ Stir the bacon into the batter, then spoon the batter into the prepared cups, filling them half-full. For even baking, half-fill any empty cups with water. Bake until risen and lightly colored, about 20 minutes. Serve hot or warm.

Corn Bread

MAKES 1 LOAF

1 cup flour
5 tablespoons superfine sugar
1 teaspoon salt
1 tablespoon baking powder
1½ cups cornmeal
1½ cups milk
2 eggs
6 tablespoons butter, melted
½ cup (1 stick) margarine, melted

1 Preheat the oven to 400°F. Line the bottom and sides of a 9- × 5-inch loaf pan with wax paper and grease.

2 Sift the flour, sugar, salt, and baking powder into a mixing bowl.

3 ▼ Add the cornmeal and stir to blend. Make a well in the center.

4 ▲ Whisk together the milk, eggs, butter, and margarine. Pour the mixture into the well. Stir until just blended; do not overmix.

5 Pour into the pan and bake until a cake tester inserted in the center comes out clean, about 45 minutes. Serve hot or at room temperature.

Tex-Mex Corn Bread

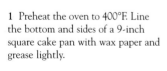

MAKES 9 SQUARES

3–4 whole canned chile peppers, drained
2 eggs
scant 2 cups buttermilk
¼ cup (½ stick) butter, melted
½ cup flour
1 teaspoon baking soda
2 teaspoons salt
1½ cups cornmeal
2 cups corn kernels

1 Preheat the oven to 400°F. Line the bottom and sides of a 9-inch square cake pan with wax paper and grease lightly.

2 ▲ With a sharp knife, chop the chiles in a fine dice and set aside.

3 ▲ In a large bowl, whisk the eggs until frothy, then whisk in the buttermilk. Add the melted butter.

4 In another large bowl, sift together the flour, baking soda, and salt. Fold into the buttermilk mixture in 3 batches, then fold in the cornmeal in 3 batches.

5 ▲ Fold in the chiles and corn.

6 Pour the batter into the prepared pan and bake until a cake tester inserted in the middle comes out clean, 25–30 minutes. Let stand 2–3 minutes before unmolding. Cut into squares and serve warm.

Corn Bread (top), Tex-Mex Corn Bread

Cranberry Orange Bread

MAKES 1 LOAF

2 cups flour

generous ¹/₂ cup superfine sugar

1 tablespoon baking powder

¹/₂ teaspoon salt

grated rind of 1 large orange

scant ³/₄ cup fresh orange juice

2 eggs, lightly beaten

6 tablespoons butter or margarine, melted

1 cup fresh cranberries

¹/₂ cup chopped walnuts

1 Preheat the oven to 350°F. Line the bottom and sides of a 9- × 5-inch loaf pan with wax paper and grease.

2 Sift the flour, sugar, baking powder, and salt into a mixing bowl.

3 ▼ Stir in the orange rind.

4 ▲ Make a well in the center and add the orange juice, eggs, and melted butter or margarine. Stir from the center until the ingredients are blended; do not overmix.

5 ▲ Add the cranberries and walnuts and stir until blended.

6 Transfer the mixture to the prepared pan and bake until a cake tester inserted in the center comes out clean, 45–50 minutes.

7 ▲ Let cool in the pan for 10 minutes before transferring to a rack to cool completely. Serve thinly sliced, toasted or plain, with butter or cream cheese, and jam.

Date and Pecan Loaf

MAKES 1 LOAF

1 cup pitted dates, chopped
³/₄ cup boiling water
¹/₄ cup unsalted butter, at room temperature
¹/₄ cup soft dark brown sugar
¹/₄ cup superfine sugar
1 egg, at room temperature
2 tablespoons brandy
1¹/₄ cups flour
2 teaspoons baking powder
¹/₂ teaspoon salt
³/₄ teaspoon freshly grated nutmeg
³/₄ cup coarsely chopped pecans

1 ▲ Place the dates in a bowl and pour over the boiling water. Set aside to cool.

2 Preheat the oven to 350°F. Line the bottom and sides of a 9- × 5-inch loaf pan with wax paper and grease.

3 ▲ With an electric mixer, cream the butter and sugars until light and fluffy. Beat in the egg and brandy, then set aside.

4 Sift the flour, baking powder, salt, and nutmeg together, 3 times.

5 ▼ Fold the dry ingredients into the sugar mixture in 3 batches, alternating with the dates and water.

6 ▲ Fold in the pecans.

7 Pour the batter into the prepared tin and bake until a cake tester inserted in the center comes out clean, 45–50 minutes. Let cool in the tin for 10 minutes before transferring to a rack to cool completely.

Orange and Honey Quick Bread

MAKES 1 LOAF

3¹/4 cups flour
2¹/2 teaspoons baking powder
¹/2 teaspoon baking soda
¹/2 teaspoon salt
2 tablespoons margarine
1 cup thin honey
1 egg, at room temperature, lightly beaten
1¹/2 tablespoons grated orange rind
³/4 cup freshly squeezed orange juice
1 cup walnuts, chopped

1 Preheat the oven to 325°F.

2 Sift together the flour, baking powder, baking soda, and salt.

3 Line the bottom and sides of a 9- × 5-inch loaf pan with wax paper and grease.

4 ▲ With an electric mixer, cream the margarine until soft. Stir in the honey until blended, then stir in the egg. Add the orange rind and stir to combine thoroughly.

5 ▲ Fold the flour mixture into the honey and egg mixture in 3 batches, alternating with the orange juice. Stir in the walnuts.

6 Pour into the pan and bake until a cake tester inserted in the center comes out clean, 60–70 minutes. Let stand 10 minutes before unmolding onto a rack to cool.

Applesauce Bread

MAKES 1 LOAF

1 egg
1 cup bottled or homemade applesauce
¹/4 cup (¹/2 stick) butter or margarine, melted
¹/2 cup soft dark brown sugar
¹/4 cup superfine sugar
2¹/2 cups flour
2 teaspoons baking powder
¹/2 teaspoon baking soda
¹/2 teaspoon salt
1 teaspoon ground cinnamon
¹/2 teaspoon freshly grated nutmeg
¹/2 cup currants or raisins
¹/3 cup pecans or walnuts, chopped

1 Preheat the oven to 350°F. Line the bottom and sides of a 9- × 5-inch loaf pan with wax paper and grease.

2 ▲ Break the egg into a bowl and beat lightly. Stir in the applesauce, butter or margarine, and both sugars. Set aside.

3 In another bowl, sift together the flour, baking powder, baking soda, salt, cinnamon, and nutmeg. Fold the dry ingredients into the applesauce mixture in 3 batches.

4 ▼ Stir in the currants or raisins, and nuts.

5 Pour into the prepared pan and bake until a cake tester inserted in the center comes out clean, about 1 hour. Let stand 10 minutes. Unmold onto a rack and cool completely.

Orange and Honey Quick Bread (top), Applesauce Bread

Lemon and Walnut Bread

MAKES 1 LOAF

¹/₂ cup (1 stick) butter or margarine, at room temperature
¹/₂ cup sugar
2 eggs, at room temperature, separated
grated rind of 2 lemons
2 tablespoons fresh lemon juice
2 cups flour
2 teaspoons baking powder
¹/₂ cup milk
¹/₃ cup walnuts, chopped
pinch of salt

1 Preheat the oven to 350°F. Line the bottom and sides of a 9- × 5-inch loaf pan with wax paper and grease.

2 With an electric mixer, cream the butter or margarine with the sugar until light and fluffy.

3 ▲ Beat in the egg yolks.

4 Add the lemon rind and juice and stir until blended. Set aside.

5 ▲ In another bowl, sift together the flour and baking powder, 3 times. Fold into the butter mixture in 3 batches, alternating with the milk. Fold in the walnuts. Set aside.

6 ▲ Beat the egg whites and salt until stiff peaks form. Fold a large dollop of the egg whites into the walnut mixture to lighten it. Fold in the remaining egg whites carefully until just blended.

7 ▲ Pour the batter into the prepared pan and bake until a cake tester inserted in the center of the loaf comes out clean, 45–50 minutes. Let stand 5 minutes before unmolding onto a rack to cool completely.

Apricot Nut Loaf

MAKES 1 LOAF

$^{1}/_{2}$ cup ready-to-eat dried apricots
1 large orange
$^{2}/_{3}$ cup raisins
$^{3}/_{4}$ cup superfine sugar
generous $^{1}/_{3}$ cup oil
2 eggs, lightly beaten
$2^{1}/_{4}$ cups flour
2 teaspoons baking powder
$^{1}/_{2}$ teaspoon salt
1 teaspoon baking soda
$^{1}/_{2}$ cup chopped walnuts

1 Preheat the oven to 350°F. Line the bottom and sides of a 9- × 5-inch loaf pan with wax paper and grease.

2 Place the apricots in a bowl, cover with lukewarm water and let stand 30 minutes.

3 ▲ With a vegetable peeler, remove the orange rind, leaving the pith.

4 With a sharp knife, finely chop the orange rind strips.

5 Drain the apricots and chop coarsely. Place in a bowl with the orange rind and raisins. Set aside.

6 Squeeze the peeled orange. Measure the juice and add enough hot water to obtain $^{3}/_{4}$ cup liquid.

7 ▼ Pour the orange juice mixture over the apricot mixture. Stir in the sugar, oil, and eggs. Set aside.

8 In another bowl, sift together the flour, baking powder, salt, and baking soda. Fold the flour mixture into the apricot mixture in 3 batches.

9 ▲ Stir in the walnuts.

10 Spoon the batter into the prepared pan and bake until a cake tester inserted in the center comes out clean, 55–60 minutes. If the loaf browns too quickly, protect the top with a sheet of foil. Let cool in the pan for 10 minutes before transferring to a rack to cool completely.

Mango Bread

MAKES 2 LOAVES

2¹/₂ cups flour

2 teaspoons baking soda

2 teaspoons ground cinnamon

¹/₂ teaspoon salt

¹/₂ cup margarine,
    at room temperature

3 eggs, at room temperature

generous 1¹/₂ cups superfine sugar

¹/₂ cup vegetable oil

1 large ripe mango, peeled and chopped

generous 1 cup dry unsweetened
    shredded coconut

¹/₂ cup raisins

1 Preheat the oven to 350°F. Line the bottom and sides of 2 9- × 5-inch loaf pans with wax paper and grease.

2 Sift together the flour, baking soda, cinnamon, and salt. Set aside.

3 With an electric mixer, cream the margarine until soft.

4 ▼ Beat in the eggs and sugar until light and fluffy. Beat in the oil.

5 Fold the dry ingredients into the creamed ingredients in 3 batches.

6 Fold in the mango, two-thirds of the coconut and the raisins.

7 ▲ Spoon the batter into the pans.

8 Sprinkle over the remaining coconut. Bake until a cake tester inserted in the center comes out clean, 50–60 minutes. Let stand 10 minutes before unmolding onto a rack to cool completely.

Zucchini Bread

MAKES 1 LOAF

¹/₄ cup (¹/₂ stick) butter

3 eggs

1 cup vegetable oil

generous 1¹/₂ cups sugar

2 medium unpeeled zucchini, grated

2¹/₂ cups flour

2 teaspoons baking soda

1 teaspoon baking powder

1 teaspoon salt

1 teaspoon ground cinnamon

1 teaspoon freshly grated nutmeg

¹/₄ teaspoon ground cloves

²/₃ cup walnuts, chopped

1 Preheat the oven to 350°F.

2 Line the bottom and sides of a 9- × 5-inch loaf pan with wax paper and grease.

3 ▲ In a saucepan, melt the butter over low heat. Set aside.

4 With an electric mixer, beat the eggs and oil together until thick. Beat in the sugar. Stir in the melted butter and grated zucchini. Set aside.

5 ▲ In another bowl, sift all the dry ingredients together 3 times. Carefully fold into the zucchini mixture. Fold in the walnuts.

6 Pour into the pan and bake until a cake tester inserted in the center comes out clean, 60–70 minutes. Let stand 10 minutes before unmolding onto a wire rack to cool completely.

Mango Bread (top), Zucchini Bread

Whole-Wheat Banana Nut Bread

MAKES 1 LOAF

$^1/_2$ cup (1 stick) butter, at room temperature
generous $^1/_2$ cup superfine sugar
2 eggs, at room temperature
1 cup flour
1 teaspoon baking soda
$^1/_4$ teaspoon salt
1 teaspoon ground cinnamon
$^1/_2$ cup whole-wheat flour
3 large ripe bananas
1 teaspoon vanilla extract
$^1/_3$ cup chopped walnuts

1 Preheat the oven to 350°F. Line the bottom and sides of a 9- × 5-inch loaf pan with wax paper and grease.

2 With an electric mixer, cream the butter and sugar together until light and fluffy.

3 ▲ Add the eggs, 1 at a time, beating well after each addition.

4 Sift the flour, baking soda, salt, and cinnamon over the butter mixture and stir to blend.

5 ▲ Stir in the whole-wheat flour.

6 ▲ With a fork, mash the bananas to a purée, then stir into the batter. Stir in the vanilla and walnuts.

7 ▲ Pour the batter into the prepared pan and spread level.

8 Bake until a cake tester inserted in the center comes out clean, about 50–60 minutes. Let stand 10 minutes before transferring to a rack.

Dried Fruit Loaf

MAKES 1 LOAF

2²/³ cups mixed dried fruit, such as
    currants, raisins, chopped ready-to-eat
    dried apricots, and dried cherries

1¼ cups cold strong tea

scant 1 cup soft dark brown sugar

grated rind and juice of 1 small orange

grated rind and juice of 1 lemon

1 egg, lightly beaten

1¾ cups flour

1 tablespoon baking powder

pinch of salt

1 ▲ In a bowl, toss together all the
dried fruit, pour over the tea and let
soak overnight.

2 Preheat the oven to 350°F. Line the
bottom and sides of a 9- × 5-inch loaf
pan with wax paper and grease.

3 ▲ Strain the fruit, reserving the
liquid. In a bowl, combine the sugar,
orange and lemon rind, and fruit.

4 ▼ Pour the orange and lemon juice
into a measuring cup; if the quantity
is less than 1 cup, complete with the
soaking liquid.

5 Stir the citrus juices and egg into
the dried fruit mixture.

6 In another bowl, sift together the
flour, baking powder, and salt. Stir
into the fruit mixture until blended.

7 Transfer to the prepared tin and
bake until a cake tester inserted in
the center comes out clean, about
1¼ hours. Let stand 10 minutes before
unmolding onto a rack to cool.

Blueberry Streusel Bread

MAKES 8 PIECES

¹/₄ cup (¹/₂ stick) butter or margarine, at room temperature
scant 1 cup superfine sugar
1 egg, at room temperature
¹/₂ cup milk
2 cups flour
2 teaspoons baking powder
¹/₂ teaspoon salt
2¹/₂ cups fresh blueberries
FOR THE TOPPING
generous ¹/₂ cup sugar
¹/₃ cup flour
¹/₂ teaspoon ground cinnamon
¹/₄ cup (¹/₂ stick) butter, cut in pieces

1 Preheat the oven to 375°F. Grease a 9-inch square baking dish.

2 With an electric mixer, cream the butter or margarine with the sugar until light and fluffy. Add the egg, beat to combine, then mix in the milk until blended.

3 ▼ Sift over the flour, baking powder, and salt, and stir just enough to blend the ingredients.

4 ▲ Add the blueberries and stir.

5 Transfer to the baking dish.

6 ▲ For the topping, place the sugar, flour, cinnamon, and butter in a mixing bowl. Cut in with a pastry blender until the mixture resembles coarse crumbs.

7 ▲ Sprinkle the topping over the batter in the baking dish.

8 Bake until a cake tester inserted into the center comes out clean, about 45 minutes. Serve warm or cold.

Chocolate Chip Walnut Loaf

MAKES 1 LOAF

¹/₂ cup superfine sugar
³/₄ cup flour
1 teaspoon baking powder
4 tablespoons cornstarch
generous ¹/₂ cup (1 stick) butter, at room temperature
2 eggs, at room temperature
1 teaspoon vanilla extract
2 tablespoons currants or raisins
¹/₄ cup walnuts, finely chopped
grated rind of ¹/₂ lemon
3 tablespoons semisweet chocolate chips
confectioners' sugar, for dusting

1 Preheat the oven to 350°F. Line an 8¹/₂- × 4¹/₂-inch loaf pan with wax paper and grease.

2 ▲ Sprinkle 1¹/₂ tablespoons of the superfine sugar into the pan and tilt to distribute the sugar in an even layer over the bottom and sides. Shake out any excess.

~ VARIATION ~

For the best results, the eggs should be at room temperature. If they are too cold when folded into the creamed butter mixture, they may separate. If this happens, add a spoonful of the flour to help stabilize the mixture.

3 ▼ Sift together the flour, baking powder, and cornstarch into a mixing bowl, 3 times. Set aside.

4 With an electric mixer, cream the butter until soft. Add the remaining sugar and continue beating until light and fluffy. Add the eggs, 1 at a time, beating to incorporate thoroughly after each addition.

5 Gently fold the dry ingredients into the butter mixture, in 3 batches; do not overmix.

6 ▲ Fold in the vanilla, currants or raisins, walnuts, lemon rind, and chocolate chips until just blended.

7 Pour the batter into the prepared pan and bake until a cake tester inserted in the center comes out clean, 45–50 minutes. Let cool in the pan for 5 minutes before transferring to a rack to cool completely. Dust over an even layer of confectioners' sugar before serving.

Glazed Banana Spice Loaf

MAKES 1 LOAF

1 large ripe banana

1/2 cup (1 stick) butter,
   at room temperature

generous 3/4 cup superfine sugar

2 eggs, at room temperature

scant 2 cups flour

1 teaspoon salt

1 teaspoon baking soda

1/2 teaspoon freshly grated nutmeg

1/4 teaspoon ground allspice

1/4 teaspoon ground cloves

3/4 cup sour cream

1 teaspoon vanilla extract

FOR THE GLAZE

1 cup confectioners' sugar

1–2 tablespoons fresh lemon juice

1 Preheat the oven to 350°F. Line an 8½- × 4½-inch loaf pan with wax paper and grease.

2 ▼ With a fork, mash the banana in a bowl. Set aside.

3 With an electric mixer, cream the butter and sugar until light and fluffy. Add the eggs 1 at a time, beating to blend well after each addition.

4 Sift together the flour, salt, baking soda, nutmeg, allspice, and cloves. Add to the butter mixture and stir to combine well.

5 ▲ Add the sour cream, banana, and vanilla and mix just enough to blend. Pour into the prepared pan.

6 ▲ Bake until the top springs back when touched lightly, 45–50 minutes. Let cool in the pan for 10 minutes. Unmold onto a wire rack to cool.

7 ▲ For the glaze, combine the confectioners' sugar and lemon juice, then stir until smooth.

8 To glaze, place the cooled loaf on a rack set over a baking sheet. Pour the glaze over the top of the loaf and allow to set.

Sweet Sesame Loaf

MAKES 1 OR 2 LOAVES

6 tablespoons sesame seeds
2½ cups flour
1 teaspoon salt
2½ teaspoons baking powder
¼ cup (½ stick) butter or margarine, at room temperature
scant ¾ cup sugar
2 eggs, at room temperature
grated rind of 1 lemon
1½ cups milk

1 Preheat the oven to 350°F. Line a 9- × 5-inch loaf pan with wax paper and grease the paper.

2 ▲ Reserve 2 tablespoons of the sesame seeds. Spread the remainder on a baking sheet and bake until lightly toasted, about 10 minutes.

3 Sift the flour, salt, and baking powder into a bowl.

4 ▲ Stir in the toasted sesame seeds and set aside.

5 With an electric mixer, cream the butter or margarine and sugar together until light and fluffy. Beat in the eggs, then stir in the lemon rind and milk.

6 ▼ Pour the milk mixture over the dry ingredients and fold in with a large metal spoon until just blended.

7 ▲ Pour into the pan and sprinkle over the reserved sesame seeds.

8 Bake until a cake tester inserted into the center comes out clean, about 1 hour. Let cool in the pan for about 10 minutes before unmolding onto a wire rack to cool completely.

Whole-Wheat Scones

Makes 16

¾ cup (1½ sticks) cold butter

3 cups whole-wheat flour

1¼ cups flour

2 tablespoons superfine sugar

½ teaspoon salt

2½ teaspoons baking soda

2 eggs

¾ cup buttermilk

2½ tablespoons raisins

1 Preheat the oven to 400°F. Grease and flour a large baking sheet.

2 ▲ Cut the butter into small pieces.

3 Combine the dry ingredients in a bowl. Add the butter and rub in with your fingertips until the mixture resembles coarse crumbs. Set aside.

4 In another bowl, whisk together the eggs and buttermilk. Set aside 2 tablespoons for glazing.

5 Stir the remaining egg mixture into the dry ingredients until it just holds together. Stir in the raisins.

6 Roll out the dough to about ¾ inch thick. Stamp out circles with a cookie cutter. Place on the prepared sheet and brush with the glaze.

7 Bake until golden, 12–15 minutes. Allow to cool slightly before serving. Split in two with a fork while still warm and spread with butter and jam, if wished.

Orange and Raisin Scones

Makes 16

2½ cups flour

1½ teaspoons baking powder

4½ tablespoons sugar

½ teaspoon salt

5 tablespoons butter, diced

5 tablespoons margarine, diced

grated rind of 1 large orange

4 tablespoons raisins

½ cup buttermilk

milk, for glazing

1 Preheat the oven to 425°F. Grease and flour a large baking sheet.

2 Combine the dry ingredients in a large bowl. Add the butter and margarine and cut in with a pastry blender until the mixture resembles coarse crumbs.

3 ▲ Add the orange rind and raisins.

4 Gradually stir in the buttermilk to form a soft dough.

5 ▲ Roll out the dough to about ¾ inch thick. Stamp out circles with a cookie cutter.

6 ▲ Place on the prepared sheet and brush the tops with milk.

7 Bake until golden, 12–15 minutes. Serve hot or warm, with butter, or whipped or clotted cream, and jam.

~ COOK'S TIP ~

For light, tender scones, handle the dough as little as possible. If you wish, split the scones when cool and toast them under a preheated broiler. Butter them while still hot.

Whole-Wheat Scones (top), Orange and Raisin Scones

Buttermilk Biscuits

MAKES 15

1³/4 cups flour

1 teaspoon salt

1 teaspoon baking powder

¹/2 teaspoon baking soda

4 tablespoons cold butter or margarine

³/4 cup buttermilk

1 Preheat the oven to 425°F. Grease and flour a baking sheet.

2 Sift the dry ingredients into a bowl. Cut in the butter or margarine with a pastry blender until the mixture resembles coarse crumbs.

3 ▼ Gradually pour in the buttermilk, stirring the mixture with a fork to form a soft dough.

4 ▲ Roll out the dough to about ¹/2 inch thick. Stamp out circles with a 2-inch cookie cutter.

5 Place on the prepared baking sheet and bake until golden, 12–15 minutes. Serve warm or at room temperature.

Baking Powder Biscuits

MAKES 8

1¹/2 cups flour

2 tablespoons sugar

1 tablespoon baking powder

pinch of salt

5 tablespoons cold butter, cut in pieces

¹/2 cup milk

1 Preheat the oven to 425°F. Grease and flour a baking sheet.

~ VARIATION ~

For Berry Shortcake, split the biscuits in half while still warm. Butter one half, top with lightly sugared fresh berries, such as strawberries, raspberries or blueberries, and sandwich with the other half. Serve at once with dollops of whipped cream.

2 ▲ Sift the flour, sugar, baking powder, and salt into a bowl.

3 Cut in the butter with a pastry blender until the mixture resembles coarse crumbs.

4 Pour in the milk and stir with a fork to form a soft dough.

5 ▲ Roll out the dough about ¹/4 inch thick. Stamp out circles using a 2¹/2-inch cookie cutter.

6 Place on the prepared sheet and bake until golden, about 12 minutes. Serve hot or warm, with butter and jam, to accompany tea or coffee.

Buttermilk Biscuits (top), Baking Powder Biscuits

Herb Popovers

MAKES 12

3 eggs

1 cup milk

2 tablespoons butter, melted

²/₃ cup flour

pinch of salt

1 small sprig each mixed fresh herbs, such as chives, tarragon, dill, and parsley

1 Preheat the oven to 425°F. Grease 12 small ramekins or popover cups.

2 With an electric mixer, beat the eggs until blended. Beat in the milk and melted butter.

3 Sift together the flour and salt, then beat into the egg mixture to combine thoroughly.

4 ▼ Strip the herb leaves from the stems and chop finely. Mix together and measure out 2 tablespoons. Stir the herbs into the batter.

5 ▲ Fill the prepared cups half-full.

6 Bake until golden, 25–30 minutes. Do not open the oven door during baking time or the popovers may collapse. For drier popovers, pierce each one with a knife after the 30-minute baking time and bake for 5 minutes more. Serve hot.

Cheese Popovers

MAKES 12

3 eggs

1 cup milk

2 tablespoons butter, melted

²/₃ cup flour

¹/₄ teaspoon salt

¹/₄ teaspoon paprika

¹/₃ cup freshly grated Parmesan cheese

~ VARIATION ~

To make Yorkshire Pudding Popovers, as an accompaniment for roast beef, omit the cheese and paprika, and use 4–6 tablespoons of the pan drippings to replace the butter. Put them into the oven in time to serve warm with the beef.

1 Preheat the oven to 425°F. Grease 12 small ramekins or popover cups.

2 ▲ With an electric mixer, beat the eggs until they are blended. Beat in the milk and melted butter.

3 ▲ Sift together the flour, salt, and paprika, then beat into the egg mixture. Add the cheese and stir.

4 Fill the prepared cups half-full and bake until golden, 25–30 minutes. Do not open the oven door or the popovers may collapse. For drier popovers, pierce each one with a knife after the 30-minute baking time and bake for 5 minutes more. Serve hot.

Herb Popovers (top), Cheese Popovers

YEAST BREADS

THOUGH THE PACE OF TODAY'S LIFE
LEAVES LITTLE TIME FOR BAKING,
BREADMAKING CAN BE VERY
THERAPEUTIC. THE PROCESS IS
SIMPLE YET INFINITELY VARIABLE,
AS THE LOAVES THAT FOLLOW
PROVE. ROLL UP YOUR SLEEVES AND
CREATE A TRADITION.

White Bread

MAKES 2 LOAVES

¹/₄ cup lukewarm water
1 package active dry yeast
2 tablespoons sugar
2 cups lukewarm milk
2 tablespoons butter or margarine, at room temperature
2 teaspoons salt
7¹/₂–8 cups strong white bread flour

1 Combine the water, dried yeast, and 1 tablespoon of the sugar in a measuring cup and leave to stand for 15 minutes until the mixture is frothy.

2 ▼ Pour the milk into a large bowl. Add the remaining sugar, the butter or margarine, and salt. Stir in the yeast mixture.

3 Stir in the flour, 1¹/₄ cups at a time, until a stiff dough is obtained. Alternatively, use a food processor.

4 ▲ Transfer the dough to a floured surface. To knead, push the dough away from you with the palm of your hand, then fold it towards you, and push it away again. Repeat until the dough is smooth and elastic.

5 Place the dough in a large greased bowl, cover with a plastic bag, and leave to rise in a warm place until doubled in volume, 2–3 hours.

6 Grease 2 9- × 5-inch loaf pans.

7 ▲ Punch down the risen dough with your fist and divide in half. Form into loaf shapes and place in the pans, seam-side down. Cover and leave to rise in a warm place until almost doubled in volume, about 45 minutes. Preheat the oven to 375°F.

8 Bake until firm and brown, about 45–50 minutes. Unmold and tap the bottom of a loaf: if it sounds hollow the loaf is done. If necessary, return to the oven and bake a few minutes more. Let cool on a rack.

Country Bread

MAKES 2 LOAVES

3 cups whole-wheat flour

3 cups flour

1¼ cups strong white bread flour

4 teaspoon salt

¼ cup butter, at room temperature

2 cups lukewarm milk

FOR THE STARTER

1 package active dry yeast

1 cup lukewarm water

1¼ cups strong white bread flour

¼ teaspoon superfine sugar

1 ▲ For the starter, combine the yeast, water, flour, and sugar in a bowl and stir with a fork. Cover and leave in a warm place for 2–3 hours, or leave overnight in a cool place.

2 Place the flours, salt, and butter in a food processor and process until just blended, 1–2 minutes.

3 Stir together the milk and starter, then slowly pour into the processor, with the motor running, until the mixture forms a dough. If necessary, add more water. Alternatively, the dough can be mixed by hand. Transfer to a floured surface and knead until smooth and elastic.

4 Place in an ungreased bowl, cover with a plastic bag, and leave to rise in a warm place until doubled in volume, about 1½ hours.

5 Transfer to a floured surface and knead briefly. Return to the bowl and leave to rise until tripled in volume, about 1½ hours.

6 ▲ Divide the dough in half. Cut off one-third of the dough from each half and shape into balls. Shape the larger remaining portion of each half into balls. Grease a baking sheet.

7 ▲ For each loaf, top the large ball with the small ball, and press the center with the handle of a wooden spoon to secure. Cover with a plastic bag, slash the top, and leave to rise.

8 Preheat the oven to 400°F. Dust the dough with whole-wheat flour and bake until the top is browned and the bottom sounds hollow when tapped, 45–50 minutes. Cool on a rack.

Braided Loaf

Makes 1 loaf

1 package active dry yeast
1 teaspoon honey
1 cup lukewarm milk
1/4 cup butter, melted
3 1/2 cups strong white bread flour
1 teaspoon salt
1 egg, lightly beaten
1 egg yolk beaten with 1 teaspoon milk, for glazing

1 ▼ Combine the yeast, honey, milk, and butter. Stir and leave for 15 minutes to dissolve.

2 In a large bowl, mix together the flour and salt. Make a well in the center and add the yeast mixture and egg. With a wooden spoon, stir from the center, incorporating flour with each turn, to obtain a rough dough.

3 Transfer to a floured surface and knead until smooth and elastic. Place in a clean bowl, cover, and leave to rise in a warm place until doubled in volume, about 1 1/2 hours.

4 Grease a baking sheet. Punch down the dough and divide into 3 equal pieces. Roll to shape each piece into a long, thin strip.

5 ▲ Begin braiding with the center strip, tucking in the ends. Cover loosely and leave to rise in a warm place for 30 minutes.

6 ▲ Preheat the oven to 375°F. Place the bread in a cool place while the oven heats. Brush with the glaze and bake until golden, 40–45 minutes. Unmold onto a rack to cool.

Sesame Seed Bread

MAKES 1 LOAF

2 teaspoons active dried yeast
1¼ cups lukewarm water
1¾ cups strong white bread flour
1¾ cups strong whole-wheat bread flour
2 teaspoons salt
5 tablespoons toasted sesame seeds
milk, for glazing
2 tablespoons sesame seeds, for sprinkling

1 Combine the yeast and ¼ cup of the water and leave to dissolve for 15 minutes. Mix the flours and salt in a large bowl. Make a well in the center and pour in the yeast mixture and remaining water.

2 ▲ With a wooden spoon, stir from the center, incorporating flour with each turn, to obtain a rough dough.

3 ▲ Transfer to a lightly floured surface. To knead, push the dough away from you with the palm of your hand, then fold it towards you, and push away again. Repeat until smooth and elastic, then return to the bowl and cover with a plastic bag. Leave the dough in a warm place for about 1½–2 hours, until doubled in volume.

4 ▲ Grease a 9-inch cake pan. Punch down the dough and knead in the sesame seeds. Divide the dough into 16 balls and place in the pan. Cover with a plastic bag and leave in a warm place until risen above the rim of the tin.

5 ▼ Preheat the oven to 425°F. Brush the loaf with milk and sprinkle with the sesame seeds. Bake for 15 minutes. Lower the heat to 375°F and bake until the bottom sounds hollow when tapped, about 30 minutes more. Cool on a rack.

Whole-Wheat Bread

MAKES 1 LOAF

5¹/₄ cups strong whole-wheat bread flour

2 teaspoons salt

4 teaspoons active dry yeast

generous 1²/₃ cups lukewarm water

2 tablespoons honey

3 tablespoons oil

1¹/₂ ounces wheatgerm

milk, for glazing

1 Combine the flour and salt in a bowl and place in the oven at its lowest setting until warmed, 8–10 minutes.

2 Meanwhile, combine the yeast with half of the water in a small bowl and leave to dissolve.

3 ▼ Make a well in the center of the flour. Pour in the yeast mixture, the remaining water, honey, oil, and wheatgerm. With a wooden spoon, stir from the center until smooth.

4 Transfer the dough to a lightly floured surface and knead just enough to shape into a loaf.

5 ▲ Grease a 9- × 5-inch loaf pan, place the dough in it and cover with a plastic bag. Leave in a warm place until the dough is about 1 inch higher than the pan rim, about 1 hour.

6 Preheat the oven to 400°F. Bake until the bottom sounds hollow when tapped, 35–40 minutes. Cool on a rack.

Rye Bread

MAKES 1 LOAF

1³/₄ cups rye flour

scant 2 cups boiling water

¹/₂ cup molasses

5 tablespoons butter, cut in pieces

1 tablespoon salt

2 tablespoons caraway seeds

1 package active dry yeast

¹/₂ cup lukewarm water

7¹/₂ cups strong white bread flour

cornmeal, for dusting

~ COOK'S TIP ~

To bring out the flavor of the caraway seeds, toast them lightly. Spread the seeds on a baking tray and place in a preheated 325°F oven for about 7 minutes.

1 ▲ Mix the rye flour, boiling water, molasses, butter, salt, and caraway seeds in a large bowl. Let cool.

2 In another bowl, mix the yeast and lukewarm water and leave to dissolve. Stir into the rye flour mixture. Stir in just enough strong flour to obtain a stiff dough. If it becomes too stiff, stir with your hands.

3 Transfer to a floured surface and knead until the dough is no longer sticky and is smooth and shiny.

4 Place in a greased bowl, cover with a plastic bag, and leave in a warm place until doubled in volume. Punch down the dough, cover, and leave to rise again for 30 minutes.

5 Preheat the oven to 350°F. Dust a baking sheet with cornmeal.

6 ▼ Shape the dough into a ball. Place on the sheet and score several times across the top. Bake until the bottom sounds hollow when tapped, about 40 minutes. Cool on a rack.

Whole-Wheat Bread (top), Rye Bread

Buttermilk Graham Bread

MAKES 8

2 teaspoons active dry yeast

½ cup lukewarm water

2 cups graham or strong whole-wheat bread flour

3 cups strong white bread flour

generous 1 cup cornmeal

2 teaspoons salt

2 tablespoons sugar

4 tablespoons butter, at room temperature

2 cups lukewarm buttermilk

1 beaten egg, for glazing

sesame seeds, for sprinkling

1 Combine the yeast and water, stir, and leave for 15 minutes to dissolve.

2 ▲ Mix together the two flours, cornmeal, salt, and sugar in a large bowl. Make a well in the center and pour in the yeast mixture, then add the butter and the buttermilk.

3 ▲ Stir from the center, mixing in the flour until a rough dough is formed. If too stiff, use your hands.

4 ▲ Transfer to a floured surface and knead until smooth. Place in a clean bowl, cover, and leave in a warm place for 2–3 hours.

5 ▲ Grease two 8-inch square baking pans. Punch down the dough. Divide into eight pieces and roll them into balls. Place four in each tin. Cover and leave in a warm place for about 1 hour.

6 Preheat the oven to 375°F. Brush with the glaze, then sprinkle over the sesame seeds. Bake until the bottoms sound hollow when tapped, about 50 minutes. Cool on a wire rack.

Multi-Grain Bread

MAKES 2 LOAVES

1 package active dry yeast
1/4 cup lukewarm water
2/3 cup rolled oats (not quick-cooking)
scant 2 cups milk
2 teaspoons salt
1/4 cup oil
1/4 cup soft light brown sugar
2 tablespoons honey
2 eggs, lightly beaten
1 ounce wheatgerm
1 1/2 cups soy flour
3 cups strong whole-wheat bread flour
about 4 cups strong white bread flour

1 Combine the yeast and water, stir, and leave for 15 minutes to dissolve.

2 ▲ Place the oats in a large bowl. Scald the milk, then pour over the rolled oats.

3 Stir in the salt, oil, sugar, and honey. Leave until lukewarm.

~ VARIATION ~

Different flours may be used in this recipe, such as rye, barley, buckwheat, or cornmeal. Try replacing the wheatgerm and the soy flour with one or two of these, using the same total amount.

4 ▲ Stir in the yeast mixture, eggs, wheatgerm, soy, and whole-wheat flours. Gradually stir in enough strong white flour to obtain a rough dough.

5 Transfer the dough to a floured surface and knead, adding flour if necessary, until smooth and elastic. Return to a clean bowl, cover, and leave to rise in a warm place until doubled in volume, about 2 1/2 hours.

6 Grease 2 8 1/2- × 4 1/2-inch bread pans. Punch down the risen dough with your fist and knead briefly.

7 Divide the dough into quarters. Roll each quarter into a cylinder 1 1/2 inches thick. Twist together 2 cylinders and put in a pan; repeat for the remaining cylinders.

8 Cover and leave to rise until doubled in size, about 1 hour.

9 Preheat the oven to 375°F.

10 ▲ Bake the loaves for about 45–50 minutes, until the bottoms sound hollow when tapped lightly. Cool on a rack.

Potato Bread

MAKES 2 LOAVES

4 teaspoons active dry yeast

1 cup lukewarm milk

8oz potatoes, boiled (reserve 1 cup of
   potato cooking liquid)

2 tablespoons oil

4 teaspoons salt

7½–8 cups strong white bread flour

1 Combine the yeast and milk in a
large bowl and leave to dissolve, about
15 minutes.

2 Meanwhile, mash the potatoes.

3 ▲ Add the potatoes, oil, and salt to
the yeast mixture and mix well. Stir in
the reserved cooking water, then stir
in the flour, 1 cup at a time, to form a
stiff dough.

4 Transfer to a floured surface and
knead until smooth and elastic. Return
to the bowl, cover, and leave in a warm
place until doubled in size, 1–1½ hours.
Punch down, then leave to rise for
another 40 minutes.

5 Grease 2 9- × 5-inch loaf pans. Roll
the dough into 20 small balls. Place 2
rows of balls in each tin. Leave until
the dough has risen above the rim of
the pans.

6 Preheat the oven to 400°F. Bake for
10 minutes, then lower the heat to
375°F. Bake until the bottoms sound
hollow when tapped, about 40 minutes.
Cool on a rack.

Irish Soda Bread

MAKES 1 LOAF

2½ cups flour

1¼ cups whole-wheat flour

1 teaspoon baking soda

1 teaspoon salt

2 tablespoons butter or margarine,
   at room temperature

1¼ cups buttermilk

1 tablespoon flour, for dusting

1 Preheat the oven to 400°F. Grease
a baking sheet.

2 Sift the flours, baking soda, and salt
together into a bowl. Make a well in
the center and add the butter or
margarine and buttermilk. Working
outwards from the center, stir with a
fork until a soft dough is formed.

3 ▲ With floured hands, gather the
dough into a ball.

4 ▲ Transfer to a floured surface and
knead for 3 minutes. Shape the dough
into a large round.

5 ▲ Place on the baking sheet. Cut
a cross in the top with a sharp knife.

6 ▲ Dust with flour. Bake until
brown, 40–50 minutes. Transfer to a
rack to cool.

Potato Bread (top), Irish Soda Bread

Anadama Bread

MAKES 2 LOAVES

2 teaspoons active dry yeast
4 tablespoons lukewarm water
¹/₂ cup cornmeal
3 tablespoons butter or margarine
4 tablespoons molasses
³/₄ cup boiling water
1 egg
3 cups strong white bread flour
2 tablespoons salt

1 Combine the yeast and lukewarm water, stir well, and leave for 15 minutes to dissolve.

2 ▼ Meanwhile, combine the cornmeal, butter or margarine, molasses, and boiling water in a large bowl. Add the yeast, egg, and half the flour. Stir together to blend.

3 ▲ Stir in the remaining flour and salt. When the dough becomes too stiff, stir with your hands until it comes away from the sides of the bowl. If it is too sticky, add more flour; if too stiff, add a little water.

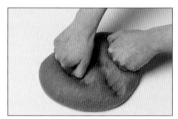

4 ▲ Transfer to a floured surface and knead until smooth and elastic. Place in a bowl, cover with a plastic bag, and leave in a warm place until doubled in size, 2–3 hours.

5 Grease 2 7- × 3-inch bread pans. Punch down the dough. Shape into 2 loaves and place in the pans, seam-side down. Cover and leave in a warm place until risen above the top of the pans.

6 ▲ Preheat the oven to 375°F. Bake for 50 minutes. Unmold and cool on a wire rack or set across the pans.

Oatmeal Bread

MAKES 2 LOAVES

scant 2 cups milk
2 tablespoons butter
1/4 cup soft dark brown sugar
2 teaspoons salt
1 package active dry yeast
1/4 cup lukewarm water
4 cups rolled oats (not quick-cooking)
6–7 1/2 cups strong white bread flour

1 ▲ Scald the milk. Remove from the heat and stir in the butter, brown sugar, and salt. Leave until lukewarm.

2 Combine the yeast and warm water in a large bowl and leave until the yeast is dissolved and the mixture is frothy. Stir in the milk mixture.

3 ▲ Add 2 1/4 cups of the oats and enough flour to obtain a soft dough.

4 Transfer to a floured surface and knead until smooth and elastic.

5 ▲ Place in a greased bowl, cover with a plastic bag, and leave until doubled in volume, 2–3 hours.

6 Grease a large baking sheet. Transfer the dough to a lightly floured surface and divide in half.

7 ▼ Shape into rounds. Place on the baking sheet, cover with a dish towel, and leave to rise until doubled in volume, about 1 hour.

8 Preheat the oven to 400°F. Score the tops and sprinkle with the remaining oats. Bake until the bottoms sound hollow when tapped, 45–50 minutes. Cool on racks.

Sourdough Bread

MAKES 1 LOAF

3 cups strong white bread flour

1 tablespoon salt

1 cup Sourdough Starter

$^{1}/_{2}$ cup lukewarm water

1 ▲ Combine the flour and salt in a large bowl. Make a well in the center and add the starter and water. With a wooden spoon, stir from the center, incorporating more flour with each turn, to obtain a rough dough.

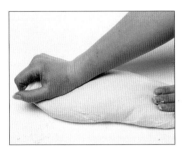

2 ▲ Transfer the dough to a floured surface. To knead, push the dough away from you with the palm of your hand, then fold it towards you, and push it away again. Repeat the process until the dough has become smooth and elastic.

3 Place in a clean bowl, cover, and leave to rise in a warm place until doubled in volume, about 2 hours.

4 Lightly grease an 8$^{1}/_{2}$- × 4$^{1}/_{2}$-inch bread pan.

5 ▼ Punch down the dough with your fist. Knead briefly, then form into a loaf shape and place in the pan, seam-side down. Cover with a plastic bag, and leave to rise in a warm place, for about 1$^{1}/_{2}$ hours.

6 Preheat the oven to 425°F. Dust the top of the loaf with flour, then score lengthwise. Bake for 15 minutes. Lower the heat to 375°F and bake for about 30 minutes more, or until the bottom sounds hollow when tapped.

Sourdough Starter

MAKES 750ML/1$^{1}/_{4}$ PINTS

1 teaspoon active dry yeast

$^{3}/_{4}$ cup lukewarm water

$^{1}/_{2}$ cup strong white bread flour

> ### ~ COOK'S TIP ~
>
> After using, feed the remaining starter with a handful of flour and enough water to restore it to a thick batter. The starter can be refrigerateed for up to 1 week, but must be brought back to room temperature before using.

1 ▲ Combine the yeast and water in a bowl, stir, and leave for 15 minutes to dissolve.

2 ▼ Sprinkle over the flour, and whisk until it forms a batter. Cover and leave to rise in a warm place for at least 24 hours or preferably 2–4 days, before using.

Sourdough French Loaves

MAKES 2 LOAVES

2 teaspoons active dry yeast
1½ cups lukewarm water
1 cup Sourdough Starter
6 cups strong white bread flour
1 tablespoon salt
1 teaspoon sugar
cornmeal, for sprinkling
1 teaspoon cornstarch
½ cup water

1 In a large bowl, combine the yeast and lukewarm water, stir, and leave for 15 minutes to dissolve.

2 ▲ Pour in the Sourdough Starter. Add 4 cups of the flour, the salt, and the sugar. Stir until smooth. Cover the bowl with a plastic bag and leave the dough to rise in a warm place until doubled in volume, about 1½ hours.

3 Stir in just enough flour to obtain a rough dough. Transfer to a floured surface and knead until the dough is smooth and elastic. Divide in half, then shape each half into a 14-inch cylinder with rounded ends.

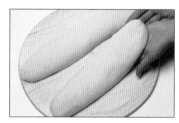

4 ▲ Place the loaves on a wooden board or tray sprinkled with cornmeal. Cover loosely with a dish towel and leave to rise in a warm place until nearly doubled in volume.

5 Preheat the oven to 425°F. Place a 15- × 12-inch baking sheet in the oven. Half-fill a shallow baking dish with hot water and put it on the bottom of the oven.

6 Mix the cornstarch and water in a small pan. Bring to the boil.

7 ▲ With a sharp knife, make several diagonal slashes across the loaves. Slide on to the hot baking sheet and brush over the cornflour mixture. Bake until the tops are golden and the bottoms sound hollow when tapped, about 25 minutes. Cool on a wire rack.

Sourdough Rye Bread

MAKES 2 LOAVES

2 teaspoons active dried yeast
$^1/_2$ cup lukewarm water
2 tablespoons butter, melted
1 tablespoon salt
1 cup strong whole-wheat bread flour
$3^1/_2$–4 cups strong white bread flour
1 egg mixed with 1 tablespoon water, for glazing

FOR THE STARTER

1 package active dry yeast
$1^1/_2$ cups lukewarm water
3 tablespoons molasses
2 tablespoons caraway seeds
$2^1/_4$ cups rye flour

1 For the starter, combine the yeast and water, stir and leave for 15 minutes to dissolve.

2 ▲ Stir in the molasses, caraway seeds, and rye flour. Cover and leave in a warm place for 2–3 days.

3 In a large bowl, combine the yeast and water, stir and leave for 10 minutes. Stir in the melted butter, salt, whole-wheat flour, and $3^1/_2$ cups of the white flour.

4 ▲ Make a well in the center and pour in the starter.

5 Stir to obtain a rough dough, then transfer to a floured surface and knead until smooth and elastic. Return to the bowl, cover, and leave to rise in a warm place until doubled in volume, about 2 hours.

6 Grease a large baking sheet. Punch down the dough and knead briefly. Cut the dough in half and form each half into a log-shaped loaf.

7 ▼ Place the loaves on the baking sheet and score the tops with a sharp knife. Cover with a clean dish towel and leave to rise in a warm place until almost doubled, about 50 minutes.

8 Preheat the oven to 375°F. Brush the loaves with the egg wash to glaze them, then bake until the bottoms sound hollow when tapped, about 50–55 minutes. If the tops of the loaves brown too quickly, place a sheet of foil over them to protect them. Cool on a wire rack.

Whole-Wheat Buttermilk Rolls

MAKES 12

2 teaspoons active dry yeast
¼ cup lukewarm water
1 teaspoon superfine sugar
¾ cup lukewarm buttermilk
¼ teaspoon baking soda
1 teaspoon salt
3 tablespoons butter, at room temperature
1¾ cups strong whole-wheat bread flour
1¼ cups strong white bread flour
1 beaten egg, for glazing

1 In a large bowl, combine the yeast, water, and sugar. Stir, and leave for 15 minutes to dissolve.

2 ▲ Add the buttermilk, baking soda, salt, and butter, and stir to blend. Stir in the whole-wheat flour.

3 Add just enough of the white flour to obtain a rough dough.

4 Transfer to a floured surface and knead until smooth and elastic. Divide into 3 equal parts. Roll each into a cylinder, then cut in 4.

5 ▼ Form the pieces into torpedo shapes. Place on a greased baking sheet, cover, and leave in a warm place until doubled in volume.

6 Preheat the oven to 400°F. Brush the rolls with the glaze. Bake until firm, 15–20 minutes. Cool on a rack.

French Bread

MAKES 2 LOAVES

1 package active dry yeast
scant 2 cups lukewarm water
1 tablespoon salt
7½–10 cups strong white bread flour
cornmeal, for sprinkling

1 Combine the yeast and water, stir, and leave for 15 minutes to dissolve. Stir in the salt.

2 Add the flour, 1 cup at a time. Beat in with a wooden spoon, adding just enough flour to obtain a smooth dough. Alternatively, use an electric mixer with a dough hook attachment.

3 Transfer to a floured surface and knead until smooth and elastic.

4 Shape into a ball, place in a greased bowl, and cover with a plastic bag. Leave to rise in a warm place until doubled in volume, 2–4 hours.

5 ▲ Transfer to a lightly floured board and shape into 2 long loaves. Place on a baking sheet sprinkled with cornmeal and leave to rise for 5 minutes.

6 ▲ Score the tops in several places with a very sharp knife. Brush with water and place in a cold oven. Set a pan of boiling water on the bottom of the oven and set the oven to 400°F. Bake until crusty and golden, about 40 minutes. Cool on a rack.

Whole-Wheat Buttermilk Rolls (top), French Bread

Parker House Rolls

MAKES 48

1 package active dry yeast
2 cups lukewarm milk
1/2 cup margarine
5 tablespoons sugar
2 teaspoons salt
2 eggs
8²/₃–10 cups strong white bread flour
1/4 cup butter

3 ▲ Pour the milk mixture into the yeast mixture. Stir in half the flour with a wooden spoon. Add the remaining flour, 1 cup at a time, until a rough dough is obtained.

1 Combine the yeast and 1/2 cup milk in a large bowl. Stir and leave for 15 minutes to dissolve.

2 Scald the remaining milk, cool for 5 minutes, then beat in the margarine, sugar, salt, and eggs. Let cool to lukewarm.

4 Transfer the dough to a lightly floured surface and knead until smooth and elastic. Place in a clean bowl, cover with a plastic bag, and leave to rise in a warm place until doubled in volume, about 2 hours.

5 In a saucepan, melt the butter and set aside. Grease 2 baking sheets.

6 Punch down the dough and divide into 4 equal pieces. Roll each piece into a 12- × 8-inch rectangle, about 1/4 inch thick.

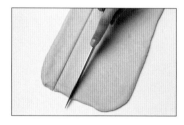

7 ▲ Cut each rectangle into 4 12- x 2-inch strips. Cut each strip into 3 4- × 2-inch rectangles.

8 ▲ Brush each rectangle with melted butter, then fold the rectangles in half, so that the top extends about 1/2 inch over the bottom.

9 ▲ Place the rectangles slightly overlapping on the baking sheet, with the longer side facing up.

10 Cover and chill for 30 minutes. Preheat the oven to 350°F. Bake until golden, 18–20 minutes. Cool slightly before slicing or breaking the rolls.

Clover Leaf Rolls

MAKES 24

1¹/₄ cups milk
2 tablespoons superfine sugar
¹/₄ cup butter, at room temperature
2 teaspoons active dry yeast
1 egg
2 teaspoons salt
4¹/₂–5 cups strong white bread flour
melted butter, for glazing

1 ▲ Heat the milk until lukewarm; test the temperature with your knuckle. Pour into a large bowl and stir in the sugar, butter, and yeast. Leave for 15 minutes to dissolve.

2 Stir the egg and salt into the yeast mixture. Gradually stir in 4¹/₂ cups of the flour. Add just enough extra flour to obtain a rough dough.

3 ▲ Transfer to a floured surface and knead until smooth and elastic. Place in a greased bowl, cover, and leave in a warm place until doubled in volume, about 1¹/₂ hours.

4 Grease 2 12-cup muffin pans.

5 ▼ Punch down the dough. Cut into 4 equal pieces. Roll each piece into a rope 14 inches long. Cut each rope into 18 pieces, then roll each into a ball.

6 ▲ Place 3 balls, side by side, in each muffin cup. Cover loosely and leave to rise in a warm place until doubled in volume, about 1¹/₂ hours.

7 Preheat the oven to 400°F. Brush the rolls with glaze. Bake until lightly browned, about 20 minutes. Cool slightly before serving.

Poppy Seed Knots

MAKES 12

1¹/₄ cups lukewarm milk

¹/₄ cup butter, at room temperature

1 teaspoon superfine sugar

2 teaspoons active dried yeast

1 egg yolk

2 teaspoons salt

4¹/₂–5 cups strong white bread flour

1 egg beaten with 2 teaspoons of water, for glazing

poppy seeds, for sprinkling

1 In a large bowl, stir together the milk, butter, sugar, and yeast. Leave for 15 minutes to dissolve.

2 Stir in the egg yolk, salt, and 2¹/₂ cups flour. Add half the remaining flour and stir to obtain a soft dough.

3 Transfer to a floured surface and knead, adding flour if necessary, until smooth and elastic. Place in a bowl, cover, and leave in a warm place until doubled in volume, 1¹/₂–2 hours.

4 ▲ Grease a baking sheet. Punch down the dough and cut into 12 pieces the size of golf balls.

5 ▲ Roll each piece to a rope, twist to form a knot and place 1 inch apart on the baking sheet. Cover loosely and leave to rise in a warm place until doubled in volume, 1–1¹/₂ hours.

6 Preheat the oven to 350°F.

7 ▲ Brush the knots with the egg glaze and sprinkle over the poppy seeds. Bake until the tops are lightly browned, 25–30 minutes. Cool slightly on a rack before serving.

Bread Sticks

MAKES 18–20

1 package active dry yeast
1¼ cups lukewarm water
3⅔ cups strong white bread flour
2 teaspoons salt
1 teaspoon superfine sugar
2 tablespoons olive oil
10 tablespoons sesame seeds
1 beaten egg, for glazing
coarse salt, for sprinkling

1 Combine the yeast and water, stir and leave for 15 minutes to dissolve.

2 ▲ Place the flour, salt, sugar, and olive oil in a food processor. With the motor running, slowly pour in the yeast mixture, and process until the dough forms a ball. If sticky, add more flour; if dry, add more water.

3 Transfer to a floured surface and knead until smooth and elastic. Place in a bowl, cover, and leave to rise in a warm place for 45 minutes.

4 ▲ Lightly toast the sesame seeds in a frying pan. Grease 2 baking sheets.

5 ▼ Roll small handfuls of dough into cylinders about 12 inches long. Place on the baking sheets.

~ VARIATION ~

If you like, use other seeds, such as poppy or caraway, or, for plain bread sticks, omit the seeds and salt.

6 ▲ Brush with egg glaze, sprinkle with the sesame seeds, then sprinkle over some coarse salt. Leave to rise, uncovered, until almost doubled in volume, about 20 minutes.

7 Preheat the oven to 400°F. Bake until golden, about 15 minutes. Turn off the heat but leave the bread sticks in the oven for 5 minutes more. Serve warm or cool.

Croissants

Makes 18

1 package active dry yeast
generous 1¼ cups lukewarm milk
2 teaspoons superfine sugar
1½ teaspoons salt
3⅔–4½ cups strong white bread flour
1 cup (2 sticks) cold unsalted butter
1 egg beaten with 2 teaspoons water, for glazing

1 In the large bowl of an electric mixer, stir together the yeast and warm milk. Leave for 15 minutes to dissolve. Stir in the sugar, salt, and 1¼ cups of the flour.

2 Using a dough hook, on low speed, gradually add the remaining flour. Beat on high until the dough pulls away from the sides of the bowl. Cover and leave to rise in a warm place until doubled, about 1½ hours.

3 On a floured surface, knead the dough until smooth. Wrap it in wax paper and refrigerate for 15 minutes.

4 ▲ Place each ½ cup (1 stick) butter between two sheets of wax paper. With a rolling pin, flatten each to form a 6- × 4-inch rectangle. Set aside.

5 ▲ On a floured surface, roll out the dough to a 12- × 8-inch rectangle. Place a butter rectangle in the center. Fold the bottom third of dough over the butter and press gently to seal. Top with the other butter rectangle, then fold over the top dough third.

6 ▲ Turn the dough so that the short side is facing you, with the long folded edge on the left and the long open edge on the right, like a book.

7 Roll the dough gently into a 12- × 8-inch rectangle; do not press the butter out. Fold in thirds again and mark one corner with your fingertip to indicate the first turn. Wrap and refrigerate for 30 minutes.

8 Repeat twice more: again position the dough like a book, roll, fold in thirds, mark, wrap, and refrigerate. After the third fold, refrigerate for at least 2 hours (or overnight).

9 Roll out the dough about ⅛-inch thick to a rectangle about 13 inches wide. Trim the sides to neaten.

10 ▲ Cut the dough in half lengthwise, then cut into triangles 6 inches high with a 4-inch base.

11 ▲ Gently go over the triangles lengthwise with a rolling pin to stretch slightly. Roll up from base to point. Place point-down on baking sheets and curve to form a crescent. Cover and leave to rise in a warm place until more than doubled in volume, 1–1½ hours. (Or, refrigerate overnight and bake the next day.)

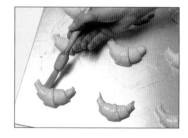

12 ▲ Preheat the oven to 475°F. Brush the crescents with the glaze. Bake for 2 minutes. Lower the heat to 375°F and bake until golden, about 10–12 more minutes. Serve warm.

Dill Bread

MAKES 2 LOAVES

4 teaspoons active dry yeast
2 cups lukewarm water
2 tablespoons sugar
9¼ cups strong white bread flour
½ onion, chopped
4 tablespoons oil
1 large bunch of dill, finely chopped
2 eggs, lightly beaten
¾ cup cottage cheese
4 teaspoons salt
milk, for glazing

1 Mix together the yeast, water, and sugar in a large bowl and leave for 15 minutes to dissolve.

2 ▼ Stir in about half of the flour. Cover and leave to rise in a warm place for 45 minutes.

3 ▲ In a skillet, cook the onion in 1 tablespoon of the oil until soft. Set aside to cool, then stir into the yeast mixture. Stir the dill, eggs, cottage cheese, salt, and remaining oil into the yeast mixture. Gradually add the remaining flour until too stiff to stir.

4 ▲ Transfer to a floured surface and knead until smooth and elastic. Place in a bowl, cover, and leave to rise until doubled in volume, 1–1½ hours.

5 ▲ Grease a large baking sheet. Cut the dough in half and shape into two rounds. Leave to rise in a warm place for 30 minutes.

6 Preheat the oven to 375°F. Score the tops, brush with the milk, and bake until browned, about 50 minutes. Cool on a rack.

Spiral Herb Bread

MAKES 2 LOAVES

2 tablespoons active dry yeast
2¹/₂ cups lukewarm water
3²/₃ cups strong white bread flour
4¹/₂ cups strong whole-wheat bread flour
3 teaspoons salt
2 tablespoons butter
1 large bunch of parsley, finely chopped
1 bunch of scallions, chopped
1 garlic clove, finely chopped
salt and ground black pepper
1 egg, lightly beaten
milk, for glazing

1 Combine the yeast and ¹/₄ cup of the water, stir, and leave for about 15 minutes to dissolve.

2 Combine the flours and salt in a large bowl. Make a well in the center and pour in the yeast mixture and the remaining water. With a wooden spoon, stir from the center, working outwards to obtain a rough dough.

3 Transfer the dough to a floured surface and knead until smooth and elastic. Return to the bowl, cover with a plastic bag, and leave until doubled in volume, about 2 hours.

4 ▲ Meanwhile, combine the butter, parsley, scallions, and garlic in a large skillet. Cook over low heat, stirring, until softened. Season with salt and pepper and set aside.

5 Grease two 9- × 5-inch bread pans. When the dough has risen, cut in half and roll each half into a rectangle about 14 × 9 inches.

6 ▼ Brush both with the beaten egg. Divide the herb mixture between the two, spreading just up to the edges.

7 ▲ Roll up to enclose the filling and pinch the short ends to seal. Place in the pans, seam-side down. Cover, and leave in a warm place until the dough rises above the rim of the pans.

8 Preheat the oven to 375°F. Brush with milk and bake until the bottoms sound hollow when tapped, about 55 minutes. Cool on a rack.

Pizza

MAKES 2

4¹/₂ cups strong white bread flour
1 teaspoon salt
2 teaspoons active dry yeast
1¹/₄ cups lukewarm water
¹/₄–¹/₂ cup extra-virgin olive oil
tomato sauce, grated cheese, olives, and herbs, for topping

1 Combine the flour and salt in a large mixing bowl. Make a well in the center and add the yeast, water, and 2 tablespoon of the olive oil. Leave for 15 minutes to dissolve the yeast.

2 With your hands, stir until the dough just holds together. Transfer to a floured surface and knead until smooth and elastic. Avoid adding too much flour while kneading.

3 ▲ Brush the inside of a clean bowl with 1 tablespoon of the oil. Place the dough in the bowl and roll around to coat with the oil. Cover with a plastic bag and leave to rise in a warm place until more than doubled in volume, about 45 minutes.

4 Divide the dough into 2 balls. Preheat the oven to 400°F.

5 ▲ Roll each ball into a 10-inch circle. Flip the circles over and onto your palm. Set each circle on the work surface and rotate, stretching the dough as you turn, until it is about 12 inches in diameter.

6 ▲ Brush 2 pizza pans with oil. Place the dough circles in the pans and neaten the edges. Brush with oil.

7 ▲ Cover with the toppings and bake until golden, 10–12 minutes.

Cheese Bread

MAKES 1 LOAF

1 package active dry yeast
1 cup lukewarm milk
2 tablespoons butter
3²/₃ cups strong white bread flour
2 teaspoons salt
3¹/₂ ounces sharp Cheddar cheese, grated

1 Combine the yeast and milk. Stir and leave for 15 minutes to dissolve.

2 Melt the butter, let cool, and add to the yeast mixture.

3 Mix the flour and salt together in a large bowl. Make a well in the center and pour in the yeast mixture.

4 With a wooden spoon, stir from the center, incorporating flour with each turn, to obtain a rough dough. If the dough seems too dry, add 2–3 tablespoons water.

5 Transfer to a floured surface and knead until smooth and elastic. Return to the bowl, cover, and leave to rise in a warm place until doubled in volume, 2–3 hours.

6 ▲ Grease a 9- × 5-inch bread pan. Punch down the dough with your fist. Knead in the cheese, distributing it as evenly as possible.

7 ▼ Twist the dough, form into a loaf shape and place in the pan, tucking the ends under. Leave in a warm place until the dough rises above the rim of the pan.

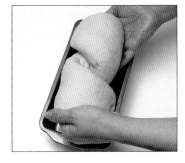

8 ▲ Preheat the oven to 400°F. Bake for 15 minutes, then lower the heat to 375°F and bake until the bottom sounds hollow when tapped, about 30 minutes more. Cool on a rack.

Italian Flat Bread with Sage

MAKES 1 LOAF

2 teaspoons active dry yeast
1 cup lukewarm water
3 cups strong white bread flour
2 teaspoons salt
5 tablespoons extra-virgin olive oil
12 fresh sage leaves, chopped

1 Combine the yeast and water, stir, and leave for 15 minutes until the yeast has completely dissolved.

2 Mix the flour and salt in a large bowl, and make a well in the center.

3 Stir in the yeast mixture and 4 tablespoons of the oil. Stir from the center, incorporating flour with each turn, to obtain a rough dough.

4 ▲ Transfer the dough to a lightly floured surface and knead until it is smooth and elastic. Shape into a ball and place in a lightly oiled bowl. Cover and leave to rise in a warm place until doubled in volume, about 2 hours.

5 Preheat the oven to 400°F and place a baking sheet in the center of the oven.

6 Punch down the dough. Knead in the sage leaves, then roll into a 12-inch circle. Leave to rise slightly.

7 ▼ Dimple the surface all over with your finger. Drizzle the remaining oil on top. Slide a floured board under the bread, carry to the oven, and slide off onto the hot baking sheet. Bake for about 35 minutes, or until golden brown. Cool on a rack.

Zucchini Yeast Bread

MAKES 1 LOAF

1 pound zucchini, grated
2 tablespoons salt
2 teaspoons active dry yeast
1¼ cups lukewarm water
3½ cups strong white bread flour
olive oil, for brushing

1 ▼ In a colander, alternate the layers of grated zucchini and salt. Leave for 30 minutes, then squeeze out the moisture with your hands.

2 Combine the yeast with ¼ cup of the warm water. Leave for 15 minutes.

3 ▲ Place the zucchini, yeast, and flour in a bowl. Stir together and add just enough of the remaining water to obtain a rough dough.

4 Transfer to a floured surface and knead until smooth and elastic. Return the dough to the bowl, cover with a plastic bag, and leave to rise in a warm place until doubled in volume, about 1½ hours.

5 Punch down the risen dough with your fist and knead into a tapered cylinder. Place on a greased baking sheet, cover, and leave to rise in a warm place until doubled in volume.

6 ▼ Preheat the oven to 425°F. Brush the bread with olive oil and bake for 40–45 minutes, or until the loaf is a golden color. Cool on a rack.

Italian Flat Bread with Sage (top), Zucchini Yeast Bread

Olive Bread

MAKES 2 LOAVES

4 teaspoons active dry yeast

2 cups warm water

3^1/$_2$ cups strong white bread flour

1^1/$_2$ cups strong whole-wheat bread flour

generous ^{1}/$_2$ cup cornmeal

2 teaspoons salt

2 tablespoons olive oil

1 cup mixed pitted green and black olives, cut in half

cornmeal, for sprinkling

1 Combine the yeast and water, stir, and leave for 5 minutes to dissolve.

2 Stir in 2 cups of the white flour, cover, and leave in a warm place for 1 hour.

3 In a large mixing bowl, combine the remaining white flour, the whole-wheat flour, cornmeal, and salt. Make a well in the center; pour in the olive oil and yeast mixture.

4 ▼ With a wooden spoon, stir from the center, incorporating flour with each turn. When the dough becomes stiff, stir with your hands until a rough dough is obtained.

5 Transfer to a floured surface and knead until smooth and elastic. Return to the bowl, cover, and leave to rise in a warm place until doubled in volume, about 1^1/$_2$ hours.

6 ▲ Punch down the dough with your fist. Add the olives and knead in as evenly as possible.

7 Cut the dough in half and shape each half into a round. Sprinkle a baking sheet with cornmeal. Place the rounds on the sheet, seam-side down. Cover with a dish towel and leave to rise until nearly doubled in volume.

8 Place a baking pan in the bottom of the oven and half fill it with hot water. Preheat the oven to 425°F.

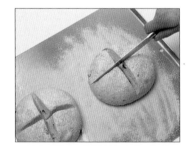

9 ▲ With a sharp knife, score the tops of the loaves. Bake for 20 minutes. Lower the heat to 375°F and bake for 25–30 minutes more, or until the bottoms of the loaves sound hollow when tapped. Remove and cool on a wire rack.

Pumpkin Spice Bread

MAKES 1 LOAF

2 packages active dry yeast
1 cup lukewarm water
2 teaspoons ground cinnamon
1 teaspoon ground ginger
1 teaspoon ground allspice
1/4 teaspoon ground cloves
1 teaspoon salt
6 tablespoons instant nonfat dry milk
6 ounces cooked or canned pumpkin
1 3/4 cups sugar
1/2 cup (1 stick) butter, melted
5 1/2 cups strong white bread flour
1/3 cup pecans, finely chopped

1 In the bowl of an electric mixer, combine the yeast and water, stir, and leave for 15 minutes to dissolve. In another bowl, mix the spices together.

2 To the yeast, add the salt, milk, pumpkin, generous 1/2 cup of the sugar, 3 tablespoons of the melted butter, 2 teaspoons of the spice mixture, and 2 cups of the flour.

3 ▲ With the dough hook, mix on low speed until blended. Gradually add the remaining flour and mix on medium speed until a rough dough is formed. Alternatively, mix by hand.

4 Transfer to a floured surface and knead until smooth. Place in a bowl, cover, and leave to rise in a warm place until doubled, 1–1 1/2 hours.

5 ▼ Punch down and knead briefly. Divide the dough into thirds. Roll each third into an 18-inch rope. Cut each rope into 18 equal pieces, then roll into balls.

6 Grease a 10-inch tube pan. Stir the remaining sugar into the remaining spice mixture. Roll the balls in the remaining melted butter, then in the sugar and spice mixture.

7 ▲ Place 18 balls in the pan and sprinkle over half the pecans. Add the remaining balls, staggering the rows, then sprinkle over the remaining pecans. Cover and leave to rise in a warm place until almost doubled, about 45 minutes.

8 Preheat the oven to 350°F. Bake for 55 minutes. Cool in the tin for about 20 minutes, then unmold. Serve warm.

Walnut Bread

MAKES 1 LOAF

3²/₃ cups strong whole-wheat bread flour
1¹/₄ cups strong white bread flour
2¹/₂ teaspoons salt
2¹/₂ cups lukewarm water
1 tablespoon honey
1 package active dry yeast
1 cup walnut pieces, plus more for decorating
1 beaten egg, for glazing

1 Combine the flours and salt in a large bowl. Make a well in the center and add 1 cup of the water, the honey, and the yeast.

2 Set aside until the yeast dissolves and the mixture is frothy.

3 Add the remaining water. With a wooden spoon, stir from the center, incorporating flour with each turn, to obtain a smooth dough. Add more flour if the dough is too sticky and use your hands if the dough becomes too stiff to stir.

4 Transfer to a floured board and knead, adding flour if necessary, until the dough is smooth and elastic. Place in a greased bowl and roll the dough around in the bowl to coat thoroughly on all sides.

5 ▲ Cover with a plastic bag and leave in a warm place until doubled in volume, about 1¹/₂ hours.

6 ▲ Punch down the dough and knead in the walnuts evenly.

7 Grease a baking sheet. Shape into a round loaf and place on the baking sheet. Press in walnut pieces to decorate the top. Cover with a damp cloth and leave to rise in a warm place until doubled, 25–30 minutes.

8 Preheat the oven to 425°F.

9 ▲ With a sharp knife, score the top. Brush with the glaze. Bake for 15 minutes. Lower the heat to 375°F and bake until the bottom sounds hollow when tapped, about 40 minutes. Cool on a rack.

Pecan Rye Bread

MAKES 2 LOAVES

1¹/₂ packages active dry yeast
2³/₄ cups lukewarm water
6 cups strong white bread flour
4¹/₂ cups rye flour
2 tablespoons salt
1 tablespoon honey
2 teaspoons caraway seeds (optional)
¹/₂ cup butter, at room temperature
1¹/₃ cups pecans, chopped

1 Combine the yeast and ¹/₂ cup of the water. Stir and leave for 15 minutes to dissolve.

2 In the bowl of an electric mixer, combine the flours, salt, honey, caraway seeds, if using, and butter. With the dough hook, mix on low speed until well blended.

3 Add the yeast mixture and the remaining water and mix on medium speed until the dough forms a ball.

4 ▲ Transfer to a floured surface and knead in the pecans.

5 Return the dough to a clean bowl, cover with a plastic bag, and leave in a warm place until doubled in volume, about 2 hours.

6 Grease 2 8¹/₂- × 4¹/₂-inch bread pans.

7 ▲ Punch down the risen dough.

8 Divide the dough in half and form into loaves. Place in the pans, seam-side down. Dust the tops with flour. Cover with plastic bags and leave to rise in a warm place until doubled in volume, about 1 hour.

9 Preheat the oven to 375°F.

10 ▼ Bake until the bottoms sound hollow when tapped, 45–50 minutes. Cool on racks.

Sticky Buns

MAKES 18

scant ³/4 cup milk

1 package active dry yeast

2 tablespoons superfine sugar

3¹/2–4 cups strong white bread flour

1 teaspoon salt

¹/2 cup (1 stick) cold butter, cut into pieces

2 eggs, lightly beaten

grated rind of 1 lemon

FOR THE TOPPING AND FILLING

1¹/4 cups soft dark brown sugar

5 tablespoons butter

¹/2 cup water

¹/2 cup pecans, chopped

3 tablespoons superfine sugar

2 teaspoons ground cinnamon

generous 1 cup raisins

1 Heat the milk to lukewarm. Add the yeast and sugar and leave until frothy, about 15 minutes.

2 Combine the flour and salt in a large mixing bowl. Add the butter and cut in with a pastry blender until the mixture resembles coarse crumbs.

3 ▲ Make a well in the center and add the yeast mixture, eggs, and lemon rind. With a wooden spoon, stir from the center, incorporating flour with each turn. When it becomes too stiff, stir by hand to obtain a rough dough.

4 Transfer to a floured surface and knead until smooth and elastic. Return to the bowl, cover with a plastic bag and leave to rise in a warm place until doubled in volume, about 2 hours.

5 Meanwhile, for the topping, make the syrup. Combine the brown sugar, butter, and water in a heavy saucepan. Bring to the boil and boil gently until thick and syrupy, about 10 minutes.

6 ▲ Place 1 tablespoon of the syrup in the bottom of each of 18 1¹/2-inch muffin cups. Sprinkle in a thin layer of chopped pecans, reserving the rest for the filling.

7 Punch down the dough and transfer to a floured surface. Roll out to an 18- × 12-inch rectangle.

8 ▲ For the filling, combine the superfine sugar, cinnamon, raisins, and reserved nuts. Sprinkle over the dough in an even layer.

9 ▲ Roll up tightly, from the long side, to form a cylinder.

10 ▲ Cut the cylinder into 1-inch rounds. Place each in a prepared muffin cup, cut-side up. Leave to rise in a warm place until increased by half, about 30 minutes.

11 Preheat the oven to 350°F. Place foil under the pans to catch any syrup that bubbles over. Bake until golden, about 25 minutes.

12 Remove from the oven and invert the tins onto a sheet of wax paper. Leave for 3–5 minutes, then remove the buns from the pans. Transfer to a rack to cool. Serve sticky-side up.

~ COOK'S TIP ~

To save time and energy, make double the recipe and freeze half for another occasion.

Raisin Bread

MAKES 2 LOAVES

1 package active dry yeast
2 cups lukewarm milk
1 cup raisins
generous 1/4 cup currants
1 tablespoon sherry or brandy
1/2 teaspoon freshly grated nutmeg
grated rind of 1 large orange
5 tablespoons sugar
1 tablespoon salt
1/2 cup (1 stick) butter, melted
6–7 1/2 cups strong white bread flour
1 egg beaten with 1 tablespoon cream, for glazing

1 Stir together the yeast and 1/2 cup of the milk and let stand for 15 minutes to dissolve.

2 ▲ Mix the raisins, currants, sherry or brandy, nutmeg, and orange rind together and set aside.

3 In another bowl, mix the remaining milk, sugar, salt, and half the butter. Add the yeast mixture. With a wooden spoon, stir in half the flour, 1 1/4 cups at a time, until blended. Add the remaining flour as needed for a stiff dough.

4 Transfer to a floured surface and knead until smooth and elastic. Place in a greased bowl, cover, and leave to rise in a warm place until doubled in volume, about 2 1/2 hours.

5 Punch down the dough, return to the bowl, cover, and leave in a warm place for 30 minutes.

6 Grease 2 8 1/2- × 4 1/2-inch bread pans. Divide the dough in half and roll each half into a rectangle about 20 × 7 inches.

7 ▲ Brush the rectangles with the remaining melted butter. Sprinkle over the raisin mixture, then roll up tightly, tucking in the ends slightly as you roll. Place in the prepared pans, cover, and leave to rise until almost doubled in volume.

8 ▲ Preheat the oven to 400°F. Brush the loaves with the glaze. Bake for 20 minutes. Lower the heat to 350°F and bake for 25–30 minutes more, until golden. Cool on racks.

Prune Bread

MAKES 1 LOAF

1 cup dried prunes
1 package active dry yeast
²/₃ cup strong whole-wheat bread flour
3¹/₄–3²/₃ cups strong white bread flour
¹/₂ teaspoon baking soda
1 teaspoon salt
1 teaspoon pepper
2 tablespoons butter, at room temperature
³/₄ cup buttermilk
¹/₃ cup walnuts, chopped
milk, for glazing

1 Simmer the prunes in water to cover until soft, or soak overnight. Drain, reserving ¹/₄ cup of the soaking liquid. Pit and chop the prunes.

2 Combine the yeast and the reserved prune liquid. Leave for 15 minutes.

3 In a large bowl, stir together the flours, baking soda, salt, and pepper. Make a well in the center.

4 ▲ Add the chopped prunes, butter, and buttermilk. Pour in the yeast mixture. With a wooden spoon, stir from the center, incorporating more flour with each turn, to obtain a rough dough.

5 Transfer to a floured surface and knead until smooth and elastic. Return to the bowl, cover with a plastic bag, and leave to rise in a warm place until doubled in volume, about 1¹/₂ hours.

6 Grease a baking sheet.

7 ▲ Punch down the dough with your fist, then knead in the walnuts.

8 Shape the dough into a long, cylindrical loaf. Place on the baking sheet, cover loosely, and leave to rise in a warm place for 45 minutes.

9 Preheat the oven to 425°F.

10 ▼ With a sharp knife, score the top deeply. Brush with milk and bake for 15 minutes. Lower the heat to 375°F and bake until the bottom sounds hollow when tapped, about 35 minutes more. Cool on a rack.

Braided Prune Bread

Makes 1 loaf

1 package active dry yeast
¹/₄ cup lukewarm water
¹/₄ cup lukewarm milk
¹/₄ cup superfine sugar
¹/₂ teaspoon salt
1 egg
¹/₄ cup (¹/₂ stick) butter, at room temperature
3²/₃–4¹/₂ cups strong white bread flour
1 egg beaten with 2 teaspoons water, for glazing

For the filling

scant 1 cup cooked prunes, pitted
2 teaspoons grated lemon rind
1 teaspoon grated orange rind
¹/₄ teaspoon freshly grated nutmeg
3 tablespoons butter, melted
¹/₄ cup very finely chopped walnuts
2 tablespoons superfine sugar

1 In a large bowl, combine the yeast and water, stir, and leave for 15 minutes to dissolve.

2 Stir in the milk, sugar, salt, egg, and butter. Gradually stir in 3 cups of the flour to obtain a soft dough.

3 Transfer to a floured surface and knead in just enough flour to obtain a dough that is smooth and elastic. Put into a clean bowl, cover, and leave to rise in a warm place until doubled in volume, about 1¹/₂ hours.

~ VARIATION ~

For Braided Apricot Bread, replace the prunes with the same amount of dried apricots. It is not necessary to cook them, but, to soften them, soak them in hot tea and discard the liquid before using.

4 ▲ Meanwhile, for the filling, combine the prunes, lemon and orange rinds, nutmeg, butter, walnuts, and sugar, and stir together to blend. Set aside.

5 Grease a large baking sheet. Punch down the dough and transfer to a lightly floured surface. Knead briefly, then roll out into a 15- × 10-inch rectangle. Carefully transfer to the baking sheet.

6 ▲ Spread the filling in the center.

7 ▲ With a sharp knife, cut 10 strips at an angle on either side of the filling, cutting just to the filling.

8 ▲ For a braided pattern, fold up one end neatly, then fold over the strips from alternating sides until all the strips are folded over. Tuck excess dough at the ends underneath.

9 ▲ Cover loosely with a dish towel and leave to rise in a warm place until almost doubled in volume.

10 ▲ Preheat the oven to 375°F. Brush with the glaze. Bake until browned, about 30 minutes. Transfer to a rack to cool.

Kugelhopf

MAKES 1 LOAF

²/₃ cup raisins

1 tablespoon Kirsch or brandy

1 package active dry yeast

¹/₂ cup lukewarm water

¹/₂ cup (1 stick) unsalted butter, at room temperature

¹/₂ cup sugar

3 eggs, at room temperature

grated rind of 1 lemon

1 teaspoon salt

¹/₂ teaspoon vanilla extract

3²/₃ cups strong white bread flour

¹/₂ cup milk

¹/₄ cup slivered almonds

scant 1 cup whole blanched almonds, chopped

confectioners' sugar, for dusting

1 ▼ In a bowl, combine the raisins and Kirsch or brandy. Set aside.

2 Combine the yeast and water, stir, and leave for 15 minutes to dissolve.

3 With an electric mixer, cream the butter and sugar until thick and fluffy. Beat in the eggs, 1 at a time. Add the lemon rind, salt, and vanilla. Stir in the yeast mixture.

4 ▲ Add the flour, alternating with the milk, until the mixture is well blended. Cover and leave to rise in a warm place until doubled in volume, about 2 hours.

5 ▲ Grease a 10 cup Kugelhopf mold, then sprinkle the slivered almonds evenly over the bottom.

6 Work the raisins and whole almonds into the dough, then spoon into the mold. Cover with a plastic bag, and leave to rise in a warm place until the dough almost reaches the top of the mold, about 1 hour.

7 Preheat the oven to 350°F.

8 Bake until golden brown, about 45 minutes. If the top browns too quickly, protect with a sheet of foil. Let cool in the mold for 15 minutes, then invert onto a rack. Dust the top lightly with confectioners' sugar before serving.

Panettone

MAKES 1 LOAF

²/₃ cup lukewarm milk
1 package active dry yeast
3–3¹/₂ cups strong white bread flour
5 tablespoons sugar
2 teaspoons salt
2 eggs
5 egg yolks
³/₄ cup (1¹/₂ sticks) unsalted butter, at room temperature
scant 1 cup raisins
grated rind of 1 lemon
¹/₂ cup candied citrus peel, chopped

1 Combine the milk and yeast in a large warmed bowl and leave for 10 minutes to dissolve.

2 Stir in 1 cup of the flour, cover loosely, and leave in a warm place for 30 minutes.

3 Sift over the remaining flour and stir into the dough mixture. Make a well in the center and add the sugar, salt, eggs, and egg yolks.

4 ▲ Stir with a wooden spoon until stiff, then stir with your hands to obtain a very elastic and sticky dough. Add a little more flour if necessary, but keep the dough as soft as possible.

5 ▲ To incorporate the butter, smear it over the dough, then work it in with your hands. When the butter is evenly distributed, cover, and leave to rise in a warm place until doubled in volume, 3–4 hours.

6 Line the bottom of an 8-cup charlotte mold or 2-pound coffee can with wax paper, then grease the bottom and sides.

7 Punch down the dough and transfer to a floured surface. Knead in the raisins, lemon rind, and citrus peel.

8 ▲ Put the dough in the mold. Cover and leave to rise in a warm place until it is well above the top of the tin, about 2 hours.

9 Preheat the oven to 400°F. Bake for 15 minutes, cover the top with foil and lower the heat to 350°F. Bake for 30 minutes more. Let cool in the mold for 5 minutes, then transfer to a rack.

Danish Wreath

SERVES 10–12

1/4 ounce active dry yeast
3/4 cup lukewarm milk
1/4 cup superfine sugar
4 cups strong white bread flour
1/2 teaspoon salt
1/2 teaspoon vanilla extract
1 egg, beaten
1 cup (2 sticks) unsalted butter
1 egg yolk beaten with 2 teaspoons water, for glazing
1 cup confectioners' sugar
1–2 tablespoons water
chopped pecans or walnuts, for sprinkling
FOR THE FILLING
scant 1 cup soft dark brown sugar
1 teaspoon ground cinnamon
1/3 cup pecans or walnuts, toasted and chopped

1 Combine the yeast, milk, and 1/2 teaspoon of the sugar. Stir and leave for 15 minutes to dissolve.

2 Combine the flour, sugar, and salt. Make a well in the center and add the yeast mixture, vanilla, and egg. Stir until a rough dough is formed.

3 Transfer to a floured surface and knead until smooth and elastic. Wrap and refrigerate for 15 minutes.

~ VARIATION ~

For a different filling, substitute 3 tart apples, peeled and grated, the grated rind of 1 lemon, 1 tablespoon lemon juice, 1/2 teaspoon ground cinnamon, 3 tablespoons sugar, 1 1/4 tablespoons currants, and 2 tablespoons chopped walnuts. Combine well and use as described.

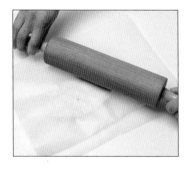

4 ▲ Meanwhile, place each 1/2 cup (1 stick) butter between two sheets of wax paper. With a rolling pin, flatten each to form a 6- × 4-inch rectangle. Set both rectangles aside.

5 ▲ Roll out the dough to a 12- × 8-inch rectangle. Place one butter rectangle in the center. Fold the bottom third of dough over the butter and seal the edge. Place the other butter rectangle on top and cover with the top third of the dough.

6 Turn the dough so the shorter side faces you. Roll into a 12- × 8-inch rectangle. Fold into thirds, and indent one edge with your finger to indicate the first turn. Wrap in wax paper and refrigerate for 30 minutes.

7 Repeat 2 more times; rolling, folding, marking, and refrigerateing between each turn. After the third fold refrigerate for 1–2 hours, or longer.

8 Grease a large baking sheet. In a bowl, stir together all the filling ingredients until blended.

9 ▲ Roll out the dough to a 25- × 6-inch strip. Spread over a thin layer of filling, leaving a 1/2-inch border.

10 Roll up the dough lengthwise into a cylinder. Place on the baking sheet and form into a circle, pinching the edges together to seal. Cover with an inverted bowl and leave in a warm place to rise for 45 minutes.

11 ▲ Preheat the oven to 400°F. Slash the top every 2 inches, cutting about 1/2 inch deep. Brush with the egg glaze. Bake until golden, about 35–40 minutes. Cool on a rack. To serve, mix the confectioners' sugar and water, then drizzle over the wreath. Sprinkle with the pecans or walnuts.

PIES &
TARTS

HERE IS EVERY SORT OF FILLING –
FROM ORCHARD FRUITS TO AUTUMN
NUTS, TANGY CITRUS TO LUSCIOUS
CHOCOLATE – FOR THE MOST
MEMORABLE PIES AND TARTS. SOME
ARE PLAIN AND SOME ARE FANCY,
BUT ALL ARE DELICIOUS.

Plum Pie

SERVES 8

2 pounds red or purple plums
grated rind of 1 lemon
1 tablespoon lemon juice
3/4–scant 1 cup superfine sugar
3 tablespoons quick-cooking tapioca
pinch of salt
1/2 teaspoon ground cinnamon
1/4 teaspoon freshly grated nutmeg
FOR THE CRUST
2 1/2 cups flour
1 teaspoon salt
6 tablespoons cold butter, cut in pieces
1/4 cup cold shortening, cut in pieces
1/4–1/2 cup ice water
milk, for glazing

1 ▼ For the crust, sift the flour and salt into a bowl. Add the butter and shortening and cut in with a pastry blender until the mixture resembles coarse crumbs.

2 Stir in just enough water to bind the dough. Gather into 2 balls, 1 slightly larger than the other. Wrap and refrigerate for 20 minutes.

3 Place a baking sheet in the center of the oven and preheat to 425°F.

4 On a lightly floured surface, roll out the larger dough ball to about 1/8 inch thick. Transfer to a 9-inch pie pan and trim the edge.

5 ▲ Halve the plums, discard the pits, and cut in large pieces. Mix all the filling ingredients together (if the plums are tart, use scant 1 cup sugar). Transfer to the pie shell.

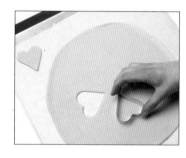

6 ▲ Roll out the remaining dough and place on a baking tray lined with wax paper. With a cutter, stamp out 4 hearts. Transfer the dough lid to the pie using the wax paper.

7 Trim to leave a 1/4-inch overhang. Fold the top edge under the bottom and pinch to seal. Arrange the dough hearts on top. Brush with the milk. Bake for 15 minutes. Reduce the heat to 350°F and bake for 30–35 minutes more. If the crust browns too quickly, protect with a sheet of foil.

Blueberry Pie

SERVES 8

1 pound blueberries
generous $1/2$ cup superfine sugar
3 tablespoons cornstarch
2 tablespoons lemon juice
2 tablespoons butter, diced
FOR THE CRUST
$2^1/2$ cups flour
$3/4$ teaspoon salt
$1/2$ cup (1 stick) cold butter, cut in pieces
3 tablespoons cold shortening, cut in pieces
5–6 tablespoons ice water
1 egg beaten with 1 tablespoon water, for glazing

1 For the crust, sift the flour and salt into a bowl. Add the butter and shortening, and cut in with a pastry blender until the mixture resembles coarse crumbs. With a fork, stir in just enough water to bind the dough. Form into 2 equal balls, wrap in wax paper, and refrigerate for 20 minutes.

2 On a floured surface, roll out 1 ball about $1/8$ inch thick. Place in a 9-inch pie pan and trim to leave a $1/2$-inch overhang. Brush the base with egg glaze.

3 ▲ Mix all the filling ingredients together, except the butter (reserve a few blueberries for decoration). Spoon into the shell and dot with the butter. Brush the egg glaze on the edge of the lower crust.

4 Place a baking sheet in the center of the oven and preheat to 425°F.

5 ▼ Roll out the remaining dough on a baking tray lined with wax paper. With a serrated pastry wheel, cut out 24 thin strips of dough. Roll out the scraps and cut out leaf shapes. Mark veins in the leaves with the point of a knife.

6 ▲ Weave the strips in a close lattice, then transfer to the pie using the wax paper. Press the edges to seal and trim. Arrange the dough leaves around the rim. Brush with egg glaze.

7 Bake for 10 minutes. Reduce the heat to 350°F and bake until the dough is golden, 40–45 minutes more. Decorate with the reserved berries.

Raspberry Tart

SERVES 8

4 egg yolks
5 tablespoons superfine sugar
3 tablespoons flour
1¼ cups milk
pinch of salt
½ teaspoon vanilla extract
2⅔ cups fresh raspberries
5 tablespoons grape jelly
1 tablespoon fresh orange juice
FOR THE CRUST
1⅔ cups flour
½ teaspoon baking powder
¼ teaspoon salt
1 tablespoon sugar
grated rind of ½ orange
6 tablespoons cold butter, cut in pieces
1 egg yolk
3–4 tablespoons whipping cream

1 For the crust, sift the flour, baking powder, and salt into a bowl. Stir in the sugar and orange rind. Add the butter and cut in with a pastry blender until the mixture resembles coarse crumbs. With a fork, stir in the egg yolk and just enough cream to bind the dough. Gather into a ball, wrap in wax paper, and refrigerate.

2 For the custard filling, beat the egg yolks and sugar until thick and lemon-colored. Gradually stir in the flour.

3 In a saucepan, bring the milk and salt just to the boil, then remove from the heat. Whisk into the egg yolk mixture, return to the pan, and continue whisking over moderately high heat until just bubbling. Cook for 3 minutes to thicken. Transfer immediately to a bowl. Add the vanilla and stir to blend.

4 ▲ Cover with wax paper to prevent a skin from forming.

5 ▲ Preheat the oven to 400°F. On a floured surface, roll out the dough ⅛ inch thick, transfer to a 10-inch tart pan and trim the edge. Prick the bottom all over with a fork and line with crumpled wax paper. Fill with pie weights and bake for 15 minutes. Remove the paper and weights. Continue baking until golden, 6–8 minutes more. Let cool.

6 ▲ Spread an even layer of the pastry cream filling in the tart shell and arrange the raspberries on top. Melt the jelly and orange juice in a saucepan and brush on top to glaze.

Rhubarb and Cherry Pie

SERVES 8

1 pound rhubarb, cut in 1-inch pieces (about 3 cups)

1 1-pound can (2 cups) pitted tart red or black cherries, drained

1½ cups superfine sugar

1 ounce quick-cooking tapioca

FOR THE CRUST

2½ cups flour

1 teaspoon salt

6 tablespoons cold butter, cut in pieces

⅓ cup cold shortening, cut in pieces

¼–½ cup ice water

milk, for glazing

1 ▲ For the crust, sift the flour and salt into a bowl. Add the butter and shortening to the dry ingredients and cut in with a pastry blender until the mixture resembles coarse crumbs.

2 With a fork, stir in just enough water to bind the dough. Gather into 2 balls, 1 slightly larger than the other. Wrap the dough in wax paper and refrigerate for at least 20 minutes.

3 Place a baking sheet in the center of the oven and preheat to 400°F.

4 On a lightly floured surface, roll out the larger dough ball to a thickness of about ⅛ inch.

5 ▼ Roll the dough around the rolling pin and transfer to a 9-inch pie pan. Trim the edge to leave a ½-inch overhang all around.

6 Refrigerate the pie shell while making the filling.

7 In a mixing bowl, combine the rhubarb, cherries, sugar, and tapioca, and spoon into the pie shell.

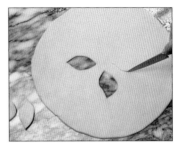

8 ▲ Roll out the remaining dough and cut out leaf shapes.

9 Transfer the dough to the pie and trim to leave a ¾-inch overhang. Fold the top edge under the bottom and flute. Roll small balls from the scraps. Mark veins in the dough leaves and place on top with the dough balls.

10 Glaze the top and bake until golden, 40–50 minutes.

Peach Leaf Pie

SERVES 8

2¹/₂ pounds ripe peaches

juice of 1 lemon

¹/₂ cup superfine sugar

3 tablespoons cornstarch

¹/₄ teaspoon grated nutmeg

¹/₂ teaspoon ground cinnamon

2 tablespoons butter, diced

FOR THE CRUST

2¹/₂ cups flour

³/₄ teaspoon salt

¹/₂ cup (1 stick) cold butter, cut in pieces

generous ¹/₃ cup cold shortening, cut in pieces

5–6 tablespoons ice water

1 egg beaten with 1 tablespoon water, for glazing

1 For the crust, sift the flour and salt into a bowl. Add the butter and shortening and cut in with a pastry blender until the mixture resembles coarse crumbs.

2 ▲ With a fork, stir in just enough water to bind the dough. Gather into 2 balls, 1 slightly larger than the other. Wrap in wax paper and refrigerate for at least 20 minutes.

3 Place a baking sheet in the center of the oven and preheat to 425°F.

4 ▲ Drop a few peaches at a time into boiling water for 20 seconds, then transfer to a bowl of cold water. When cool, peel off the skins.

5 Slice the peaches and combine with the lemon juice, sugar, cornstarch, and spices. Set aside.

6 ▲ On a lightly floured surface, roll out the larger dough ball to about ¹/₈ inch thick. Transfer to a 9-inch pie pan and trim. Refrigerate.

7 ▲ Roll out the remaining dough ¹/₄ inch thick. Cut out leaf shapes 3 inches long, using a template if needed. Mark veins with a knife. With the scraps, roll a few balls.

8 ▲ Brush the bottom of the pie shell with egg glaze. Add the peaches, piling them higher in the center. Dot with the butter.

9 ▲ To assemble, start from the outside edge and cover the peaches with a ring of leaves. Place a second ring of leaves above, staggering the positions. Continue with rows of leaves until covered. Place the balls in the center. Brush with glaze.

10 Bake the pie for 10 minutes. Lower the heat to 350°F and bake for 35–40 minutes more.

~ COOK'S TIP ~

Baking the pie on a preheated baking sheet helps to make the bottom crust crisp. The moisture from the filling keeps the bottom crust more humid than the top, but this baking method helps to compensate for the top crust being more exposed to the heat source.

Peach Tart with Almond Cream

SERVES 8–10

4 large ripe peaches

²/₃ cup blanched almonds

2 tablespoons flour

7 tablespoons unsalted butter,
    at room temperature

¹/₂ cup plus 2 tablespoons superfine sugar

1 egg

1 egg yolk

¹/₂ teaspoon vanilla extract,
    or 2 teaspoons rum

FOR THE CRUST

1²/₃ cups flour

³/₄ teaspoon salt

7 tablespoons cold unsalted butter,
    cut in pieces

1 egg yolk

2¹/₂–3 tablespoons ice water

1 ▲ For the crust, sift the flour and salt into a bowl.

2 Add the butter and cut in with a pastry blender until the mixture resembles coarse crumbs. Stir in the egg yolk and just enough water to bind the dough. Gather into a ball, wrap in wax paper, and refrigerate for at least 20 minutes.

3 Place a baking sheet in the center of the oven and preheat to 400°F.

4 ▲ On a floured surface, roll out the dough to ¹/₈ inch thick. Transfer to a 10-inch tart pan. Trim the edge, prick the bottom, and refrigerate.

5 ▲ Score the bottoms of the peaches. Drop the peaches, 1 at a time, into boiling water. Boil for 20 seconds, then dip in cold water. Peel off the skins using a sharp knife.

6 ▲ Grind the almonds finely with the flour in a food processor, blender, or nut grinder. With an electric mixer, cream the butter and generous ¹/₂ cup of the sugar until light and fluffy. Gradually beat in the egg and yolk. Stir in the almonds and vanilla or rum. Spread in the pastry shell.

7 ▲ Halve the peaches and remove the pits. Cut crossways in thin slices and arrange on top of the almond cream like the spokes of a wheel; keep the slices of each peach half together. Fan out by pressing down gently at a slight angle.

8 ▲ Bake until the pastry begins to brown, 10–15 minutes. Lower the heat to 350°F and continue baking until the almond cream sets, about 15 minutes more. Ten minutes before the end of the cooking time, sprinkle with the remaining 2 tablespoons of sugar.

~ VARIATION ~

For a Nectarine and Apricot Tart with Almond Cream, replace the peaches with nectarines, prepared and arranged the same way. Peel and chop 3 fresh apricots. Fill the spaces between the fanned-out nectarines with 1 tablespoon of chopped apricots. Bake as above.

Apple and Cranberry Lattice Pie

SERVES 8

grated rind of 1 orange
3 tablespoons fresh orange juice
2 large, tart cooking apples
1¹/₂ cups cranberries
¹/₂ cup raisins
2 tablespoons walnuts, chopped
generous 1 cup superfine sugar
¹/₂ cup soft dark brown sugar
2 tablespoons flour
FOR THE CRUST
2¹/₂ cups flour
¹/₂ teaspoon salt
6 tablespoons cold butter, cut in pieces
¹/₂ cup cold shortening, cut in pieces
¹/₄–¹/₂ cup ice water

1 ▼ For the crust, sift the flour and salt into a bowl. Add the butter and shortening and cut in with a pastry blender until the mixture resembles coarse crumbs. With a fork, stir in just enough water to bind the dough. Gather into 2 equal balls, wrap in wax paper, and refrigerate for at least 20 minutes.

2 ▲ Put the orange rind and juice into a mixing bowl. Peel and core the apples and grate into the bowl. Stir in the cranberries, raisins, walnuts, all except 1 tablespoon of the superfine sugar, the brown sugar, and flour.

3 Place a baking sheet in the center of the oven and preheat to 400°F.

4 On a lightly floured surface, roll out 1 ball of dough to about ¹/₈ inch thick. Transfer to a 9-inch pie pan and trim. Spoon the cranberry and apple mixture into the shell.

5 ▲ Roll out the remaining dough to a circle about 11 inches in diameter. With a serrated pastry wheel, cut the dough into 10 strips, ³/₄ inch wide. Place 5 strips horizontally across the top of the tart at 1-inch intervals. Weave in 5 vertical strips and trim the edges. Sprinkle the top with the remaining sugar.

6 Bake for 20 minutes. Reduce the heat to 350°F and bake for about 15 minutes more, until the crust is golden and the filling is bubbling.

Open Apple Pie

SERVES 8

3 pounds sweet-tart firm eating or cooking apples
1/4 cup superfine sugar
2 teaspoons ground cinnamon
grated rind and juice of 1 lemon
2 tablespoons butter, diced
2–3 tablespoons honey
FOR THE CRUST
2 1/2 cups flour
1/2 teaspoon salt
1/2 cup cold butter, cut in pieces
generous 1/3 cup shortening, cut in pieces
5–6 tablespoons ice water

1 For the crust, sift the flour and salt into a bowl. Add the butter and shortening and cut in with a pastry blender until the mixture resembles coarse crumbs.

2 ▲ With a fork, stir in just enough water to bind the dough. Gather into a ball, wrap in wax paper, and refrigerate for at least 20 minutes.

3 Place a baking sheet in the center of the oven and preheat to 400°F.

4 ▼ Peel, core, and slice the apples. Combine the sugar and cinnamon in a bowl. Add the apples, lemon rind, and juice and stir.

5 On a lightly floured surface, roll out the dough to a circle about 12 inches in diameter. Transfer to a 9-inch diameter deep pie dish; leave the dough hanging over the edge. Fill with the apple slices.

6 ▲ Fold in the edges and crimp loosely for a decorative border. Dot the apples with diced butter.

7 Bake on the hot baking sheet until the dough is golden and the apples are tender, about 45 minutes.

8 Melt the honey in a saucepan and brush over the apples to glaze. Serve warm or at room temperature.

Apple Pie

SERVES 8

2 pounds tart cooking apples

2 tablespoons flour

generous $^{1}/_{2}$ cup superfine sugar

$1^{1}/_{2}$ tablespoons fresh lemon juice

$^{1}/_{2}$ teaspoon ground cinnamon

$^{1}/_{2}$ teaspoon ground allspice

$^{1}/_{4}$ teaspoon ground ginger

$^{1}/_{4}$ teaspoon freshly grated nutmeg

$^{1}/_{4}$ teaspoon salt

$^{1}/_{4}$ cup butter, diced

FOR THE CRUST

$2^{1}/_{2}$ cups flour

1 teaspoon salt

6 tablespoons cold butter, cut in pieces

$^{1}/_{3}$ cup cold shortening, cut in pieces

$^{1}/_{4}$–$^{1}/_{2}$ cup ice water

1 ▲ For the crust, sift the flour and salt into a bowl.

2 Add the butter and shortening and cut in with a pastry blender until the mixture resembles coarse crumbs. With a fork, stir in just enough water to bind the dough.

3 ▲ Gather into 2 balls, wrap in wax paper, and refrigerate for 20 minutes.

4 ▲ On a lightly floured surface, roll out 1 ball $^{1}/_{8}$ inch thick. Transfer to a 9-inch pie pan and trim the edge. Place a baking sheet in the center of the oven and preheat to 425°F.

5 ▲ Peel, core, and slice the apples into a bowl. Toss with the flour, sugar, lemon juice, spices, and salt. Spoon into the pie shell and dot with butter.

6 ▲ Roll out the remaining dough. Place on top of the pie and trim to leave a $^{3}/_{4}$-inch overhang. Fold the overhang under the bottom dough and press to seal. Crimp the edge.

7 ▲ Roll out the scraps and cut out leaf shapes and roll balls. Arrange on top of the pie. Cut steam vents.

8 Bake for 10 minutes. Reduce the heat to 350°F and bake until golden, 40–45 minutes more. If the pie browns too quickly, protect with foil.

~ COOK'S TIP ~

Instead of using cooking apples, choose crisp eaters such as Granny Smith, which will not soften too much during cooking.

Pear and Apple Crumb Pie

SERVES 8

3 firm pears

4 tart cooking apples

scant 1 cup superfine sugar

2 tablespoons cornstarch

pinch of salt

grated rind of 1 lemon

2 tablespoons fresh lemon juice

²/₃ cup raisins

²/₃ cup flour

1 teaspoon ground cinnamon

6 tablespoons cold butter, cut in pieces

FOR THE CRUST

1¹/₄ cups flour

¹/₂ teaspoon salt

scant ¹/₂ cup cold shortening, cut in pieces

2 tablespoons ice water

1 For the crust, sift the flour and salt into a bowl. Add the shortening and cut in with a pastry blender until the mixture resembles coarse crumbs. Stir in just enough water to bind the dough. Gather into a ball and transfer to a lightly floured surface. Roll out ¹/₈ inch thick.

2 ▲ Transfer to a shallow 9-inch pie pan and trim to leave a ¹/₂-inch overhang. Fold the overhang under for double thickness. Flute the edge with your fingers. Refrigerate.

3 Place a baking sheet in the center of the oven and preheat to 450°F.

4 ▲ Peel and core the pears. Slice them into a bowl. Peel, core, and slice the apples. Add to the pears. Stir in one-third of the sugar, the cornstarch, salt, and lemon rind. Add the lemon juice and raisins and stir to blend.

5 For the crumb topping, combine the remaining sugar, flour, cinnamon, and butter in a bowl. Blend with your fingertips until the mixture resembles coarse crumbs. Set aside.

6 ▲ Spoon the fruit filling into the pie shell. Sprinkle the crumbs lightly and evenly over the top.

7 Bake for 10 minutes, then reduce the heat to 350°F. Cover the top of the pie loosely with a sheet of foil and continue baking until browned, about 35–40 minutes more.

Chocolate Pear Tart

SERVES 8

4 1-ounce squares semisweet chocolate, grated
3 large firm, ripe pears
1 egg
1 egg yolk
1/2 cup light cream
1/2 teaspoon vanilla extract
3 tablespoons superfine sugar
FOR THE CRUST
1 1/4 cups flour
pinch of salt
2 tablespoons sugar
1/2 cup (1 stick) cold unsalted butter, cut in pieces
1 egg yolk
1 tablespoon fresh lemon juice

1 For the crust, sift the flour and salt into a bowl. Add the sugar and butter. Cut in with a pastry blender until the mixture resembles coarse crumbs. With a fork, stir in the egg yolk and lemon juice until the mixture forms a dough. Gather into a ball, wrap in wax paper, and refrigerate for at least 20 minutes.

2 Place a baking sheet in the center of the oven and preheat to 400°F.

3 On a lightly floured surface, roll out the dough 1/8 inch thick. Transfer to a 10-inch tart pan and trim the edge.

4 ▲ Sprinkle the bottom of the tart shell with the grated chocolate.

5 ▲ Peel, halve, and core the pears. Cut in thin slices crossways, then fan them out slightly.

6 Transfer the pear halves to the tart with the help of a metal spatula and arrange on top of the chocolate like the spokes of a wheel.

7 ▼ Whisk together the egg and egg yolk, cream, and vanilla. Ladle over the pears, then sprinkle with sugar.

8 Bake for 10 minutes. Reduce the heat to 350°F and cook until the custard is set and the pears begin to caramelize, about 20 minutes more. Serve warm.

Caramelized Upside-Down Pear Pie

SERVES 8

5–6 firm, ripe pears
scant 1 cup sugar
$1/2$ cup (1 stick) unsalted butter
whipped cream, for serving
FOR THE CRUST
1 cup flour
$1/4$ teaspoon salt
generous $1/2$ cup (1 stick) cold butter, cut in pieces
$1/4$ cup ($1/2$ stick) cold shortening, cut in pieces
4 tablespoons ice water

1 ▲ For the crust, sift the flour and salt into a bowl. Add the butter and shortening and cut in with a pastry blender until the mixture resembles coarse crumbs. With a fork, stir in enough ice water to bind the dough. Gather into a ball, wrap in wax paper, and refrigerate for at least 20 minutes. Preheat the oven to 400°F.

~ VARIATION ~

For Caramelized Upside-Down Apple Pie, replace the pears with 8–9 firm, tart apples. There may seem to be too many apples, but they shrink slightly as they cook.

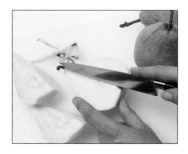

2 ▲ Quarter, peel, and core the pears. Place in a bowl and toss with a few tablespoons of the sugar.

3 ▲ In a $10^{1}/_{2}$-inch ovenproof skillet, melt the butter over moderately high heat. Add the remaining sugar. When the mixture starts to color, arrange the pears evenly around the edge and in the center.

4 ▲ Continue cooking, uncovered, until caramelized, about 20 minutes.

5 ▲ Leave the fruit to cool. Roll out a circle of dough slightly larger than the diameter of the skillet. Place the dough on top of the pears, tucking it around the edges. Transfer the pan to the oven and bake for 15 minutes, then reduce the heat to 350°F. Bake the pie until golden, about 15 minutes more.

6 ▲ Let the pie cool in the skillet for about 3–4 minutes. Run a knife around the edge to loosen the pie, ensuring that the knife reaches down to the bottom of the skillet. Invert a plate on top and, protecting your hands with oven gloves, hold plate and skillet firmly, and turn them both over quickly.

7 Lift off the skillet. If any pears stick to it, remove them gently with a metal spatula and replace them carefully on the pie. Serve warm, with the whipped cream passed separately.

Key Lime Pie

SERVES 8

3 large egg yolks

1 14-ounce can sweetened
   condensed milk

1 tablespoon grated lime rind

1/2 cup fresh lime juice

green food coloring (optional)

1/2 cup whipping cream

FOR THE CRUST

2 cups graham crackers, crushed

5 tablespoons butter or margarine, melted

1 Preheat the oven to 350°F.

2 ▲ For the crust, place the crushed crackers in a bowl and add the butter or margarine. Mix to combine.

> ~ VARIATION ~
>
> Use lemons instead of limes,
> with yellow food coloring.

3 Press the mixture evenly over the bottom and sides of a 9-inch pie pan. Bake for 8 minutes. Let cool.

4 ▲ Beat the yolks until thick. Beat in the milk, lime rind and juice, and coloring, if using. Pour into the prebaked crust and refrigerate until set, about 4 hours. To serve, whip the cream and pipe a lattice pattern on top.

Fruit Tartlets

MAKES 8

3/4 cup red currant or grape jelly

1 tablespoon fresh lemon juice

3/4 cup whipping cream

1 1/2 pounds fresh fruit, such as
   strawberries, raspberries, kiwi fruit,
   peaches, grapes, or blueberries, peeled
   and sliced as necessary

FOR THE CRUST

10 tablespoons cold butter, cut in pieces

generous 1/4 cup soft dark brown sugar

3 tablespoons unsweetened cocoa powder

1 3/4 cups flour

1 egg white

1 For the crust, combine the butter, brown sugar, and cocoa over low heat. When the butter is melted, remove from the heat and sift over the flour. Stir, then add just enough egg white to bind the mixture. Gather into a ball, wrap in wax paper, and refrigerate for 30 minutes.

2 ▲ Grease 8 3-inch tartlet pans. Roll out the dough between 2 sheets of wax paper. Stamp out 8 4-inch rounds with a fluted cutter.

3 Line the tartlet pans with dough. Prick the bottoms. Refrigerate for 15 minutes. Preheat the oven to 350°F.

4 Bake until firm, 20–25 minutes. Cool, then remove from the pans.

5 ▲ Melt the jelly with the lemon juice. Brush a thin layer in the bottom of the tartlets. Whip the cream and spread a thin layer in the tartlet cases. Arrange the fruit on top. Brush with the glaze and serve.

Key Lime Pie (top), Fruit Tartlets

Chocolate Lemon Tart

SERVES 8–10

1¼ cups superfine sugar
6 eggs
grated rind of 2 lemons
¾ cup lemon juice
¾ cup whipping cream
chocolate curls, for decorating
FOR THE CRUST
1⅔ cups flour
2 tablespoons unsweetened cocoa powder
¼ cup confectioners' sugar
½ teaspoon salt
½ cup butter or margarine
1 tablespoon water

1 ▲ Grease a 10-inch tart pan.

2 For the crust, sift the flour, cocoa powder, confectioners' sugar, and salt into a bowl. Set aside.

3 ▲ Melt the butter and water over a low heat. Pour over the flour mixture and stir with a wooden spoon until the dough is smooth and the flour has absorbed all the liquid.

4 Press the dough evenly over the base and side of the prepared tart pan. Refrigerate the pie shell while preparing the filling.

5 Place a baking sheet in the center of the oven and preheat to 375°F.

6 ▲ Whisk the sugar and eggs until the sugar is dissolved. Add the lemon rind and juice and mix well. Add the cream. Taste the mixture and add more lemon juice or sugar if needed. It should taste tart but also sweet.

7 Pour the filling into the tart shell and bake on the hot sheet until the filling is set, 20–25 minutes. Cool on a rack. When cool, sprinkle with the chocolate curls.

Lemon Almond Tart

SERVES 8

scant 1 cup whole blanched almonds

$^1/_2$ cup sugar

2 eggs

grated rind and juice of $1^1/_2$ lemons

$^1/_2$ cup (1 stick) butter, melted

strips of lemon rind, for decorating

FOR THE CRUST

$1^2/_3$ cups flour

1 tablespoon superfine sugar

$^1/_2$ teaspoon salt

$^1/_2$ teaspoon baking powder

6 tablespoons cold unsalted butter,
  cut in pieces

3–4 tablespoons whipping cream

1 For the crust, sift the flour, sugar, salt, and baking powder into a bowl. Add the butter and cut in with a pastry blender until the mixture resembles coarse crumbs.

2 ▲ With a fork, stir in just enough cream to bind the dough.

3 Gather into a ball and transfer to a lightly floured surface. Roll out the dough about $^1/_8$ inch thick and carefully transfer to a 9-inch tart pan. Trim and prick the bottom all over with a fork. Refrigerate for at least 20 minutes.

4 Place a baking sheet in the center of the oven and preheat to 400°F.

5 Line the tart shell with crumpled wax paper and fill with pie weights. Bake for 12 minutes. Remove the paper and weights and continue baking until golden, 6–8 minutes more. Remove the shell and reduce the oven temperature to 350°F.

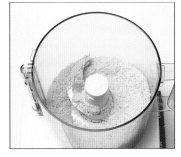

6 ▲ Grind the almonds finely with 1 tablespoon of the sugar in a food processor, blender, or nut grinder.

7 ▲ Set a mixing bowl over a pan of hot water. Add the eggs and the remaining sugar, and beat with an electric mixer until the mixture is thick enough to leave a ribbon trail when the beaters are lifted.

8 Stir in the lemon rind and juice, butter, and ground almonds.

9 Pour into the prebaked shell. Bake until the filling is golden and set, about 35 minutes. Decorate with lemon rind.

Lemon Meringue Pie

SERVES 8

grated rind and juice of 1 large lemon
1 cup plus 1 tablespoon cold water
generous $1/2$ cup plus 6 tablespoons superfine sugar
2 tablespoons butter
3 tablespoons cornstarch
3 eggs, separated
pinch of salt
pinch of cream of tartar
FOR THE CRUST
$1^1/4$ cups flour
$1/2$ teaspoon salt
scant $1/2$ cup cold shortening, cut in pieces
2 tablespoons ice water

1 For the crust, sift the flour and salt into a bowl. Add the shortening and cut in with a pastry blender until the mixture resembles coarse crumbs. With a fork, stir in just enough water to bind the mixture. Gather into a ball.

2 ▲ On a lightly floured surface, roll out the dough about $1/8$ inch thick. Transfer to a 9-inch pie pan and trim the edge to leave a $1/2$-inch overhang.

3 ▲ Fold the overhang under and crimp the edge. Refrigerate the pie shell for at least 20 minutes.

4 Preheat the oven to 400°F.

5 ▲ Prick the case all over with a fork. Line with crumpled wax paper and fill with pie weights. Bake for 12 minutes. Remove the paper and weights and continue baking until golden, 6–8 minutes more.

6 In a saucepan, combine the lemon rind and juice, 1 cup of the water, generous $1/2$ cup of the sugar, and butter. Bring the mixture to the boil.

7 Meanwhile, in a mixing bowl, dissolve the cornstarch in the remaining water. Add the egg yolks.

> ~ **VARIATION** ~
>
> For Lime Meringue Pie, substitute the grated rind and juice of two medium-sized limes for the lemon.

8 ▲ Add the egg yolk mixture to the lemon mixture and return to the boil, whisking continuously until the mixture thickens, about 5 minutes.

9 Cover the surface with wax paper to prevent a skin forming and let cool.

10 ▲ For the meringue, using an electric mixer beat the egg whites with the salt and cream of tartar until they hold stiff peaks. Add the remaining sugar and beat until glossy.

11 ▲ Spoon the lemon mixture into the pie shell and spread level. Spoon the meringue on top, smoothing it up to the edge of the crust to seal. Bake until golden, 12–15 minutes.

Orange Tart

SERVES 8

1 cup sugar

1 cup fresh orange juice, strained

2 large navel oranges

scant 1 cup whole blanched almonds

1/4 cup (1/2 stick) butter

1 egg

1 tablespoon flour

3 tablespoons apricot jam

FOR THE CRUST

scant 2 cups flour

1/2 teaspoon salt

1/4 cup (1/2 stick) cold butter, cut in pieces

3 tablespoons cold margarine,
cut in pieces

3–4 tablespoons ice water

1 For the crust, sift the flour and salt into a bowl. Add the butter and margarine and cut in with a pastry blender until the mixture resembles coarse crumbs. Stir in just enough water to bind the dough. Gather into a ball, wrap in wax paper, and refrigerate for at least 20 minutes.

2 On a lightly floured surface, roll out the dough 1/4 inch thick and transfer to an 8-inch tart pan. Trim off the overhang. Refrigerate until needed.

3 In a pan, combine generous 3/4 cup of the sugar and the orange juice and boil until thick and syrupy, about 10 minutes.

4 ▲ Cut the oranges into 1/4-inch slices. Do not peel. Add to the syrup. Simmer gently for 10 minutes, or until glazed. Transfer to a rack to dry. When cool, cut in half. Reserve the syrup. Place a baking sheet in the oven and heat to 400°F.

5 Grind the almonds finely in a food processor, blender, or nut grinder. With an electric mixer, cream the butter and remaining sugar until light and fluffy. Beat in the egg and 2 tablespoons of the orange syrup. Stir in the almonds and flour.

6 Melt the jam over a low heat, then brush over the tart shell. Pour in the almond mixture. Bake until set, about 20 minutes. Leave to cool.

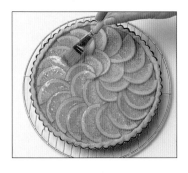

7 ▲ Arrange overlapping orange slices on top. Boil the remaining syrup until thick. Brush on top to glaze.

Pumpkin Pie

SERVES 8

1 pound cooked or canned pumpkin
1 cup whipping cream
2 eggs
$1/2$ cup soft dark brown sugar
4 tablespoons light corn syrup
$1^1/2$ teaspoons ground cinnamon
1 teaspoon ground ginger
$1/4$ teaspoon ground cloves
$1/2$ teaspoon salt
FOR THE CRUST
$1^1/2$ cups flour
$1/2$ teaspoon salt
6 tablespoons cold butter, cut in pieces
3 tablespoons cold shortening, cut in pieces
3–4 tablespoons ice water

1 For the crust, sift the flour and salt into a bowl. Cut in the butter and shortening with a pastry blender until the mixture resembles coarse crumbs. Bind with ice water. Wrap in wax paper and refrigerate for 20 minutes.

2 Roll out the dough and line a 9-inch pie pan. Trim off the overhang. Roll out the trimmings and cut out leaf shapes. Wet the rim with a brush and water.

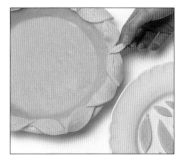

3 ▲ Place the dough leaves around the edge. Refrigerate for 20 minutes. Preheat the oven to 400°F.

4 ▲ Prick the bottom with a fork and line with crumpled wax paper. Fill with pie weights and bake for 12 minutes. Remove paper and weights and bake until golden, 6–8 minutes more. Reduce the heat to 375°F.

5 ▼ Beat together the pumpkin, cream, eggs, sugar, corn syrup, spices, and salt. Pour into the shell and bake until set, about 40 minutes.

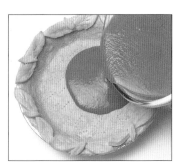

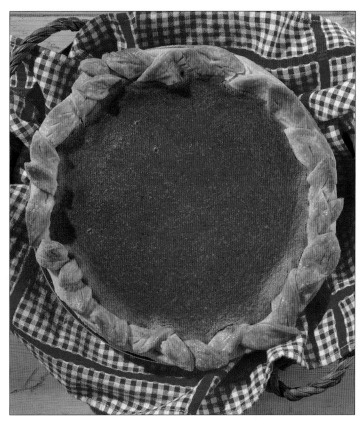

Maple Walnut Pie

SERVES 8

3 eggs

pinch of salt

1/4 cup superfine sugar

1/4 cup (1/2 stick) butter or margarine, melted

1 cup pure maple syrup

1 cup chopped walnuts

whipped cream, for decorating (optional)

FOR THE CRUST

9 tablespoons flour

9 tablespoons whole-wheat flour

pinch of salt

1/4 cup (1/2 stick) cold butter, cut in pieces

3 tablespoons cold shortening,
   cut in pieces

1 egg yolk

2–3 tablespoons ice water

1 ▼ For the crust, sift the flours and salt into a bowl. Add the butter and shortening and cut in with a pastry blender until the mixture resembles coarse crumbs. With a fork, stir in the egg yolk and just enough water to bind the dough. Form into a ball.

2 Wrap in wax paper and refrigerate for at least 20 minutes.

3 Preheat the oven to 425°F.

4 On a lightly floured surface, roll out the dough about 1/8 inch thick and transfer to a 9-inch pie pan. Trim the edge. To decorate, roll out the trimmings. With a small heart-shaped cutter, stamp out enough hearts to go around the rim of the pie. Brush the edge with water, then arrange the dough hearts all around.

5 ▲ Prick the bottom with a fork. Line with crumpled wax paper and fill with pie weights. Bake for 10 minutes. Remove the paper and weights and continue baking until golden brown, 3–6 minutes more.

6 In a bowl, whisk the eggs, salt, and sugar together. Stir in the butter or margarine and maple syrup.

7 ▲ Set the pie shell on a baking sheet. Pour in the filling, then sprinkle the nuts over the top.

8 Bake until just set, about 35 minutes. Cool on a rack. Decorate with whipped cream, if wished.

Pecan Tart

SERVES 8

3 eggs
pinch of salt
scant 1 cup soft dark brown sugar
$^{1}/_{2}$ cup dark corn syrup
2 tablespoons fresh lemon juice
6 tablespoons butter, melted
1$^{1}/_{4}$ cups chopped pecans
$^{1}/_{2}$ cup pecan halves
FOR THE CRUST
1$^{1}/_{2}$ cups flour
1 tablespoon superfine sugar
1 teaspoon baking powder
$^{1}/_{2}$ teaspoon salt
6 tablespoons cold unsalted butter, cut in pieces
1 egg yolk
3–4 tablespoons whipping cream

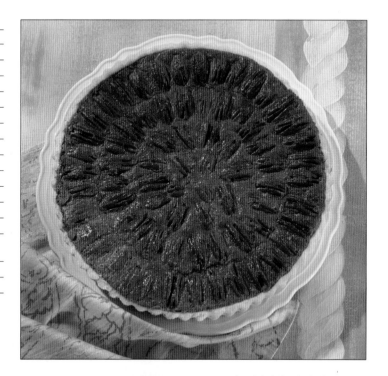

1 For the crust, sift the flour, sugar, baking powder, and salt into a bowl. Add the butter and cut in with a pastry blender until the mixture resembles coarse crumbs.

2 ▼ In a bowl, beat together the egg yolk and cream until blended.

~ COOK'S TIP ~

Serve this tart warm, accompanied by ice cream or whipped cream, if wished.

3 ▲ Pour the cream mixture into the flour mixture and stir with a fork.

4 Gather the dough into a ball. On a lightly floured surface, roll out $^{1}/_{8}$ inch thick and transfer to a 9-inch tart pan. Trim the overhang and flute the edge with your fingers. Refrigerate for at least 20 minutes.

5 Place a baking sheet in the center of the oven and preheat to 400°F.

6 In a bowl, lightly whisk the eggs and salt. Add the sugar, corn syrup, lemon juice, and butter. Mix well and stir in the chopped nuts.

7 ▲ Pour into the pastry shell and arrange the pecan halves in concentric circles on top.

8 Bake for 10 minutes. Reduce the heat to 325°F and continue baking for 25 minutes more.

Mince Pies

MAKES 36

1¹/₂ cups finely chopped
   blanched almonds

generous ¹/₂ cup ready-to-eat dried
   apricots, finely chopped

generous 1 cup raisins

²/₃ cup currants

²/₃ cup candied cherries, chopped

³/₄ cup candied citrus peel, chopped

1 cup finely chopped beef suet

grated rind and juice of 2 lemons

grated rind and juice of 1 orange

scant 1 cup soft dark brown sugar

4 tart cooking apples, peeled, cored,
   and chopped

2 teaspoons ground cinnamon

1 teaspoon freshly grated nutmeg

¹/₂ teaspoon ground cloves

1 cup brandy

1 cup cream cheese

2 tablespoons superfine sugar

confectioners' sugar, for dusting

FOR THE CRUST

3¹/₂ cups flour

1¹/₄ cups confectioners' sugar

1¹/₂ cups (3 sticks) cold butter, cut in pieces

grated rind and juice of 1 orange

milk, for glazing

1 Mix the nuts, dried and candied fruit, suet, citrus rind and juice, brown sugar, apples, and spices.

2 ▲ Stir in the brandy. Cover and leave in a cool place for 2 days.

3 For the crust, sift the flour and confectioners' sugar into a bowl. Cut in the butter with a pastry blender until the mixture resembles coarse crumbs.

4 ▲ Add the orange rind. Stir in just enough orange juice to bind. Gather into a ball, wrap in wax paper, and refrigerate for at least 20 minutes.

5 Preheat the oven to 425°F. Grease 2–3 muffin pans. Beat together the cream cheese and sugar.

6 ▲ Roll out the pastry ¹/₄ inch thick. With a fluted pastry cutter, stamp out 36 3-inch rounds.

> ~ COOK'S TIP ~
>
> The mincemeat mixture may be packed into sterilized jars and sealed. It will keep refrigerated for several months. Add a few tablespoonfuls to give apple pies a lift, or make small mincemeat-filled parcels using phyllo pastry.

7 ▲ Transfer the rounds to the muffin pans. Fill halfway with mincemeat. Top with a teaspoonful of the cream cheese mixture.

8 ▲ Roll out the pastry trimmings and stamp out 36 2-inch rounds with a fluted cutter. Brush the edges of the pies with milk, then set the rounds on top. Cut a small steam vent in the top of each pie.

9 ▲ Brush lightly with milk. Bake until golden, 15–20 minutes. Leave to cool for 10 minutes before unmolding. Dust with confectioners' sugar.

Shoofly Pie

SERVES 8

| 1 cup flour |
| 1 cup soft dark brown sugar |
| 1/4 teaspoon each salt, ground ginger, cinnamon, mace, and grated nutmeg |
| 6 tablespoons cold butter, cut in pieces |
| 2 eggs |
| 1/2 cup molasses |
| 1/2 cup boiling water |
| 1/2 teaspoon baking soda |
| FOR THE CRUST |
| 1/2 cup cream cheese, at room temperature, cut in pieces |
| 1/2 cup (1 stick) cold butter, at room temperature, cut in pieces |
| 1 cup flour |

1 For the crust, put the cream cheese and butter in a mixing bowl. Sift over the flour.

2 ▲ Cut in with a pastry blender until the dough just holds together. Wrap in wax paper and refrigerate for at least 30 minutes.

3 Place a baking sheet in the center of the oven and preheat to 375°F.

4 In a bowl, mix together the flour, sugar, salt, spices, and cold butter pieces. Blend with your fingertips until the mixture resembles coarse crumbs. Set aside.

5 On a lightly floured surface, roll out the dough 1/8 inch thick and transfer to a 9-inch pie pan. Trim the overhanging dough and flute the rim.

6 ▲ Spoon one-third of the crumbs into the pie shell.

7 ▲ To complete the filling, whisk the eggs with the molasses in a large bowl until combined.

8 Pour the boiling water into a small bowl. Stir in the bicarbonate of soda; the mixture will foam. Immediately whisk into the egg mixture. Pour carefully into the pie shell and sprinkle the remaining crumbs evenly over the top.

9 Stand on the hot sheet and bake until browned, about 35 minutes. Let cool to room temperature, then serve.

Treacle Tart

SERVES 4–6

³/₄ cup dark corn syrup
1¹/₂ cups fresh white bread crumbs
grated rind of 1 lemon
2 tablespoons fresh lemon juice
FOR THE CRUST
1¹/₂ cups flour
¹/₂ teaspoon salt
6 tablespoons cold butter, cut in pieces
3 tablespoons cold margarine, cut in pieces
3–4 tablespoons ice water

1 For the crust, combine the flour and salt in a bowl. Add the butter and margarine and cut in with a pastry blender until the mixture resembles coarse crumbs.

2 ▲ With a fork, stir in just enough water to bind the dough. Gather into a ball, wrap in wax paper, and refrigerate for at least 20 minutes.

3 On a lightly floured surface, roll out the dough ¹/₈ inch thick. Transfer to an 8-inch tart pan and trim off the overhang. Refrigerate for at least 20 minutes. Reserve the trimmings for the lattice top.

4 Place a baking sheet at the top of the oven and preheat to 400°F.

5 In a saucepan, warm the syrup until thin and runny.

6 ▲ Remove from the heat and stir in the bread crumbs and lemon rind. Let sit for 10 minutes so that the bread can absorb the syrup. Add more bread crumbs if the mixture is thin. Stir in the lemon juice and spread evenly in the pastry shell.

7 Roll out the pastry trimmings and cut into 10–12 thin strips.

8 ▼ Lay half the strips on the filling, then lay the remaining strips at an angle over them to form a lattice.

9 Place on the hot sheet and bake for 10 minutes. Lower the heat to 375°F. Bake until golden, about 15 minutes more. Serve warm or cold.

Chess Pie

SERVES 8

2 eggs

3 tablespoons whipping cream

1/2 cup soft dark brown sugar

2 tablespoons sugar

2 tablespoons flour

1 tablespoon whisky

3 tablespoons butter, melted

1/2 cup chopped walnuts

1/2 cup pitted dates, chopped

whipped cream, for serving

FOR THE CRUST

6 tablespoons cold butter

3 tablespoons cold shortening

1 1/2 cups flour

1/2 teaspoon salt

3–4 tablespoons ice water

1 ▲ For the crust, cut the butter and shortening into small pieces.

2 Sift the flour and salt into a bowl. With a pastry blender, cut in the butter and shortening until the mixture resembles coarse crumbs. Stir in just enough water to bind. Gather into a ball, wrap in wax paper, and refrigerate for at least 20 minutes.

3 Place a baking sheet in the oven and preheat it to 375°F.

4 Roll out the dough thinly and line a 9-inch pie pan. Trim the edge. Roll out the trimmings, cut thin strips and braid them. Brush the edge of the pie shell with water and fit the pastry braids around the rim.

5 ▲ In a mixing bowl, whisk together the eggs and cream.

6 Add both sugars and beat until well combined. Sift over 15ml/ 1 tablespoon of the flour and stir in. Add the whisky, the melted butter, and the walnuts. Stir to combine.

7 ▲ Mix the dates with the remaining flour and stir into the walnut mixture.

8 Pour into the pastry case and bake until the pastry is golden and the filling puffed up, about 35 minutes. Serve at room temperature, with whipped cream if desired.

Coconut Cream Pie

SERVES 8

scant 1¹/₂ cups dry unsweetened
   shredded coconut

³/₄ cup superfine sugar

4 tablespoons cornstarch

pinch of salt

2¹/₂ cups milk

¹/₄ cup whipping cream

2 egg yolks

2 tablespoons unsalted butter

2 teaspoons vanilla extract

FOR THE CRUST

1¹/₄ cups flour

¹/₄ teaspoon salt

3 tablespoons cold butter, cut in pieces

2 tablespoons cold shortening,
   cut in pieces

2–3 tablespoons ice water

1 For the crust, sift the flour and salt, then cut in the butter and shortening until it resembles coarse crumbs.

2 ▲ With a fork, stir in just enough water to bind the dough. Gather into a ball, wrap in wax paper, and refrigerate for 20 minutes.

3 Preheat the oven to 425°F. Roll out the dough ¹/₈ inch thick. Transfer to a 9-inch pie pan. Trim and flute the edges. Prick the bottom. Line with crumpled wax paper and fill with pie weights. Bake for 10–12 minutes. Remove the paper and weights, reduce the heat to 350°F, and bake until brown, 10–15 minutes.

4 ▲ Spread 2 ounces of the coconut on a baking sheet and toast in the oven until golden, 6–8 minutes, stirring often. Set aside for decorating.

5 Put the sugar, cornstarch, and salt in a saucepan. In a bowl, whisk the milk, cream, and egg yolks. Add the egg mixture to the saucepan.

6 ▼ Cook over a low heat, stirring constantly, until the mixture comes to a boil. Boil for 1 minute, then remove from the heat. Add the butter, vanilla, and remaining coconut.

7 Pour into the prebaked pie shell. When cool, sprinkle toasted coconut in a ring in the center.

Black Bottom Pie

SERVES 8

2 teaspoons unflavored gelatin
3 tablespoons cold water
2 eggs, separated
1¼ cups superfine sugar
2 tablespoons cornstarch
½ teaspoon salt
2 cups milk
2 1-ounce squares semisweet chocolate, finely chopped
2 tablespoons rum
¼ teaspoon cream of tartar
chocolate curls, for decorating
FOR THE CRUST
3 cups gingersnaps, crushed
5 tablespoons butter, melted

1 Preheat the oven to 350°F.

2 For the crust, mix the crushed gingersnaps and melted butter.

3 ▲ Press the mixture evenly over the bottom and sides of a 9-inch pie pan. Bake for 6 minutes. Let cool.

4 Sprinkle the gelatin over the water and let stand to soften.

5 Beat the egg yolks in a large mixing bowl and set aside.

6 In a saucepan, combine half the sugar, the cornstarch, and salt. Gradually stir in the milk. Boil for 1 minute, stirring constantly.

7 ▲ Whisk the hot milk mixture into the yolks, then pour it all back into the saucepan and return to a boil, whisking. Cook for 1 minute, still whisking. Remove from the heat.

8 ▲ Measure out 1 cup of the hot custard mixture and pour into a bowl. Add the chopped chocolate to the custard mixture, and stir until melted. Stir in half the rum and pour into the pie crust.

9 ▲ Whisk the softened gelatin into the plain custard until it has dissolved, then stir in the remaining rum. Set the pan in cold water until it reaches room temperature.

10 ▲ With an electric mixer, beat the egg whites and cream of tartar until they hold stiff peaks. Add the remaining sugar gradually, beating or whisking thoroughly at each addition.

11 ▲ Fold the custard into the egg whites, then spoon over the chocolate mixture in the pie shell. Refrigerate until set, about 2 hours.

12 Decorate the top with chocolate curls. Keep the pie refrigerateed until ready to serve.

~ COOK'S TIP ~

To make chocolate curls, melt 8 1-ounce squares semisweet chocolate over hot water, stir in 1 tablespoon shortening and mould in a small foil-lined loaf pan. For large curls, soften the bar between your hands and scrape off curls from the wide side with a vegetable peeler; for small curls, grate from the narrow side using a box grater.

Velvety Mocha Tart

SERVES 8

2 teaspoons instant espresso coffee

2 tablespoons hot water

1¹/₂ cups whipping cream

6 1-ounce squares semisweet chocolate

1 1-ounce square bittersweet
   cooking chocolate

¹/₂ cup whipped cream, for decorating

chocolate-covered coffee beans,
   for decorating

FOR THE CRUST

2¹/₂ cups chocolate wafers, crushed

2 tablespoons superfine sugar

5 tablespoons butter, melted

1 ▲ For the crust, mix the crushed
chocolate wafers and sugar together,
then stir in the melted butter.

2 Press the mixture evenly over the
bottom and sides of a 9-inch pie pan.
Refrigerate until firm.

3 In a bowl, dissolve the coffee in the
water and set aside.

5 Melt both the chocolates in the top
of a double boiler, or in a heatproof
bowl set over a pan of hot water.
Remove from the heat when nearly
melted and stir to continue melting.
Set the bottom of the pan in cool
water to reduce the temperature. Be
careful not to splash any water on the
chocolate or it will become grainy.

4 Pour the cream into a mixing
bowl. Set the bowl in hot water to
warm the cream, bringing it closer to
the temperature of the chocolate.

6 ▲ With an electric mixer, whip
the cream until it is lightly fluffy.
Add the dissolved coffee and whip
until the cream just holds its shape.

7 ▲ When the chocolate is at room
temperature, fold it gently into the
cream with a large metal spoon.

8 Pour into the chilled biscuit crust
and refrigerate until firm. To serve,
pipe a ring of whipped cream rosettes
around the edge, then place a
chocolate-covered coffee bean in the
center of each rosette.

Brandy Alexander Tart

SERVES 8

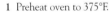

¹/₂ cup cold water

1 tablespoon unflavored gelatin

generous ¹/₂ cup superfine sugar

3 eggs, separated

4 tablespoons brandy

4 tablespoons crème de cacao

pinch of salt

1¹/₄ cups whipping cream

chocolate curls, for decorating

FOR THE CRUST

4 cups graham crackers, crumbed

5 tablespoons butter, melted

1 tablespoon superfine sugar

1 Preheat oven to 375°F.

2 For the crust, mix the cracker crumbs with the butter and sugar in a bowl.

3 ▲ Press the crumbs evenly on to the bottom and sides of a 9-inch tart pan. Bake until just brown, about 10 minutes. Cool on a rack.

4 Place the water in the top of a double boiler set over hot water. Sprinkle over the gelatin and let stand for 5 minutes to soften. Add half the sugar and the egg yolks. Whisk constantly over a very low heat until the gelatin dissolves and the mixture thickens slightly. Do not allow the mixture to boil.

5 ▲ Remove from the heat and stir in the brandy and crème de cacao.

6 Set the pan over ice water and stir occasionally until it cools and thickens; it should not set firmly.

7 With an electric mixer, beat the egg whites and salt until they hold stiff peaks. Beat in the remaining sugar. Spoon a dollop of whites into the yolk mixture and fold in to lighten.

8 ▼ Pour the egg yolk mixture over the remaining whites and fold together.

9 Whip the cream until soft peaks form, then gently fold into the filling. Spoon into the prebaked crust and refrigerate until set, 3–4 hours. Decorate the top with chocolate curls before serving.

Nesselrode Pie

SERVES 10

1 tablespoon rum
1/4 cup candied fruit, chopped
scant 2 cups milk
4 teaspoons unflavored gelatin
1/2 cup superfine sugar
1/2 teaspoon salt
3 eggs, separated
1 cup whipping cream
chocolate curls, for decorating
FOR THE CRUST
3 cups graham crackers, crushed
5 tablespoons butter, melted
1 tablespoon sugar

1 For the crust, mix the crushed graham crackers, butter, and sugar. Press evenly and firmly over the bottom and sides of a 9-inch pie pan. Refrigerate until firm.

2 ▲ In a bowl, stir together the rum and candied fruit. Set aside.

3 Pour 1/2 cup of the milk into a bowl. Sprinkle over the gelatin and let stand 5 minutes to soften.

4 ▲ In the top of a double boiler, combine 1/4 cup of the sugar, the remaining milk, and salt. Stir in the gelatin mixture. Cook over hot water, stirring, until the gelatin dissolves.

5 Whisk in the egg yolks and cook, stirring, until thick enough to coat a spoon. Do not boil. Pour the custard over the candied fruit mixture. Set in a bowl of ice water to cool.

6 Whip the cream lightly. Set aside.

7 With an electric mixer, beat the egg whites until they hold soft peaks. Add the remaining sugar and beat just enough to blend. Fold a large dollop of the egg whites into the cooled gelatin mixture. Pour into the remaining egg whites and carefully fold together. Fold in the cream.

8 ▲ Pour into the pie shell and refrigerate until firm. Decorate the top with chocolate curls.

Chocolate Chiffon Pie

SERVES 8

7 1-ounce squares semisweet chocolate

1 cup milk

1 tablespoon unflavored gelatin

$^{1}/_{2}$ cup sugar

2 extra-large eggs, separated

1 teaspoon vanilla extract

1$^{1}/_{2}$ cups whipping cream

pinch of salt

whipped cream and chocolate curls,
   for decorating

FOR THE CRUST

3$^{1}/_{2}$ cups graham crackers, crushed

6 tablespoons butter, melted

1 Place a baking sheet in the oven
and preheat to 350°F.

2 For the crust, mix the crushed
graham crackers and butter in a bowl.
Press the crumbs evenly over the
bottom and sides of a 9-inch pie plate.
Bake for 8 minutes. Let cool.

3 Chop the chocolate, then grind in
a food processor or blender. Set aside.

4 Place the milk in the top of a
double boiler. Sprinkle over the
gelatin. Let stand 5 minutes to soften.

5 ▲ Set the top of a double boiler
over hot water. Add 3 tablespoons of
the sugar, the chocolate, and egg
yolks. Stir until dissolved. Add the
vanilla extract.

6 ▲ Set the top of the double boiler
in a bowl of ice and stir until the
mixture reaches room temperature.
Remove from the ice and set aside.

7 Whip the cream lightly. Set aside.
With an electric mixer, beat the egg
whites and salt until they hold soft
peaks. Add the remaining sugar and
beat only enough to blend.

8 Fold a dollop of egg whites into
the chocolate mixture, then pour
back into the whites and fold in.

9 ▲ Fold in the whipped cream
and pour into the pie shell. Put
in the freezer until just set, about 5
minutes. If the centre sinks, fill with
any remaining mixture. Refrigerate for
3–4 hours. Decorate with whipped
cream and chocolate curls. Serve cold.

Chocolate Cheesecake Pie

SERVES 8

1½ cups cream cheese

4 tablespoons whipping cream

generous 1 cup superfine sugar

½ cup unsweetened cocoa powder

½ teaspoon ground cinnamon

3 eggs

whipped cream, for decorating

chocolate curls, for decorating

FOR THE BASE

1½ cups graham crackers, crushed

¾ cup crushed amaretti biscuits
(if unavailable, use extra crushed
graham crackers)

6 tablespoons butter, melted

1 Place a baking sheet in the center of the oven and preheat to 350°F.

2 For the crust, mix the crushed crackers and butter in a bowl.

3 ▲ With a spoon, press the crumbs over the bottom and sides of a 9-inch pie pan. Bake for 8 minutes. Let cool. Keep the oven on.

4 With an electric mixer, beat the cheese and cream together until smooth. Beat in the sugar, cocoa, and cinnamon until blended.

5 ▼ Add the eggs, one at a time, beating just enough to blend.

6 Pour into the pie shell and bake on the hot baking sheet for about 25–30 minutes. The filling will sink down as it cools. Decorate with whipped cream and chocolate curls.

Frozen Strawberry Pie

SERVES 8

1 cup cream cheese

1 cup sour cream

2 10-ounce packages frozen sliced
strawberries, thawed

FOR THE CRUST

2 cups graham crackers, crushed

1 tablespoon superfine sugar

5 tablespoons butter, melted

~ VARIATION ~

For Frozen Raspberry Pie, use raspberries in place of the strawberries, and prepare the same way, or try other frozen fruit.

1 ▲ For the crust, mix together the crushed crackers, sugar, and butter.

2 Press the crumbs evenly and firmly over the bottom and sides of a 9-inch pie pan. Freeze until firm.

3 ▼ Blend together the cream cheese and sour cream. Reserve 6 tablespoons of the strawberries. Add the remainder to the cream cheese mixture.

4 Pour the filling into the crust and freeze for 6–8 hours until firm. To serve, spoon some of the reserved berries and juice on top.

Chocolate Cheesecake Pie (top), Frozen Strawberry Pie

Kiwi Ricotta Cheese Tart

SERVES 8

¹/₂ cup blanched almonds
¹/₂ cup superfine sugar
4 cups ricotta cheese
1 cup whipping cream
1 egg and 3 egg yolks
1 tablespoon flour
pinch of salt
2 tablespoons rum
grated rind of 1 lemon
2¹/₂ tablespoons lemon juice
2 tablespoons honey
5 kiwi fruit
FOR THE CRUST
1¹/₄ cups flour
1 tablespoon superfine sugar
¹/₂ teaspoon salt
¹/₂ teaspoon baking powder
6 tablespoons cold butter, cut in pieces
1 egg yolk
3–4 tablespoons whipping cream

1 For the crust, mix together the flour, sugar, salt, and baking powder in a large bowl. Cut in the butter with a pastry blender until the mixture resembles coarse crumbs. Mix together the egg yolk and cream. Stir in just enough to bind the dough.

2 ▲ Transfer to a lightly floured surface, flatten slightly, wrap in wax paper, and refrigerate for 30 minutes. Preheat the oven to 425°F.

3 ▲ On a lightly floured surface, roll out the dough to ¹/₈-inch thickness. Transfer to a 9-inch springform pan. Crimp the edge decoratively.

4 ▲ Prick the bottom of the dough with a fork. Line with crumpled wax paper and fill with pie weights. Bake for 10 minutes. Remove the paper and weights and bake for 6–8 minutes more, until golden. Leave to cool. Reduce the temperature to 350°F.

5 ▲ Grind the almonds finely with 1 tablespoon of the sugar in a food processor, blender, or nut grinder.

6 Beat the ricotta until creamy. Add the cream, egg, yolks, remaining sugar, flour, salt, rum, lemon rind, and 2 tablespoons of lemon juice. Combine.

7 ▲ Stir in the ground almonds until well blended.

8 Pour into the shell, bake for 1 hour, let cool then refrigerate, loosely covered for 2–3 hours. Unmold on to a plate.

9 Combine the honey and remaining lemon juice for the glaze.

10 ▲ Peel the kiwis. Halve them lengthwise, then cut crosswise into ¹/₄ inch slices. Arrange the slices in rows across the top of the tart. Just before serving, brush with the glaze.

Apple Strudel

SERVES 10–12

generous $^1\!/_2$ cup raisins
2 tablespoons brandy
5 eating apples, such as Granny Smith or Jonathan
3 large, tart cooking apples
scant $^1\!/_2$ cup soft dark brown sugar
1 teaspoon ground cinnamon
grated rind and juice of 1 lemon
$^1\!/_2$ cup dry bread crumbs
$^1\!/_2$ cup chopped pecans or walnuts
12 sheets phyllo pastry
$^3\!/_4$ cup (1$^1\!/_2$ sticks) butter, melted
confectioners' sugar, for dusting

1 Soak the raisins in the brandy for at least 15 minutes.

2 ▼ Peel, core, and thinly slice the apples. In a bowl, combine the sugar, cinnamon, and lemon rind. Stir in the apples and half the bread crumbs.

3 Add the raisins, nuts, and lemon juice, and stir until blended.

4 Preheat the oven to 375°F. Grease 2 baking sheets.

5 ▲ Carefully unfold the phyllo sheets. Keep the unused sheets covered with wax paper. Lift off one sheet, place on a clean surface, and brush with melted butter. Lay a second sheet on top and brush with butter. Continue until you have a stack of 6 buttered sheets.

6 Sprinkle a few tablespoons of bread crumbs over the last sheet and spoon half the apple mixture along the bottom edge of the strip.

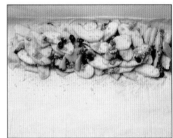

7 ▲ Starting at the apple-filled end, roll up the pastry, as for a jelly roll. Place on a baking sheet, seam-side down, and carefully fold under the ends to seal. Repeat the procedure to make a second strudel. Brush both with butter.

8 Bake the strudels for 45 minutes. Let cool slightly. Using a small sieve, dust with a fine layer of confectioners' sugar. Serve warm with whipped cream.

Cherry Strudel

SERVES 8

generous 1 cup fresh bread crumbs
3/4 cup (1 1/2 sticks) butter, melted
1 cup superfine sugar
1 tablespoon ground cinnamon
1 teaspoon grated lemon rind
1 pound sour cherries, pitted
8 sheets phyllo pastry
confectioners' sugar, for dusting

1 Lightly fry the fresh bread crumbs in 2 1/2 ounces of the melted butter until golden. Set aside to cool.

2 ▲ In a large mixing bowl, toss together the sugar, cinnamon, and lemon rind.

3 Stir in the cherries.

4 Preheat the oven to 375°F. Grease a baking sheet.

5 Carefully unfold the phyllo sheets. Keep the unused sheets covered with wax paper. Lift off one sheet, place on a flat surface lined with wax paper. Brush the pastry with melted butter. Sprinkle about one-eighth of the bread crumbs evenly over the surface.

6 ▲ Lay a second sheet of phyllo on top, brush with butter and sprinkle with crumbs. Continue until you have a stack of 8 buttered, crumbed sheets.

7 Spoon the cherry mixture along the bottom edge of the strip. Starting at the cherry-filled end, roll up the dough as for a jelly roll. Use the wax paper to help flip the strudel on to the baking sheet, seam-side down.

8 ▼ Carefully fold under the ends to seal in the fruit. Brush the top with any remaining butter.

9 Bake the strudel for 45 minutes. Let cool slightly. Using a small sieve, dust with a fine layer of confectioners' sugar.

Mushroom Quiche

SERVES 8

1 pound fresh mushrooms
2 tablespoons olive oil
1 tablespoon butter
1 clove garlic, finely chopped
1 tablespoon lemon juice
2 tablespoons finely chopped fresh parsley
3 eggs
1¹/₂ cups whipping cream
³/₄ cup freshly grated Parmesan cheese
salt and ground black pepper
FOR THE CRUST
1²/₃ cups flour
¹/₂ teaspoon salt
6 tablespoons cold butter, cut in pieces
3 tablespoons cold margarine, cut in pieces
3–4 tablespoons ice water

1 For the crust, sift the flour and salt into a bowl. Cut in the butter and margarine with a pastry blender until the mixture resembles coarse crumbs. Stir in enough water to bind.

2 Gather into a ball, wrap in wax paper, and refrigerate for 20 minutes.

3 Place a baking sheet in the center of the oven and preheat to 375°F.

4 Roll out the dough ¹/₈ inch thick. Transfer to a 9-inch tart pan and trim the edge. Prick the bottom all over with a fork. Line with crumpled wax paper and fill with pie weights. Bake for 12 minutes. Remove the paper and weights and continue baking until golden, about 5 minutes more.

5 ▲ Wipe the mushrooms with a damp paper towel to remove any dirt. Trim the ends of the stalks, place on a cutting board, and slice thinly.

6 Heat the oil and butter in a frying pan. Stir in the mushrooms, garlic, and lemon juice. Season with salt and pepper. Cook until the mushrooms render their liquid, then raise the heat and cook until dry.

7 ▼ Stir in the parsley and add more salt and pepper if necessary.

8 Whisk the eggs and cream together, then stir in the mushrooms. Sprinkle the cheese over the bottom of the prebaked pie shell and pour the mushroom filling over the top.

9 Bake until puffed and brown, about 30 minutes. Serve the quiche warm.

Bacon and Cheese Quiche

SERVES 8

4 ounces medium-thick bacon slices
3 eggs
1¹/₂ cups whipping cream
3¹/₂oz Swiss cheese, grated
pinch of freshly grated nutmeg
salt and ground black pepper
FOR THE CRUST
1²/₃ cups flour
¹/₂ teaspoon salt
6 tablespoons cold butter, cut in pieces
3 tablespoons cold margarine, cut in pieces
3–4 tablespoons ice water

1 Make the crust as per steps 1–4 above. Maintain the oven at 375°F.

2 ▲ Fry the bacon until crisp. Drain, then crumble into small pieces. Sprinkle in the pie shell.

3 ▲ Beat together the eggs, cream, cheese, nutmeg, salt, and pepper. Pour over the bacon and bake until puffed and brown, about 30 minutes. Serve the quiche warm.

Mushroom Quiche (top), Bacon and Cheese Quiche

Cheese and Tomato Quiche

Serves 6–8

10 medium-sized tomatoes

1 2-ounce can anchovy fillets, drained and finely chopped

1/2 cup whipping cream

1 3/4 cups grated Monterey Jack cheese

1/2 cup whole-wheat bread crumbs

1/2 teaspoon dried thyme

salt and ground black pepper

For the crust

scant 2 cups flour

1/2 teaspoon salt

1/2 cup (1 stick) cold butter, cut in pieces

1 egg yolk

2–3 tablespoons ice water

1 For the crust, sift the flour and salt into a bowl. Cut in the butter with a pastry blender until the mixture resembles coarse crumbs.

2 ▲ With a fork, stir in the egg yolk and enough water to bind the dough.

3 Roll out the dough about 1/8 inch thick and transfer to a 9-inch tart pan. Refrigerate until needed. Preheat the oven to 400°F.

4 ▲ Score the bottoms of the tomatoes. Plunge in boiling water for 1 minute. Remove and peel off the skin with a knife. Cut in quarters and remove the seeds with a spoon.

5 ▲ In a bowl, mix the anchovies and cream. Stir in the cheese.

6 Sprinkle the bread crumbs in the crust. Arrange the tomatoes on top. Season with thyme, salt, and pepper.

7 ▲ Spoon the cheese mixture on top. Bake until golden, 25–30 minutes. Serve warm.

Onion and Anchovy Tart

SERVES 8

4 tablespoons olive oil

2 pounds onions, sliced

1 teaspoon dried thyme

2–3 tomatoes, sliced

24 small black olives, pitted

1 2-ounce can anchovy fillets,
    drained and sliced

6 sun-dried tomatoes, cut in slivers

salt and ground black pepper

FOR THE CRUST

1²/₃ cups flour

¹/₂ teaspoon salt

¹/₂ cup (1 stick) cold butter, cut in pieces

1 egg yolk

2–3 tablespoons ice water

3 ▲ Heat the oil in a frying pan.
Add the onions, thyme, and seasoning.
Cook over low heat, covered, for
25 minutes. Uncover and continue
cooking until soft. Let cool. Preheat
the oven to 400°F.

4 ▼ Spoon the onions into the tart
shell and top with the tomato slices.
Arrange the olives in rows. Make a
lattice pattern, alternating lines of
anchovies and sun-dried tomatoes.
Bake until golden, 20–25 minutes.

1 ▲ For the crust, sift the flour and
salt into a bowl. Cut in the butter with
a pastry blender until the mixture
resembles coarse crumbs. Stir in the
yolk and just enough water to bind.

2 ▲ Roll out the dough to about
¹/₈ inch thick. Transfer to a 9-inch tart
pan, using the rolling pin, and trim
the edge. Refrigerate until needed.

Ricotta and Basil Tart

Serves 8–10

2 cups basil leaves, tightly packed
1 cup flat-leaf parsley
1/2 cup extra-virgin olive oil
2 eggs
1 egg yolk
3 1/2 cups ricotta cheese
scant 1 cup black olives, pitted
3/4 cup freshly grated Parmesan cheese
salt and ground black pepper
For the crust
1 2/3 cups flour
1/2 teaspoon salt
6 tablespoons cold butter, cut in pieces
3 tablespoons cold margarine, cut in pieces
3–4 tablespoons ice water

1 ▲ For the crust, sift the flour and salt into a bowl. Add the butter and margarine.

2 Cut in with a pastry blender until the mixture resembles coarse crumbs. With a fork, stir in just enough water to bind the dough. Gather into a ball, wrap in wax paper, and refrigerate for at least 20 minutes.

3 Place a baking sheet in the center of the oven and preheat to 375°F.

4 Roll out the dough 1/8 inch thick and transfer to a 10-inch tart pan. Prick the bottom with a fork and line with crumpled wax paper. Fill with pie weights and bake for 12 minutes. Remove the paper and weights and bake until golden, 3–5 minutes more. Lower the heat to 350°F.

5 ▲ In a food processor or blender, combine the basil, parsley, and olive oil. Season well with salt and pepper and process until finely chopped.

6 In a bowl, whisk the eggs and yolk to blend. Gently fold in the ricotta.

7 ▲ Fold in the basil mixture and olives until well combined. Stir in the Parmesan and adjust the seasoning.

8 Pour into the prebaked shell and bake until set, 30–35 minutes.

Pennsylvania Dutch Ham and Apple Pie

SERVES 6–8

5 tart cooking apples
4 tablespoons soft light brown sugar
1 tablespoon flour
pinch of ground cloves
pinch of ground black pepper
6 ounces sliced baked ham
2 tablespoons butter or margarine
4 tablespoons whipping cream
1 egg yolk
FOR THE CRUST
2 cups flour
1/2 teaspoon salt
6 tablespoons cold butter, cut in pieces
4 tablespoons cold margarine, cut in pieces
4–8 tablespoons ice water

1 For the crust, sift the flour and salt into a large bowl. Cut in the butter and margarine with a pastry blender until the mixture resembles coarse crumbs. Stir in enough water to bind together, gather into 2 balls, and wrap in wax paper. Chill for 20 minutes. Preheat the oven to 425°F.

2 ▲ Quarter, core, peel, and thinly slice the apples. Place in a bowl and toss with the sugar, flour, cloves, and pepper to coat evenly. Set aside.

3 Roll out 1 dough ball 1/8 inch thick and line a 10-inch pie pan, letting the excess pastry hang over the edge.

4 Arrange half the ham slices in the bottom of the pastry case. Top with a ring of spiced apple slices, then dot with half the butter or margarine.

5 ▲ Repeat the layers, finishing with apples. Dot with butter or margarine. Pour over 3 tablespoons of the cream.

6 Roll out the remaining pastry to make a lid. Place it on top, fold the top edge under the bottom and press.

7 ▲ Roll out the dough scraps and cut out decorative shapes. Arrange on top of the pie. Ruffle the edge, using your fingers and a fork. Cut steam vents at regular intervals. Mix the egg yolk and remaining cream and brush on top to glaze, including the dough shapes.

8 Bake for 10 minutes. Reduce the heat to 350°F and bake until golden, 30–35 minutes more. Serve hot.

CAKES & TORTES

AS DELICIOUS AS THEY ARE
BEAUTIFUL, THESE CAKES AND
TORTES ARE PERFECT TO SERVE AT
TEATIME OR FOR DESSERT. THE
DELIGHTFUL PARTY CAKES MAKE
SPECIAL OCCASIONS MEMORABLE.

Angel Food Cake

SERVES 12–14

generous 1 cup flour

2 tablespoons cornstarch

generous 1¹/₂ cups superfine sugar

10–11 ounces egg whites
(about 10–11 eggs)

1¹/₄ teaspoons cream of tartar

¹/₄ teaspoon salt

1 teaspoon vanilla extract

¹/₄ teaspoon almond extract

confectioners' sugar, for dusting

1 Preheat the oven to 325°F.

2 ▼ Sift the flours before measuring, then sift them 4 times with ¹/₂ cup of the sugar. Transfer to a bowl.

3 With an electric mixer, beat the egg whites until foamy. Sift over the cream of tartar and salt, and continue to beat until the whites hold soft peaks when the beaters are lifted.

4 ▲ Add the remaining sugar in 3 batches, beating well after each addition. Stir in the vanilla and almond extracts.

5 ▲ Add the flour mixture, in 2 batches, and fold in with a large metal spoon after each addition.

6 Transfer to an ungreased 10-inch tube pan and bake until just browned on top, about 1 hour.

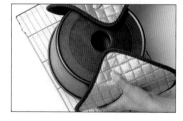

7 ▲ Turn the pan upside down onto a cake rack and let cool 1 hour. If the cake does not unmold, run a knife around the edge to loosen it. Invert onto a serving plate.

8 When cool, lay a star-shaped template on top of the cake, sift over confectioners' sugar, and lift off.

Black and White Pound Cake

SERVES 16

4 1-ounce squares semisweet chocolate
3 cups flour
1 teaspoon baking powder
2 cups (4 sticks) butter, at room temperature
3½ cups superfine sugar
1 tablespoon vanilla extract
10 eggs, at room temperature
confectioners' sugar, for dusting

1 ▲ Preheat the oven to 350°F. Line a 10-inch tube pan with wax paper and grease the paper. Dust with flour and spread evenly with a brush.

2 ▲ Melt the chocolate in the top of a double boiler, or in a heatproof bowl set over a saucepan of hot water. Stir occasionally. Set aside.

3 In a bowl, sift together the flour and baking powder. In another bowl, cream the butter, sugar, and vanilla with an electric mixer until light and fluffy. Add the eggs, 2 at a time, then gradually incorporate the flour mixture on low speed.

4 ▲ Spoon half of the batter into the prepared pan.

5 ▲ Stir the chocolate into the remaining batter, then spoon into the pan. With a metal spatula, swirl the two batters for a marbled effect.

6 Bake until a cake tester inserted into the center comes out clean, about 1 hour 45 minutes. Cover with foil halfway through baking. Let stand 15 minutes, then unmold and transfer to a rack. To serve, dust with confectioners' sugar.

Chiffon Cake

SERVES 16

2¹/₂ cups flour
1 tablespoon baking powder
1 teaspoon salt
1³/₄ cups superfine sugar
¹/₂ cup vegetable oil
7 eggs, at room temperature, separated
³/₄ cup cold water
2 teaspoons vanilla extract
2 teaspoons grated lemon rind
¹/₂ teaspoon cream of tartar
FOR THE FROSTING
5¹/₂oz unsalted butter
5 cups confectioners' sugar
4 teaspoons instant coffee dissolved in 4 tablespoons hot water

1 Preheat the oven to 325°F.

2 ▼ Sift the flour, baking powder, and salt into a bowl. Stir in 8 ounces of the sugar. Make a well in the center and add the oil, egg yolks, water, vanilla, and lemon rind. Beat with a whisk or metal spoon until the mixture is smooth.

3 With an electric mixer, beat the egg whites with the cream of tartar until they hold soft peaks. Add the remaining sugar and beat until the mixture holds stiff peaks.

4 ▲ Pour the flour mixture over the whites in 3 batches, folding well after each addition.

5 Transfer the batter to an ungreased 10- × 4-inch tube pan and bake until the top springs back when touched lightly, about 1 hour.

6 ▲ When baked, remove from the oven and immediately hang the cake upside-down over the neck of a funnel or a narrow bottle. Let cool. To remove the cake, run a knife around the inside to loosen, then turn the tin over and tap the sides sharply. Invert the cake onto a serving plate.

7 For the frosting, beat together the butter and confectioners' sugar with an electric mixer until smooth. Add the coffee and beat until fluffy. With a metal spatula, spread over the sides and top of the cake.

Spice Cake

SERVES 10–12

1¹/₄ cups milk
2 tablespoons dark corn syrup
2 teaspoons vanilla extract
¹/₂ cup walnuts, chopped
³/₄ cup (1¹/₂ sticks) butter, at room temperature
generous 1¹/₂ cups superfine sugar
1 egg, at room temperature
3 egg yolks, at room temperature
2¹/₂ cups flour
1 tablespoon baking powder
1 teaspoon freshly grated nutmeg
1 teaspoon ground cinnamon
¹/₂ teaspoon ground cloves
¹/₄ teaspoon ground ginger
¹/₄ teaspoon ground allspice
FOR THE FROSTING
³/₄ cup cream cheese
2 tablespoons unsalted butter
1³/₄ cups confectioners' sugar
2 tablespoons finely chopped stem ginger
2 tablespoons syrup from stem ginger
stem ginger pieces, for decorating

1 Preheat the oven to 350°F. Line 3 8-inch cake pans with wax paper and grease. In a bowl, combine the milk, syrup, vanilla, and walnuts.

2 ▼ With an electric mixer, cream the butter and sugar until light and fluffy. Beat in the egg and egg yolks. Add the milk mixture and stir well.

3 Sift together the flour, baking powder, and spices 3 times.

4 ▲ Add the flour mixture to the egg mixture in 4 batches, and fold in carefully after each addition.

5 Divide the batter between the tins. Bake until the cakes spring back when touched lightly, about 25 minutes. Let stand 5 minutes, then unmold and cool on a rack.

6 ▼ For the frosting, combine all the ingredients and beat with an electric mixer. Spread the frosting between the layers and over the top. Decorate with pieces of stem ginger.

Caramel Layer Cake

SERVES 8–10

2¹/₂ cups flour

1¹/₂ teaspoons baking powder

³/₄ cup (1¹/₂ sticks) butter,
     at room temperature

generous ³/₄ cup superfine sugar

4 eggs, at room temperature, beaten

1 teaspoon vanilla extract

¹/₂ cup milk

whipped cream, for decorating

caramel threads, for decorating
     (optional, see below)

FOR THE FROSTING

scant 1¹/₃ cups soft dark brown sugar

1 cup milk

2 tablespoons unsalted butter

3–5 tablespoons whipping cream

1 Preheat the oven to 350°F. Line
2 8-inch cake pans with wax paper and
grease lightly.

2 ▲ Sift the flour and baking powder
together 3 times. Set aside.

~ COOK'S TIP ~

To make caramel threads, combine
5 tablespoons sugar and ¹/₄ cup water
in a heavy saucepan. Boil until light
brown. Dip the pan in cold water to
halt cooking. Trail from a spoon on
an oiled baking sheet.

3 With an electric mixer, cream the
butter and superfine sugar until light
and fluffy.

4 ▲ Slowly mix in the beaten eggs.
Add the vanilla. Fold in the flour
mixture, alternating with the milk.

5 ▲ Divide the batter between the
prepared tins and spread evenly,
hollowing out the centers slightly.

6 Bake until the cakes pull away from
the sides of the tin, about 30 minutes.
Let stand 5 minutes, then unmold
and cool on a rack.

7 ▲ For the frosting, combine the
brown sugar and milk in a saucepan.

8 Bring to the boil, cover, and cook
for 3 minutes. Remove the lid and
continue to boil, without stirring,
until the mixture reaches 238°F on a
sugar thermometer.

9 ▲ Immediately remove the
saucepan from the heat and add the
butter, but do not stir it in. Cool until
lukewarm, then beat until the mixture
is smooth and creamy.

10 Stir in enough cream to obtain a
spreadable consistency. If necessary,
refrigerate to thicken more.

11 ▲ Spread a layer of frosting on
top of one cake. Sandwich with the
second cake, then spread the top and
sides with the rest of the frosting and
smooth the surface.

12 To decorate, pipe whipped cream
rosettes around the edge. If using,
place a mound of caramel threads
in the center before serving.

Lady Baltimore Cake

SERVES 8–10

2½ cups flour
2½ teaspoons baking powder
½ teaspoon salt
4 eggs
1¾ cups superfine sugar
grated rind of 1 large orange
1 cup fresh orange juice
1 cup vegetable oil
18 pecan halves, for decorating
FOR THE FROSTING
2 egg whites
1¾ cups superfine sugar
5 tablespoons cold water
¼ teaspoon cream of tartar
1 teaspoon vanilla extract
⅓ cup pecans, finely chopped
⅔ cup raisins, chopped
3 dried figs, finely chopped

1 Preheat the oven to 350°F. Line 2 9-inch round cake pans with wax paper and grease the paper.

2 In a bowl, sift together the flour, baking powder, and salt. Set aside.

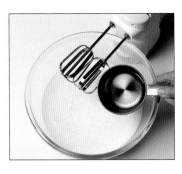

3 ▲ With an electric mixer, beat the eggs and sugar until thick and lemon-colored. Beat in the orange rind and juice, then the oil.

4 On low speed, beat in the flour mixture in 3 batches. Divide the cake mixture between the prepared pans.

5 ▲ Bake until a cake tester inserted in the center comes out clean, about 30 minutes. Let stand 15 minutes, then run a knife around the inside edge and transfer the cakes to racks to cool completely.

6 ▲ For the frosting, combine the egg whites, sugar, water, and cream of tartar in the top of a double boiler, or in a heatproof bowl set over boiling water. With an electric mixer, beat until glossy and thick. Off the heat, add the vanilla extract and continue beating until thick. Fold in the pecans, raisins, and figs.

8 Spread a layer of frosting on top of one cake. Sandwich with the second cake, then spread the top and sides with the rest of the frosting. Arrange the pecan halves on top.

Carrot Cake with Maple Butter Frosting

SERVES 12

1 pound carrots, peeled
1¹/₂ cups flour
2 teaspoons baking powder
¹/₂ teaspoon baking soda
1 teaspoon salt
2 teaspoons ground cinnamon
4 eggs
2 teaspoons vanilla extract
¹/₂ cup soft dark brown sugar
¹/₄ cup superfine sugar
1¹/₄ cups sunflower oil
1 cup finely chopped walnuts
²/₃ cup raisins
walnut halves, for decorating (optional)

FOR THE FROSTING

6 tablespoons unsalted butter
3 cups confectioners' sugar
¹/₄ cup maple syrup

1 Preheat the oven to 350°F. Line an 11- × 8-inch rectangular baking pan with wax paper and grease.

2 ▲ Grate the carrots and set aside.

3 Sift the flour, baking powder, baking soda, salt, and cinnamon into a bowl. Set aside.

4 With an electric mixer, beat the eggs until blended. Add the vanilla, sugars, and oil; beat to incorporate. Add the dry ingredients, in 3 batches, folding in well after each addition.

5 ▲ Add the carrots, walnuts, and raisins and fold in thoroughly.

6 Pour the batter into the prepared pan and bake until the cake springs back when touched lightly, 40–45 minutes. Let stand 10 minutes, then unmold and transfer to a rack.

7 ▼ For the frosting, cream the butter with half the sugar until soft. Add the syrup, then beat in the remaining sugar until blended.

8 Spread the frosting over the top of the cake. Using a metal spatula, make decorative ridges in the frosting. Cut into squares. Decorate with walnut halves, if wished.

Cranberry Upside-Down Cake

SERVES 8

3–3¹/₂ cups fresh cranberries

¹/₄ cup (¹/₂ stick) butter

³/₄ cup superfine sugar

FOR THE CAKE MIXTURE

9 tablespoons flour

1 teaspoon baking powder

3 eggs

generous ¹/₂ cup sugar

grated rind of 1 orange

3 tablespoons butter, melted

1 Preheat the oven to 350°F. Place a baking sheet on the middle shelf of the oven.

2 Wash the cranberries and pat dry. Thickly smear the butter on the bottom and sides of a 9- × 2-inch round cake pan. Add the sugar and swirl the pan to coat evenly.

3 ▲ Add the cranberries and spread in an even layer over the bottom of the pan.

4 For the batter, sift the flour and baking powder twice. Set aside.

5 ▲ Combine the eggs, sugar, and orange rind in a heatproof bowl set over a pan of hot but not boiling water. With an electric mixer, beat until the eggs leave a ribbon trail when the beaters are lifted.

6 Add the flour mixture in 3 batches, folding in well after each addition. Gently fold in the melted butter, then pour over the cranberries.

7 Bake for 40 minutes. Let cool for 5 minutes, then run a knife around the inside edge to loosen.

8 ▲ While the cake is still warm, place a flat plate on top of the pan. Protecting your hands with oven gloves, hold the plate and pan firmly and turn them both over quickly. Lift off the pan carefully.

Pineapple Upside-Down Cake

SERVES 8

¹/₂ cup (1 stick) butter
scant 1 cup soft dark brown sugar
1 16-ounce can pineapple slices, drained
4 eggs, separated
grated rind of 1 lemon
pinch of salt
generous ¹/₂ cup superfine sugar
²/₃ cup flour
1 teaspoon baking powder

1 Preheat the oven to 350°F.

2 Melt the butter in a 10-inch ovenproof skillet. Remove about 1 tablespoon of the melted butter and set aside.

3 ▲ Add the brown sugar to the skillet and stir until blended. Place the drained pineapple slices on top in one layer. Set aside.

~ VARIATION ~

For Apricot Upside-down Cake, replace the pineapple slices with 1 cup ready-to-eat dried apricots. If they need softening, simmer them in about ¹/₂ cup orange juice until plump and soft. Drain the apricots and discard any remaining cooking liquid.

4 In a bowl, whisk together the egg yolks, reserved butter, and lemon rind until well blended. Set aside.

5 ▼ With an electric mixer, beat the egg whites with the salt until they are stiff. Fold in the superfine sugar, 2 tablespoons at a time. Fold in the egg yolk mixture.

6 Sift the flour and baking powder together. Carefully fold into the egg mixture in 3 batches.

7 ▲ Pour the mixture over the pineapple and smooth level.

8 Bake until a cake tester inserted into the center comes out clean, about 30 minutes.

9 While still hot, place a serving plate on top of the pan, bottom-side up. Holding them tightly together with oven gloves, quickly flip over. Serve hot or cold.

Lemon Coconut Layer Cake

SERVES 8–10

1¹/₂ cups flour
¹/₄ teaspoon salt
7 eggs
1³/₄ cups sugar
1 tablespoon grated orange rind
grated rind of 1¹/₂ lemons
juice of 1 lemon
scant 1 cup dry unsweetened shredded coconut
1 tablespoon cornstarch
¹/₂ cup water
3 tablespoons butter
FOR THE FROSTING
6 tablespoons unsalted butter
1¹/₂ cups confectioners' sugar
grated rind of 1¹/₂ lemons
2 tablespoons lemon juice
2¹/₂ cups dry unsweetened shredded coconut

1 Preheat the oven to 350°F. Line 3 8-inch cake pans with wax paper and grease. In a bowl, sift together the flour and salt and set aside.

2 ▲ Place 6 of the eggs in a large heatproof bowl set over hot water. With an electric mixer, beat until frothy. Gradually beat in 1 cup of the sugar until the mixture doubles in volume and is thick enough to leave a ribbon trail when the beaters are lifted, about 10 minutes.

3 ▲ Remove the bowl from the hot water. Fold in the orange rind, half the grated lemon rind, and 1 tablespoon of the lemon juice until blended. Fold in the coconut.

4 Sift over the flour mixture in 3 batches, gently folding in thoroughly after each addition.

5 ▲ Divide the mixture between the prepared pans.

6 Bake until the cakes pull away from the sides of the pans, 20–25 minutes. Let stand 3–5 minutes, then unmold and cool on a rack.

7 In a bowl, blend the cornstarch with a little cold water to dissolve. Whisk in the remaining egg until just blended. Set aside.

8 ▲ In a saucepan, combine the remaining lemon rind and juice, the water, remaining sugar, and butter.

9 Over moderate heat, bring the mixture to a boil. Whisk in the eggs and cornstarch mixture, and return to the boil. Whisk continuously until thick, about 5 minutes. Remove from the heat and pour into a bowl. Cover with wax paper and set aside to cool.

10 ▲ For the frosting, cream the butter and confectioners' sugar until smooth. Stir in the lemon rind and enough lemon juice to obtain a thick, spreadable consistency.

11 Sandwich the 3 cake layers with the lemon custard mixture. Spread the frosting over the top and sides. Cover the cake with the coconut, pressing it in gently.

Lemon Yogurt Ring

Serves 12

1 cup (2 sticks) butter, at room temperature
generous 1¹/₂ cups superfine sugar
4 eggs, at room temperature, separated
2 teaspoons grated lemon rind
generous ¹/₃ cup lemon juice
1 cup plain yogurt
2¹/₂ cups flour
2 teaspoons baking powder
1 teaspoon baking soda
¹/₂ teaspoon salt

For the glaze

1 cup confectioners' sugar
2 tablespoons lemon juice
3–4 tablespoons plain yogurt

1 Preheat the oven to 350°F. Grease a 13¹/₄-cup bundt or fluted tube pan and dust with flour.

2 With an electric mixer, cream the butter and superfine sugar until light and fluffy. Add the egg yolks, 1 at a time, beating well after each addition.

3 ▲ Add the lemon rind, juice, and yogurt and stir to blend.

4 Sift together the flour, baking powder, and baking soda. In another bowl, beat the egg whites and salt until they hold stiff peaks.

5 ▲ Fold the dry ingredients into the butter mixture, then fold in a dollop of egg whites. Fold in the remaining whites until blended.

6 Pour into the pan and bake until a cake tester inserted into the center comes out clean, about 50 minutes. Let stand 15 minutes, then unmold and cool on a rack.

7 For the glaze, sift the confectioners' sugar into a bowl. Stir in the lemon juice and just enough yogurt to make a smooth glaze.

8 ▲ Set the cooled cake on the rack over a sheet of wax paper or a baking sheet. Pour over the glaze and let it drip down the sides. Allow the glaze to set before serving.

Sour Cream Streusel Cake

SERVES 12–14

¹/₂ cup (1 stick) butter, at room temperature
scant ³/₄ cup superfine sugar
3 eggs, at room temperature
scant 2 cups flour
1 teaspoon baking soda
1 teaspoon baking powder
1 cup sour cream
FOR THE TOPPING
1 cup soft dark brown sugar
2 teaspoons ground cinnamon
²/₃ cup walnuts, finely chopped
¹/₄ cup cold butter, cut in pieces

1 Preheat the oven to 350°F. Line the base of a 9-inch square cake pan with wax paper and grease.

2 ▲ For the topping, place the brown sugar, cinnamon, and walnuts in a bowl. Mix with your fingertips, then add the butter and continue working with your fingertips until the mixture resembles coarse crumbs.

3 To make the cake, cream the butter with an electric mixer until soft. Add the sugar and continue beating until the mixture is light and fluffy.

4 Add the eggs, 1 at a time, beating well after each addition.

5 In another bowl, sift the flour, baking soda, and baking powder together 3 times.

6 ▲ Fold the dry ingredients into the butter mixture in 3 batches, alternating with the sour cream. Fold until blended after each addition.

7 ▲ Pour half of the batter into the prepared pan and sprinkle over half the walnut crumb topping mixture.

8 Pour the remaining batter on top and sprinkle over the remaining walnut mixture.

9 Bake until browned, about 60–70 minutes. Let stand 5 minutes, then unmold and cool on a rack.

Plum Crumbcake

SERVES 8–10

10 tablespoons butter or margarine, at room temperature
³/4 cup superfine sugar
4 eggs, at room temperature
1¹/2 teaspoons vanilla extract
1¹/4 cups flour
1 teaspoon baking powder
1¹/2 pounds purple plums, halved and pitted
FOR THE TOPPING
1 cup flour
generous ¹/2 cup soft light brown sugar
1¹/2 teaspoons ground cinnamon
6 tablespoons butter, cut in pieces

1 Preheat the oven to 350°F.

2 For the topping, combine the flour, light brown sugar, and cinnamon in a bowl. Add the butter and work the mixture lightly with your fingertips until it resembles coarse crumbs. Set aside.

3 ▲ Line a 10- × 2-inch round cake pan with wax paper and grease.

4 Cream the butter or margarine and sugar until light and fluffy.

5 ▲ Beat in the eggs, 1 at a time. Stir in the vanilla.

6 In a bowl, sift together the flour and baking powder, then fold into the butter mixture in 3 batches.

7 ▲ Pour the batter into the tin. Arrange the plums on top.

8 ▲ Sprinkle the topping over the plums in an even layer.

9 Bake until a cake tester inserted in the center comes out clean, about 45 minutes. Let cool in the pan.

10 To serve, run a knife around the inside edge and invert onto a plate. Invert again onto a serving plate so that the topping is right-side up.

~ VARIATION ~

This cake can also be made with the same quantity of apricots, peeled, if preferred, or pitted cherries, or use a mixture of fruit, such as red or yellow plums, greengage plums, and apricots.

Peach Torte

SERVES 8

1 cup flour
1 teaspoon baking powder
pinch of salt
$^1/_2$ cup (1 stick) unsalted butter, at room temperature
scant 1 cup superfine sugar
2 eggs, at room temperature
6–7 peaches
sugar and lemon juice, for sprinkling
whipped cream, for serving (optional)

1 Preheat the oven to 350°F. Grease a 10-inch springform pan.

2 ▲ Sift together the flour, baking powder, and salt. Set aside.

3 With an electric mixer, cream the butter and sugar until light and fluffy. Beat in the eggs, then fold in the dry ingredients until blended.

4 ▲ Spoon the mixture into the pan and smooth it to make an even layer over the bottom.

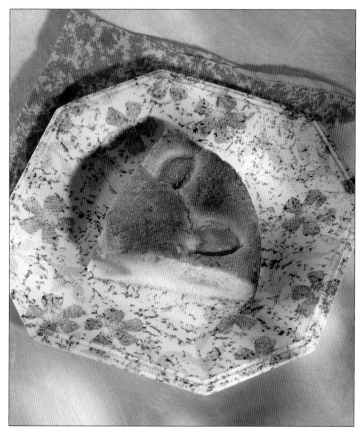

5 ▼ To skin the peaches, drop several at a time into a pan of gently boiling water. Boil for 10 seconds, then remove with a slotted spoon. Peel off the skin with the aid of a sharp knife. Cut the peaches in half and discard the stones.

6 ▲ Arrange the peach halves on top of the batter. Sprinkle lightly with sugar and lemon juice.

7 Bake until golden brown and set, 50–60 minutes. Serve warm, with whipped cream, if desired.

Apple Ring Cake

SERVES 12

7 eating apples, such as Jonathan or
  Granny Smith

1¹/₂ cups vegetable oil

2¹/₄ cups superfine sugar

3 eggs

3¹/₂ cups flour

1 teaspoon salt

1 teaspoon baking soda

1 teaspoon ground cinnamon

1 teaspoon vanilla extract

1 cup chopped walnuts

generous 1 cup raisins

confectioners' sugar, for dusting

1 Preheat the oven to 350°F. Grease a
9-inch tube pan.

2 ▲ Quarter, peel, core, and slice the
apples into a bowl. Set aside.

3 With an electric mixer, beat the oil
and sugar together until blended. Add
the eggs and continue beating until
the mixture is creamy.

4 Sift together the flour, salt, baking
soda, and cinnamon.

5 ▼ Fold the flour mixture into the
egg mixture with the vanilla. Stir in
the apples, walnuts, and raisins.

6 Pour into the pan and bake until the
cake springs back when touched
lightly, about 1¹/₄ hours. Let stand
15 minutes, then unmold and transfer
to a cooling rack. Dust with a layer of
confectioners' sugar before serving.

Orange Cake

SERVES 6

1¹/₂ cups flour

pinch of salt

1¹/₂ teaspoons baking powder

¹/₂ cup (1 stick) butter or margarine,
  at room temperature

generous ¹/₂ cup superfine sugar

grated rind of 1 large orange

2 eggs, at room temperature

2 tablespoons milk

FOR THE SYRUP AND DECORATION

generous ¹/₂ cup superfine sugar

1 cup fresh orange juice, strained

3 orange slices, for decorating

1 Preheat the oven to 350°F. Line an
8-inch cake pan with wax paper and
grease the paper.

2 ▲ Sift the flour, salt, and baking
powder onto a square of wax paper.

3 With an electric mixer, cream the
butter or margarine until soft. Add
the sugar and orange rind, and beat
until light and fluffy. Beat in the
eggs, 1 at a time. Fold in the flour in
3 batches, then add the milk.

4 Spoon into the pan and bake until
the cake pulls away from the sides,
about 30 minutes. Remove from the
oven but leave in the pan.

5 Meanwhile, for the syrup, dissolve
the sugar in the orange juice over low
heat. Add the orange slices and
simmer for 10 minutes. Remove and
drain. Let the syrup cool.

6 ▲ Prick the cake all over with a
fine skewer. Pour the syrup over the
hot cake. It may seem at first that
there is too much syrup for the cake
to absorb, but it will soak it all up.
Unmold when completely cooled and
decorate with small triangles of the
orange slices arranged on top.

Apple Ring Cake (top), Orange Cake

Orange and Walnut Roll

4 eggs, separated
generous $^1/_2$ cup superfine sugar
1 cup very finely chopped walnuts
pinch of cream of tartar
pinch of salt
confectioners' sugar, for dusting
FOR THE FILLING
1$^1/_4$ cups whipping cream
1 tablespoon superfine sugar
grated rind of 1 orange
1 tablespoon orange liqueur, such as Grand Marnier

1 Preheat the oven to 350°F. Line a 12- × 9$^1/_2$-inch jelly roll pan with wax paper and grease the paper.

2 With an electric mixer, beat the egg yolks and sugar until thick.

3 ▲ Stir in the walnuts.

4 In another bowl, beat the egg whites with the cream of tartar and salt until they hold stiff peaks. Fold gently but thoroughly into the walnut mixture.

5 Pour the mixture into the prepared pan and spread level with a spatula. Bake for 15 minutes.

6 Run a knife along the inside edge to loosen, then invert the cake onto a sheet of wax paper dusted with confectioners' sugar.

7 ▲ Peel off the wax paper. Roll up the cake while it is still warm with the help of the sugared paper. Set aside to cool.

8 For the filling, whip the cream until it holds soft peaks. Stir together the superfine sugar and orange rind, then fold into the whipped cream. Add the liqueur.

9 ▲ Gently unroll the cake. Spread the inside with a layer of orange whipped cream, then re-roll. Keep refrigerated until ready to serve. Dust the top with confectioners' sugar just before serving.

Chocolate Roll

SERVES 10

8 1-ounce squares semisweet chocolate
3 tablespoons water
2 tablespoons rum, brandy, or strong coffee
7 eggs, separated
scant 1 cup superfine sugar
pinch of salt
1½ cups whipping cream
confectioners' sugar, for dusting

1 Preheat the oven to 350°F. Line a 15- × 13-inch jelly roll pan with wax paper and grease the paper.

2 ▲ Combine the chocolate, water, and rum or other flavoring in the top of a double boiler, or in a heatproof bowl set over hot water. Heat until melted. Set aside.

3 With an electric mixer, beat the egg yolks and sugar until thick.

4 ▲ Stir in the melted chocolate.

5 In another bowl, beat the egg whites and salt until they hold stiff peaks. Fold a large dollop of the egg whites into the yolk mixture to lighten it, then carefully fold in the rest of the whites.

6 ▼ Pour the mixture into the pan; smooth evenly with a metal spatula.

7 Bake for 15 minutes. Remove from the oven, cover with wax paper and a damp dish towel. Let stand 1–2 hours.

8 With an electric mixer, whip the cream until stiff. Set aside.

9 Run a knife along the inside edge to loosen, then invert the cake on to a sheet of wax paper that has been dusted with confectioners' sugar.

10 Peel off the wax paper. Spread with an even layer of whipped cream, then roll up the cake with the help of the sugared paper. The cake may crack.

11 Refrigerate for several hours. Before serving, dust with an even layer of confectioners' sugar.

Chocolate Frosted Layer Cake

SERVES 8

1 cup (2 sticks) butter or margarine, at room temperature
generous 1½ cups superfine sugar
4 eggs, at room temperature, separated
2 teaspoons vanilla extract
3⅓ cups flour
2 teaspoons baking powder
pinch of salt
1 cup milk
FOR THE FROSTING
5 1-ounce squares semisweet chocolate
½ cup sour cream
pinch of salt

1 Preheat the oven to 350°F. Line 2 8-inch round cake pans with wax paper and grease. Dust with flour and shake to distribute. Tap to dislodge any excess flour.

2 With an electric mixer, cream the butter or margarine until soft. Gradually add the sugar and continue beating until light and fluffy.

3 ▲ Lightly beat the egg yolks, then mix into the creamed butter and sugar with the vanilla.

4 Sift the flour with the baking powder 3 times. Set aside.

5 In another bowl, beat the egg whites with the salt until they hold stiff peaks. Set aside.

6 ▲ Gently fold the dry ingredients into the butter mixture in 3 batches, alternating with the milk.

7 Add a large dollop of the whites and fold in to lighten the mixture. Carefully fold in the remaining whites until just blended.

8 Divide the batter between the pans and bake until the cakes pull away from the sides of the tins, about 30 minutes. Let stand 5 minutes. Unmold and cool on a rack.

9 ▲ For the frosting, melt the chocolate in the top of a double boiler, or a bowl set over hot water. When cool, stir in the sour cream and salt.

10 Sandwich the layers with frosting, then spread on the top and side.

Devil's Food Cake with Orange Frosting

SERVES 8–10

¹/₂ cup unsweetened cocoa powder
³/₄ cup boiling water
³/₄ cup (1¹/₂ sticks) butter, at room temperature
1¹/₂ cups soft dark brown sugar
3 eggs, at room temperature
2¹/₂ cups flour
1¹/₂ teaspoons baking soda
¹/₄ teaspoon baking powder
¹/₂ cup sour cream
orange rind strips, for decoration
FOR THE FROSTING
generous 1¹/₂ cups superfine sugar
2 egg whites
4 tablespoons frozen orange juice concentrate
1 tablespoon lemon juice
grated rind of 1 orange

1 Preheat the oven to 350°F. Line 2 9-inch cake pans with wax paper and grease. In a bowl, mix the cocoa and water until smooth. Set aside.

2 With an electric mixer, cream the butter and sugar until light and fluffy. Add the eggs, 1 at a time, beating well after each addition.

3 ▲ When the cocoa mixture is lukewarm, add to the butter mixture.

4 ▼ Sift together the flour, baking soda, and baking powder twice. Fold into the cocoa mixture in 3 batches, alternating with the sour cream.

5 Pour into the pans and bake until the cakes pull away from the sides of the tins, 30–35 minutes. Let stand 15 minutes. Unmold onto a rack.

6 Thinly slice the orange rind strips. Blanch in boiling water for 1 minute.

7 ▲ For the frosting, place all the ingredients in the top of a double boiler, or in a bowl set over hot water. With an electric mixer, beat until the mixture holds soft peaks. Continue beating off the heat until thick enough to spread.

8 Sandwich the cake layers with frosting, then spread over the top and side. Arrange the blanched orange rind strips on top of the cake.

Best-Ever Chocolate Cake

SERVES 12–14

¹/₂ cup (1 stick) unsalted butter
1 cup flour
¹/₂ cup unsweetened cocoa powder
1 teaspoon baking powder
pinch of salt
6 eggs
generous 1 cup superfine sugar
2 teaspoons vanilla extract
FOR THE FROSTING
8 1-ounce squares semisweet chocolate, chopped
6 tablespoons unsalted butter
3 eggs, separated
1 cup whipping cream
3 tablespoons superfine sugar

1 Preheat the oven to 350°F. Line 3 8- × 1¹/₂-in round cake pans with wax paper and grease.

2 ▲ Dust evenly with flour and spread with a brush. Set aside.

~ VARIATION ~

For a simpler frosting, combine 1 cup whipping cream with 8 ounces finely chopped semisweet chocolate in a saucepan. Stir over low heat until the chocolate has melted. Cool and whisk to spreading consistency.

3 ▲ Melt the butter over a low heat. With a spoon, skim off any foam that rises to the surface. Set aside.

4 ▲ Sift the flour, cocoa, baking powder, and salt together 3 times and set aside.

5 Place the eggs and sugar in a large heatproof bowl set over a pan of hot water. With an electric mixer, beat until the mixture doubles in volume and is thick enough to leave a ribbon trail when the beaters are lifted, about 10 minutes. Add the vanilla.

6 ▲ Sift over the dry ingredients in 3 batches, folding in carefully after each addition. Fold in the butter.

7 Divide the batter between the pans and bake until the cakes pull away from the sides of the pan, about 25 minutes. Transfer to a rack.

8 For the frosting, chop the chocolate and melt in the top of a double boiler, or in a heatproof bowl set over hot water.

9 ▲ Off the heat, stir in the butter and egg yolks. Return to low heat and stir until thick. Remove from the heat and set aside.

10 Whip the cream until firm; set aside. In another bowl, beat the egg whites until stiff. Add the sugar and beat until glossy.

11 Fold the cream into the chocolate mixture, then carefully fold in the egg whites. Refrigerate for 20 minutes to thicken the frosting.

12 ▲ Sandwich the cake layers with frosting, stacking them carefully. Spread the remaining frosting evenly over the top and sides of the cake.

Rich Chocolate Nut Cake

SERVES 10

1 cup (2 sticks) butter

8 1-ounce squares semisweet chocolate

1 cup unsweetened cocoa powder

1¾ cups superfine sugar

6 eggs

generous ⅓ cup brandy or cognac

2 cups finely chopped hazelnuts

FOR THE GLAZE

¼ cup (½ stick) butter

5 1-ounce squares bittersweet chocolate

2 tablespoons milk

1 teaspoon vanilla extract

1 Preheat the oven to 350°F. Line a 9- × 2-in round cake pan with wax paper and grease.

2 Melt the butter and chocolate together in the top of a double boiler, or in a heatproof bowl set over hot water. Set aside to cool.

3 ▼ Sift the cocoa into a bowl. Add the sugar and eggs, and stir until just combined. Pour in the melted chocolate mixture and brandy.

4 Fold in three-quarters of the nuts, then pour the batter into the prepared pan.

5 ▲ Set the pan inside a large pan and pour 1 inch of hot water into the outer pan. Bake until the cake is firm to the touch, about 45 minutes. Let stand 15 minutes, then unmold and transfer to a cooling rack.

6 Wrap the cake in wax paper and refrigerate for at least 6 hours.

7 For the glaze, combine the butter, chocolate, milk, and vanilla in the top of a double boiler, or in a heatproof bowl set over hot water, until melted.

8 Place a piece of wax paper under the cake, then drizzle spoonfuls of glaze along the edge to drip down and coat the sides. Pour the remaining glaze on top of the cake.

9 ▲ Cover the sides of the cake with the remaining nuts, gently pressing them on with the palm of your hand.

Chocolate Brownie Cake

SERVES 8–10

4 1-ounce squares semisweet chocolate
3/4 cup butter
2 1/4 cups superfine sugar
3 eggs
1 teaspoon vanilla extract
1 1/2 cups flour
1 teaspoon baking powder
1 cup chopped walnuts
FOR THE TOPPING
1 1/2 cups whipping cream
8 1-ounce squares semiswect chocolate
1 tablespoon vegetable oil

1 Preheat the oven to 350°F. Line 2 8-inch cake pans, at least 1 3/4 inches deep, with wax paper and grease the paper.

2 Melt the chocolate and butter together in the top of a double boiler, or in a heatproof bowl set over a saucepan of hot water.

4 ▲ Sift over the flour and baking powder. Stir in the walnuts.

5 Divide the batter between the prepared tins and spread level.

6 Bake until a cake tester inserted in the center comes out clean, about 30 minutes. Let stand 10 minutes, then unmold and transfer to a rack.

7 When the cakes are cool, whip the cream until firm. With a long serrated knife, carefully slice each cake in half horizontally.

8 Sandwich the layers with some of the whipped cream and spread the remainder over the top and sides of the cake. Refrigerate until needed.

9 ▼ For the chocolate curls, melt the chocolate and oil in the top of a double boiler or a bowl set over hot water. Transfer to a non-porous surface. Spread to a 1/2-in thick rectangle. Just before the chocolate sets, hold the blade of a straight knife at an angle to the chocolate and scrape across the surface to make curls. Place on top of the cake.

3 ▲ Transfer to a mixing bowl and stir in the sugar. Add the eggs and vanilla, and mix until well blended.

~ VARIATION ~

To make Chocolate Brownie Ice Cream Cake, sandwich the cake layers with softened vanilla ice cream. Freeze before serving.

Sachertorte

SERVES 8–10

4 1-ounce squares semisweet chocolate
6 tablespoons unsalted butter, at room temperature
1/4 cup superfine sugar
4 eggs, separated
1 extra egg white
1/4 teaspoon salt
9 tablespoons flour, sifted
FOR THE TOPPING
5 tablespoons apricot jam
1 cup plus 1 tablespoon water
1 tablespoon unsalted butter
6 1-ounce squares semisweet chocolate
scant 1/2 cup superfine sugar
ready-made chocolate decorating frosting (optional)

1 Preheat the oven to 325°F. Line a 9- × 2-inch cake pan with wax paper and grease.

2 ▲ Melt the chocolate in the top of a double boiler, or in a heatproof bowl set over hot water. Set aside.

3 With an electric mixer, cream the butter and sugar until light and fluffy. Stir in the chocolate.

4 ▲ Beat in the yolks, 1 at a time.

5 In another bowl, beat the egg whites with the salt until stiff.

6 ▲ Fold a dollop of whites into the chocolate mixture to lighten it. Fold in the remaining whites in 3 batches, alternating with the sifted flour.

7 ▲ Pour into the pan and bake until a cake tester comes out clean, about 45 minutes. Unmold onto a rack.

8 ▲ Meanwhile, melt the jam with 1 tablespoon of the water over low heat, then strain for a smooth consistency.

9 For the frosting, melt the butter and chocolate in the top of a double boiler, or a bowl set over hot water.

10 ▲ In a heavy pan, dissolve the sugar in the remaining water over low heat. Raise the heat and boil until it reaches 225°F on a sugar thermometer. Immediately plunge the bottom of the pan into cold water for 1 minute. Pour into the chocolate mixture and stir to blend. Let cool for a few minutes.

11 To assemble, brush the warm jam over the cake. Starting in the center, pour over the frosting and work outward in a circular movement. Tilt the rack to spread; use a metal spatula to smooth the sides of the cake. Let set overnight. If wished, decorate with chocolate frosting.

Raspberry and Hazelnut Meringue Cake

SERVES 8

1¹/₄ cups hazelnuts

4 egg whites

pinch of salt

1 cup superfine sugar

¹/₂ teaspoon vanilla extract

FOR THE FILLING

1¹/₄ cups whipping cream

1¹/₂ pounds raspberries, about 3 pints

1 Preheat the oven to 350°F. Line the bottom of 2 8-inch cake pans with wax paper and grease.

2 Spread the hazelnuts on a baking sheet and bake until lightly toasted, about 8 minutes. Let cool slightly.

3 ▲ Rub the hazelnuts vigorously in a clean dish towel to remove most of the skins.

4 Grind the nuts in a food processor, blender, or nut grinder until they are the consistency of coarse sand.

5 Reduce the oven to 300°F.

6 With an electric mixer, beat the egg whites and salt until they hold stiff peaks. Beat in 2 tablespoons of the sugar, then fold in the remaining sugar, a few tablespoons at a time, with a rubber spatula. Fold in the vanilla and the hazelnuts.

7 ▲ Divide the batter between the prepared pans and spread level.

8 Bake for 1¹/₄ hours. If the meringues brown too quickly, protect with a sheet of foil. Let stand 5 minutes, then carefully run a knife around the inside edge of the pans to loosen. Unmold onto a rack to cool.

9 For the filling, whip the cream until just firm.

10 ▲ Spread half the cream in an even layer on one meringue round and top with half the raspberries.

11 Top with the other meringue round. Spread the remaining cream on top and arrange the remaining raspberries over the cream. Refrigerate for 1 hour for easy cutting.

Forgotten Torte

SERVES 6

6 egg whites, at room temperature

$^1/_2$ teaspoon cream of tartar

pinch of salt

generous $1^1/_2$ cups superfine sugar

1 teaspoon vanilla extract

$^3/_4$ cup whipping cream

FOR THE SAUCE

2 cups fresh or thawed
    frozen raspberries

2–3 tablespoons confectioners' sugar

1 Preheat the oven to 450°F.

2 ▲ Grease a 6$^1/_4$-cup ring mold. With an electric mixer, beat the egg whites, cream of tartar, and salt until they hold soft peaks. Add the sugar and beat until glossy and stiff. Fold in the vanilla.

3 ▲ Spoon into the prepared pan and smooth the top level.

4 Place in the oven, then turn the oven off. Leave overnight; do not open the oven door at any time.

5 ▼ To serve, gently loosen the edge with a sharp knife and unmold onto a serving plate. Whip the cream until firm. Spread it over the top and upper sides of the meringue and decorate with any meringue crumbs.

6 ▲ For the sauce, purée the fruit, then strain. Sweeten to taste. Serve with the torte.

~ COOK'S TIP ~

This recipe is not suitable for fan assisted and solid fuel ovens.

Nut and Apple Torte

SERVES 8

²/₃ cup pecans or walnuts
¹/₂ cup flour
2 teaspoons baking powder
¹/₄ teaspoon salt
2 large cooking apples
3 eggs
generous 1 cup superfine sugar
1 teaspoon vanilla extract
³/₄ cup whipping cream

1 Preheat the oven to 325°F. Line 2 9-inch cake pans with wax paper and grease the paper. Spread the nuts on a baking sheet and bake for 10 minutes.

2 Finely chop the nuts. Reserve 1¹/₂ tablespoons and place the rest in a mixing bowl. Sift over the flour, baking powder, and salt and stir.

3 ▲ Quarter, core, and peel the apples. Cut into ¹/₈-inch dice, then stir into the nut-flour mixture.

4 ▲ With an electric mixer, beat the eggs until frothy. Gradually add the sugar and vanilla and beat until a ribbon forms, about 8 minutes. Gently fold in the flour mixture.

5 Pour into the pans and level the tops. Bake until a cake tester inserted in the center comes out clean, about 35 minutes. Let stand 10 minutes.

6 ▲ To loosen, run a knife around the inside edge of each pan. Let cool.

7 ▲ Whip the cream until firm. Spread half over the cake. Top with the second cake. Pipe whipped cream rosettes on top and sprinkle over the reserved nuts before serving.

Almond Cake

SERVES 4–6

| 1¹/₃ cups blanched whole almonds, plus more for decorating |
| 2 tablespoons butter |
| 6 tablespoons confectioners' sugar |
| 3 eggs |
| ¹/₂ teaspoon almond extract |
| ¹/₄ cup flour |
| 3 egg whites |
| 1 tablespoon superfine sugar |

1 ▲ Preheat the oven to 325°F. Line a 9-inch round cake pan with wax paper and grease.

2 ▲ Spread the almonds in a baking tray and toast for 10 minutes. Cool, then coarsely chop generous 1 cup.

3 Melt the butter and set aside. Increase the oven temperature to 400°F.

4 Grind the chopped almonds with half the confectioners' sugar in a food processor, blender, or nut grinder. Transfer to a mixing bowl.

5 ▲ Add the whole eggs and remaining confectioners' sugar. With an electric mixer, beat until the mixture forms a ribbon when the beaters are lifted. Mix in the butter and almond extract. Sift over the flour and fold in gently.

6 With an electric mixer, beat the egg whites until they hold soft peaks. Add the superfine sugar and beat until stiff and glossy.

7 ▲ Fold the whites into the almond mixture in 4 batches.

8 Spoon the batter into the prepared pan and bake in the center of the oven until golden brown, about 15–20 minutes. Decorate the top with the remaining toasted whole almonds. Serve warm.

Walnut Coffee Torte

SERVES 8–10

1¹/₄ cups walnuts
generous ³/₄ cup superfine sugar
5 eggs, separated
1 cup dry bread crumbs
1 tablespoon unsweetened cocoa powder
1 tablespoon instant coffee
2 tablespoons rum or lemon juice
pinch of salt
6 tablespoons grape or red currant jelly
chopped walnuts, for decorating
FOR THE FROSTING
8 1-ounce squares semisweet chocolate
3 cups whipping cream

1 ▲ For the frosting, combine the chocolate and cream in the top of a double boiler, or in a heatproof bowl set over simmering water. Stir until the chocolate melts. Let cool, then cover and refrigerate overnight or until the mixture is firm.

2 Preheat the oven to 350°F. Line a 9- × 2-inch cake pan with wax paper and grease.

3 ▲ Grind the nuts in a food processor, blender, or nut grinder with 3 tablespoons of the sugar.

4 With an electric mixer, beat the egg yolks and remaining sugar until thick and lemon-colored.

5 ▲ Fold in the walnuts. Stir in the bread crumbs, cocoa, coffee, and rum or lemon juice.

6 ▲ In another bowl, beat the egg whites with the salt until they hold stiff peaks. Fold carefully into the walnut mixture with a rubber spatula.

7 Pour the meringue batter into the prepared pan and bake until the top of the cake springs back when touched lightly, about 45 minutes. Let the cake stand for 5 minutes, then unmold and cool on a rack.

8 ▲ When cool, slice the cake in half horizontally.

9 With an electric mixer, beat the chocolate frosting mixture on low speed until it becomes lighter, about 30 seconds. Do not overbeat or it may become grainy.

10 ▲ Warm the jelly in a saucepan until melted, then brush over the cut cake layer. Spread with some of the chocolate frosting, then sandwich with the remaining cake layer. Brush the top of the cake with jelly, then cover the sides and top with the remaining chocolate frosting. Make a starburst pattern by pressing gently with a table knife in lines radiating from the center. Arrange the chopped walnuts around the edge.

Light Fruit Cake

MAKES 2 LOAVES

1 cup ready-to-eat prunes
1¹/₂ cups dates
1 cup currants
1¹/₃ cups golden raisins
1 cup dry white wine
1 cup rum
3 cups flour
2 teaspoons baking powder
1 teaspoon ground cinnamon
¹/₂ teaspoon freshly grated nutmeg
1 cup (2 sticks) butter, at room temperature
generous 1 cup superfine sugar
4 eggs, at room temperature, lightly beaten
1 teaspoon vanilla extract

1 Pit the prunes and dates and chop finely. Place in a bowl with the currants and raisins.

2 ▲ Stir in the wine and rum and leave to stand, covered, for 48 hours. Stir occasionally.

3 Preheat the oven to 300°F and place a tray of hot water on the bottom of the oven. Line 2 9- × 5- × 3-inch pans with wax paper and grease.

4 Sift together the flour, baking powder, cinnamon, and nutmeg.

5 ▲ With an electric mixer, cream the butter and sugar together until light and fluffy.

6 Gradually add the eggs and vanilla. Fold in the flour mixture in 3 batches. Fold in the dried fruit mixture and its macerating liquid.

7 ▲ Divide the mixture between the pans and bake until a cake tester inserted in the center comes out clean, about 1¹/₂ hours.

8 Let stand 20 minutes, then unmold and transfer to a cooling rack. Wrap in foil or wax paper and store in an airtight container. If possible, leave for at least 1 week before serving to allow the flavors to mellow.

Dark Fruit Cake

SERVES 12

²/₃ cup currants
generous 1 cup raisins
¹/₃ cup golden raisins
¹/₄ cup candied cherries, halved
3 tablespoons Madeira or sherry wine
³/₄ cup (1¹/₂ sticks) butter
scant 1 cup soft dark brown sugar
2 eggs, at room temperature
1³/₄ cups flour
2 teaspoons baking powder
2 teaspoons each ground ginger, allspice, and cinnamon
1 tablespoon dark corn syrup
1 tablespoon milk
¹/₃ cup mixed candied fruit, chopped
1 cup chopped walnuts
FOR THE DECORATION
generous 1 cup superfine sugar
¹/₂ cup water
1 lemon, thinly sliced
¹/₂ orange, thinly sliced
¹/₂ cup orange marmalade
candied cherries

6 Bake until a cake tester inserted in the center comes out clean, about 2¹/₂–3 hours. Cover with foil when the top is golden to prevent over-browning. Cool in the pan on a rack.

1 One day before preparing, combine the currants, both raisins, and the cherries in a bowl. Stir in the Madeira or sherry. Cover and let stand overnight to macerate.

2 Preheat the oven to 300°F. Line a 9- × 3-inch springform pan with wax paper and grease. Place a tray of hot water on the bottom of the oven.

3 With an electric mixer, cream the butter and sugar until light and fluffy. Beat in the eggs, 1 at a time.

4 ▲ Sift the flour, baking powder, and spices together 3 times. Fold into the butter mixture in 3 batches. Fold in the syrup, milk, dried fruit and liquid, candied fruit, and nuts.

5 ▲ Spoon into the pan, spreading out so there is a slight depression in the center of the batter.

7 ▲ For the decoration, combine the sugar and water in a saucepan and bring to a boil. Add the lemon and orange slices and cook until candied, about 20 minutes. Work in batches, if necessary. Remove the fruit with a slotted spoon. Pour the remaining syrup over the cake and let cool. Melt the marmalade over low heat, then brush over the top of the cake. Decorate with the candied citrus slices and cherries.

Whiskey Cake

MAKES 1 LOAF

1½ cups chopped walnuts

⅔ cup raisins, chopped

⅔ cup currants

1 cup flour

1 teaspoon baking powder

¼ teaspoon salt

½ cup (1 stick) butter

1 cup superfine sugar

3 eggs, at room temperature, separated

1 teaspoon freshly grated nutmeg

½ teaspoon ground cinnamon

generous ⅓ cup bourbon whiskey

confectioners' sugar, for dusting

1 ▼ Preheat the oven to 325°F. Line a 9- × 5- x 3-inch loaf pan with wax paper. Grease the paper and sides of the pan.

2 ▲ Place the walnuts, raisins, and currants in a bowl. Sprinkle over 2 tablespoons of the flour, mix and set aside. Sift together the remaining flour, baking powder, and salt.

3 ▲ Cream the butter and sugar until light and fluffy. Beat in the egg yolks.

4 Mix the nutmeg, cinnamon, and whiskey. Fold into the butter mixture, alternating with the flour mixture.

5 ▲ In another bowl, beat the egg whites until stiff. Fold into the whiskey mixture until just blended. Fold in the walnut mixture.

6 Bake until a cake tester inserted in the center comes out clean, about 1 hour. Let cool in the pan. Dust with confectioners' sugar over a template.

Gingerbread

SERVES 8–10

1 tablespoon vinegar
³/₄ cup milk
1¹/₂ cups flour
2 teaspoons baking powder
¹/₄ teaspoon baking soda
¹/₂ teaspoon salt
2 teaspoons ground ginger
1 teaspoon ground cinnamon
¹/₄ teaspoon ground cloves
¹/₂ cup (1 stick) butter, at room temperature
generous ¹/₂ cup superfine sugar
1 egg, at room temperature
³/₄ cup molasses
whipped cream, for serving
chopped stem ginger, for decorating

1 ▲ Preheat the oven to 350°F. Line the bottom of an 8-inch square cake pan with wax paper and grease the paper and the sides of the pan.

2 ▲ Add the vinegar to the milk and set aside. It will curdle.

3 In another mixing bowl, sift all the dry ingredients together 3 times and set aside.

4 With an electric mixer, cream the butter and sugar until light and fluffy. Beat in the egg until well combined.

5 ▼ Stir in the molasses.

6 ▲ Fold in the dry ingredients in 4 batches, alternating with the curdled milk. Mix only enough to blend.

7 Pour into the prepared pan and bake until firm, 45–50 minutes. Cut into squares and serve warm, with whipped cream. Decorate with the stem ginger.

Classic Cheesecake

SERVES 8

1 cup graham cracker crumbs
4 cups cream cheese, at room temperature
scant 1¼ cups superfine sugar
grated rind of 1 lemon
3 tablespoons lemon juice
1 teaspoon vanilla extract
4 eggs, at room temperature

1 Preheat the oven to 325°F. Grease an 8-inch springform pan. Place on a round of foil 4–5 inches larger than the diameter of the pan. Press it up the sides to seal tightly.

2 Sprinkle the crumbs in the base of the pan. Press to form an even layer.

3 With an electric mixer, beat the cream cheese until smooth. Add the sugar, lemon rind and juice, and vanilla, and beat until blended. Beat in the eggs, 1 at a time. Beat just enough to blend thoroughly.

4 ▲ Pour into the prepared pan. Set the pan in a larger baking pan and pour enough hot water in the outer pan to come 1 inch up the side of the pan. Place in the oven.

5 Bake until the top of the cake is golden brown, about 1½ hours. Let cool in the pan.

6 ▼ Run a knife around the edge to loosen, then remove the rim of the pan. Refrigerate for at least 4 hours before serving.

Chocolate Cheesecake

SERVES 10–12

10 1-ounce squares semisweet chocolate
5 cups cream cheese, at room temperature
1 cup superfine sugar
2 teaspoons vanilla extract
4 eggs, at room temperature
¾ cup sour cream
1 tablespoon unsweetened cocoa powder
FOR THE BASE
3½ cups chocolate wafer crumbs
6 tablespoons butter, melted
½ teaspoon ground cinnamon

1 Preheat the oven to 350°F. Grease the bottom and sides of a 9- × 3-inch springform pan.

2 ▲ For the crust, mix the chocolate crumbs with the butter and cinnamon. Press evenly in the bottom of the pan.

3 Melt the chocolate in the top of a double boiler, or in a heatproof bowl set over hot water. Set aside.

4 Beat the cream cheese until smooth, then beat in the sugar and vanilla. Add the eggs, 1 at a time.

5 Stir the sour cream into the cocoa powder to form a paste. Add to the cream cheese mixture. Stir in the melted chocolate.

6 ▼ Pour into the crust. Bake for 1 hour. Let cool in the pan; remove the rim. Refrigerate before serving.

Classic Cheesecake (top), Chocolate Cheesecake

Lemon Mousse Cheesecake

Serves 10–12

5 cups cream cheese, at room temperature
1¾ cups superfine sugar
⅓ cup flour
4 eggs, at room temperature, separated
½ cup fresh lemon juice
grated rind of 2 lemons
2 cups graham cracker crumbs

1 Preheat the oven to 325°F. Line a 10- × 2-inch round cake pan with wax paper and grease the paper.

2 With an electric mixer, beat the cream cheese until smooth. Gradually add 1½ cups of the sugar, and beat until light. Beat in the flour.

3 ▲ Add the egg yolks, and lemon juice and rind, and beat until smooth and well blended.

4 In another bowl, beat the egg whites until they hold soft peaks. Add the remaining sugar and beat until stiff and glossy.

5 ▲ Add the egg whites to the cream cheese mixture and gently fold in.

6 Pour the batter into the prepared pan. Set the pan in a larger baking pan and pour enough hot water in the outer pan to come 1 inch up the side of the pan. Place in the oven.

7 Bake until golden, 60–65 minutes. Let cool in the pan on a rack. Cover and refrigerate for at least 4 hours.

8 To unmold, run a knife around the inside edge. Place a flat plate, bottom-side up, over the pan and invert onto the plate. Smooth the top with a metal spatula.

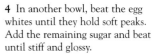

9 ▲ Sprinkle the cracker crumbs over the top in an even layer, pressing down slightly to make a top crust.

10 To serve, cut slices with a sharp knife dipped in hot water.

Marbled Cheesecake

SERVES 10

1/2 cup unsweetened cocoa powder
5 tablespoons hot water
4 cups cream cheese, at room temperature
1 cup superfine sugar
4 eggs
1 teaspoon vanilla extract
1 1/4 cups graham cracker crumbs

1 Preheat the oven to 350°F. Line an 8- × 3-inch cake pan with wax paper and grease.

2 Sift the cocoa powder into a bowl. Pour over the hot water and stir to dissolve. Set aside.

3 With an electric mixer, beat the cheese until smooth and creamy. Add the sugar and beat to incorporate. Beat in the eggs, 1 at a time. Do not overmix.

4 Divide the batter evenly between 2 bowls. Stir the chocolate batter into one, then add the vanilla to the remaining batter.

5 ▲ Pour a cupful of the plain batter into the center of the pan; it will spread out into an even layer. Slowly pour over a cupful of chocolate batter in the center.

6 ▲ Repeat alternating cupfuls of the batters in a circular pattern until both are used up.

7 Set the pan in a roasting pan and pour in hot water to come 1 1/2 inches up the sides of the cake pan.

8 Bake until the top of the cake is golden, about 1 1/2 hours. It will rise during baking but will sink later. Let cool in the pan on a rack.

9 To unmold, run a knife around the inside edge. Place a flat plate, bottom-side up, over the pan and invert onto the plate.

10 ▼ Sprinkle the crumbs evenly over the base, gently place another plate over them, and invert again. Cover and refrigerate for at least 3 hours, or overnight. To serve, cut slices with a sharp knife dipped in hot water.

Heart Cake

MAKES 1 CAKE

1 cup butter or margarine, at room temperature
generous 1 cup superfine sugar
4 eggs, at room temperature
1¹/₂ cups flour
1 teaspoon baking powder
¹/₂ teaspoon baking soda
2 tablespoons milk
1 teaspoon vanilla extract
FOR FROSTING AND DECORATING
3 egg whites
1³/₄ cups superfine sugar
2 tablespoons cold water
2 tablespoons fresh lemon juice
¹/₄ teaspoon cream of tartar
pink food coloring
6–8 tablespoons confectioners' sugar

1 Preheat the oven to 350°F. Line an 8-inch heart-shaped cake pan with wax paper and grease.

2 ▲ With an electric mixer, cream the butter or margarine and sugar until light and fluffy. Add the eggs, 1 at a time, beating thoroughly after each addition.

3 Sift the flour, baking powder, and baking soda together. Fold the dry ingredients into the butter mixture in 3 batches, alternating with the milk. Stir in the vanilla.

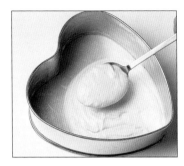

4 ▲ Spoon the batter into the prepared pan and bake until a cake tester inserted in the center comes out clean, 35–40 minutes. Let the cake stand in the pan for 5 minutes, then unmold and transfer to a rack to cool completely.

5 For the frosting, combine 2 of the egg whites, the superfine sugar, water, lemon juice, and cream of tartar in the top of a double boiler, or in a bowl set over simmering water. With an electric mixer, beat until thick and holding soft peaks, about 7 minutes. Remove from the heat and continue beating until the mixture is thick enough to spread. Tint the frosting with the pink food coloring.

6 ▲ Put the cake on a board, about 12 inches square, covered in foil or in paper suitable for contact with food. Spread the frosting evenly on the cake. Smooth the top and sides. Leave to set 3–4 hours, or overnight.

7 ▲ For the paper piping bags, fold an 11- × 8-inch sheet of parchment or wax paper in half diagonally, then cut into 2 pieces along the fold mark. Roll over the short side, so that it meets the right-angled corner and forms a cone. To form the piping bag, hold the cone in place with one hand, wrap the point of the long side of the triangle around the cone, and tuck inside, folding over twice to secure. Snip a hole in the pointed end and slip in a small metal piping tip to extend about ¹/₄ inch.

8 For the piped decorations, place 1 tablespoon of the remaining egg white in a bowl and whisk until frothy. Gradually beat in enough confectioners' sugar to make a stiff mixture suitable for piping.

9 ▲ Spoon into a paper piping bag to half-fill. Fold over the top and squeeze to pipe decorations on the top and sides of the cake.

Cup Cakes

1/2 cup (1 stick) butter, at room temperature

generous 1 cup superfine sugar

2 eggs, at room temperature

1 1/2 cups flour

1/4 teaspoon salt

1 1/2 teaspoons baking powder

1/2 cup plus 1 tablespoon milk

1 teaspoon vanilla extract

FOR FROSTING AND DECORATING

2 large egg whites

3 1/2 cups sifted confectioners' sugar

1–2 drops glycerin

juice of 1 lemon

food colorings

hundreds and thousands, for decorating

candied lemon and orange slices

1 Preheat the oven to 375°F.

2 ▲ Line 16 muffin cups with fluted paper baking liners, or grease.

~ COOK'S TIP ~

Ready-made cake decorating products are widely available, and may be used, if preferred, instead of the recipes given for frosting and decorating. Colored gel in tubes with piping tips is useful.

3 With an electric mixer, cream the butter and sugar until light and fluffy. Add the eggs, 1 at a time, beating well after each addition.

4 Sift together the flour, salt, and baking powder. Stir into the butter mixture, alternating with the milk. Stir in the vanilla.

5 ▲ Fill the cups half-full and bake until the tops spring back when touched lightly, about 20 minutes. Let the cup cakes stand in the pan for 5 minutes, then unmold and transfer to a rack to cool completely.

6 For the frosting, beat the egg whites until stiff but not dry. Gradually add the sugar, glycerin, and lemon juice, and continue beating for 1 minute. The consistency should be spreadable. If necessary, thin with a little water or add more sifted confectioners' sugar.

7 ▲ Divide the frosting between several bowls and tint with food colorings. Spread different colored frostings over the cooled cup cakes.

8 ▲ Decorate the cakes as wished, with sugar decorations such as colored sprinkles.

9 ▲ Other decorations include candied orange and lemon slices. Cut into small pieces and arrange on top of the cup cakes. Alternatively, use other suitable candies.

10 ▲ To make freehand iced decorations, fill paper pastry bags with different colored frostings. Pipe on faces, or make other designs.

Snake Cake

SERVES 10–12

1 cup butter or margarine,
    at room temperature

grated rind and juice of 1 small orange

generous 1 cup superfine sugar

4 eggs, at room temperature, separated

1$\frac{1}{2}$ cups flour

1 teaspoon baking powder

pinch of salt

FOR THE FROSTING AND DECORATING

2 tablespoons butter, at room temperature

3 cups confectioners' sugar

5 1-ounce squares semisweet chocolate

pinch of salt

$\frac{1}{2}$ cup sour cream

1 egg white

green and blue food colorings

1 Preheat the oven to 375°F. Grease 2 8$\frac{1}{2}$-inch ring molds and dust them with flour.

2 With an electric mixer, cream the butter or margarine, orange rind, and sugar until light. Beat in the egg yolks, 1 at a time.

3 Sift the flour and baking powder. Fold into the butter mixture, alternating with the orange juice.

4 ▲ In another bowl, beat the egg whites and salt until stiff.

5 Fold a large dollop of the egg whites into the creamed butter mixture to lighten it, then gently fold in the remaining whites.

6 Divide the batter between the prepared pans and bake until a cake tester inserted in the center comes out clean, about 25 minutes. Let stand 5 minutes, then unmold onto a wire rack to cool.

7 Prepare a board, 24 × 8 inches, covered in paper suitable for contact with food, or in foil.

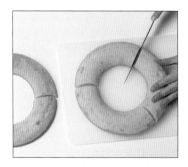

8 ▲ Cut the cakes in 3 even pieces. Trim to level the flat side, if necessary, and shape the head by cutting off wedges from the front. Shape the tail in the same way.

9 ▲ For the butter frosting, mix the butter with scant $\frac{1}{2}$ cup of the sugar. Use to join the cake segments and arrange on the board.

10 ▲ For the chocolate frosting, melt the chocolate. Stir in the salt and sour cream. When cool, spread over the cake and smooth the surface.

11 ▲ For the decoration, beat the egg white until frothy. Add enough of the remaining confectioners' sugar to obtain a thick mixture. Divide among several bowls and add food colorings.

12 ▲ Fill paper piping bags with frosting, and pipe decorations along the top of the cake.

Sun Cake

1/2 cup (1 stick) unsalted butter

6 eggs

generous 1 cup superfine sugar

1 cup flour

1/2 teaspoon salt

1 teaspoon vanilla extract

For frosting and decorating

2 tablespoons unsalted butter,
    at room temperature

4 cups sifted confectioners' sugar

1/2 cup apricot jam

2 tablespoons water

2 large egg whites

1–2 drops glycerin

juice of 1 lemon

yellow and orange food colorings

1 Preheat the oven to 350°F. Line
2 8- × 2-inch round cake pans, then
grease and flour.

2 In a pan, melt the butter over very
low heat. Skim off any foam that rises
to the surface, then set aside.

3 ▲ Place a heatproof bowl over a
saucepan of hot water. Add the eggs
and sugar. Beat with an electric mixer
until the mixture doubles in volume
and is thick enough to leave a ribbon
trail when the beaters are lifted,
8–10 minutes.

4 Sift the flour and salt together
3 times. Sift over the egg mixture in
3 batches, folding in well after each
addition. Fold in the melted butter
and vanilla.

5 Divide the batter between the pans.
Level the surfaces and bake until the
cakes shrink slightly from the sides of
the pans, 25–30 minutes. Let stand
5 minutes, then unmold and transfer
to a cooling rack.

6 Prepare a board, 16 inches square,
covered in paper suitable for contact
with food, or in foil.

7 ▲ For the sunbeams, cut 1 of the
cakes into 8 equal wedges. Cut away a
rounded piece from the base of each
so that they fit neatly up against the
sides of the whole cake.

8 ▲ For the butter frosting, mix the
butter and 1/4 cup of the confectioners'
sugar. Use to attach the sunbeams.

9 ▲ Melt the jam with the water and
brush over the cake. Place on the
board and straighten, if necessary.

10 ▲ For the frosting, beat the
egg whites until stiff but not dry.
Gradually add 3 1/2 cups of the
confectioners' sugar, the glycerin, and
lemon juice, and continue beating for
1 minute. If necessary, thin with water
or add a little more sugar. Tint with
yellow food coloring and spread over
the cake.

11 ▲ Divide the remaining frosting
in half and tint with more food
coloring to obtain bright yellow and
orange. Pipe decorative zig-zags on the
sunbeams and a face in the middle.

Jack-O'-Lantern Cake

SERVES 8–10

1¹/₂ cups flour	
2¹/₂ teaspoons baking powder	
pinch of salt	
¹/₂ cup (1 stick) butter, at room temperature	
generous 1 cup superfine sugar	
3 egg yolks, at room temperature, well beaten	
1 teaspoon grated lemon rind	
³/₄ cup milk	
FOR THE CAKE COVERING	
5–6 cups confectioners' sugar	
2 egg whites	
2 tablespoons liquid glucose	
orange and black food colorings	

1 Preheat the oven to 375°F. Line an 8-inch round cake pan with wax paper and grease.

2 Sift together the flour, baking powder, and salt. Set aside.

3 With an electric mixer, cream the butter and sugar until light and fluffy. Gradually beat in the egg yolks, then add the lemon rind. Fold in the flour mixture in 3 batches, alternating with the milk.

4 Spoon the mixture into the prepared pan. Bake until a cake tester inserted in the center comes out clean, about 35 minutes. Let stand 5 minutes then unmold onto a rack.

~ COOK'S TIP ~

If you prefer, use ready-made roll-out cake covering or rolled fondant, available at cake decorating supply shops and some supermarkets. Knead in food coloring, if required.

---

5 For the frosting, sift 5 cups of the confectioners' sugar into a bowl. Make a well in the center, add 1 egg white, the glucose, and orange food coloring. Stir until a dough forms.

6 ▲ Transfer to a clean work surface dusted with confectioners' sugar and knead briefly.

7 ▲ Carefully roll out the orange cake covering to a thin sheet.

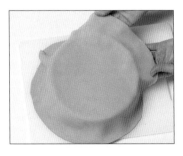

8 ▲ Place the sheet on top of the cooled cake and smooth the sides. Trim the excess covering and reserve.

9 ▲ From the trimmings, cut shapes for the lid. Tint the remaining cake covering trimmings with black food coloring. Roll out thinly and cut shapes for the face.

10 ▲ Brush the undersides with water and arrange the face on top of the cake. Also put the lid in place.

11 ▲ Place 1 tablespoon of the remaining egg white in a bowl and stir in enough confectioners' sugar to make a thick frosting. Tint with black food coloring, fill a paper piping bag and pipe the outline of the lid.

Stars and Stripes Cake

1 cup (2 sticks) butter or margarine, at room temperature

1 cup soft dark brown sugar

generous 1 cup sugar

5 eggs, at room temperature

2¹/₂ cups flour

2 teaspoons baking powder

1 teaspoon baking soda

1 teaspoon ground cinnamon

1 teaspoon ground ginger

¹/₂ teaspoon ground allspice

¹/₄ teaspoon ground cloves

¹/₄ teaspoon salt

1¹/₂ cups buttermilk

¹/₂ cup raisins

FOR THE FROSTING AND CAKE COVERING

2 tablespoons butter

9–10 cups confectioners' sugar

3 egg whites

4 tablespoons liquid glucose

red and blue food colorings

1 Preheat the oven to 350°F. Line a 12- × 9-inch baking pan with wax paper and lightly grease.

2 With an electric mixer, cream the butter or margarine and sugars until light and fluffy. Gradually beat in the eggs, 1 at a time, beating well after each addition.

3 Sift together the flour, baking powder, baking soda, spices, and salt. Fold into the butter mixture in 3 batches, alternating with the buttermilk. Stir in the raisins.

4 Pour the batter into the prepared pan and bake until the cake springs back when touched lightly, about 35 minutes. Let stand 10 minutes, then unmold onto a wire rack.

5 Make the butter frosting by mixing the butter with scant ¹/₂ cup of the confectioners' sugar.

6 ▲ When the cake is cool, cut a curved shape from the top.

7 ▲ Attach it to the bottom of the cake with the butter frosting.

8 Prepare a board, about 16 × 12 inches, covered in paper suitable for contact with food, or in foil. Transfer the cake to the board.

9 For the cake covering, sift 9 cups of the confectioners' sugar into a bowl. Add 2 of the egg whites and the liquid glucose. Stir until the mixture forms a dough.

10 Cover and set aside half of the covering. On a clean work surface lightly dusted with confectioners' sugar, roll out the remaining covering to a sheet. Carefully transfer to the cake. Smooth the sides and trim any excess from the bottom edges.

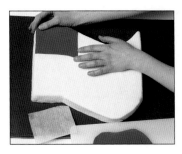

11 ▲ Tint one-quarter of the remaining covering blue and tint the rest red. Roll out the blue to a thin sheet and cut out the background for the stars. Place on the cake.

12 ▲ Roll out the red covering, cut out stripes, and place on the cake.

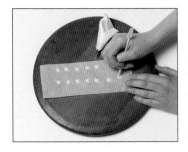

13 ▲ For the stars, mix 1 tablespoon of the egg white with just enough confectioners' sugar to thicken. Pipe small stars onto a sheet of wax paper and leave to set. When dry, peel them off and place on the blue background.

INDEX

Z